OPERATING SYSTEMS
Concepts and Applications

OPERATING SYSTEMS
Concepts and Applications

Donald R. Horner, Ph.D.
Eastern Washington University

Scott, Foresman and Company
Glenview, Illinois   London

UNIX™ is a trademark of Bell Laboratories, Incorporated.
XENIX™ is a trademark of Microsoft Corporation.
VAX™ is a trademark of Digital Equipment Corporation.
MVS™ and VM™ are trademarks of International Business Machines
Corporation.

Library of Congress Cataloging-in-Publication Data

Horner, Donald.
   Operating systems.

   Bibliography: P.
   Includes index.
   1. Operating systems (Computers) 2. Microcomputers
(Computer science) I. Title
QA76.74.Q63H46   1989   005.4'46   88-25822
ISBN 0-673-38065-3

ISBN 0-673-38065-3

   2 3 4 5 6 RRC 93 92 91 90 89

To   Donna
Sherry
J
JR
Ryan
Jerod
Janelle
Kyle
DeAnna
Juanita
John

Preface

The breadth of topics required of Operating Systems courses rank those courses among the hardest to teach—and their textbooks among the hardest to write. Until the early 1980s, there were at most a half dozen books available on the subject. By the time this text was being developed the numbers had jumped to about a dozen; currently there are almost two dozen good textbooks on this topic.

Operating Systems: Concepts and Applications is designed for a first under-graduate course surveying the principles central to operating system design. The conceptual approach was chosen to meet the requirements of students who either do not need a high level of algorithmic detail or who will get the more detailed information and practice in a second course. The exercise sections include many problems encountered by those who major in Management Information Systems and Computer Information Systems—students whose needs are generally overlooked by the existing textbooks. This text also provides enough information for a second course surveying currently popular operating system implementations.

The background required to understand the text's material can be as minimal as a thorough introduction to programming. Chapter 2 (essentially a condensation of much of Adair's *Computer Organization and Architecture*—used by permission) fills in enough information on computer organization and architecture to do the rest. Of course, the more exposure to data structures, assembly language, and organization and architecture, the better.

In writing this book my major goal has been to strike a balance between the theory of operating system design and the use of that theory in the daily choices made by most users. A foremost desire is that readers understand the concepts well enough to interact intelligently, meaningfully, and efficiently with operating systems in whatever user-capacity they find themselves. There has been a conscious effort to introduce the rightful place of microcomputers and their specific operating systems.

The text is organized in four major sections:
- Operating Systems Overview
- Operating Systems Theory
- Management Issues
- Operating Systems Applications

Part One provides a brief history, offers a review of computer organization and architecture, and discusses the nature and importance of the user interface (an important issue in operating system design that is all too often ignored). While each of the three chapters from this part may be skipped by the reader with previous background in this field, the chapters provide an insightful overview for many of the concepts that follow.

The theory of operating systems as presented in Part Two covers the usual topics, albeit in an unusual order. Chapter 4 not only discusses file systems but introduces input/output concepts later covered in Chapter 5. Chapter 5 previews the notions of concurrent processing, synchronization and deadlock. Chapter 6 describes various techniques for memory management. Chapters 7, 8, and 9 deal with the progressively more sophisticated topics related to process scheduling for single CPU systems, multiple processor systems, and networks. These discussions of multiple processor systems and networks create a platform for understanding computer systems of the very near future. As the topics of Part Two increase in the level of sophistication, the text becomes progressively more conceptual and less theoretical.

Part Three treats a set of topics not usually found in operating systems texts, as it addresses numerous management issues related to the acquisition, operation, and management of specific computer systems. These topics have particular significance for students from MIS, CIS, and other business-related programs.

Part Four offers overviews of several of today's more popular operating systems. These include microcomputer operating systems found on the Macintosh and IBM microcomputers (among them, MS-DOS and OS/2). The highly portable and successful UNIX operating system is discussed. Digital's VAX VMS and several of IBM's mini- and mainframe operating systems are previewed. This material can be incorporated into the earlier chapters as specific implementations of the concepts, or it can be used as the basis for a second course—moving abstract concepts into the practical world of available operating systems choices.

The overall organization of the text includes the use of principles supported by examples and exercises. The exercise sets are quite different in their range and type. Many exercises require serious thought about the impact of the theory on real world decisions. Significant terms are emphasized by **boldface** type when first introduced.

A special word of thanks is due to Dr. Roland "Skip" Keefer, longtime "Mr. Computer Science" at Eastern Washington University. Others to be recognized as contributing through the review process include series editor Fred McFadden, University of Colorado—Colorado Springs; Robert Duvall, Virginia Commonwealth University; George Rice, DeAnza College; Henry A. Etlinger, Rochester Institute of Technology; John K. Gotwals, Purdue University; John Carsen, George Washington University; Curt White, Illinois State University—Normal; James E. Benjamin, Southern Illinois University at Edwardsville; and Charles R. Taylor, Southwest Missouri State University. Thanks also go to Susan Nelle as sponsoring editor and Amy Rood as production editor.

Contents

ONE

Operating Systems Overview

1 Introduction

The study of operating systems can take any one of several possible directions: It can be designed for a number of different groups of users, classified according to their technical expertise and the type of activities they perform. **End users** tend to be less technically inclined; they use computers to run programs to perform a personal or organizational task. **Professional users** generally create and support the hardware and software systems. These two groups usually see the computer from quite different perspectives.

The **skilled user** is a special subcategory of end user who specializes in using the computer for only one task and is not expected to use programs unrelated to that task (for example, data entry clerks and word processors). The **power user,** one who goes beyond using a single software package to perform a particular task, may also be in the end user group. Power users are harder to classify, however, since they are often enthusiasts continually searching for improved software packages or innovative ways to use existing software. Still, they may share a reduced level of technical need with the other end users, particularly where operating systems are concerned.

Professional users include those who will design operating systems. **System programmers,** who develop the underlying software that drives the computer system and who continually "tweak" existing operating systems to meet particular goals, have needs similar to those of the designers. **Application programmers,** who create the programs that end users actually see and operate, are professional users with somewhat different requirements.

The operating system designers and system programmers form a small group. Most of those using computers will limit their involvement to crafting or simply manipulating, application programs. While it may not be apparent, a conceptual understanding of operating systems is valuable, if not essential, for all users.

This text is designed to meet the needs of the application programmer *and* the end user. It, nonetheless, does serve as a useful introduction for system designers and system programmers who will have more technical follow-up courses.

The Operating System

In the simplest terms, an **operating system** is a set of programs. When the computer is running, the operating system is executing in an endless loop, waiting for someone or some program to make a request. When a request is made, the operating system directs all action taken to satisfy it.

While the previous paragraph seems to say very little, it does indicate the two fundamental categories of operating system activity. The operating system must be able to **communicate** with the party making the request and to **control** the computer's resources to satisfy that request. Various authors have described these two aspects as the **superstructure** and **kernel** (Barron [1]), the **beautification** and **resource management** (Finkel [5]), or the **system services** and **kernel** (Massie [8]).

Control
: The computer is a potentially powerful electromechanical system of resources that must be harnessed to do productive work for users. Its potential is realized only through proper control and use. That part of an operating system given to the control function will usually be called the **kernel** in this text although terms such as **monitor, supervisor, resource manager** or **resource executive** may also appear.

The resources controlled include the **central processor (CPU), main memory, secondary mass storage, peripheral (input/output, I/O) devices, programs,** and **data.** Resources may be controlled for use by one program at a time or by several programs. They may be controlled for use by one person at a time or by several people. Facilities may be controlled for **interactive** computing, where the user may intervene to direct the execution, or for **batch** processing, where no user intervention is exercised. A system may be controlled for one specialized purpose or for many general uses.

The User Interface
: Users generally take the operating system's control function for granted. That control is **transparent** (invisible) most of the time, and it takes place without the user's awareness. While the application program is running, the user sees only the application, even though the operating system is quietly linking the application with the hardware. Most user interaction with the operating system occurs when no application is running—and then only to signal which application should run next.

The user's view of the computer system is, for the most part, shaped by what he or she must do to signal the operating system. The **user interface** manages the user-to-machine and machine-to-user communications when no application is running, and it includes the language and graphics employed in the process. If that communication is cryptic, difficult to learn, difficult to use, prone to errors, or narrow in capability, the user will have a negative picture of the entire computer system, no matter how excellent the hardware and control mechanism may be. On the other hand, if the user can learn to use the system quickly and easily, has confidence that disaster will not strike, and can accomplish what he or she wants, the system will be thought an excellent one, regardless of the hardware and how control is accomplished. In short, most users seldom "see" the hardware or control mechanisms but base their impressions of the entire system on the user interface.

System Services
: System services form an extension to the user interface. Programs called **system programs** have been placed in three groups (Calengaert [4]): **operating system** (or kernel), **utilities,** and **language system.**

For the end user wishing to compute interactively, an operating system provides a **command interpreter** (the visible evidence of the user interface) for communication. The interpreter accepts commands such as setting up operating parameters, displaying information about the system or its files, displaying information contained in files, and selecting and running programs. From the user's point of view, when an application runs, it replaces the command interpreter.

Each operating system has some routines to support the execution of application programs. Additional routines operate the hardware, including peripheral devices such as printers, terminals, and so on. Still others allow the user to input data into running programs interactively and to maintain file systems. All of this can be accomplished without the worry that many other users may be doing the same things on the same machine at the same time. These functions may be referred to as the **hardware interface:** the links that enable software to communicate with and control hardware.

An often overlooked, but extremely important, function of the operating system is the handling and reporting of **errors** that occur. Errors must be handled in a way that keeps disaster minimized; they should also be reported in a fashion that permits an understanding of the problem and its likely solutions.

Utilities are actually a loose collection of application programs developed over a number of years and available to all in the community of users. In a real sense, they are not part of the operating system, but they allow the system to be used more fully. Editors, word processors, spreadsheets, database handlers, sorting routines, text formatters, and other tools fall into this category.

The language system consists of the **translators** (compilers, interpreters, and assemblers) for program code written in assembly and high-level languages. **Loaders** (to place programs in the computer for execution) and **linkers** (to make large executable programs from several smaller ones) are needed to make programs runnable. Debugging tools and other routines smoothing the development of application programs are a desirable part of any language system. A library of routines that can be "pulled into" the development of application programs is a worthwhile feature if such work takes place.

Measures of Efficiency and Effectiveness

The effectiveness and efficiency of a computer system is of great concern to users. **Effectiveness** deals with whether or not the system does what it was purchased to do and whether it does so in a reasonable manner. **Efficiency** compares reality with what is possible, making productivity versus waste comparisons. Some measures center on time. **Turnaround time** indicates how long noninteractive (batch) jobs take for completion; **response time** measures the equivalent of turnaround time for interactive jobs. **Reaction time** measures the delay between a request and the machine's first action to satisfy it.

Capacity measures the raw horsepower or capability of a computer and is contrasted with **utilization,** which is the percentage of capacity being used. **Throughput** represents the amount of work completed *per unit of time* and stands in contrast to **workload** (an indicator of how much work the system is asked to do). **Availability** measures how easy or difficult it is to gain access to a particular system resource (for example, whether a user often has to wait for a terminal or printer).

The measures covered earlier may be reinterpreted when costs are factored in. It might seem reasonable to simply purchase the most powerful system available and continually upgrade it to increase horsepower whenever possible. Improvements in performance, however, can be expensive. Any improvement in performance that costs more than the user or organization believes the performance is worth will not be purchased.

While security measures incorporated in a system do not contribute directly to performance, they are nonetheless worth evaluating and measuring. Equipment, software, and data security can have significant dollar values attached. Data, in particular, is becoming a high-cost and highly valuable resource that must be protected adequately.

Operating System Goals

At the most general level, the goal of an operating system is to provide the greatest return on computer investments. What that actually means depends on how return on investment is calculated. If the system is the data processing heart for a timesharing service, dollars earned would represent the value returned. If the computer is part of a decision support system for a top-level executive, value might be measured in terms of personal productivity. If the machine is a research tool for laboratory scientists, the return on investment could be totally subjective and couched in terms of increased creativity. If the goal is to do process control for a chemical factory, any calamities prevented and lives saved might figure in the value returned on the investment.

If **machine productivity** is the focus of goal setting, then the numbers game will enter into the equation. Throughput, utilization, number of users, response times, and so on will be the dominant concern. If, however, **user productivity** is the primary focus, then ease of learning, ease of use, the availability of tools, and such considerations will predominate.

In any case, the computer will be expected to offer solutions to some set of problems. The goals for the operating system, given in terms of problem solving, are then reflected in the range and types of problems to be solved. Is the system to solve a narrow range of problems or any problem in general? Is the level of service provided to problem solvers to be limited or open-ended?

At the more detailed level, the operating system strives to create a reliable, consistent environment for each user. Never overlook the importance of consistency: It reduces learning time, user errors, and frustration while encouraging confidence. Reliability involves the security and well-being of programs and data, as well as the ability to meet deadlines.

Users should find it convenient to use the system (that is, the system should be "user friendly"). And the operating system should make particularly convenient those activities performed most often or considered most important. One way for this to be accomplished is by having a "customizable" operating system that can be fine-tuned to accommodate each user.

Users must be protected from each other's errors. Their programs and files must be secured from intentional alteration and observation by unauthorized programs and persons, for programs and data represent a large organizational or personal investment. Both data and security are valuable concerns.

Any system should provide ample language service and other tools to facilitate all user activity. But users should be able to easily pick and choose those of value to them. The volume of services should not prove overwhelming or intimidating.

Finally, the user should not have to worry about how the operating system does what it does to manage their programs.

To sum up, each computer, as an electromechanical device or set of devices, creates an unreservedly hostile environment for human existence. In spite of this, almost everyone wants to use a computer to solve one or more problems of interest. While solving problems, the user does not want to worry about courtesy, protocol, coordination, and sharing with other users. Neither, however, does he or she wish to engage in cutthroat competition for the system's resources.

The user would like to "turn a key" and have the machine roar into action. **Programs** provide this controlled and channeled action. Think of programs as the tools used by computers to solve problems. One major problem to be solved is the writing of the programs themselves. If the machine is to be really useful, it should provide assistance for the craftsmen who create these tools users want and need.

Thus there are myriad competing needs. The craftsman, when writing an application program for a user, generally writes in some high-level language and needs the system to "be" a Pascal, BASIC, LISP, or whatever machine. Meanwhile, the user doesn't care one bit about Pascal, BASIC or LISP but wants the computer to be an accounting machine, a graphics machine, a wordprocessor, or whatever. Somehow, systems must be capable of being all things to all people—*and* easy to use and foolproof.

This responsibility lies on the shoulders of the operating system. The quality or success of each computer is almost exclusively based on the success of its operating system in general and the user interface in particular.

Why Study Operating Systems?

Only a few people will ever design operating systems, and only another small group will be system programmers. For the majority who simply use operating systems, this text must serve a support function.

Anyone who has studied computers has experienced those times when his or her knowledge seemed disjointed, the pieces unrelated. Much of what was known and experienced seemed unrelated to anything else. Studying what operating systems do and how they do it can serve to integrate all this knowledge and experience that has gone before.

The study of operating systems also focuses previous learning and experience on the design considerations that shape these systems. It is most helpful to know how operating systems evolved and what features are commonly found. The ability to use an operating system confidently and effectively is enhanced through such understanding, and the learning curve for users of new operating systems is somewhat flattened.

Application programmers will not write their most efficient software without a reasonable understanding of the role, nature, and functioning of the operating system being used. Most professionals will be asked to participate in the evaluation, reevaluation, acquisition, reconfiguration, or fine-tuning of some computer system. A study of operating systems discloses the design tradeoffs made between time (speed), space (memory), and functionality—or the tradeoffs between tasks accomplished through hardware and through software. Without an understanding of operating system concepts, this involvement may be cursory and disappointing—even harmful!

Some History

The history of computers can be examined in terms of four tracks of development: mainframe systems, minicomputers, microcomputers, and multiple processor systems/ networks. The periods of development overlapped and contained many similarities. Each new development track had a compressed time frame when compared with the one preceding it.

The 1960s stand as the period of rapid development for mainframe computers. Some of the most important features introduced at this time were a comprehensive operating system, multiprogramming, multiprocessing, multiprocessors, cache memory, specialized I/O devices, large on-line storage, large fixed disks, and removable disk packs.

The initial rate of mainframe improvement was rapid but is now slowing down. This slowing is due to the architecture itself beginning to limit how much advantage can be taken of improvements in the technology. The design of today's mainframe computers has largely reached the stage where further increases in performance can only be provided by raw speed increases in the electronic circuitry, rather than by improvements in the basic design.

The development of the minicomputer followed much the same path as the mainframe had nearly a decade before. Early minicomputers held the promise of dramatic improvement in the ratio of performance to cost. Minicomputers were used in areas such as engineering and science that required intensive computation on relatively small amounts of data. Word processing was one of the first widespread applications of minicomputers in business. Because they were used independently of any other computer and performed only the one task, these early word processors were known as *stand-alone* systems and were said to use a *dedicated* computer.

However, the same effect noted earlier for mainframes is also beginning to happen with minicomputers. The rate of development for the established minicomputer architectures is flattening off as they begin to reach performance limits imposed by their architectures.

The computer-on-a-chip (micro) created a new starting point for computing. The chips were designed to mimic the features of successful minicomputer CPUs, such as the DEC PDP-11 series. A CPU on every desk became a reality in the 1980s. Microcomputers experienced a compressed development cycle that has not yet peaked. Their size has made them ideal for the creation of hardware with tens, hundreds, or even thousands of CPUs.

The competition between high-performance personal computers and minicomputers has grown quite intense. While a CPU on every desk is possible, independent personal computers incur extra costs with respect to peripheral devices. For example, it is usually cheaper to provide each user with access to part of a single, large-capacity, high-performance disk storage unit than to provide each individual with a separate, proportionately smaller unit. Networking offers some compromises, but the greatest functional difference between using individual computers and using a single timeshared computer in business is the way data is handled.

Raw Machine In the beginning, all computers were personal computers in the sense that the entire machine was dedicated to one individual for the duration of his or her session. But that wasn't necessarily good: These machines did not have operating systems to perform any control, and they could accommodate only one user at a time. The machines were, in fact, hand operated. Programming was accomplished by hand-wiring panels that were then plugged into the machine. To change programs meant changing wires or changing plug-in panels. Running the programs required hand operation of the switches on the various control panels. This made the computer a huge personal workstation (with the emphasis on work). Needless to say, there were no casual users in those dark ages (1940s through 1950s).

But then conditions improved: Users graduated from hand wired panels to instructions on **punched cards** or **paper tape. Card readers** and **tape readers** could be used to load programs into the machine. A simple, often overlooked concept made the use of these input devices possible: instead of **hardwiring** the instructions into the machine, the instructions were stored in memory. Still, virtually all users had to be programmers—and machine language programmers at that!

In any case, imagine the time taken in setting up a program to run—and in reversing the process when the run finished. Or worse yet, imagine the problem when an error terminated execution. The processor spent almost all its time waiting for something to do. (Wait for setup. Wait for teardown. Wait for input. Wait for output.) Since machines in those days were extremely expensive to buy, power, and maintain—and programmer time was cheap by comparison—it became clear that wasted processor time had to be reduced.

Satellite I/O Several solutions were found. First, card readers were faster than plug-in panels, but **magnetic tape** machines were faster than card readers. It soon became widespread practice to have **offline** satellite workstations read cards onto magnetic tape. The magnetic tape could be hand carried to the computer room, mounted on a drive mechanism connected to the computer, and then read at high speed.

Two other ideas became clear. If job setup and teardown could be automated, the most significant processor waits would be markedly shortened. If **input/output (I/O)** operations could be accomplished *independent* of the processor, the processor could do other work required by the program while I/O proceeded **concurrently.** I/O wait would be reduced.

Somewhere during this evolution, several other events made programmers' lives easier. **Libraries** of often used routines were collected to cut down on "reinventing-the-wheel" time. Programs that communicate with peripheral devices (**device drivers**) were among the first to be cast into libraries. Closely related was the notion of **logical** or **symbolic names** for devices: They allowed the calling programs to call a printer, tape, or whatever without having to worry about physical characteristics and addresses. In addition, high-level languages and their translators began to appear.

Batch Systems **Automated job sequencing** resulted in the first operating system (called a **monitor**). The idea was to **batch** jobs (programs) one after the other in a stack of cards placed in a card reader or as a sequence of magnetic blips on tape. This formed a **job stream** that could supply a more or less continuous flow of jobs into the system.

Several problems had to be solved. First, the monitor had to coexist in memory along with the program being run. Next, the monitor had to be protected from alteration by the executing program's instructions. Then, each job stream required the use of **control statements** to mark the beginning and ending of each program, to mark the beginning and ending of code and data, and to indicate what system capabilities (for example, compilers, tape drives, printers, and so on) would be required. Control statements were grouped and developed into **job control languages (JCL).**

Another subtle problem involved communication between the "pieces" of a given program. For example, a **source program** written in a high-level language might be loaded and then compiled into machine language. The output of the compiler then needs to be used as input for the **loader,** whose responsibility is to place the machine code into memory for the start of execution. However, if the job's card stack includes cards for several **library routines,** these need to be coordinated (**linked**) with the compiled code. Execution is just the final phase. In short, the card stack for a single job is really a small job stream *within* the larger job stream.

Here's another important concern with automatic job sequencing: What does the system do when a runtime error occurs? Monitors had to realize errors, report errors, and respond without a total disaster occurring. Monitors had to be **fault-tolerant.**

Not only did monitors take up memory, they utilized processor time to manage the job stream. That is, operating systems became an **overhead** cost for system management. The plan was for increased processor productivity (through less wait time) to be worth more than the overhead cost. In the beginning, that was easy to accomplish on a heavily loaded system, regardless of how efficient or inefficient the monitor seemed to be.

I/O Channels

The idea of satellite I/O was mentioned earlier as one way to cut down on processor wait times: Use the fastest I/O devices on the computer system, while using slower devices offline only. Another development soon had an impact: Imagine I/O devices that are capable of being tied to a computer system but which can operate autonomously. That is, if an output device can get its information from memory and perform output without the processor directing the action, output can occur concurrently with processing. Similarly, if an input device can place information into memory without processor intervention, input and processing can occur concurrently. Thus, many activities can go on at once. The processor can give more of its time to computing and much less to waiting. This was made possible by the development of **I/O channels** (essentially complete, specialized computer systems that exist within the larger system). Now, input, processing, and output can occur simultaneously.

Satellite I/O thus became less attractive. A slow I/O device running on a channel no longer wastes so much processor time. Putting offline activities back online through I/O channels led to the notion of a **virtual device.** The processor thought it was talking to a card reader, when in reality it was a reading a file or buffer (a segment of storage) created and filled by the card reader/channel combination.

SPOOLing

SPOOLing (Simultaneous Peripheral Operation OnLine) resulted from the development of channels. The only catch was how to notify the processor that input was finished or to signal that output needed some information. Two ways were developed to handle the problem: **polling** and **hardware interrupts.** Polling required that the processor regularly check a channel to see if servicing was needed. Hardware interrupts seemed better; they allow the channel to interrupt the processor when service is required. That way, the processor could continue on its way without regard for what the channel was doing, knowing that an interrupt would tell when service was needed. An interrupt may be thought of as a signal that can't be ignored for very long, a signal that causes the processor to shift gears and undertake some new specific action.

The advent of **disk systems** meant that spooling systems offered other choices. The jobs coming as input arrived sequentially but could be stored temporarily on disk. A **scheduler** then selected the jobs from the **pool** in any desired order (determined by some priority). Similarly, jobs being pooled for printing could be printed at convenience and in any chosen order. The lock-step of sequential response (brought about by the nature of card readers and magnetic tape devices) was broken. Spooling systems, therefore, consist of a writer mechanism, a reader mechanism, and a scheduler.

Multi-programming

Just as channels issue interrupts to get the main processor's attention, application programs can issue (software) interrupts. Moreover, interrupts can be used to cause processing to switch from one program to another.

The interrupt was central to the development of **multiprogramming** (the act of placing more than one application in main memory at once). If, during the execution of program A, the processor must suspend execution of A pending an I/O operation, it can then change focus to program B (which is also in memory) and begin execution, continuing until another interrupt occurs. The processor will eventually return to computation for program A.

Prior to multiprogramming, input and output activities for a program could occur concurrently with processing for the *same* program. With the advent of multiprogramming, input and output for one program was allowed to overlap the processing of a *different* program. Interactive programming, coupled with multiprogramming, gives a user flexibility in running several jobs simultaneously, interacting with whichever he or she chooses. Executing programs in such a way that they appear to be running simultaneously is called **multitasking.**

Time Sharing

Interrupts triggered by the **system clock** allow the operating system to switch processing from one program to another at timed intervals. That is the essence of **time sharing,** whose purpose is to make the computer's power available to as many users as possible. Each user has control of the computer for a short period of time on a regular basis. Because the processor is so fast in comparison with I/O devices and users, enough work can be done during the short **time slice** to give the user the impression that the entire system and its resources belong to him or her alone.

Types of Systems

Time sharing and multiprogramming gave rise to a number of different kinds of computer systems. One example is the narrow purpose, **online transaction processing** system, exemplified by airline reservation systems. This stands in contrast to the **general purpose** system which serves many users and many different applications. General purpose systems may be batch-oriented or promote interactive computing (batch and interactive refer to styles of programming and computing, not to multiprogramming and timesharing). **Process control** systems are **real time** systems that are even narrower in scope and function than the transaction processing systems.

Microcomputers

Microcomputers popularized interactive computing, made a CPU available locally to each user, and created the notion of an **intelligent workstation** or **productivity tool.** Desktop computing came on the scene, followed quickly by the intelligent workstation, which could function on a **stand alone** basis or as an **intelligent terminal** accessing a mainframe or minicomputer system. For a variety of reasons, microcomputer software was better designed for a less technical audience than software for minicomputers and mainframe systems. Accordingly, computing power became available to and usable by people who were not computer specialists. With the intelligent terminal/workstation, users choose the lesser power of the desktop unit or the greater power (and complexity) of the larger systems as needed.

It is interesting to note that the evolution of microcomputers parallels that of the larger early systems but with a compressed time frame. In the late 1970s, almost all microcomputers were single user, **single tasking** (only one application program sharing memory with the operating system). The operating systems offered only rudimentary services. By the mid-1980s, it was fairly common to find single user, **multitasking** (multiprogramming) microcomputers. Even a few multiuser timesharing microcomputer systems were appearing as the power, main memory capacity, and secondary storage capacity grew rapidly. Multiprogramming microcomputer systems will soon be the norm with multiuser microsystems also commonplace.

From a business perspective, the personal computer introduced by IBM in 1981 and given the name IBM PC had the most dramatic impact on the way many people used computers. Prior to IBM's entry into the field, most businesses were reluctant to use microcomputers due to a history of rapid change and poor support. IBM's entrance into the field represented a kind of stability that had been missing. Almost two years later, Apple Corporation introduced the Macintosh personal computer, which altered the way people interact with their machines. The original PC and the Macintosh represented almost totally opposite philosophies of what a personal computer should be; this began a battle for the business market that is still being fought. The introduction of desktop publishing in 1985 established the Macintosh in business applications because of its high-resolution graphics, its ability to drive a laser printer, and the availability of desktop publishing software. Yet the Macintosh did not match the IBM PC as a general purpose device in the office. The battle between the two vendors is still unfolding today in the form of the IBM Personal System/2 and the Macintosh II.

Perhaps the IBM PC became the industry standard because IBM understood the difference between computer architecture and computer organization (discussed in Chapter 2). IBM already had two major successes with the S/360 in 1963 and the S/370 in 1970. Its established customers believed that the first IBM PC was really the introduction of a *line* of personal computers, a commitment from IBM that future developments would go into improving the organization and allowing the architecture, and therefore the software base, to mature. In contrast, many manufacturers sold their systems on the strength of new architectural features while ignoring the disruptions and extra expense involved in changing software to run in each new machine. They quickly realized the significance of IBM's promise of a system that would continue to grow while still running all of the earlier software. Almost all other manufacturers were forced to adopt the PC architecture: The major exception is Apple Corporation with its Macintosh family of computers.

Networks

Computers hooked together in cooperative efforts can provide significant increases in the availability and distribution of computer power. In fact, many of the newer, more powerful computers being developed really consist of several smaller processors configured in a **network** arrangement and packaged as a single (**multiprocessing**) unit. Normally the processors are **tightly coupled,** meaning that all processors share a common main memory. On the other end of the spectrum, multiple standalone computers located at a variety of (perhaps very remote) sites are connected for purposes of **distributed** access. Coordination occurs over a communication network managed by **message passing.**

Networks may exist within a single hardware box, may be scattered throughout a huge office complex, may be spread over a major metropolitan area, or may be flung across the world. The parts may be interconnected by wires, phonelines, light pulses, microwaves, or satellite signals. The possibilities are seemingly endless.

Any number of vendors have been developing networking tools for such activity. For example, IBM has adopted a plan called **systems application architecture (SAA),** which is designed to remove the barriers between mainframes, minicomputers, and personal computers. SAA bridges the different architectures by setting several conditions that a program must satisfy. The conditions constrict the languages that may be used, the way a program must interact with users, and the way one program may communicate with another program. Networking efforts and conventions are in a very great state of flux at this time.

Trends

Timesharing mainframes extended computing power to a greater number of users. Minicomputers fueled the race to lower computing costs. Microcomputers brought the CPU to the user on his or her desk and made interactive processing the norm. The man/machine interface of these small powerhouses brought computer use to the nontechnical user and contributed to an explosion in computer literate users. The microcomputer revolution drove down the cost of computing.

The general trends have always included the drive for more power, more utility, more accessibility, and lower cost per unit of power. The current movement toward networking and multiprocessor systems reflects those same goals. The emphasis is moving toward functionality and connectivity. Users want to know what a system can do on its own, how expandable it is for meeting increased demands, and what it can be connected to. The major trends involve multiple processor systems, migration of popular/critical applications to the operating system, and better user interfaces.

It is currently possible to take a microcomputer (for example, an IBM PC or Macintosh) and add special computers called **transputers** as peripheral devices to create a **microsupercomputer** (not super microcomputer) at a comparatively low cost.

However, technology always precedes its application by some period of time. The applications for such systems will be mounting for several years. The use of thousands of transputers allows researchers to work on problems previously considered impossible or impractical.

In the commercial world, personal computers are giving way to the more powerful, graphics-driven workstations capable of standalone computing but designed to greatly multiply their power by participating in a network arrangement. Personal computers have typically been designed with *local* processing in mind; computer communications was an afterthought. Workstations of the Sun, Apollo, TeleVideo, Hewlett Packard, and VAX class have been designed to *incorporate communications from the beginning*. Workstations may be networked with each other, with minicomputers, and with mainframe systems. These workstations typically have more powerful CPUs than personal computers, better graphics capabilities, several megabytes' more main memory, and multitasking. Networks of workstations provide a resource base and flexibility unknown just a few years ago, even with the largest timesharing mainframe systems. It is also true, however, that the distinction between low-end workstations and high-end personal computers is blurring rapidly.

Networking is becoming so pervasive that OS/2, the operating system for PS/2, has been designed with a LAN (Local Area Network) manager as an integral part. The Macintosh operating system, Finder, is undergoing alteration so that it, too, has flexible communications built-in. Operating systems in general are now being designed to incorporate communication capabilities to achieve maximum connectivity with other systems. Communications has been an applications add-on until just recently.

Aside from communications, operating systems *as resource managers* are changing very little, particularly for single CPU systems. However, operating systems for networks and multiprocessor systems are changing dramatically. In general, the one trend common to most operating system redesigns (and most new operating systems) is the incorporation of functions that used to be considered applications *outside* the realm of the operating system. In addition to communications, database management systems are being added as operating system responsibilities. (The Pick operating system and IBM's S/3X are two popular examples.) These databases will be **hypermedia** databases that contain numeric, textual, graphical, and audio data that can be mixed and matched at will. Certain graphics capabilities and some applications of artificial intelligence (such as inference engines and expert systems) will also find their way into most operating systems of tomorrow. Typical applications such as spreadsheets and wordprocessors will also be incorporated into the operating system. Other support tools used by programmers and decision support tools used by managers will be added to the operating system as well.

Some of the most striking recent changes that will be carried into the future deal with the way users interact with their machines. While menus gave a friendlier interface than the ancient mainframe command line, the Macintosh operating system has been the commercial leader in changing interfaces. The Macintosh introduced the public at large to *object oriented* interfaces, where users give commands by manipulating graphic icons. Windowing (the ability to have multiple active displays on one video screen) is fast becoming standard, particularly when coupled with iconic interfaces. As operating systems incorporate more of the current application programs, developers will be constrained to present a consistent user interface across all applications for a given system, making new applications easier to learn.

These trends declare that operating systems are going to get larger and use greater system resources themselves, requiring more processing power and greater main memory capacities. In order to make the increased services faster and more efficient, parts of the operating system will be incorporated into the hardware itself.

As systems grow more powerful and easier to use, there will be a change in the way people think about computing. It will be technically possible to solve problems that are not even given current consideration.

In short, the operating system is to: make the system work, make it work efficiently, make it available, make it easy to use, make its use relatively error-free, make it pleasant to use, and make it provide a return on investment.

Exercises

Most of the exercises below do not follow as easy extensions of the chapter's discussion. Rather, these exercises ask you to begin the thinking and evaluation processes that will increase the effectiveness and meaning of the coming chapters.

1. Discuss the statement: The operating system is a resource sharing executive.
2. List the resources an operating system might control.
3. Why is an operating system said to be event driven?
4. Why would you expect an operating system for a personal computer to have more superstructure and less kernel than a timesharing system?
5. Application programs are said to serve users individually, while operating systems serve users collectively. Explain.
6. In the BOS (before operating system) days, how were runtime errors likely to be handled? Remember that without an operating system, there was no automatic error messaging.
7. When automated job sequencing (batch) was first introduced, what was likely to happen to a program with an error? How would a computer operator be helpful?
8. Before SPOOLing, batch jobs were executed in the order in which they were "fed" into the machine. Why?
9. What does a user accomplish by interactive computing that is not accomplished otherwise?
10. Compare/contrast multiprogramming and timesharing.
11. Why is timesharing attractive?
12. Some have said that JCL for batch processing is more complex than is required for interactive processing. Why?
13. **Buffering** refers to Mechanism A's placement (writing) of data into a storage segment for later retrieval (reading) by Mechanism B. Describe some uses of buffering.
14. Consider the statement: In a modern computer system, no resource is directly available to a user. How does the user gain access to a resource?
15. Compare/contrast the terms **online** and **real time.**
16. Interactive multitasking allows a user to have a **foreground** (interactive) job and one or more **background** (noninteractive) tasks. Give an example of how that might be useful on a single user system.

17. Why is the amount of main memory likely to be important in a multiprocessing system?

18. What is meant by the computing environment?

19. Finkel's [5] *beautification principle* says: An operating system hides the hardware and provides a pleasant environment. What does this mean?

20. Why might the **variance** in response time be as important an indication of service as the mininum response time figure?

21. In a large timesharing system, which measures of efficiency would likely be of primary concern?

22. Describe security concerns for the users of an *in-house* timesharing system. What if the timesharing system belongs to a *data processing service?* If there is phone access to the timesharing service?

23. Compare/contrast the desire to maximize machine efficiency with the desire to maximize user productivity. Which is likely to be preferred? Why and under what conditions?

24. What is likely meant by the term "turnkey application"? For example, a PC is sold with a software package that makes it a turnkey accounting system. What does this imply? Why would it be desirable? To whom?

25. What would one look for in a system with very high utilization but very low throughput?

26. Make a list of utilities that would be useful for writing application programs.

27. Why would a designer write most system services as application programs rather than as part of the operating system?

28. In some quarters, multitasking and multiprogramming are considered to be different terms. Multitasking is sometimes taken to mean that each user may have several programs executing concurrently. In such a case, how might the two terms really differ?

29. List some devices where data must be accessed **serially.** What are some devices where data is naturally accessed **randomly?**

30. Suppose Machine A can accomplish some act by use of a single hardware instruction. Machine B does not have such a hardware instruction but can accomplish the same thing through its operating system software. Speculate why the hardware solution might be preferred.

31. Discuss the importance of intelligent workstations in terms of online and offline processing.

32. Describe the characteristics of systems where measures of efficiency are most important.

33. Capacity is a measure: What "quantities" might have meaningful capacities? Which capacity is likely considered most important? By whom and for what reasons?

34. The term **virtual** is used often in computing circles. It means *something seeming to have all the properties of another object without being that object.* A programmer writing COBOL programs views his computer as a virtual COBOL machine. What does this mean?

35. Using the discussion from Exercise 34, answer the following: An international computer network has a standardized virtual terminal. If a user has two different kinds of terminals, can both be used to access the network? Explain.

2 Organization and Architecture

Overview
The concentric model portrays a computer system as constructed of layers of software and hardware, arranged rather like the layers of an onion. This arrangement suggests the structured approach that modern computer systems use and graphically illustrates the relationships among the various hardware and software components.

Computer architecture is those aspects of a computer that directly relate to the way it executes (runs) programs; computers with the same architecture can execute the same programs. **Computer organization** is the way a particular architecture is implemented: What components are used and how they are connected. In other words, computer architecture determines **what** a computer can do; computer organization determines **how** a computer does that work.

Computer organization describes the way a manufacturer chooses to construct a computer; it is independent of the architecture. Manufacturers can provide various organizations for the same architecture. This allows them to offer a **family** of computer systems. The two most notable examples of successful computer architectures are the IBM System/370 (introduced in 1970) and the DEC VAX family (introduced in 1978). It is no coincidence that IBM (International Business Machines) and DEC (Digital Equipment Corporation) are now the world's largest and second largest manufacturers of computer systems.

Architectural features that influence the operation of a computer include the following five factors: **word size, register organization, control unit organization, instruction set,** and **available addressing modes.** Organizational features that influence the operation of a computer include technology, clock speed, amount of memory fitted, and the design of the buses. Organizational features are transparent (invisible) to the operation of the software, apart from affecting the speed of execution.

For most users, the software hides the architecture and organization of a computer from view. However, the architecture determines what software runs on the machine and must be considered when purchasing software. The organization of a computer determines factors such as speed, capacity, and cost, and it is therefore of primary importance when selecting a system or adding components.

Figure 2.1

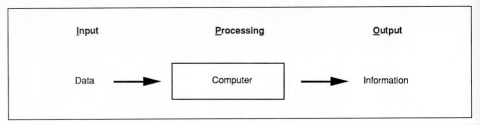

Figure 2.1 shows a model of the computer commonly known as the input/process/output model or more briefly, the **IPO** model. Figure 2.2 depicts the relationship between people and computer information systems as an iterative (cycling) process. Information produced by the computer system influences decisions. New decisions lead to the creation of more data that in turn, processed by the computer, influence the next level of decision making.

Figure 2.2

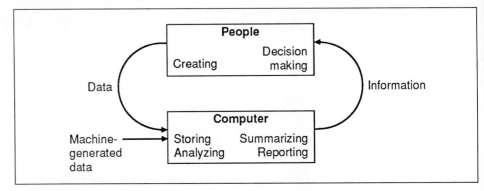

The Concentric Circle Model

The concentric circle model shows what each part of the computer system does and where the boundaries are. Any user asked to describe the operation of a computer will give a very personal view. A user who does word processing only will give a picture of the word processor, perhaps as shown in Figure 2.3. The outer word processing "layer"

Figure 2.3

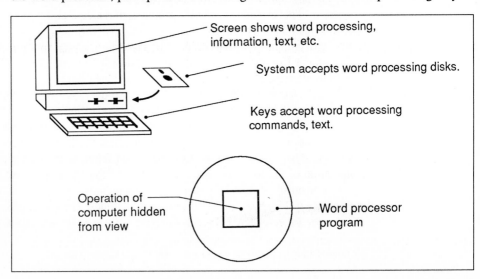

Figure 2.4

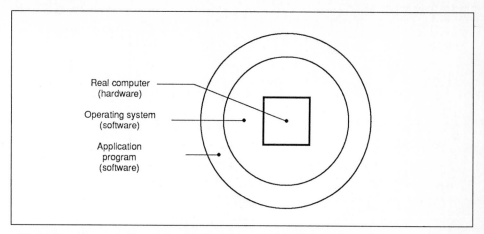

Real computer
(hardware)

Operating system
(software)

Application
program
(software)

effectively separates the user from the inner circle of hardware. All user interaction is with the running program.

A user who runs two or more programs is aware that the computer has a different "look and feel" for each. For example, the way in which the user enters commands from the keyboard and the way the computer displays information on the screen vary from program to program. In running several programs, the user discovers the existence of the operating system, which runs as a sort of master organizer that can accept commands whenever no user program is running. Sooner or later, he or she discovers that the operating system is actually an integral part of the computer system, linking the hardware and the programs. This view is seen in Figure 2.4.

Hardware

The very center of the concentric circle model (the hardware and innermost layer of software) includes a number of physical components. The most common general architecture (and the one examined here) is the **Von Neumann** architecture, whose most important contribution to computing is the **stored program** concept. Prior to this design, computers were programmed by wiring pluggable panels or reading long streams of punched paper tape. Reading instructions from memory was a thousand times faster than paper tape. Moreover, the computer gained an ability to read the instructions *in whatever order was required.* That is, the computer became able to keep track of sequencing.

CPU Elements

There are six functional sections in any computer. These are shown symbolically in Figure 2.5. Several of these units are often considered to be part of a larger unit called the **central processing unit (CPU),** which is shown as a dotted box in Figure 2.5.

Arithmetic and logic unit (ALU). As its name suggests, the ALU performs arithmetical and logical operations on numbers in a computer. It is here that "computing" takes place during the execution part of the machine cycle to be discussed in the following sections.

Registers. The registers form the first level of memory available to the CPU. They are a "fast" form of memory. (In a physical sense, there are only two ways in which data

Figure 2.5

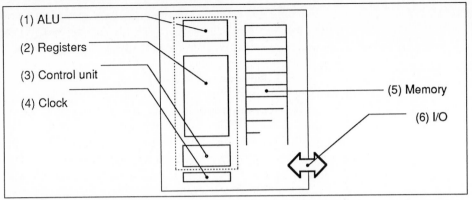

data and addressing information can exist inside a computer. They are either stored in registers or memory or else they take the form of an electrical signal that is moving through wires from one point to another.) The size and organization of the registers in a CPU determine the major characteristics of that particular computer—that is, the registers play a major role in defining the architecture of a computer. Figure 2.6 shows the so-called **visible registers** associated with the functional components from Figure 2.5.

Figure 2.6

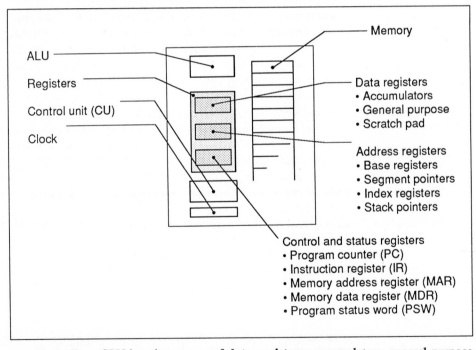

Typically, a CPU has three types of **data registers:** accumulators, general-purpose registers, and scratchpads. The name "accumulator" is a holdover from early mechanical calculating machines in which the answer was "accumulated" in a mechanical register. Most machines have several accumulators used in conjunction with the ALU. General-purpose registers have the characteristics of an accumulator. Scratchpad registers are used to temporarily hold data (such as intermediate results).

The **program status word (PSW)** is a collection of information that indicates the current status of the program. It consists of the **program counter** (instruction pointer) and a **flag register** (condition codes register). There are also some bits in the PSW that control CPU functions (such as turning the hardware interrupts on and off).

The program counter is an address register that always points to the next instruction to be executed. The CPU keeps track of where it is in a program by storing the address of the next instruction in this special CPU register. In order to alter the order of execution of instructions, a branching instruction loads the program counter with a new address that is either calculated by the CPU or supplied as part of the instruction. The contents of the program counter are also modified when an interrupt occurs. The initial loading of the program counter is performed by a hardware "reset."

The **stack pointer** is an address register that points to a region of memory that has been set aside for a **stack.** A stack is defined as a linear list of information where all accesses, insertions, and removals are made at one end of the list, called the **top of stack** (a LIFO structure). The stack is typically used by the system for temporary storage when switching execution from one activity to another.

An **index register** is a special form of base address register that is used as a pointer to memory in operations that manipulate strings and arrays of data.

Control unit (CU). The control unit translates program instructions into electronic signals that control the operation of the entire computer. It orchestrates all of the activities in the CPU. One of the control unit's primary functions is to decode program instructions and translate them into sequences of signals for controlling the CPU. Program instructions consist of two parts: (1) an operation code (**op code**) that specifies the operation to be performed and (2) an operand that supplies either the data to be operated on or the address of the data to be operated on.

There is a great similarity between the operation of the control unit and the operation of the CPU itself. Both perform tasks that are specified by stored instructions. In each case, the instructions reduce down to a sequence of smaller steps, and from time to time they both perform tests to determine what the next instruction should be. Microprogrammed controllers exploit this similarity by using a simple computer (called a **microcontrol**) to generate the control sequences. Figure 2.7 on the following page shows one of the forms a microcontrol can take. In the system depicted here, a microprogram memory (almost always a ROM) contains a list of micro-instructions. A sequence of micro-instructions is necessary to execute every program instruction. Micro-instructions execute in a reserved, very high speed memory. Thus, microprogramming forms a thin layer around the hardware that generates the machine language instructions.

Clock. Information in a computer is physically represented as electronic signals. The clock generates streams of clock pulses that synchronize all the operations. In the same fashion that the rising and falling of a conductor's baton synchronizes musicians in an orchestra, the rising and falling voltage in a **clock signal** synchronizes the operation of circuits in a computer. Everything a computer does is done in time to a clock pulse.

Clock pulses are often described by a **frequency,** such as 8-megahertz (Hz). This frequency is a measure of how many clock pulses occur in one second; an 8-megahertz

Figure 2.7

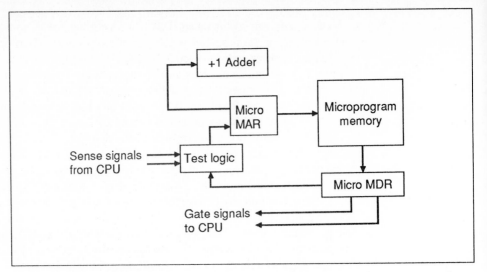

clock has eight million pulses every second. The higher the clock frequency, the faster the operation of the computer.

Memory.   The memory in a computer performs two roles. It stores (in binary form) programs that are executed by the computer and data that is processed by the programs. The memory is organized in a hierarchy of **bits, bytes** (8 bits), and **words** (of 8, 16, 32, or 64 bits). The word size is an architectural feature and depends on the particular system. The addresses in memory point to the smallest **addressable unit,** either a byte or word. A computer's memory requirements fall into two major categories: internal and external.

Input/Output (I/O).   I/O provides communications between the computer and any external devices. I/O is handled in a number of different ways, depending on the amount of data to be handled and the speed with which it must be transferred. The peripheral devices may be connected to the system directly or through cables. An interface of some sort is required.

   Spooling consists of transferring data to or from an I/O device through an intermediate store, so it can be transferred at a more convenient time or so that a section of the data that is generated separately can be transferred in bulk. The process is shown in Figure 2.8. Spooling can be used with any I/O device or communication channel (described in sections that follow), but the intermediate store is almost always a disk file.

   Buffering is a programming technique used to compensate for the slow and possibly erratic rate at which a peripheral device consumes or generates data. If a peripheral communicates directly with a program, the program must run in exact synchrony with the peripheral. Buffering allows the program and device to each run at its own speed: The writer puts data into the buffer at the writer's speed, while the other later reads it at the reader's speed.

General operation.   A computer operates by working through a list of instructions stored in part of the memory. Before a program can be executed, it (or at least a part of

Figure 2.8

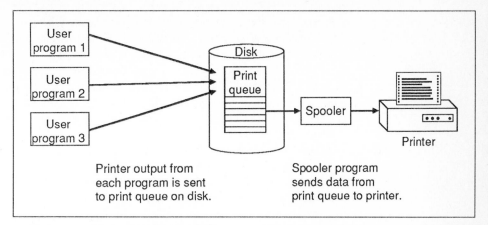

Printer output from
each program is sent
to print queue on disk.

Spooler program
sends data from
print queue to printer.

it) must be loaded into memory. Execution follows a cycle known as **fetch-decode-execute.**

Execution begins when the operating system transfers control to the memory location of the first instruction. The machine **fetches** the instruction in the following manner: A clock pulse triggers the CU, the memory address of the next instruction is found in the program counter, the instruction is copied from memory to the instruction register, and the program counter is updated to the next instruction's address. The instruction in the instruction register is **decoded** by the control unit. Finally, the ALU carries out the **execution** of the instruction. This cycle repeats itself until the program is completed.

Pipelining is a technique for minimizing the amount of time the CPU spends waiting for instructions to be read from memory. Without pipelining, a CPU sequentially fetches an instruction, decodes it, and then executes it. Only after it completes the execution of an instruction does it begin to fetch the next instruction from memory. This results in a stop-start action for the CPU. When the system uses pipelining, it has a mechanism for fetching the next instruction *while the current instruction is still being executed* (see Figure 2.9). Pipelining is used extensively on larger machines.

The CPU must access memory at least once in every instruction cycle to fetch

Figure 2.9

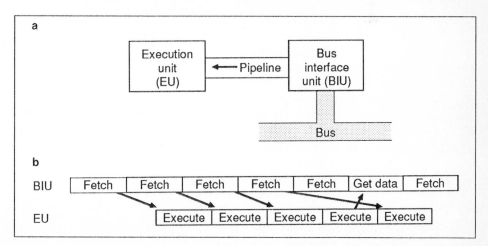

the instruction—and more than once if operands must be fetched or results must be written. The rate at which a CPU can execute instructions therefore depends on the **memory cycle time.** Since main memory cycle time is two to ten times greater than that of the CPU, a small amount of very fast **cache memory** may be interposed between the CPU and main memory. Programs tend to execute clusters of instructions: If the proper instructions are in cache, the execution time is reduced. A variety of caching algorithms have been established to make sure that the correct instructions are usually in cache.

Cache memories often use special addressing schemes such as **content-addressable memory** to further improve access times. Content-addressable memory, otherwise known as **associative memory,** finds information quickly; this is done by examining all the words in a memory simultaneously to see if any match a particular specification, rather than stepping through and testing each one in turn. This is somewhat like trying to find all the Smiths in a room full of people by saying "All Smiths step forward," rather than asking each person in turn whether his or her name is Smith.

Buses   Wires connect sources of data to destinations of data within a computer. A separate wire is used for each bit of data transferred as a unit. These groups of wires are called **buses.** A bus transfers data from a source to a destination. Figure 2.10 shows how three separate buses are used in a typical computer, each carrying a particular type of information. They are the **data bus,** the **address bus,** and the **control bus.**

Figure 2.10

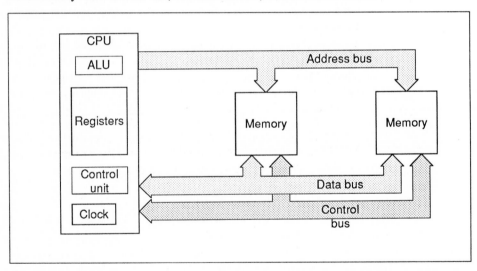

Data Bus.   The data bus transfers data between registers or between registers and memory locations. The **width** (number of wires) of the data bus greatly influences the speed of the computer. The more wires it contains, the greater the number of bits it can move at a time—and hence the more data it can shift at a time. Small microcomputers have 8-bit buses for moving a byte at a time. High-performance microcomputers, minicomputers, and many mainframes have 32-bit data buses (4 bytes); some mainframes have 64-bit data buses. Data can flow in either direction on a data bus. When many devices are connected to a bus, they must all take their turns at using it.

The width of the data path between the CPU and memory is one organizational feature that often differs among members of the same family of computers. This variation occurs in both the IBM PC family and the System/370, where narrower data paths are used on some models to reduce hardware costs while accepting the penalty of reduced processing speed.

Address bus.   The address bus carries binary signals for selecting the memory storage locations to be used when data is read from or written to the memory. The number of unique addresses that can be carried (one at a time) by an address bus is the nth power of 2 where n is the number of wires (**width** of the bus). A 16-wire address bus gives an address range of 64K (65,636) addresses, each address pointing to a byte or word. A 32-wire bus gives an address range of 4 gigabytes for a byte-addressable machine.

Modern computers use large amounts of memory, thereby requiring large addresses to access any individual location. Computers such as these use anywhere from 20-bit (as in the Intel 8086/8088) to 32-bit addresses (as in the Intel 80386).

Control bus.   The control bus carries signals that tell devices when they may use the bus and sets up the circuits on the bus for data flow toward or away from the memory. The control bus always includes the following functions in some form:

1. A signal that signifies whether an operation is reading data from memory or writing data to memory. Some systems use separate read and write lines to distribute this information.
2. A signal to say when the information on the address bus is ready to use.

Since the data and address buses are shared by all of the system components, it is necessary to synchronize their actions. Control wires convey command and timing signals between system components. Typical control signals include memory write, memory read, I/O write, I/O read, bus request (indicates that one of the system modules wants to take control of the bus), bus grant, interrupt request (indicates that an interrupt has been requested), interrupt acknowledge, system clock (synchronizes all operations), and reset (sets all modules to their initial startup conditions).

Memory   **Internal memory** is connected to the system buses and holds programs and data that must be immediately accessible to the CPU. **External memory** communicates with the CPU through an I/O mechanism and holds programs and data for which some access delay can be tolerated.

There are two classes of internal memory:

1. **Random-access memory (RAM)** is memory the computer can read data from or store data to.
2. **Read-only memory (ROM)** is memory the computer can read from but cannot write to. ROM has data or program information stored into it during manufacture.

Internal memory is always electronic and is referred to as **system memory, main memory, main store,** or **core memory.**

External memory is usually in the form of magnetically recorded disks or tape, but some optically recorded systems have appeared. External memory is often referred to as **backing store, bulk storage, auxiliary storage, secondary store,** or **secondary memory.**

Selecting the best combination of memory for a computer is usually a matter of working out the best compromise in speed, capacity, and cost. A hierarchy of different devices is used. Sufficient high-speed memory is used to enable the CPU to operate efficiently, and then progressively larger amounts are used of each of the slower memories. Figure 2.11 shows how the types of memory used in a computer system form a pyramid, ranging from a base of slow, low-cost optical or magnetic storage through to a peak of very fast and very expensive internal CPU registers. Almost all computer systems include CPU registers, main memory, and magnetic disk. High-speed applications include cache memory to bridge the gap in speed between the CPU and main memory.

Figure 2.11

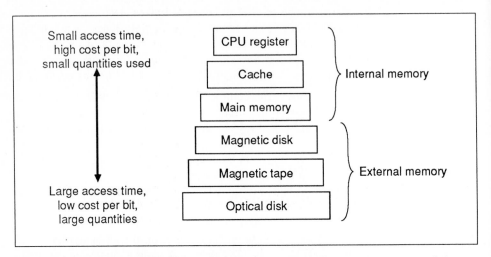

Input/Output   I/O can be handled in a number of different ways depending on the amount of data to be moved and the speed with which it must be transferred. In small systems (such as most personal computers and some minicomputers) I/O is handled by **I/O controller** devices that are managed directly by the CPU. In larger systems the I/O is handled by secondary processors called **I/O channels,** which transfer data directly to and from main memory.

Polled I/O.   When a CPU is communicating with an external device, there is usually a great discrepancy between the speeds of the CPU and the device. The data transfer can be made more efficient by having a control register associated with the I/O port; the control register is read by the CPU just as if it were memory. One of the bits in the control register is used as a flag to indicate whether the I/O device is ready to transfer another character. The CPU periodically checks the flag for **device ready** status, effectively asking the device if it's ready to continue—this is known as **polling.**

Interrupt-Driven I/O.   A more efficient way to accomplish the coordination is through the use of **interrupts,** whereby the CPU ignores the peripheral device until the device actively signals it. The interrupt process (Figure 2.12) consists of the following steps:

1. The device sends a signal known as an interrupt to the CPU to signal its readiness.

Figure 2.12

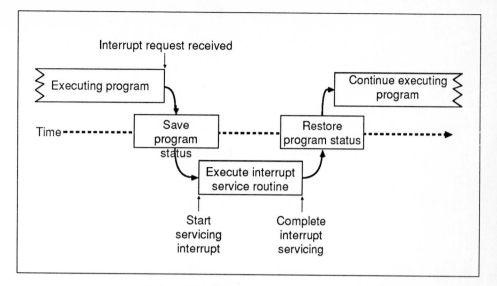

2. The CPU receives the interrupt (signal) and stops executing the program in progress, saves the status of the program in memory or special registers, and then begins executing an interrupt service routine to take care of its part of the next phase of I/O. After the I/O activity, the CPU retrieves the interrupted program's status and continues as if nothing had happened.
3. The I/O device takes care of its responsibility, sending another interrupt when finished.

The use of interrupts enables the CPU to handle a variety of different tasks, each of which may be executing at different speeds. A separate interrupt servicing routine is stored in memory for each of the interrupt tasks to be performed.

DMA and I/O channels.   When polled and interrupt-driven I/O must pass through the CPU (that is, when the CPU must manage the byte-by-byte data transfer to and from memory), there is an upper limit to the transfer speed that can be handled. For high-speed I/O, there is another technique known as **direct memory access (DMA)**. This method effectively bypasses CPU involvement by transferring data directly between the I/O device and main memory. An I/O **controller** or **channel** does the work independent of the CPU after being given general instructions. A block of data, rather than a character (byte), is transferred between interrupts. This reduces the CPU involvement dramatically. DMA is often described as **cycle-stealing** since the unit has priority over the CPU for memory accesses. When the channel needs to access memory, it signals the CPU, which is then put on hold until the block of data is transferred. Because I/O is relatively slow and DMA uses very few memory cycles, overall processing speed is increased by offloading the data transfer to the DMA units and giving priority to the I/O activity.

I/O channels come in two general varieties: **selectors** and **multiplexors.** Selectors serve peripheral devices one at a time for high-speed data I/O. A single selector normally services several devices but creates a data stream for only one at a time. A multiplexor, on the other hand, interleaves I/O streams for several devices to create a data

Figure 2.13

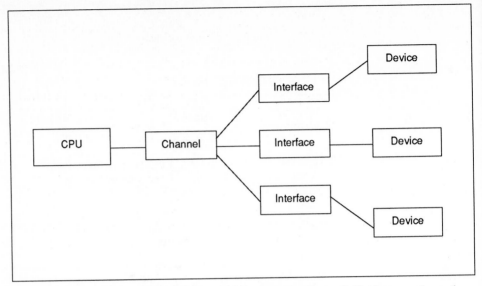

transfer servicing several peripheral units at one time. Figure 2.13 shows a channel arrangement.

I/O Connections.   Peripheral devices may be connected to a computer by direct connection to a bus or through a port via cables. Two types of data communication are
used between the I/O ports of the computer and the external devices (see Figure 2.14).
Parallel communication is similar to the flow of data inside a computer, where an entire word is transmitted at a time: All the data bits in a binary output word are sent
simultaneously over separate wires. In addition, extra wires are needed for control signals. **Serial communication** sends words of data one bit at a time over fewer wires.

Figure 2.14

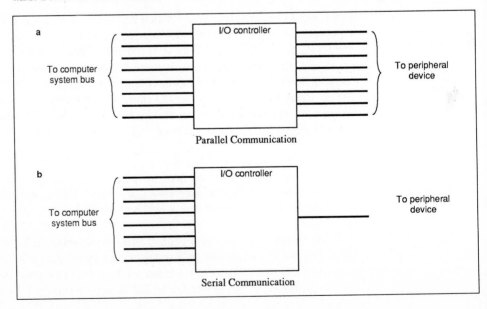

If directly connected to a bus, the peripheral communicates with the computer through an electronic interface. The interface translates between the device-independent symbolic instruction the user initiates (for example, read or write) and the complex set of physical activities required to carry it out. This arrangement is commonly set up for peripherals (such as tapes and disks) that must transfer large amounts of data in and out of main memory very quickly. The peripheral device itself may be connected to the interface through a cable. The use of "cards" plugged into a PC is a good example of this mechanism.

Instruction Set

The repertoire of instructions for a particular CPU is called its **instruction set.** In modern hardware systems, the instruction set is often determined by a process known as **microcoding.** The microcode consists of a thin layer of **firmware** (programs written in a special, low-level language and "burned" into ROM) that effectively isolates the system programmer from the hardware by generating the instruction set that controls the machine. (See Figure 2.15.) At this level, machine language instructions are required for machine control.

Figure 2.15

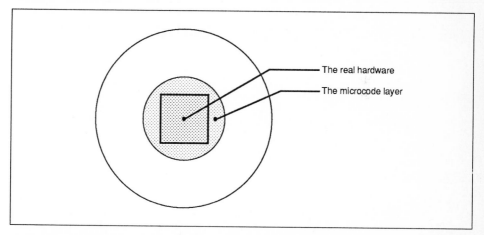

The real hardware

The microcode layer

Large and powerful machine instructions make it easier to express problems in machine-executable form, but they execute more slowly. Modern trends have been to supply more powerful machine instructions to make programming easier and less expensive. Another, more recent approach reduces the instruction set to a small number of carefully chosen instructions that allow the computer to operate at very high execution speeds. These **reduced instruction set computers (RISC)** are still able to perform complex tasks by combining several of the simpler instructions.

The word size of the hardware affects the instruction set, particularly in terms of their number. A machine with 32-bit words, for example, can give many more bits to the **opcode** representing an instruction than can one using 8-bit words. More bits in the opcode translate into more opcodes; hence more instructions can be defined.

As an example of this point, the IBM S/370 handles eight bytes in some instructions, and the DEC VAX handles instructions with up to almost forty bytes. Because instructions can have a wide variety of lengths, the word size for a particular computer is usually taken as the number of bits used in the majority of instructions. The IBM

Figure 2.16

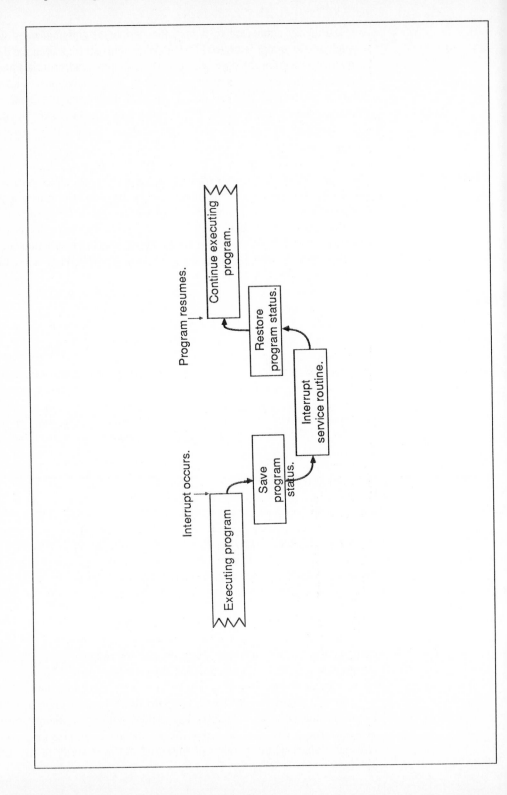

S/370 is considered to have a 32-bit word size, even though it can handle 8-, 16-, 32- and 64-bit quantities. Note that the DEC VAX has a 32-bit word size, the 8086/88 used in the original IBM PC has a 16-bit word size, and the 80386 used in some of the IBM PS/2 personal computers has a 32-bit word size.

Interrupt Handling

Interrupts are performed by a combination of special software and hardware functions that cause a computer's CPU to suspend the program it is executing and transfer to another program (called an **interrupt handler**). Interrupts are a way of getting the CPU's immediate attention and service. The interrupt handler determines the cause of the interrupt, performs the appropriate operation, and then returns control to the suspended program. Figure 2.16 shows the sequence of events that occurs when a program is interrupted.

Software interrupts are used primarily to request service from operating system routines. System calls are effectively software interrupts whose purpose is to get the operating system to perform some action on behalf of the program. Hardware interrupts are initiated by signals from events external to the CPU (for example, timer out, I/O device requires attention, or a hardware failure has been detected).

It is necessary for CPUs to be able to block interrupts while they are executing critical sections of code. In most systems, interrupts can be temporarily disabled. However, there may be one or more interrupts (reserved for events of catastrophic importance) that cannot be disabled.

To minimize the time spent determining the cause of an interrupt, each interrupt type will have a reserved memory location that contains the address (**interrupt vector**) of the appropriate interrupt handler routine. The use of vectors speeds up the CPU's response to interrupts by enabling it to transfer directly to the appropriate handler routine without needing to perform tests on the hardware to determine which device generated the interrupt.

Many of the functions in an operating system are time-dependent. The operating system uses a software clock that is initialized from a hardware clock during booting and then updated at regular intervals by a hardware timer.

System Software

Virtually every computer uses an operating system to manage its hardware, software, and data resources and to provide support for application software. The basic purpose is to provide a link between the application programs and the hardware. The concentric circle model shows this link as a number of layers of software between the physical hardware and the application software (Figure 2.17). Access to the operating system occurs in the form of system

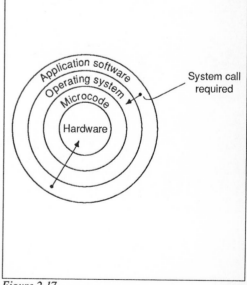

Figure 2.17

Figure 2.18

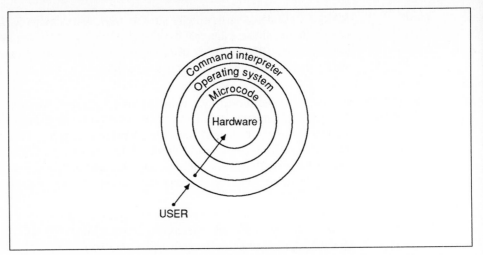

calls that are effectively extended instructions. The operating system enhances the system by adding features that neither the hardware nor instruction set provides directly. These added features (**extended instructions**) behave like extensions that make the basic hardware more powerful and easier to use. The system calls act as the programmer's interface to the system: They represent how the programmer gets the operating system to perform the functions needed by the application.

Whenever application programs are not executing, the operating system provides its own outer layer in the form of a command processor that accepts user commands. This is the lowest level user interface outside the system calls (Figure 2.18). Application programs have a separate user interface that replaces the operating system's command processor while the application program is executing. (See Figure 2.19.) In this way the application effectively hides the operating system from the user's view. However, the operating system is still present beneath the application software, providing (via commands and system calls) the necessary links to the hardware.

The operating system manages the hardware and software resources of the com-

Figure 2.19

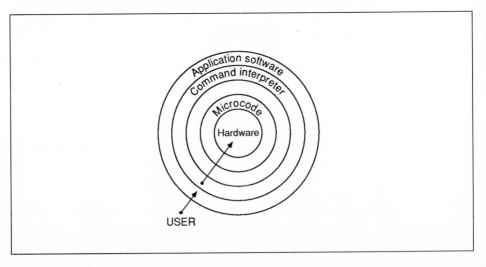

puter and makes them available to the user, either by accepting commands typed directly into it through the command processor or by providing support for application programs. Regardless of the size of the system, the primary purposes of an operating system remain the same: *to make the computer system operate efficiently and to make it easy to use.*

Basic Layers

Broadly speaking, an operating system performs three main functions: It manages the hardware, it supports and controls programs, and it processes commands. Figure 2.20 shows the operating system comprised of three layers of software: the **hardware interface,** the **run-time support,** and the **user interface.**

Figure 2.20

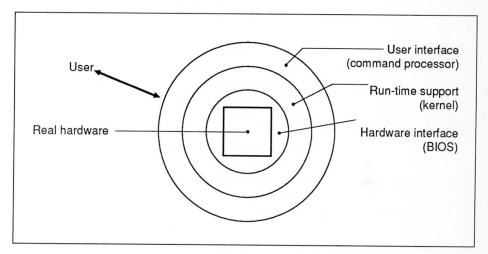

The hardware interface provides the links (system calls) that enable the software to communicate with and control the hardware. It simplifies the user's view of the intricate processes required to direct hardware actions. At each stage, these complicated procedures require extensive, precise knowledge about the properties and management of the computer hardware. The operating system makes these complicated actions available through a single instruction (system call), handling each hardware function in a consistent manner and presenting a simplified view of it to the user program.

This simplified view has two advantages: It simplifies operations that require hardware activity, and it provides a standard way for the user programs to interact with hardware. This last point is important to manufacturers of computers that are similar but not identical. In this way, it is unnecessary for the user program to know the details of how each function is carried out.

The operating system's second major task, controlling programs, involves loading programs from the system's storage device, setting up the environment in the computer for the particular program, and providing a variety of support functions while the program is executing. Generally, the operating system also provides access to other system software and utilities.

The third major task performed by the operating system is to provide an interface between the user and the computer. This task involves two separate functions: (1) displaying information for the user and (2) carrying out commands entered by the user.

The design of the user interface, whether in the operating system or in a user program, is extremely important because it is the part to which most people are exposed.

Operating System Types

Operating systems are often classified on each of the following bases:

1. Number of users that can be supported simultaneously (single user or multiple users).
2. Number of jobs that can be run at the same time (single tasking or multitasking).
3. Number of processors used in the system (single processor or multiple processors).

Because a CPU generally processes data much faster than the data can be moved in or out of the system, the CPU in a single tasking system is often idle while it waits for data I/O operations to be completed. Timesharing (dividing the CPU's time into short slices and apportioning them among several jobs), keeps the CPU busy while it waits for the I/O for each task.

Multiprocessor operating systems support more than one CPU at the same time and can be described as either loosely coupled (or linked) systems, as in Figure 2.21(a), or tightly coupled, as in Figure 2.21(b). In a loosely coupled system, each CPU has its own resources and communicates with other CPUs over a communications link. The operating system coordinates the individual actions of the CPUs. Tightly coupled multiprocessing systems differ by combining all the system resources so that all the resources are accessible to all the processors. This design leads to extremely complex operating systems.

Process Scheduling

The operating system uses a special technique called **scheduling** to manage the loading and execution of multiple programs. Three commonly needed types of scheduling are

Figure 2.21

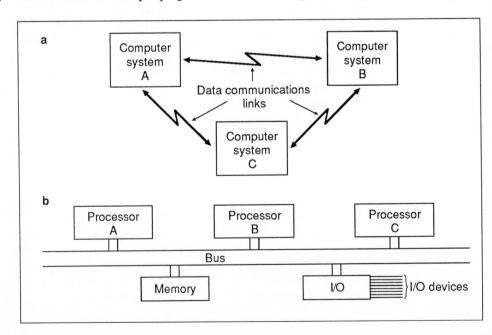

often employed. A **high-level (long-term)** scheduler determines when particular pro-grams should be loaded into the memory for execution. A **short-term** scheduler (**dis-patcher**) determines which process is to be executed next by the CPU. An **I/O sched-uler (medium-term)** determines which I/O device will be used to service a particular I/O request. During the time that a process exists in memory, it will typically be in one of several possible conditions referred to as **states.** These states and the paths between them are shown in Figure 2.22.

Figure 2.22

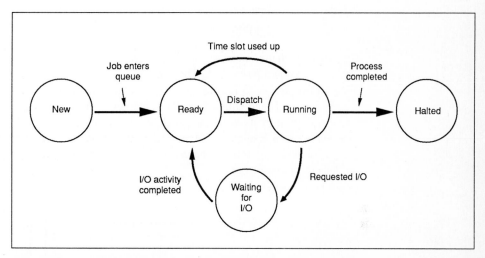

Memory Management

In a computer that runs only one user program at a time, the main memory is divided into two parts: (1) a part for the memory resident portion of the operating system and (2) a part for the program being executed. In a multitasking system, the user portion of the main memory must be further divided among the multiple programs. However, such partitioning may not allow enough programs in main memory concurrently to keep the CPU busy. In such a case, some of the waiting processes may be temporarily trans-ferred from memory to disk storage in a process called **swapping.** (See Figure 2.23.) The purpose in swapping out one waiting program is to swap in another ready one. If done properly, the CPU efficiency increases.

Figure 2.23

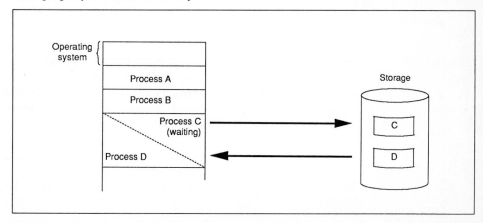

Contiguous memory allocation.   Finding suitable areas of vacant memory for each process can be complicated. A number of strategies are used to divide the available memory; **partitioning** (memory is divided into separate contiguous regions called **partitions** each of which is allocated to one program) is just one such strategy. The partitions may all be of the same size or, more likely, of differing sizes. The partitioning may be static (fixed) or dynamic, in which case the partitions and their sizes are determined when a program is to be loaded. Regardless of the type of partitioning, main memory is wasted by **internal fragmentation** (fixed partitions are only partially used by the program) or **external fragmentation** (unallocated chunks of memory may be too small to hold a program).

Paging and virtual memory.   All but the smallest modern systems use a different technique known as **paging.** The main memory is divided into relatively small, fixed-size partitions called **frames,** and the programs are divided into equal-sized portions called **pages.** Fragmentation is not a problem since, whatever the size of a program, only a fraction of its last frame will be wasted (Figure 2.24). When pages of a process are loaded into frames of memory, the frames need not be adjacent to each other. A special addressing scheme based on logical addresses allows the pages to be placed anywhere in main store.

Figure 2.24

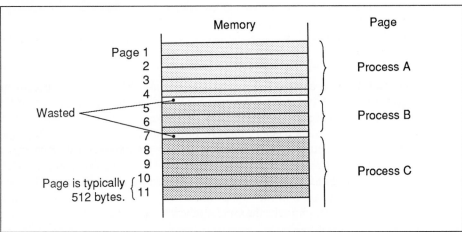

A paging system maintains a table of pages for each program that shows which main memory frame is allocated to each page of the program. **Demand paging,** keeping only those pages in memory that are currently required to continue execution, allows the number of concurrently loaded programs to increase dramatically. Pages not currently required reside in secondary store. Since only a few pages of a program need to be memory in a paged system, programs may actually be larger than all of main memory. Generally, the only limitation is the amount of disk storage available. Such systems are said to use **virtual memory,** because disk storage is virtually the same as real memory insofar as the program is concerned. Virtual addresses, measured as offsets from the start of the virtual code image, are not tied to main memory addresses at all. Programmers no longer need to worry about the size of their programs and data structures.

Figure 2.25

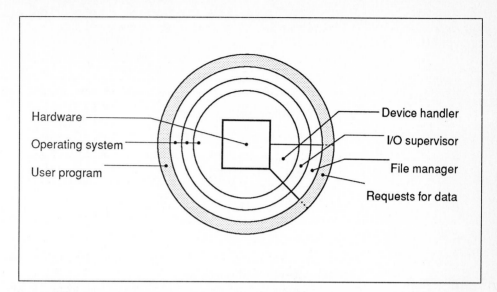

Hardware

Operating system

User program

Device handler

I/O supervisor

File manager

Requests for data

File Handling The operating system provides a variety of services that enable user programs to access stored data without knowledge of the physical process. Figure 2.25 shows the relationship of the **file manager** to the user program and to the routines that handle the device I/O.

To convert the user's logical request into a physical request, the file manager must first obtain information about the location and structure of the file. This information is usually kept in a structure known as a **directory** or **catalog.** The file manager begins processing a file by creating a small data structure in main memory called a **file control block (FCB).** The FCB holds information about the file and the I/O device that will be used.

The details of how files are physically arranged on a storage medium (such as magnetic tape or magnetic disk) vary from device to device and from operating system to operating system. Records within files can be either of fixed length or of variable length. Fixed-length records are relatively easy to work with, since the start of any particular record is simple to calculate from a knowledge of the starting address of the first entry and the number of bytes in each record. Because of this, fixed-length records can be easily read in random order. Variable-length records, on the other hand, require an end-of-record character or a field indicating the record's length. Variable-length records are normally read in sequential order unless special measures are taken to build extra tables (indexes) that show where each record starts.

Databases **Databases** are collections of interrelated data of such a nature that the collections can be represented as a number of files but not a single file. Depending on the database management system used, these files may be integrated permanently into a single connected structure or integrated temporarily for each interrogation, known as a **query.** The organization of a database is such that data stored in the files can be used as keys to find interrelated data. Items of data within the database are primarily linked together in units called records. Data are retrieved by specifying the values of some of the data items and causing the system to return all or part of any records where there is a match

Figure 2.26

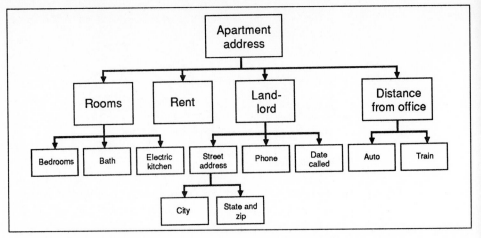

with the specified items. There are three common types of database organization: **hierarchical, network,** and **relational.**

A hierarchical database system exhibits a data hierarchy whereby each record is owned by another record (its owner) and each member record type can be owned by only one owner record type. The only way to get to a subordinate record is by entering at the topmost record and working down through the levels until you reach the record you require (see Figure 2.26).

A network database system is similar to a hierarchical database system, but each record may have more than one owner, making it possible to reach a record by more than one path (see Figure 2.27).

A relational database is so named not because it relates one file to another, but because it uses a mathematical construct called a **relation.** A relation is nothing more than a table of **rows** (records) and **columns** (fields). Relations can be linked together on the basis of a common field. The relational system is structured at the time each query is posed, rather than at the time the database is established (as in the case of the hierarchical and network systems). The relational database can structure a wider range

Figure 2.27

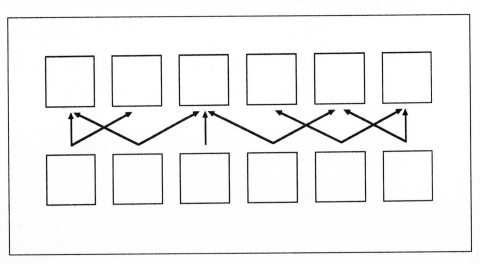

of queries at runtime than other systems. Relational databases can also use more system resources in the process.

Executing Programs

Compilers translate high-level source code to object code. Each statement of source code usually generates several object code statements. Some compilers translate into assembly language code which must, in turn, be assembled into machine code. Other compilers translate directly into machine code. Once a program is satisfactorily compiled, it can be used without further compiling.

The machine code may be **absolutely addressed** or **relatively addressed.** Absolute addressing requires the code to be loaded at the same specific memory address every time. Relatively addressed code is **relocatable:** it can be loaded wherever space is found. Relative addresses are measured as offsets from the start of the code (virtual address zero). Virtual memory techniques use relative addressing.

A related term is **address binding,** the act of associating code addresses to physical addresses in main memory. Binding may be accomplished by the programmer writing absolute code, an assembler or compiler generating absolute code, or by linkers and loaders (described below) placing relatively addressed code in memory. The closer to execution that the binding of addresses takes place, the more flexibility the operating system has in managing programs and memory. In paged virtual memory systems, binding is dynamic and is performed *during execution,* with a page of code possibly occupying different addresses at different points of execution.

Programmers frequently create large programs as a number of smaller, more manageable modules, or they make use of libraries containing useful prewritten modules of object code. The **linker** is a utility program that performs the task of combining specified modules into a single, executable object-code program.

A **loader** is a utility program that loads an executable program into memory and prepares it for execution. The exact functions performed depend on the operating system. Loading is the final stage in preparation for execution. A **linking loader** combines the work of a linker and a loader to link and load programs for execution; that is, programs are linked every time they are loaded. A **link editor,** on the other hand, links the various parts of a program into a single executable image stored on disk. Loading, then, does not require the linking effort every time the program is loaded.

Exercises

1. Answer each of the following questions for the computer system you use most often.
   a. Can you expand memory? If so, by how much?
   b. Can you add more disk drives?
   c. What kind of bus system does this system use? How does this affect the type of peripherals you can use?
   d. Are the data and address buses of the same size?
   e. Is the accumulator the same size as the data bus?
   f. Describe the registers for this machine.
   g. Are machine instructions hardwired or microcoded?
   h. What is the clock speed? Is it variable? Can it be speeded up?
   i. How many instructions can this machine execute per minute?

    j. Which operating system commands/programs are memory resident? Which are nonresident?

    k. Find a program that will not run on this machine for architectural reasons.

    l. Find a program that will not run on this machine for organizational reasons. What organizational changes are required to make it runnable?

2. How does clock speed affect the performance of the computer? What do you suspect defines the upper limit of clock speed?

3. Explain the Fetch-Decode-Execute cycle.

4. Compare/contrast microcode instructions, machine instructions, and operating system calls.

5. On your system you have a single keystroke that will stop the execution of a running program. Describe what is actually happening when this keystroke is pressed.

6. Describe DMA and cycle stealing. When interrupts occur, the "environment" of the executing program is saved to be restored later. Why is this not necessary during cycle stealing?

7. What do you suspect is the difference between synchronous and asynchronous buses?

8. Describe the difference between absolute addressing and relative addressing.

9. Describe the general nature and purpose of paging.

10. What is the advantage of a memory-resident operating system command/program over a nonresident one?

11. How does the end user's view of an operating system differ from that of an application programmer?

12. Draw a diagram showing how input spooling works. Do the same for output spooling.

13. Describe the role of an I/O channel and the general types.

14. What is the general role of the bus system?

15. What is the general role of buffering?

16. Compare/contrast the use of interrupts for data input activity and data output activity.

17. Describe each of the following.

    a. assembling

    b. compiling

    c. loading

    d. linking

    Show where each fits in the general concentric circle model.

18. Compare/contrast a linking loader and a linkage editor.

19. Draw a concentric circle diagram showing where a windowing system fits in a system whose operating system provides only a command interpreter.

20. In Exercise 19, an expert system program runs with the aid of the windowing system. Draw a concentric circle diagram showing the nature of the system.

21. How will increased user-friendliness of application programs affect the skills needed by business people to effectively use the computer?

22. You work in a marketing department. You suggest to your boss that instead of relying on DP, you'd like to get your own system. He says, "Write me a proposal for a

system, given a budget of $10,000 for hardware, software, and training." Write the proposal using real costs from today's marketplace.

23. Continue with the scenario in Exercise 22: Your boss is fired. His replacement is willing to go along with your suggestion but will only allot $4,000. Prepare a new proposal.

24. Take a look at one family of computers (HP, Apple, IBM, DEC) and determine the compatibility among models.

25. Compare a specific micro, a specific mini, and a specific mainframe computer system in terms of the following operating system capabilities.
    a. Number of users
    b. Number of concurrent tasks
    c. Batch capabilities
    d. Spooling
    e. Buffering
    f. Hardware speed
    g. Size
    h. I/O speed and capabilities

26. Describe how one microcoded machine might be altered to emulate another of different architecture.

27. Describe the hardware needed to do each of the following:
    a. Desktop publishing
    b. Presentation graphics
    c. CAD (Computer Assisted Design)
    d. Telecommunication

28. What kinds of activities are normally done through the command interpreter using a keyboard?

3 User Interface

Anyone who uses a computer for any purpose must have some means of indicating his or her needs. The **user interface** allows the user to interact with the machine to get the work done. This interface determines how the person thinks about, talks about, and perceives the computer—as a tool. Most systems have several different interfaces or interface levels, each tailored for a variety of uses and users.

Each interface has one primary goal: to act as a **communication channel** between two entities. For user interfaces, that communication is between a machine and the person hoping to use that machine to solve a problem. The user interface determines how any communication takes place.

By contrast, a user interface is an **insulator** between the communicating parties and can be viewed as a translator or go-between. Typically translation is required because the machine and the user do not speak even remotely similar languages.

This chapter looks at these matters from the user's point of view. The user has a number of desires and tasks that shape his or her needs and the goals for the machine-user and user-machine communication.

The user must **logon** (or start) and **logout** (or terminate) each **session.** In many systems there is a need for security; for example, identity and privileges may need to be verified for each user. Programs need to be scheduled, loaded, and executed. Users often need to interact with running programs. Main memory and secondary memory need to be allocated and managed. Virtually all activity requires that file systems be manipulated and managed. Peripheral devices need to be accessed by users who neither know nor want to know how the devices actually work. Many systems maintain a **history** of activity related to users, programs, and file systems. If it is needed, **resource accounting** information should be maintained without requiring user intervention. **Electronic mail** systems and online **help facilities** are almost universal except for some standalone, single-user systems.

Most programs require input, followed by some transformation or function using that input; then they generate output (as in the IPO model seen in Figure 2.1). The input comes from somewhere, and the output is then deposited someplace. Many programs can take their input from a variety of different sources (mostly file systems) and write their output to a variety of destinations (again, mostly file systems). User interfaces for most modern operating systems allow the **redirection of I/O;** in this way, the source for input and destination for output can be determined dynamically at runtime as opposed to being "fixed" during the program's development.

The goal of a user interface is to make it possible, convenient, and easy for the user to accomplish a set of tasks. An interface that can be tailored or customized for each user and set of tasks has a major advantage, as it is easy to learn, generates confidence, and shortens the learning time. An interface that users consider "safe" will help improve productivity by removing fear and hesitation. In short, each user must feel comfortable with and find success in using the system for his or her set of activities without a long training period.

Layers of Interface

Almost every text on operating systems illustrates the **layered** view of a computer system, as was described in Chapter 2 of this book. In Figure 3.1, the hardware of the computer is shown as the innermost part. If that were all (as in the "good old days"), the user's environment would be a nasty one. This type of machine is not hospitable, not understanding, and not able to communicate in "human" terms.

Figure 3.1

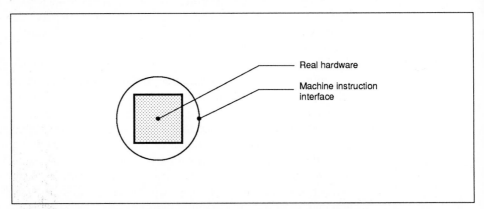

The addition of software layer upon layer around the hardware moves the system toward a civilized state. Figure 3.1 shows only one "thin" software layer used to create the machine language instruction set. The user is required to communicate with the hardware by use of these machine-language instructions and is thus isolated from the machine. The thin layer translates those instructions into the required hardware activities. The interface at this level is unattractive to most users but useful for developing operating systems. Machines of different architectures will have different instruction sets, with interfaces that are **machine** (or architecture) **dependent.** Moving to another machine generally means learning the new interface from scratch.

Fortunately, designers recognize this problem and create additional layers providing a variety of interfaces. Each added layer provides a specific set of facilities for the user. As layers are added, the user is removed further from direct interaction with the hardware. The interfaces become increasingly **hardware independent.** That is, with enough layers of the proper kind, it is possible to design a user interface that looks and acts the same on all machines. Ideally, a user familiar with the interface on one machine can move to a different machine without any down time for learning.

The Kernel: A Programmer's Interface

Figure 3.2 shows an added layer **encapsulating** the hardware and all the inhospitable environment contained therein. The **kernel** layer (first layer of the operating system) contains primitive routines for managing the interrupts, the CPU, the memory, the peripheral devices, the file system (usually), and so on. The kernel builds a wall around the instruction set interface, a wall that has windows called **service calls** or **system calls.**

Figure 3.2

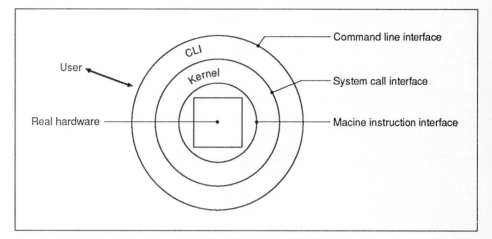

The kernel constitutes a new programmer interface that allow the user to make system calls (for example, CREAT, READ, OPEN, TIME, WRITE), rather than write a series of binary codes representing the corresponding set of machine instructions. For this reason, system calls are also called **extended instructions;** in this case, the programmer's system call is translated by the kernel layer into the proper **set** of machine-language instructions that accomplish the desired task. Thus, the programmer may think in terms of a more natural system call rather than machine language instructions.

At this point, operating systems can become portable across machines of differing architectures and organizations. Designers of the operating system merely specify the set of service calls that represent what the system will do. Note that this specification can be made independent of any actual piece of hardware. When an underlying machine is chosen, the kernel program is written to translate the machine independent service calls into the appropriate machine dependent instruction set. The kernel, then, translates between the machine dependent interface (instruction set) and the machine independent one (set of system calls).

The encapsulated hardware has become a **black box** with an input slot, a few buttons, and an output slot. For proper use, one must place the service call parameters (data about the call) in the input slot and then press the correct button (service call). The black box will perform the prescribed action, generating any required output. The programmer only needs to know which system call performs the desired activity and what parameters are required as input. He or she does not need to know how the kernel makes the machine do what it does, only that, in fact, the expected action will take place.

The kernel layer defines an **abstract machine** in the following sense: The programmer's mental picture is not of the hardware but rather a collection of service calls that cause predictable actions to take place. An understanding of how to use the service calls to accomplish a given task is all that is needed: Just place the correct parameters in the slot, punch the correct button, and wait for the result.

The kernel is a programmer's interface in the sense that the programmer "speaks" to the system via service calls. The kernel translates the service calls into machine understandable instructions; that is, the kernel intervenes on behalf of the programmer in order to accomplish his or her goals. Conversely, the kernel translates the results of machine activity by returning "programmer-readable" output from the service call. As will be seen later, service calls are generally implemented using interrupts.

The encapsulation described earlier is also known as **information hiding**—a powerful software engineering technique. Information hiding includes a contract between the software designer and the software user: If the user agrees to follow the specifications set forth in terms of the conditions of use and proper input, the designer guarantees a specific resulting action and/or output—*even if the software is redesigned internally.* Such a contract is what allows an application program to continue working properly even if operating system designers change the internal workings of the kernel. Operating system upgrades need not cause all application programs to be rewritten.

Machine Independence

The kernel, as mentioned earlier, creates a **machine independent** interface or basis for an operating system. If all of the machine dependent code is contained in the kernel, the outer layers are designed to use the system calls and not the instruction set or hardware used to implement the system. When built in this manner, an operating system can easily be **ported** from one member of a computer family to another (or from one manufacturer's equipment to another) by merely rewriting the machine dependent code in the relatively small kernel. The outer layers do not know or care which machine is hiding behind the kernel. Access by way of the system calls provides the information hiding needed for machine independence; only the kernel is machine dependent.

System Programs: The User's Interface

System programs constitute the next layer surrounding the kernel. As with each layer before, this layer defines a new abstract machine and a new interface. This time, the interface defined is more general, more "human-friendly," and more appropriate for the nonprogramming end user.

Note that the system programs under discussion here vary greatly. In many operating systems, they are written and executed as application programs rather than part of the kernel or operating system. This keeps the operating system small while extended capabilities are added at each site. Even within a given installation, the users will pick and choose only a small subset of the programs from this layer to meet his or her needs. Each user, therefore, may have a different view of the system due to the use of different facilities.

The traditional focus in this layer has been the **command language** and the **command language interpreter** (CLI). (See Figure 3.2.) The command language, often a fully programmable language, allows users to enter commands describing what is to be done (for example, COPY *myfile* [to] *yourfile*). The CLI interprets the requests and summons the appropriate action *through system calls.* Generally, the CLI is constructed to accept commands from the keyboard and deposit responses on the video screen, although redirection is often possible. The CLI approach is ancient; it was developed on mainframe systems, carried to minicomputer competitors, and finally incorporated in the first standard operating system for microcomputers (CP/M). MS-DOS, developed from CP/M and continually tailored to look more like UNIX, carried the CLI model of user interface forward.

Where the CLI is implemented as an application program, it is **extensible** (can be tailored). It is common to have more than one version available at multiuser sites, each version tailored to the individual user's needs.

Command Language

The command language is the communication medium by which the user makes requests of the operating system. In fact, the command language defines the interface; the user no longer thinks in terms of system calls but in the more descriptive commands processed by the CLI. The use of command languages varies depending on whether interactive or batch processing is being done.

Batch processing makes more demands of the command language since the user is not present to direct, intervene, or react to events and errors. Batch jobs require a complete sequence of control statements, which guide the operating system through the execution of a job. (See Figure 3.3 for a simple job.) Each statement assumes that all previous steps have been completed successfully. Any problem or error will normally cause the run to be aborted with appropriate error messages. Interactive jobs, however, allow user intervention for problem solving in the case of error. In the remaining discussion, interactive computing is assumed.

Figure 3.3

```
// JOB DOIT
// EXEC MAINT
 CATALP MYPROC
// DLBL IJSYSUC,'MY.JOBS.CAT',,VSAM                    L1
// DLBL PROGIN,'GENERAL.DATA.FILE',,VSAM               L2
// DLBL PROGOUT,'GENERAL.OUT.FILE',120,VSAM            L3
// DLBL YOURS,'GENERAL.ERROR.FILE',95/1,VSAM           L4
// EXEC MYPROG                                         L5
/+
/*
/&
```

Several command language characteristics are critical. First, the language must be easy and fast to learn. Normally the user must be able to do some computing by using only a very small set of instructions. In addition to getting started faster when only an small set must be learned, the user tends to make fewer mistakes early on and gains confidence rapidly. The user can then increase his or her knowledge by learning new commands only as they are required by the work.

Commands. Descriptive commands normally follow the verb/noun format with the verbs (command names) specifying the action to be taken. The arguments or parameters are considered to be the nouns (objects of the action). Generally, the command consists of up to three parts:

command name + options + arguments

The **options** (sometimes called **flags**) specify variations in the performance of the command. **Arguments** describe inputs and outputs for the most part.

However, the simple format just described can be deceiving. If commands that do similar kinds of things have different formats in terms of the options and parameters (suppose, for example,

COPY myfile yourfile

copies *myfile* to *yourfile* but

RENAME myfile fileB

changes the name of *fileB* to *myfile*), the language is confusing and hard to learn; mistakes will be numerous. If the command names do not relate to anything the user knows, they are not descriptive and are found hard to learn and remember. Or if two commands sound or look alike while producing totally different actions, confusion will occur (for example, suppose

REMOVE fileA

erases all versions of *fileA* from the file system but

DELETE fileA

eliminates only the latest version, leaving the previous version in its place). The choice of the symbols (typically space, semicolon, and so on) to represent field separators or **delimiters** can also make the command easy or difficult to read.

Shortcuts.   To make things easier, quicker, and more convenient for the user, most command languages have **default** values for the options and arguments. If the option flag or one or more arguments are omitted from the command line, the system supplies missing values from a predetermined list or pattern. The user, knowing the defaults, can often enter an abbreviated command (for example, SAVE without a file name or a disk name stores the current file being used, identifies it with a name specified during the session, and stores it in a disk location authorized for this user).

Where defaults are not appropriate, the operating system may enter into a **dialog** with the user for missing values (for example,

SAVE
? file name? myfile
? disk? DUA0:

where *myfile* and *DUA0:* are user responses to the prompting).

Additionally, many of the commands have shorthand versions allowing the command name itself to be abbreviated (for example, DEL for DELETE). While the short "nickname" means less typing, the shortened version may be cryptic and not easily associated with the command. The novice will likely use the full command name, while the expert prefers the shorter one. One of the goals in designing a command language is to create a package that is easy for the newcomer to learn without being cumbersome for the seasoned user.

Wildcards.   A **wild card** is a **metacharacter** (character that represents something other than itself) used to create **patterns**. For example, the asterisk in *F*.out* may be a wildcard meaning "replace by any string of characters." Thus, *F1.out, File.out,* and

F.out are names that fit the **template** or pattern *F*.out*. *F*.out* represents the set of all names that start with *F* and end with *.out*. Writing a pattern using a wildcard can accomplish a great many tasks with a single invocation. Other kinds of wildcards also exist.

Extensibility. A command language is most valuable if it is **extensible**: that is, the most versatile command languages allow the user to add commands (commands are often just executable programs placed so the system can find them) to the language and to offer **aliases** (alternative names) for other commands. For instance, the directory listing command in UNIX is *ls:* The user may establish *dir* as an alias and use it. The alias can make life easier for the novice and expert alike.

Most command languages are high-level, block-structured programming languages equipped with control statements (IF-THEN-ELSE, for example) and looping mechanisms (such as FOR, WHILE, UNTIL). The greater the number of features, the more powerful the language—and the more complicated the learning process. These more powerful features should be considered optional and for use only by the expert.

The CLI

The program that interprets the command language commands and executes them is also the program that is normally running when the user "logs on" to a large system or boots up a microcomputer. This command language interpreter operates in a simple *do forever* pattern: Wait for input, verify the command syntax, execute the command, report on success/failure, wait for input, and so on.

Commands are used to invoke programs or to cancel program execution; they may be used to gain information about the status of the system and the user. The CLI may be used to issue commands for file system manipulation and file modification or for program language support. There will be commands for intervening in currently executing programs.

The CLI can be used to issue calls for help facilities or "learn" facilities maintained by the system for user assistance. The help may be **context sensitive:** Rather than providing general help, it provides assistance specific to the problem being encountered. The **shell** (as the CLI is often called) may have an **undo** feature and other capabilities for recovery from errors or potentially disastrous situations. Speaking of errors, the CLI responses to errors must be controlled, not chaotic, and the messages must be understandable.

The shell is capable of executing built-in commands from the language (generally **intrinsic** commands are quite few in number) or **extrinsic** load-and-go commands that are disk resident. These disk resident commands may be either natural to the command language or user-defined extensions. Many of these commands fill out the layer in which the shell resides and form the user's real view of what the computer system is like. To most users, the computer is a machine that executes system and user-defined programs. At this level (Figure 3.2), system calls are seldom, if ever, seen. The CLI interfaces to the kernel via system calls, and the entire layer is portable to any machine on which the kernel has been implemented.

Human beings like feedback in response to their actions, and the CLI is designed to give that feedback. While a command is being executed, the shell gives some indication that execution is taking place (as opposed to the machine's appearing to go dead, for example). Even a few seconds' delay between the initiation of action and some indication of progress tends to frustrate most users.

Scripts.   One very powerful feature of most command interpreters is the ability to execute not only the commands associated with the command language and the user's application programs but also **shell scripts** or **command files**. A shell script is an executable file of command language commands (see Figure 3.4 for a script named *my_command*). The CLI executes these scripts just as if the user were typing them in from a keyboard. Sequences of commands are thereby executed as if they were a single (**macro**) command. This capability greatly eases the user's work.

Figure 3.4

```
echo "Trying it again today?"
date
echo "Here's your mail."
mail
echo "Here's who's on now."
who
echo "Here's the word for today."
fortune
msg n
```

Most systems allow a user "login file" to be executed upon logging in. A login file is usually a shell script executed at the start of each session. The purpose is to tailor the environment automatically to meet the user's needs and desires. Such a file generally includes the use of aliases, preferred prompts and messages, the type of terminal, and so on.

Redirection.   I/O **redirection** and **piping** are managed by some shells. Redirection allows commands to be very flexible. If a command takes its input from a file and puts its output to a file, then redirection gives the user a runtime ability to specify where input is to be collected and output is to be deposited (for example,

```
type <myfile >yourfile
```

takes input from *myfile* and *types* it to *yourfile,* creating *yourfile* as a new file if needed while

```
type <myfile
```

types **myfile** to the video screen). If, in addition, devices (such as printers and terminals) are treated like files, input and output can also be directed to physical devices as well as electronic files. For instance,

```
type <myfile >lpr
```

types the contents of **myfile** to the line printer for hardcopy.

Piping funnels the output of one command as input for a following command. With piping, a chain of commands can be invoked to perform a series of simple actions whose combined effect is quite complex (for example,

```
who | grep sam | wc -l
```

produces a listing (not seen) of those logged into the system, filters out all those whose name is not **sam** and finally counts the lines of output containing **sam**; that is, the pipeline of commands counts the number of **sam**s logged in). Piping encourages the development of complex programs through the packaging of short, simple, well-defined modules.

There is a rule of thumb: The more a CLI does for the user the more complex it will be. A widely overlooked point is that the more "friendly" the shell, the more complex it will be. Also note that the more complex a piece of software, the more costly it will be to produce, purchase, and maintain.

Other Applications   The outer layer of Figure 3.5 represents a running application. In the layered format, the application replaces the CLI (in the user's view) and presents its own interface. One of the major difficulties with application software has been the problems the user faces when using several different applications, each with its own unique interface.

Figure 3.5

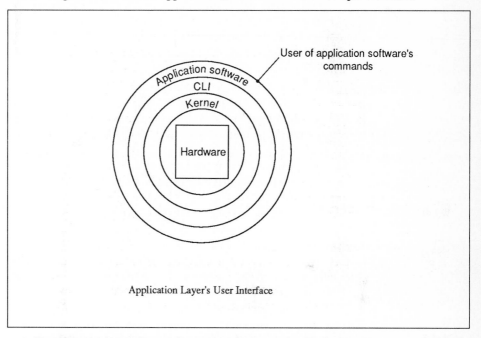

Application Layer's User Interface

Text preparation software is commonly found in this layer and is used for document preparation, program development or file creation, and alteration. Some examples are text editors and wordprocessors, formatters for printing or record shaping, spelling checkers, style checkers, index and contents creators, footnoters, and so on.

It is also in this layer that assemblers, language compilers, interpreters, and other program development tools are found. These tools are usually managed as community tools rather than private programs. Information analysis software also falls into this category (database language devices, spreadsheets, graphics tools, code generators, application generators). Communication software often resides in this layer (terminal emulators, file transfer programs, network interface devices) if it is not designed as part of the operating system itself.

Again, the application layer creates another user view of the system, particularly for **skilled users** (defined as those who specialize in the use of one application package only). The same is true for those who use several applications running in an **integrated software environment.** This environment (which presents the user with a single interface across the several applications) —not the operating system—creates the predominant user view. To this type of user, the computer is a machine that creates and manages the integrated environment. Many factors go into the creation of an integrated environment (such as uniformity of keystroke use between applications, uniformity of screen appearances, ability to automatically pass output from one program as input to another, and ability to quickly and easily switch between applications).

Such a composition of software, sitting on top of the operating system and forming a layer in its own right, hides the operating system from the user and becomes a surrogate controlling system. Each added layer creates a new abstract machine "seen" by the user. It shapes the user's perception of what can be done and how problems can be solved. These layers hide the technical detail of dealing with the machine and the CLI (good in most cases), while at the same time building a wall isolating the user from access to the full power of the machine (bad in a few cases). Such tradeoffs (ease of use versus extent of control) are typical decisions the designer and user must make.

Interface Types

Interfaces are designed to take advantage of what the user already knows; that is why **metaphor** (the use of one object, such as an icon, to represent another) is used so heavily. Building on what the user knows shortens the learning time. Various kinds of user interfacing techniques have been developed, as described in the following sections.

Keyboard/Video. The most familiar interface device is the keyboard/video display combination. Keyboard typing (a widely held skill) creates the input. The visual output on the video display unit may be either textual or graphical. For textual displays, the interface takes on the appearance of a printed dialogue between person and machine. The earlier CLI discussions used this kind of communication. The dialog uses commands and responses that are descriptive of the activity. While this process is simple and flexible, it is not usually the easiest to learn. The variety and number of commands, as well as the quality of their descriptive character, may challenge the cognitive ability of users.

Keyboard-in/text-out interfaces can be tailored for individual users and improved with several extensions. **Programmable function keys** can be assigned to trigger often-used commands by a single keystroke, avoiding keyboard entry of a rather lengthy command line; thus typing is significantly reduced. **Macrocommands** (a sequence of *several* commands stored and executed as a *single* command) speed up the command entry process.

Command Line Prompting. CLI communication can challenge the user's ability to remember command names, formats, options, and parameter requirements. The problem is significantly reduced where the shell is smart enough to **prompt** the user in case of error or omission on command entry. The dialog/prompting technique shown earlier reduces the user's cognitive load, speeds up the learning process, and instills a greater level of confidence. Formats need not be remembered in detail since the dialog secures the needed information through prompting. The underlying CLI process is still operational.

Voice-Driven Interfaces. **Voice-driven interfaces** may supplant much of the keyboard work associated with the use of the CLI. Voice-driven devices promise to reduce the need for keyboard entry and pointing devices. Voice recognition capabilities simply allow text to be generated without the use of hands. The commands and their formats still present the same problems as with the CLI. If voice input is to do more than free up the user's hands, the command language will have to become more nearly like the natural language of the user. In the future, the real value of voice will probably be tied to increased use of artificial intelligence concepts.

Artificial Intelligence. There is a move, slow but steady, toward interfaces that are more **intelligent.** For example, as the user does his or her work, every action choice allows the system to "learn" something about the user. The interface can remember most often used defaults or options or parameter combinations and supply them as the user's personal set of defaults. **Natural language interfaces** offer the user a potential for using his or her native language to control the machine. Intelligent operating systems will be able to speculate about the consequences of a user's choices and offer advice. Intelligent operating systems will even be able to give the user information about the loading of the system and its impact on what he or she wants to do. (Intelligent systems are already dynamically tuning computer systems according to loading conditions.)

Menu-Driven Interfaces

A text-oriented **menu system** is easier for nonexpert users than the CLI interface. Normally a hierarchy of menus and submenus guides the user through each command sequence. Rather than typing command sequences, the user selects from among a list of choices, usually by a single keystroke. That choice leads to a (sub)menu from which a choice is made that leads to another (sub)menu from which a ... (See Figure 3.6).

Menus are easy to use and confidence-building for the novice; there is not the pressing need to memorize all command formats, options, and parameters. Expert users, however, consider menu systems clumsy, slow, and limiting, unless there exists an **override mechanism** (for example, allow normal CLI use from the keyboard or allow entry of several keystrokes at once, thereby navigating through the entire menu maze sight unseen).

Pointing Devices. **Pointing devices** such as mice, trackballs, light pens, and fingers (for touch screens) allow menu selections to be made without use of the keyboard. The point-and-poke technique is such a comfortable way for most people to make menu selections that pointing devices have become quite popular.

Cursor keys can be used as substitutes for pointing devices, particularly with menu systems that are textual in nature or applications that are text-producing. The cursor keys are used to position a selector at the proper menu item much in the same way a pointing device would be used. They are a widely used intermediate position between normal keyboard use and external pointing devices. They are particularly useful for

Figure 3.6

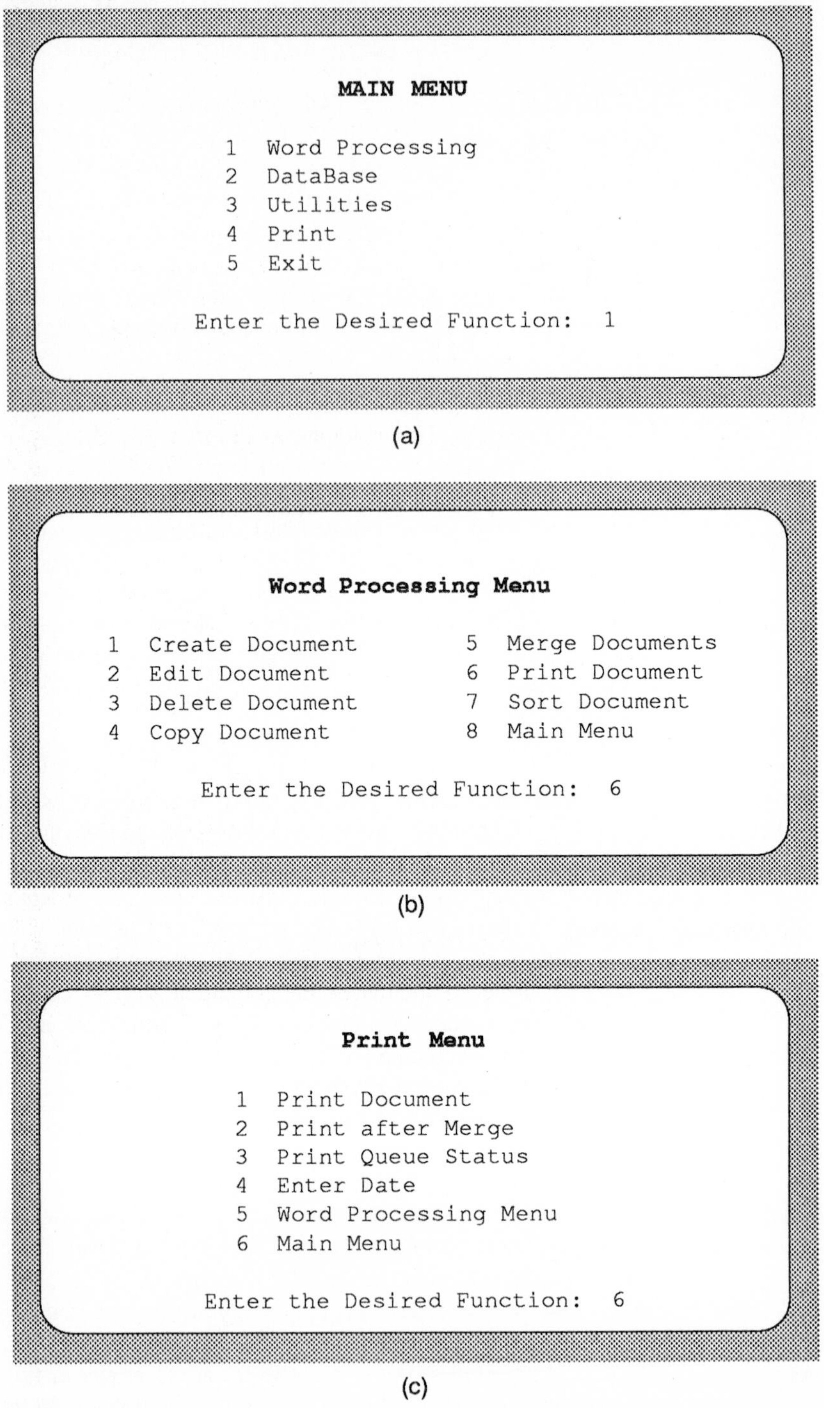

```
                    MAIN MENU

            1  Word Processing
            2  DataBase
            3  Utilities
            4  Print
            5  Exit


        Enter the Desired Function:   1
```

(a)

```
             Word Processing Menu

      1  Create Document      5  Merge Documents
      2  Edit Document        6  Print Document
      3  Delete Document      7  Sort Document
      4  Copy Document        8  Main Menu


          Enter the Desired Function:   6
```

(b)

```
                  Print Menu

            1  Print Document
            2  Print after Merge
            3  Print Queue Status
            4  Enter Date
            5  Word Processing Menu
            6  Main Menu

        Enter the Desired Function:   6
```

(c)

Figure 3.7

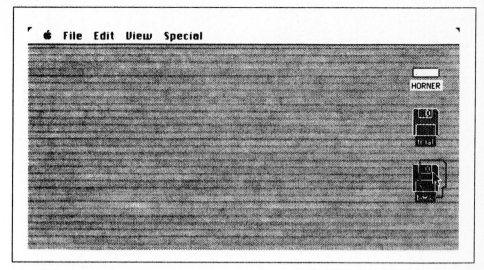

skilled touch typists who find the cursor keys more natural and faster than moving from the keyboard to a pointing device.

**Object-Oriented
Interfaces**

Menu devices are attractive because they reduce the technical demands placed on the user. **Object-oriented interfaces**, using graphics rather than text, offer even greater opportunities for simplifying the communication between computer and user. **Graphic interfaces** use **icons** (pictures) to represent ideas and objects to be manipulated by a pointing device. A mouse or other device can be used to *point* to an icon, *select* the icon, or *drag* (move) the icon to a new position. In Figure 3.7, for instance, the mouse may be used to point to the *trial* icon, select it, and drag the icon to superimpose it over *book*. In Figure 3.7, you see the icon in movement, *before* it is in place in its new position.

Figure 3.8

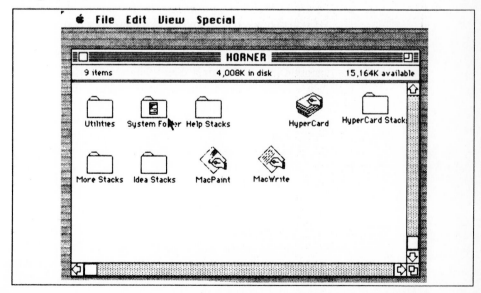

Figure 3.9

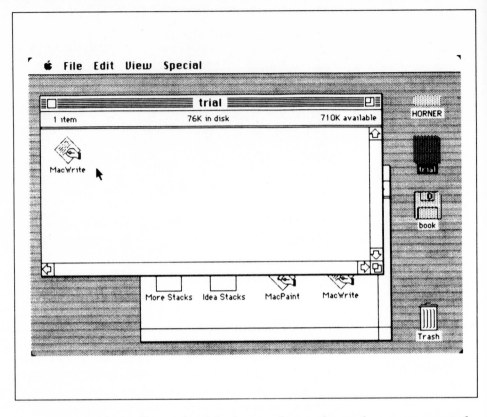

In Figure 3.8, the files *trial* and *book* are no longer shown; they may appear to be no longer available, but they can be retrieved from *Trash*. Figure 3.9 shows the contents of *trial* once it's retrieved from *Trash*. Emptying *Trash* (done through a menu selection) would remove any file in *Trash* from the system and make it nonretrievable.

Each action taken with an object represents a command line that would otherwise be typed at the keyboard. The use of graphics reduces the apparent complexity of operation: There are few conventions (how to point, select, and drag) to remember, and the operation gives the user a direct feeling of performing the command. Part of the feeling is a result of the continual visual feedback during the manipulation. The metaphors used are almost always more natural (for example, dragging a file to the waste basket to throw away or delete the file) than the corresponding command line, regardless of how descriptive the command is. Moreover, many users prefer to think in terms of manipulating objects rather than typing in relatively cryptic command lines. However, the experienced user may find the usefulness of "point-and-poke" to be restricted to only a few operations and may feel that the technique is too limiting or slow in other cases.

Apple Computer's Macintosh system introduced the computing public to this object-oriented world of user interfacing. The system's roots are found in the **Smalltalk** research activities conducted at Xerox's Palo Alto Research Center and even earlier to a group of researchers at Stanford University. A number of Xerox's employees carried their experiences to Apple where the technology was used for the short-lived **Lisa** pro-

Figure 3.10

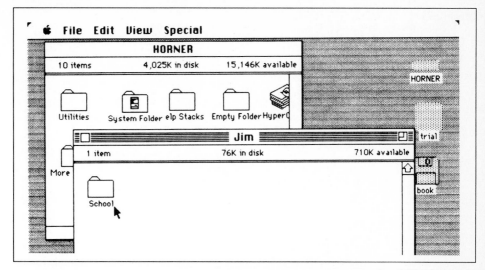

ject. The Macintosh system gained much from the Lisa activities and not only survived but flourished to become the first commercially successful application of its type.

Besides the icons representing the usual objects (files, disks, directories, and so on), there are objects of other kinds. **Windows** are objects defined for purposes of communicating with a program or examining a file. **Menus** are also objects available to this kind of interface. Dialog boxes are available for special machine/user communication needs. (See Figures 3.10, 3.11, and 3.12 for some examples of windows, menus, and boxes.)

Icons, windows, menus, and dialog boxes, like all objects, can be manipulated by the pointing device. A sample session with the Macintosh interface is found in Chapter 13. CLI sessions, for comparison, can be found in those chapters relating to MS-DOS, UNIX, and VMS.

Figure 3.11

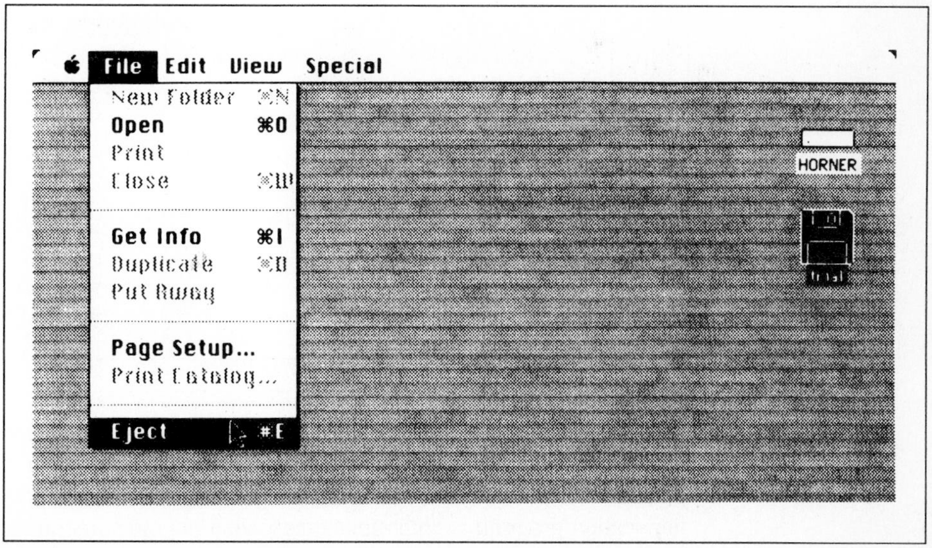

Figure 3.12

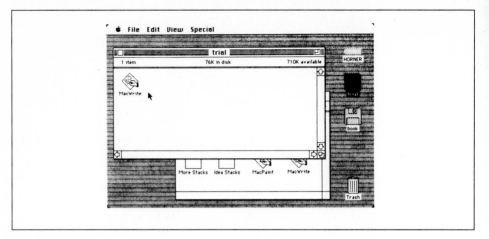

Windows
Several figures have shown **windows** which may be used with any of the interfacing mechanisms discussed above. The idea is simple enough in concept: For each running program or task, the user may have a window in which to view the activity. The window is (a portion of) the video display in which input and output activity is shown. The window may or may not be visible on the video display at any point in time, and the display unit may show more than window at a time. As seen in Figure 3.10, multiple windows may overlap with the user able to specify which window is to be dominant or "on top." If windows are constrained to be nonoverlapping, the scheme is called **tiling** (Figure 3.13).

Figure 3.13

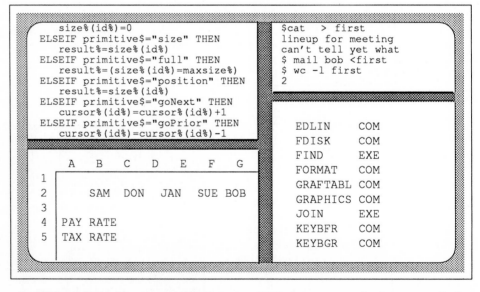

With a windowing system, the user may watch the progress of a large compilation in Window1, move text from fileA in Window2 to be included in fileB that is displayed in Window3, track the execution of a Pascal program in Window4 while a communication program is communicating with a remote computer system in Window5.

Other System Considerations

Operating systems come into being through design and implementation. Both acts are massive undertakings and require computer assistance. That is, operating systems are brought into existence through the use of a previously existing operating system. After being written, the operating system must still be installed on the machine. That installation process is often called **system generation (SYSGEN)**.

System generation may be as simple as plugging a **read only memory** chip **(ROM)** into a microcomputer and turning it on. But, usually, it is much more complicated. In any event, the goal is to get a copy of the operating system into memory. Generally, each machine has a "hardcoded" (e.g., ROM) set of instructions for booting up a system. Execution of these instructions loads further information from disk or tape.

In true SYSGEN for larger machines, the operating system, as it is to be installed on the system, is read into memory from tape. Generally, an interactive session is then initiated. During that session, the installer inputs information about the CPU (processor) for his or her machine, the amount of main memory available and a list of all peripheral devices and their characteristics. The system then customizes itself to accommodate the configuration on which it is to run. At that time, the actual operating system will be loaded and tested. Installing a system in this manner may take several days (or longer for massive systems).

A similar procedure must take place whenever the operating system is upgraded (changed), or when the physical configuration of the machine is altered (as in the addition of peripheral devices). A related activity occurs whenever the system is tuned to improve performance: Some of the choices made during SYSGEN are altered.

Even if an operating system has been installed, there is need for a boot process after the machine has been down (turned off). The ROM information normally supplies the instructions for starting the boot process. Those instructions will then load a larger set of instructions from disk and begin their execution. This latter set continues the process of loading the operating system into main memory and securing from the operator any information needed to complete the configuration.

Of course, the mechanism is simpler for microcomputers: Turn on the machine and watch the rest happen automatically. Still, the boot steps are there in some form. The system installation procedure is not generally realized by most microcomputer users, even though it is present. For example, when a printer, modem, or other peripheral is hooked to the microcomputer the user may have to install a device driver (the machine dependent software that allows the operating system to manage the device for the user) before the peripheral can be used. Disks must be initialized before they are useful and may need reformatting to be read by an upgraded version of the microcomputer's operating system.

One thing is clear, installing an operating system, upgrading an operating system, tuning an operating system, reconfiguring the physical system, and planning for change all require "down time." During such periods, the system will perform no productive work for the user. Neither will it produce revenue or return value on investment. This is an overhead cost.

Exercises

1. Describe how the terms *encapsulation* and *information hiding* have been used in this chapter. Why are they considered good software engineering practices?

2. Describe how the terms *machine dependence* and *machine independence* have been used in this chapter. Why is machine independence a good idea for programmers? For users?

3. Describe how the terms *interface* and *user interface* have been used in this chapter.

4. Describe how the terms *user view* and *abstract machine* have been used.

5. In Chapter 1, operating systems were said to be event-driven. Some say they are command-driven. Explain.

6. What prices are paid by the piling of layer upon layer of software around the hardware? What are the advantages? What factors help determine how much is enough?

7. It is not uncommon for a microcomputer user to be less sophisticated than most mainframe users. What requirements does this place on the microcomputer's interface? What kinds of problems can it create?

8. Give some examples of context-sensitive help.

9. What is likely meant by the term *resource accounting?* What resources are being referred to here?

10. Describe the use and value of defaults.

11. Describe the use and value of wildcards. Describe three different kinds of wildcards (note that one was given in this chapter).

12. Why might icons be easier to understand than printed commands? Why might they be easier to use? What kind of user might not prefer their use? Why?

13. What kind of user might find menu-driven systems difficult to manipulate? Why?

14. What kind of user would like prompting for command line inputs? Why? How should the prompting be constructed so as not to frustrate the experienced user?

15. What kind of user might prefer the use of cursor keys and programmable function keys over pointing devices? Why? How can the complaints of these users (relating to pointing devices) be overcome while retaining the pointing devices?

16. What is likely meant by the term *keystroke uniformity across applications?* Why is it important?

17. Suppose a firm has a "bare-bones" microcomputer with a popular, but stark, operating system. How can the responsible person go about purchasing software to create an appropriate user interface? What factors must be considered?

18. Describe some differences in feature preferences between an experienced user and a new user.

19. Why do operating system upgrades exist? Give at least two important reasons.

20. How would the manager of a medium-to-large system know that the system needed tuning?

21. Describe several activities for microcomputers that might be considered system configuration activities.

22. Suppose **command>file** means that the output of **command** is placed in **file** and that **command<file** implies that the input for **command** is taken from **file**. What do you think

         mail karen pete <letter

    means?

23. Suppose **command1 | command2** means that the output of **command1** is piped to **command2** as its input. If the command **who** generates a list of the users (one per line) logged onto the system and **lc** counts the number of lines in a file, what must

who | lc

generate as output?

TWO

Operating Systems Theory

4 File Systems

Virtually all computer system users have a need to store information from one session to the next. The operating system itself creates and stores information critical to its functioning. Secondary storage, usually in the form of magnetic disk media, allows for bulk storage on a semipermanent basis.

The operating system must address two fundamental problems:
- Stored data doesn't organize itself either logically or physically.
- Users must be able to access specific data elements.

Therefore, data must be physically placed on secondary storage media and logically organized for the user. Translation between the user's logical view and physical reality is a major file handling responsibility of the operating system. Some operating systems (for example, UNIX) provide very limited translation services, relying heavily on application programs to provide what the users want and need.

The nontechnical end user, the application programmer, the system programmer, and the file system implementor each has a different view of the file system. At the least technical levels, the user is concerned with the meaning of the data stored in individual files and the use of that data to solve problems. The user works with symbolic **file names** to create, update, and delete files. Symbolic **data element names** are used to add, delete, update, and read data elements. The nontechnical user seldom cares how information gets placed on the disk, where it is located, or how it is retrieved; the user does care about the safety and integrity of data. The end user prefers to remain at the symbolic (that is, file name, record, field) level. Note that the end user is responsible for attaching final meaning to the stored data: The operating system will not do that.

Writers of application programs, however, must know what kinds of files are maintained by the system and the various file manipulations the operating system will perform. Application programmers need to know how to translate between the user's mental picture of data and the operating system's structure of stored information (that is, the file's physical organization). They must be able to find their way around the file system to locate individual files, and they need to know how to navigate through the data in a given file to find a specific bit or byte.

System programmers require a greater technical knowledge of how data is actually transferred between the application program, the operating system, and the secondary storage device. That knowledge requires an understanding of the file handling system, the device drivers, and the characteristics of the storage media.

Implementors of file systems are concerned with assigning disk space to files, knowing which space on the device is free for further use, locating the existing data for each file stored, and reading and writing bits of data as required. At any point in time, the operating system must keep track of who has what files open, where each read and write is taking place within the file, and other file management information. Implementors are also concerned with efficiency, reliability, and security. Designers must choose the dividing line between those services and structures that will be managed by the operating system and those left for the application programmer to incorporate into his or her work.

Chapter 4 mainly refers to the storage of files on magnetic disk, although the discussions are generally applicable to other media as well.

The Views of the File System

The user often refers to a file system road map known as the **directory system**, which shows the names of files, certain relationships between files, and other information such as file type, size, and owner. Files are physically created and stored according to some **file organization** scheme. The nontechnical user seldom cares about this aspect of a file. Application and system programmers, however, must choose the file organization to be used even though many of the details are hidden by the operating system. The **access structure** for a file describes the manner by which specific data pieces may be located. Each file may be used with several access methods regardless of its organization. Note that how one navigates through the data in a file is directed by the access structure, which may be the responsibility of either the operating system or some application software.

A device called the **disk controller** manages the actual physical formatting, reading, and writing of the disk. Other low-level routines of the operating system's I/O mechanism serve as bridges between the processor and the device (see Figure 4.1). System programmers (and application programmers to a lesser extent) are concerned with such matters. These physical considerations are covered in more detail in Chapter 5.

Figure 4.1

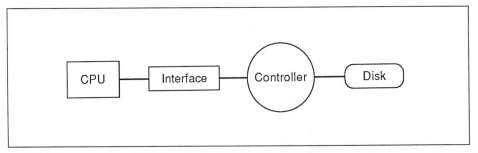

User Perceptions of Files

Files are actually collections of bits on some storage media but they represent whatever the beholder needs them to represent. From the operating system's point of view, a file is a **named** collection of bits or bytes, together with information about that collection.

The operating system may attach some structure (for example, record, field, subfield) to the data, but probably no meaning. To the end user, however, a file may represent a textual document, the source code for some COBOL program, the object code for a compiled C program, accounts receivable data, and so on.

One constant remains: The user does not see files as simple, unstructured masses of bits or bytes. Data is placed in a file for some reason known to the user, and the data usually has some logical form to it. At the least, the user who placed it there sees form in the data, and the data has logical organization. For example, the file may be seen as a collection of subunits called **records,** which may be comprised of subdivisions called **fields.** Records in a file will have some logical and, perhaps, physical uniformity among themselves. In particular, all records in a given file are likely to be subdivided into the same fields and may be composed of the same number of bytes. The operating system, while managing the file as a resource, may not have any knowledge of these logical factors.

Directories

Files stored within the system have symbolic names closely tied to the **directory system.** The directory mechanism allows users to inventory these stored files; note that a number of directory schemes are used.

Flat Directory Schemes. A **flat directory** mechanism, such as that used by CP/M (the first significant portable operating system for 8-bit microcomputers), maintains a *single* directory for an entire floppy disk. Figure 4.2 shows an example. The directory is often called the **volume directory** and is a list of **directory entries.** Each entry holds information about one file including name, type, size, creation time/date, last modification time/date, locations of the data, or pointers to another structure that does hold the information. Again, there is only one directory—the volume directory.

File names are relatively simple, generally consisting of a **primary name** and an **extension.** The primary name (often called simply **the name**) is chosen by the user to have some personal significance. The extension identifies the "kind" of file (for example, **.PAS** is a Pascal source file, **.OBJ** is an object file, **.TXT** is a text file). Extensions may be required by the operating system and other utility routines. Every

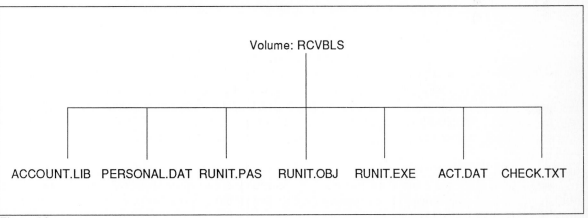

Figure 4.2

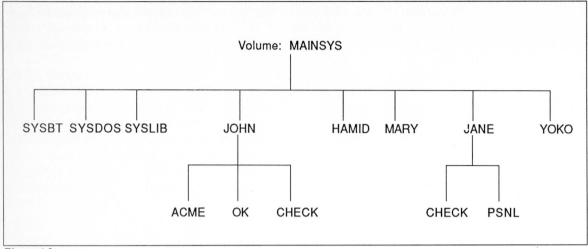

Figure 4.3

file must have a unique name, and flat directory systems do not allow two users to have personal files with the same name on the same disk. For example, even though both **User1** and **User2** wish to create a personal file called *ACCTS*, one of them will have to choose a substitute name; otherwise, the operating system won't know that they are two different files. Because of this restriction, the flat directory is simple, convenient, and efficient but useful for low-volume disk storage only. Multiuser systems and disk systems with extremely large capacities generally use a different directory mechanism.

Two-Level Directory Schemes.   **Two-level directory** mechanisms offer some improvement over the flat directories. The volume directory lists several system files or directories together with **a subdirectory for each user** (see Figure 4.3). This scheme effectively separates the files of one user from those of another. All user files are listed in the appropriate directory.

As with the flat directories, the volume directory and the subdirectories are essentially lists of entries holding the appropriate file information. The "file" described in the volume directory may actually be another directory. Directories exist in the first two levels only: Note that the third (bottom) level in Figure 4.3 consists of nondirectory files only.

Two files belonging to different users may now have the same name. John's file *Check* is never confused with Jane's file *Check* because the operating system knows to search the user's directory for a requested file. Flat directories do not permit this duplication of file names, since their files are not directly associated with a given user. A two-level system allows the operating system to create private areas (through user directories), making it easier to protect one user's files from other users.

CP/M, described earlier as having a flat directory system, actually allows a variant of the two-level scheme. However, instead of user directories, **user areas** (numbered 0 through 15) effectively partition the disk into subdisks. Users execute within the context of one user area at any time. User area 0 is often the system area, holding operating system and other files.

Hierarchical Directory Schemes. Figure 4.4 illustrates the notion of a **hierarchical** or **tree directory** structure. Tree structures extend the multilevel concept beyond a second level. Tree-structured directory systems allow entries in a user directory to be directories as well as ordinary files. In Figure 4.4, *ACME* and *OK* are two of *JOHN*'s subdirectories since they have entries themselves. Entries in a directory are called **children:** The directory itself is their **parent.** Each file (or directory) in a hierarchical system is known as a **node.** A node having no children is a **leaf** node; a nonleaf node, then, has at least one child and must be a directory. A node having no parent (the "top" node) is the **root** node, and the root itself is always a directory. MS-DOS, OS/2, UNIX, and VAX VMS, among others, use hierarchical file systems.

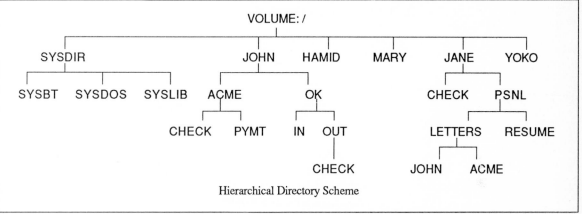

Hierarchical Directory Scheme

Figure 4.4

Flexibility in naming files is the key: John's subdirectory is the root of an eight-node tree holding two files named *CHECK*. This is permitted since the two *CHECK*s do not have the same parent directory. A file is identified by its **pathname** traced from the root. John's two *CHECK*s for example, have the following pathnames:

/JOHN/ACME/CHECK
/JOHN/OK/OUT/CHECK

The / at the start tells the operating system (and user) that the pathname is an **absolute** pathname traced from the **root directory** (called /). The subsequent /'s separate **components** of the pathname; the components are merely the subdirectories to be passed through on the way to the file in question.

Generally, the login mechanism establishes a **working** or **current directory** for the user, which the user may reset. **Partial pathnames** (identified by the lack of a starting /) describe how to arrive at the desired file by starting from the working directory. For example, if *JOHN* is the working directory, John's two *CHECK* files have partial pathnames, as in the following:

ACME/CHECK
OK/OUT/CHECK

If the working directory is *JANE*, Jane's *CHECK* has a partial pathname of

CHECK

and absolute pathname of

/JANE/CHECK

If the working directory is *JANE,* access to either of John's two *CHECK*s requires an absolute pathname since there is no path from Jane to any of John's files. Note that all lines connecting files in Figure 4.4 are assumed to be one-way paths of *downward* direction.

Links/Aliases.   While hierarchical directory mechanisms are quite flexible and very powerful, some feel they fall short in the area of file sharing. Most file systems (including hierarchical ones) allow the **owner** of the file to set **protections** or **access privileges** that allow or prohibit access to his or her files by pathname. For large systems, this facility may not be enough.

File sharing can occur in at least three ways:
- To allow another user access through the absolute pathname;
- To allow another user access by permitting the file to be copied to his or her directory;
- To allow another user to establish a symbolic link to the file.

The first two options are traditional; the third, however, can be very useful and efficient. Figure 4.5 shows one link—the dotted line from /MARY/PAPER to /JOHN/OK/OUT/CHECK. The name /MARY/PAPER is a second pathname to the file /JOHN/OK/OUT/CHECK. Only one copy of the file exists; the link simply creates an **alias** (a second pathname) of /JOHN/OK/OUT/CHECK.

While John could set permissions to allow Mary to use the pathname /JOHN/OK/OUT/CHECK, requiring her to use /MARY/PAPER has added security benefits. (If she has permissions to use /JOHN/OK/OUT/CHECK, she may accidentally be able to access files in /JOHN, /JOHN/OK, and /JOHN/OK/OUT.) Additionally, links *save file system space by avoiding file duplication* while permitting sharing.

The use of duplicate files to allow sharing creates another problem: As each user updates his or her own copy, the multiple copies become different even though they are

Figure 4.5

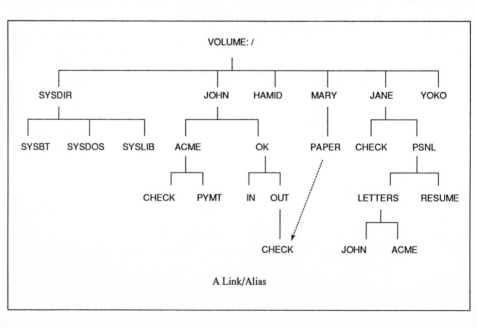

A Link/Alias

supposed to represent the same file. This is known as a problem of **consistency:** Which copy of the file, if any, represents the true state? Links avoid the consistency problem since *only one copy of the file exists.*

The fact that two directories (/JOHN/OK/OUT and /MARY) point to the same file means that the directory structure is no longer a tree (in a tree, nodes have at most one parent). The structure is known as a **directed acyclic graph (DAG).** The acyclic part

Figure 4.6

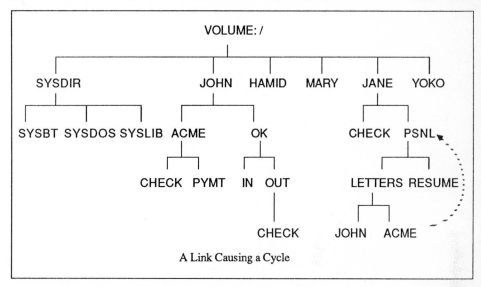

A Link Causing a Cycle

means that no path in the graph can be traced in a circle, as the links never point upward to an ancestor. Figure 4.6 illustrates such a prohibited cycle. The UNIX directory scheme is, in fact, a DAG scheme (although generally advertised as hierarchical).

However, links or aliases cause concern for the operating system. Which pathname reflects the owner? Does John or Mary own the file discussed earlier? When may a file with links be deleted? Who may delete a file with links? Who should be charged for the storage space used by the file? Does every user with a link have full owner rights? These problems complicate the directory management process and must be weighed against the advantages.

General Graph Directory Mechanisms.   Some systems go beyond the DAG and allow cycles to exist in the directory scheme (as in Figure 4.6). Such systems are known as **general graph directories.** However, hierarchical directory mechanisms with aliasing or linking are far more common.

File Operations

The end user generally requires only a few basic operations to manipulate files. With a sophisticated data management package, the user may be aware of only four data-level operations: **add** a record, **delete** a record, **update** (alter) a record, and **retrieve** (read) a record. He or she will generally be aware of the file-level instructions that **create** and **delete** a file.

Application programmers, however, will be aware of the following actions: **create, delete, open, close, read, write, EOF** (detect end of file), and **seek** (move to a particular byte position within the file). Often these will be operating system calls—those extended instructions that buffer the application programmer from the realities of the physical storage system.

File Organization

File organization is important because it governs the system and application programmers' thought processes when working with files. Some operating systems make several file organizations available, while others such as UNIX do not. The file organization has several ramifications for the **access method** to be used for data-level operations.

Serial and Sequential Files.   **Serial files** are constructed by storing data in the linear order created by data entry; that is, each newly written data element is appended to the end of the data already stored (a kind of first-come, first-written style). If data is entered in random order, the resulting serial file will hold its data in random order. There is no correspondence between a data value and its location in the file.

Sequential files, like serial files, are linear structures. However, the data in a sequentially ordered file is positioned according to some **key** value; that is, the data is aligned in such a way that its keys appear in sorted order. An ordered, singly linked list is a reasonable conceptual model.

Serial or sequential structures are imposed by the use of magnetic tape storage media. On tape, pieces of data are stored physically one after the other, in whatever order they are written. The records are read one after the other in that same data entry order. If the data entry order is random, the file will be a serial file. However, if the data is sorted by the order of its key values before being written, the tape file will be of a sequential organization. This is a case where the physical nature of the media coincides with the file's organization.

Disk files may be constructed as sequential files, even though disk media is direct access by nature (rather than serial). The read/write heads of a disk system can be positioned to any storage address directly. On direct access devices, any given address takes the same average length of time to find as any other address, but that is not true for a magnetic tape. In the case of serial/sequential files stored on disk, the physical media structure and the file organization obviously differ.

Text files and executable code files are familiar examples of sequential files. Libraries of programs are, then, collections of sequential files. Any file that is a collection of sequential subfiles is said to be **partitioned.** A library of code files, if organized as a file itself, is an example of a partitioned file.

Sequential files are typically written from beginning to end in one pass (as their physical structure makes the insertion or updating of individual data items difficult at best). Serial files may be written in smaller increments, since writing is restricted to appending data at the end. Serial and sequential files alike are normally used in applications where entire files are read with each use.

For example, the billing department of a local utility might maintain its customer accounts in a sequential file with the account number as the key. The company meter readers accumulate utility readings (transactions) in hand-held computers as they walk their rounds. In so far as account numbers are concerned, the data entry is randomly ordered. At the end of each reading period, those transactions are dumped into the main frame and sorted by customer identification number into a **sequentially organized transaction file.** The customer billing file is maintained in the same order. By reading the customer file and the transaction file in parallel and in their entirety, an updated customer file is produced by merging the information from the two. Thus the updated customer file becomes the new customer file, while the original customer file, together with the transaction file, will be archived. This is a typical application for sequential files and is also a reasonable use of magnetic tape media.

Direct Files.   **Direct files,** often called **random access files,** are files whose specific parts may be read or written individually without reading or writing other parts. This is in direct contrast to the nature of serial/sequential file organizations. Any data item in a direct file can be found as quickly as any other. For serial/sequential files, however, the time needed to locate a data item is in direct proportion to its position within the file.

It is typical for each record in a direct file to be identified by some **key value** or **(relative) record number.** The operating system translates the identifying key or record number into a media address, and the controlling mechanism moves the read/write heads directly to that location.

Direct files are attractive for applications in which only one or a few of the records are accessed at a time. Organizationally, a direct file may be pictured as an array of records, particularly if a relative record number is used. Think of the record number as the index used to locate the record within the array.

A major problem with direct access files lies in maintaining a clear relationship between each record and the key (or combination of keys) used to locate it. This is particularly true where the number of records is quite high or where the key information is not easily related to storage addresses. In particular, if the information has a natural, sequential order, that order may not be reflected in the assignment of addresses. These considerations may, of course, be of little concern to most users but of major concern to system and application programmers. Choices like these involve performance concerns as a key issue.

Indexed/Mapped Files.   An **indexed file** is conceptually a file with another file (or **index**) as the roadmap to its data. Indexed files provide some middle ground between sequential and direct organizations; they also provide considerable extension to both organization methods.

The idea is simple: Store the records anywhere on disk. In this case, physical location is not a constraint. It is possible to use any collection of desired and available addresses; then, in a comparatively small file, establish a table that maps (associates) each record with its address. Next, maintain the index file in whatever natural order is required for the application (for example, linear or hierarchical). To locate a given record, **look in the index file for the address** and then go to that location on the disk to find the record.

Why is the user interested in indexed file mechanisms? The explanation is that the index can create any view the user needs. Consider that three users might look at a given file of data from three different perspectives. Figure 4.7 shows three different indexes for the same file. One index "sees" the file's records as ordered by name, one

Figure 4.7

Record Number	Name	Account Number	Credit Limit	Current Balance	Amount Due
1	Syborski	1421	2000	500	50
2	Krookczek	0026	1000	980	100
3	Adams	9673	3000	250	25
4	Smauley	3621	2000	0	0
5	Robinson	0562	3500	1575	175

THE FILE

Name	Record Number	Account Number	Record Number	Amount Due	Record Number
Adams	3	0026	2	0	4
Krookczek	2	0562	5	25	3
Robinson	5	1421	1	50	1
Smauley	4	3621	4	100	2
Syborski	1	9673	3	175	5
Index 1		Index 2		Index 3	

INDEXED FILE

by account number, and the third by amount due. The file is the same set of stored bits and bytes but the organizations appear different.

Structured Files.   Some operating systems allow a file to be created by defining a mask or template to specify the record structure. The representative record is then subdivided into fields. Searching such a file often involves the use of one or more of its fields as **key fields.** By specifying the key fields and values, the user may ask the operating system to find particular records.

File Access Methods

An access method describes the way data elements are found within a given file. The common access methods are **serial, sequential, direct,** and **indexed.** The access method is not fixed or predetermined by the file's organization, but that organization has a strong impact (as the overlap of names might indicate).

For example, sequential access to a serial file would be a nightmare. Since the data in a serial file has a random key sequence, sequential access requires reading all data items from the beginning until the correct key is found. After a first data item is located, finding a second data item forces the whole procedure to be repeated, since there is no way of knowing whether the second data item occurred before or after the one just read. Moreover, if a data item being sought is not in the serially organized file, the entire file will have to be read before that is known. Missing data items are more efficiently detected in a sequential file: As soon as the system reads past where a data item should be, the data keys being read jump beyond the target key value.

Direct access to data elements in a sequentially organized file is possible. By specifying the data item's key, the system can start reading data and stop when the given key is found (or passed if no such key exists). Since all data items between the starting point and the final point must be read, this is very slow (and painful!). Direct access is much more efficient for files organized for direct access.

Conversely, to read a direct file in a serial fashion is to read the file by consecutive key or record number. To read it sequentially can be more difficult, since there must be a translation between keys/record numbers and the sequential order of the file's data. Another factor slows sequential access for direct files: While serial/sequential files are often placed on the disk in such a way that reading all data items serially/sequentially is very fast, random files are seldom arranged in this way. Reading an entire direct file in a sequential fashion is seldom efficient.

Indexed files are more flexible and offer a compromise where multiple access methods are required. Indexed sequential files, for instance, are stored much like sequential files; the sequential processing is relatively efficient while an index is maintained for direct processing. But note that the index takes additional storage space not required by the sequential file, and the reading of the index takes additional processing time not required for direct access of direct files. Still, indexed sequential organization is one of the most popular organizations for large-scale data processing.

Thus it is essential to select an access method that optimizes the kind of processing being done and then choose a file organization that best fits that method. If multiple access methods are required, select the organization representing the best compromise.

Implementation /Physical Representation

In order to manage a file system, the operating system must have several capabilities. The notions of reading and writing data are fundamental, but additional capabilities are also required.

Like the user, the operating system must be able to find files. For the system, this means that it must be able to "read" disks. It must be able to find the main directory, read its entries, follow a pathname by following the component directories, and ultimately find the entry for the file in question. The system must then read that entry to physically locate the file's data on the disk.

The operating system needs the ability to allocate and deallocate space on the storage media. In most systems, this is done by the allocation of **blocks** of space—a block usually being 512 bytes or a multiple of 1K bytes of storage. Besides having some **map** of the space allocated to every file, the system must have a map showing which space is currently **free** (unallocated).

The system must be able to read data from a given file and write data back. Note that the sector or block is the smallest unit of storage normally read or written by the system. Therefore, reading and writing a file requires that the system know how to read and write any particular sector or block on the device.

How does it all get started? Hardware systems, particularly mini and micro systems, usually have a ROM program that directs the hardware to read the first one or two logical blocks from the disk and then load the contents into memory at a prespecified address. Those contents are the code for a **bootstrap program**, which is then executed. The bootstrap program's purpose is to load the operating system into main memory, initialize the system's data structures, and check the file system. When completed, control passes to the operating system so that processing may begin.

Physical Organization

The storage space for a file may be organized in three general ways: **contiguous allocation, linked allocation,** and **indexed allocation.** Each has its own advantages and disadvantages.

If the method is contiguous, the file is allocated a fixed number of logically (and perhaps physically) contiguous blocks for use over its lifetime. Those blocks are numbered from zero through the largest block number. Contiguous allocation makes for fast access, since the contents of the entire file may be read or written with relatively little head movement. (See Chapter 5 for more information on disk organization.) Contiguous allocation, however, causes **external fragmentation** (unallocated chunks too small to hold a file) as the files are created and destroyed by system activity. As the number of files grows, it may be necessary to collect unallocated space into one large contiguous free section of disk. Moving files to accomplish this is called **compaction**—a slow and expensive process for large-volume disk systems. Since storage for a file is allocated when the file is created, this static allocation of storage is not space efficient: Space allocated but not currently used (**internal fragmentation**) cannot be reclaimed. See Figure 4.8 for a conceptual view of contiguous memory allocation.

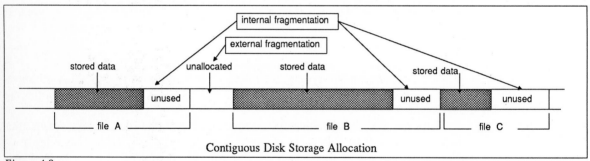

Contiguous Disk Storage Allocation

Figure 4.8

Linked allocation schemes create what are essentially serial files. The file system maintains a pointer to the first block assigned to a file, and the blocks of the file are maintained in a linked list. As mentioned, file data is accessed serially by following the pointers. While this may seem cumbersome, naturally sequential files can be reasonably implemented in this way. Fragmentation is not a problem, since only a single block need be allocated to a file at any time. Moreover, file sizes are dynamic rather than static, with blocks being added and removed as required. Accessing the entire contents of the file may cause a great amount of movement for read/write heads, since the allocated blocks are likely to be randomly placed throughout the disk. The pointers (links) take up storage space; finding a particular data element by following the pointers takes several or even many disk reads (see Figure 4.9).

Indexed allocation is quite flexible and can be used to implement files of a wide variety of logical structures. The index is merely a table of pointers locating the blocks assigned to the file. Like linked allocation schemes, fragmentation is not a concern, and file sizes are dynamic. Like linked allocation schemes, there is overhead: The

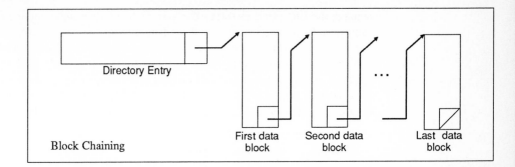

Block Chaining

First data block — Second data block — ... — Last data block

Figure 4.9

index must be stored and managed. Indexed allocation schemes generally require fewer disk reads in order to find a particular data element than is the case with linked schemes. Indexed schemes seem to be the most popular form of physical allocation (see Figure 4.10).

Figure 4.10

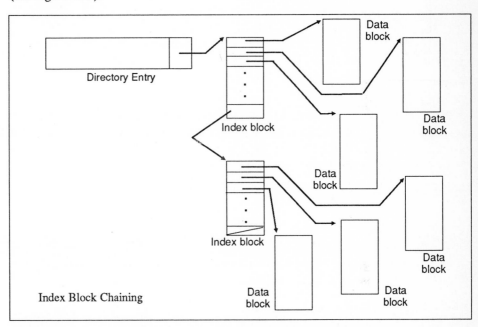

Index Block Chaining

File Control Information

The directory entries for files contain the information used for keeping track of files during processing. The information is sometimes called a **file control block (FCB).** If the directory entry does not hold such information itself, it has pointers showing where the information can be found. Several implementations are discussed in the following sections.

CP/M. While CP/M is no longer considered a major operating system, it does provide some good examples. Figure 4.11 shows a typical volume directory entry for an old CP/M diskette. When a file is open, its entry in the volume directory is loaded into main memory and becomes the **file control block** used by the operating system to manage the file. Each directory entry is 32 bytes long and contains the file name and extension. Other information such as file length, number of directory entries for this file, user area number, and permissions is also found. Sixteen bytes are given to a map of the file's logical blocks: block pointers (numbers) are one byte in length for small capacity diskettes and two bytes for larger volume disks. A pointer shows where the next 32 byte entry for this file is found (for files requiring more blocks than may be mapped with one 16 byte map).

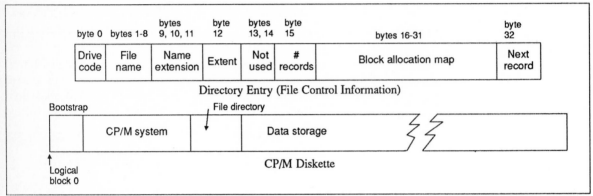

Figure 4.11

Figure 4.11 also shows a CP/M diskette as a sequence of logical blocks, picturing the location of the bootblock, the directory area, and the data area. To find the directory entry for a given file, the system merely searches sequentially through the directory area.

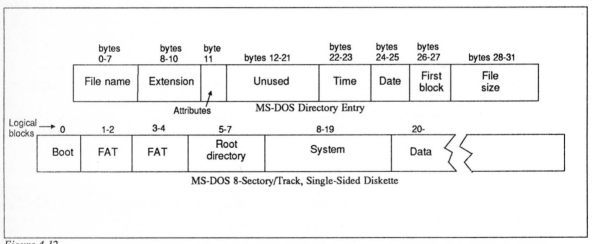

Figure 4.12

MS-DOS.   Figure 4.12 shows a typical MS-DOS directory entry and logical diskette layout. Much of the information found in the file control block for CP/M is found here as well. Note the time/date slots for time stamping files during creation or modification. The entry contains no map of the logical blocks assigned to the file. Instead, there is a pointer to the file's first logical block. This pointer is also an offset into the **File Allocation Table (FAT)** where the allocation maps for all files are managed. The use of the FAT will be shown later.

The file control information is maintained in main memory for each open file and is written back to disk when the file is closed. A copy of the FAT is also maintained in memory during execution. MS-DOS is cautious and copies the incore FAT to disk for updating whenever a change to the FAT occurs.

The boot block, two copies of the FAT, the directory section and data sections comprise an MS-DOS diskette.

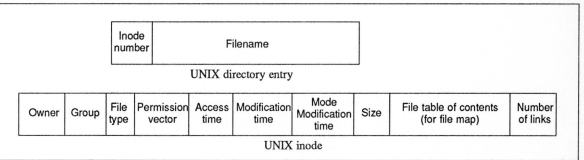

Figure 4.13

UNIX. Figure 4.13 illustrates directory entries for UNIX. These are obviously very simple entries (16 bytes in length) consisting of only a name and a pointer known as an **inode number.** For UNIX the inode corresponds more nearly to the file control block concept. Figure 4.13 also shows the inode structure.

The inode contains information about the user, the user's working group, the file type, file size (offset to the last byte of the file), various times, number of links (number of pathnames by which the file is known), and a table of contents for the blocks holding the data. There are thirteen entries in this table of contents: Their use will be discussed shortly. A copy of the inode for any open file is kept in main memory: The main memory version contains additional information. The incore inodes are written to disk regularly when altered and again when the associated file is closed.

Figure 4.14 illustrates the layout of a UNIX file system with respect to how its logical blocks are utilized. The boot block is shown along with the **superblock, inode**

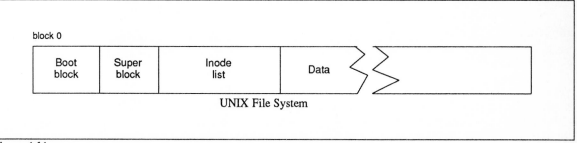

Figure 4.14

list, and **data portions.** There is no directory portion since directories are merely stored as data files, the data being the directory entries. Of special interest is the super-block which contains information pertinent to the entire system.

The superblock contains information about the size of the file system and the number of free blocks. It holds a cache mechanism for the free block list and another a cache mechanism for the free inode list. It also has fields for *locking* the free lists of inodes and blocks (for purposes of synchronization). A copy of the superblock is kept in main store and written out regularly if changes have been made.

The operating system locates each file by parsing its pathname (a hierarchical directory system with linking). The root directory or working directory (depending on whether the pathname is absolute or partial) is searched sequentially for the first component. When found, the entry's inode is examined and the directory or file located. If this is not the file in question, the next component is parsed and the present directory is searched for a match. This process continues until the desired file is found or an error state is signaled.

ProDOS.   An Apple ProDOS file directory entry is shown in Figure 4.15 (the volume directory entry is slightly different). The diskette layout shown there depicts something not seen in the previously discussed systems: ProDOS uses a diskette **bit map** (a sequence of bytes whose total bit count equals the block count of the disk, with each bit telling whether its associated data block is allocated or free) to mark each block as free or allocated. The nature of the hierarchical file system and the pathname usage is very similar to those from UNIX.

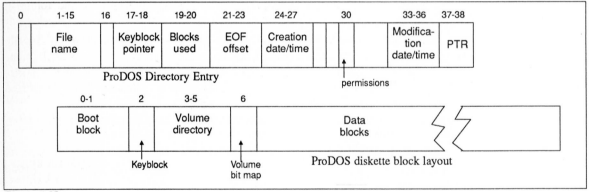

Figure 4.15

Allocation of   Noncontiguous allocation of storage space on a disk system requires the maintenance
Storage Blocks   of a list of blocks already assigned to each file and a list of unassigned or free blocks.
                     There are a number of ways to accomplish the allocation tasks but they essentially re-
                     quire the use of a table, linked lists, bit maps or some combination of these. In [3] the
                     general techniques are classified as **block chaining, index block chaining,** and **block-
                     oriented file mapping.**

Figure 4.9 illustrates block chaining. The directory entry points to the first assigned block for the file. Each data block in turn contains a pointer to the next data block forming a linked list of blocks. Of course, it is possible to use doubly linked chaining if desired. However, the use of several bytes in the data block for pointers means that the size of the data block and the number of bytes of actual data differ. It is preferred that the size of the data block and the data byte count in each block agree.

Figure 4.10 shows index block chaining. In this case, the directory entry for the file has a pointer locating the first index block. Each index block contains pointers to data blocks and one or more pointers to other index blocks; that is, the index blocks form a linked list of some variety. No data block space is given to pointers. The data byte count and the size of the block agree.

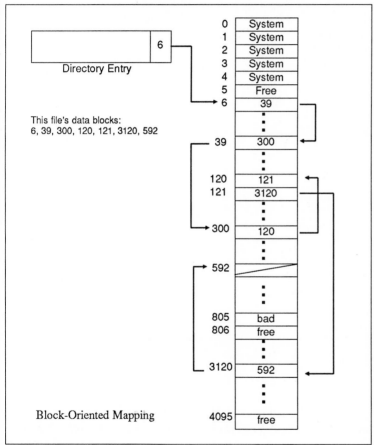

Block-oriented file mapping is shown in Figure 4.16. A map or table of all blocks is maintained on the disk. The directory entry for each file has a pointer which has two meanings: It is the *block number* of the first block assigned to the file and it is also the *offset into the block map*. Each entry in the block map is a pointer to the next block assigned to the file or indicates that the block is free or bad (unusable). In Figure 4.16 the logical blocks assigned to that file are 6, 39, 300, 120, 121, 3120, and 592. Locating the blocks assigned to a given file merely requires starting at the directory and following the pointers through the block map. Here again, the data byte count of each block agrees with the block size.

The free blocks in a block-oriented mapping arrangement may be kept as a linked list within the map or, more likely, free blocks may be found simply by searching the map. Block chaining and index block chaining, however, require a separate mechanism for keeping track of free blocks. The usual choices are linked list and bit map.

Figure 4.16

CP/M. CP/M, as mentioned earlier, keeps a block map for each file within its directory entry (Figure 4.11). In a sense it is a block-oriented file mapping except that there is no single, complete map of the entire disk nor is there a stored free block list. *At boot time,* CP/M reads the individual map for each file and constructs a bit map in main memory showing the free/allocated status for each block on the disk. Such a bit map is constructed for each disk drive. This is why CP/M cautions the user not to

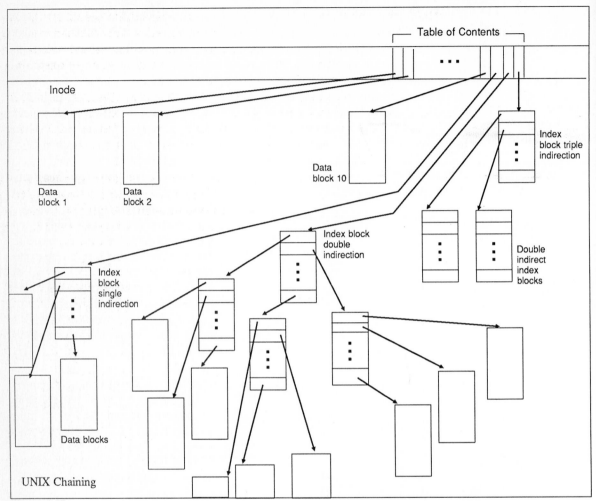

Figure 4.17

change diskettes in a drive without notifying the system: The system will attempt to use the old diskette's bit map in assigning space on the new diskette.

MS-DOS. MS-DOS uses a **File Allocation Table (FAT)** which is nothing more than the block map for the entire disk and looks essentially like Figure 4.16. For safety purposes, MS-DOS diskettes contain two copies of the FAT. An incore copy of the FAT is maintained during execution in order to speed up the allocation process. Because of this, it is possible for the memory-held copy and the disk-held copies to differ for some periods of time.

The free list is maintained in the FAT. A free block is represented by a FAT entry of zero. Simply searching for a zero locates a free block for allocation.

UNIX. UNIX has one variation on the index chaining method. Recall that the inode for each file contains a table of contents. This table holds thirteen block numbers. The first ten block numbers are **direct pointers,** each being the block number of a data block. (See Figure 4.17.) If the file requires more than ten blocks (most do not) then the **indirect pointers** come into play. Pointer number eleven is a **single indirect pointer:** It points to a block each of whose entries in turn point to a data block. If even more data blocks are required, pointer twelve in the table of contents, the **double indirect pointer,** points to an index block whose entries are pointers to *blocks of pointers* which point to data blocks. If the file is unusually large, it may require the use of the final **triple indirect pointer.** Figure 4.17 illustrates this concept.

The free list mechanism is a little more complicated than with MS-DOS or CP/M. The superblock has space allocated for pointers to a limited number of free blocks (see Figure 4.18). One of those pointers is special: It points to a free block which contains another list of free blocks. When the superblock free cache is emptied, the list from this special free block is loaded into the superblock's free cache to refill it. One of the pointers loaded is another special pointer. Figure 4.18 shows how the free blocks are maintained as a linked list of sorts through this process.

Figure 4.18

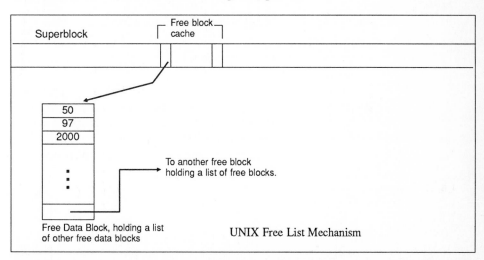

UNIX Free List Mechanism

ProDOS. ProDOS has an interesting twist on the UNIX block chaining. If the file size requires no more than one data block, the **keyblock** pointer in the directory points to the data block, as in Figure 4.19. When the size of the file grows beyond one data block, an **index block** is established and the keyblock pointer points to the index block.

Figure 4.19

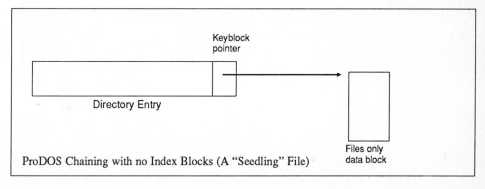

ProDOS Chaining with no Index Blocks (A "Seedling" File)

Figure 4.20

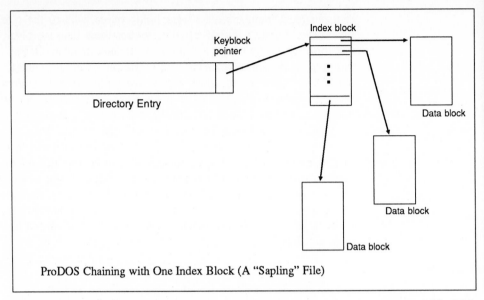

ProDOS Chaining with One Index Block (A "Sapling" File)

The index block holds pointers to the actual data blocks as shown in Figure 4.20. (This is similar to the UNIX single indirection.) If the file grows so large that the index block cannot hold enough pointers, a **master index block** is created and the keyblock pointer points to it. The master index block entries are *block numbers for index blocks*. As before, the index blocks hold pointers to data blocks. Examine Figure 4.21 and then compare it with the UNIX double indirection.

ProDOS maintains the free block list as a bit map stored on diskette.

Figure 4.21

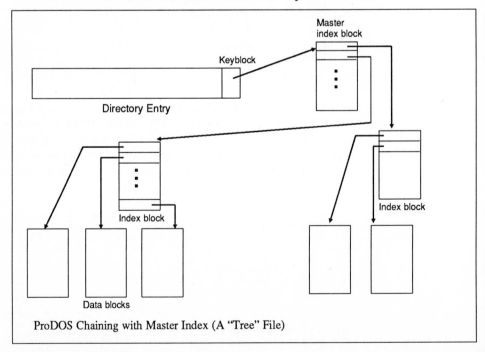

ProDOS Chaining with Master Index (A "Tree" File)

Buffering/ Caching

File system I/O makes heavy use of caching and buffering. Generally, systems create a pool (or cache) of buffers for reading and writing file blocks. Any read that takes place copies a block of data from the file system to one of the buffers. Any writing done to the file system transfers a block of data from a buffer to the disk.

During processing, the buffers hold the most current data for a file. For example, when a block of data is read into memory and altered by the application routine, the buffer data is now different from that on disk. Only when the buffer's contents are written back to disk will the disk file be current.

In more sophisticated systems, the operating system knows not only which file and block the data in a buffer belongs to, but whether that data has been modified since being read. When an application issues a write command, the operating system may either write the contents of the buffer to disk or it may decline. The system may decline to write because the data in the buffer is identical to what is already on the disk (that is, there has been no alteration of the data) and an I/O call can be saved. Generally, however, a decision to decline is due to a **delayed write** mechanism: Don't write the data out to disk until the buffer holding it must be used for some other purpose or until the file is closed. This can save I/O calls (some process might request a read of that block while it is being held).

On some occasions, the system may be able to **prefetch** a block of data by reading it before it is requested. For example, an application might request a read of the first block from a sequential file. While the application is processing that block of data, the operating system may concurrently read in the second block, suspecting that it will be required soon. When the application routine gets around to asking for the second block, there will be no I/O wait required. Some call this prefetching **queued access**.

Security

Data is an extremely important and valuable (at least expensive) resource. Users are correct in being very concerned with the safety of the data and files they manage and use. Data may become unusable through alterations to the directory mechanism or through alterations to the files holding it. The privacy of data may be compromised through unauthorized viewing.

Damage to the integrity of a directory can make it impossible for application programs to locate any given file on the media. The file may be intact with good data, but without the roadmap offered by the directory system the contents of a particular file many not be easily retrievable. Most systems are blessed with routines for repairing many problems of this type.

Data loss and data corruption essentially come about by unauthorized or improper updates to the file data. Unauthorized updates may reflect unauthorized access to and manipulation of the files in either an intentional or unintentional fashion. Improper updates also include well intentioned but erroneous data manipulations by authorized persons. They may be caused by malfunctioning read/write heads and imperfect disk media, a fire or earthquake, or even a robbery.

The problem comes from a simple source: Stored data is subject to two opposing goals. Data storage must provide for the sharing of data among authorized users yet provide privacy as required.

File Security Provisions

Some mechanical procedures are used to minimize the damage from data corruption or loss. **Data validation** procedures may be used in an attempt to insure that changes being made are reasonable changes. **Backup** copies of data files can be maintained on a regular basis. Backup copies may be made for all files (a **full dump**) or for only those that have been altered since the last backup (an **incremental dump**). Several of the most recent backup copies may be retained (in alternate, safe locations preferably). Loss of data in a file then requires *only* the reconstruction of the changes from the most recent backup, a hurtful but less odious task than starting from scratch.

Control of access by unauthorized persons takes a number of forms but usually includes file protection mechanisms. A file's owner can set a **permissions vector** allowing or disallowing read, write, and execute activity (among others). In some systems, owners may invoke this kind of permission vector at the record level, permitting or denying access to each record. It may even be possible to control access at the field level. The smallest unit for which a permission vector may be set is called the **granularity** of the security. A password may be attached to any file with access depending on its knowledge.

Privacy concerns are an issue with users. Intrusion, even to read data, by unauthorized persons should be guarded against. Data, in certain instances, can be compromised simply by being known by unauthorized persons. The permissions mechanisms and password techniques described above also assist in this matter. **Data encryption,** the encoding of data, is another technique used to make it difficult for any but authorized people to view data. Data encryption is also used for **data compaction,** of interest to users where storage space is at a premium or where storage space is a chargeback item.

There are two more subtle but important sources of difficulties with data in files. On multiuser systems, or even multitasking with a single careless user, it is possible for several programs to attempt concurrent access to a given file. Reading and writing files under concurrent processing must be carefully synchronized to prevent corruption. Secondly, where multiple copies of a given file exist, alterations to the data must be made in every copy of the file. Otherwise, the data will not be **consistent** across the several copies. Having several copies of a given file, each with different data, does not lead to useful information.

The Access Matrix

One of the simplest ways to view file security is by way of an **access matrix,** a two dimensional table whose rows represent users (or subjects) and whose columns represent the resources (or objects) being accessed. Figure 4.22 illustrates a matrix where the objects are files in the system. Depending on the granularity, objects might be as finely drawn as records from a file or fields from a record.

Each entry in the access matrix represents a **privilege vector** describing the kind of access (for example, read, write append, execute, delete) the user (row header) is permitted to the object (column header). Note that U1 in Figure 4.22 has no access to F2 but may read, write and execute F6. The matrix as a whole gives the complete set of access rights for all users and all objects.

Each *row* of the access matrix declares the **capability list** for a given user, describing the user's abilities to access the various objects. For example, in Figure 4.22 U3 has only execute permission for files F1 through F5 and read only access to F6.

Figure 4.22

	F1	F2	F3	F4	F5	F6	
U1	R,A	None	E	E	R,W	R,W,E	
U2	None	R,W,D	None	E	None	R,D	
U3	E	E	E	E	E	R	
U4	R,W	R,A	R,E	R	R,D	R,W,E	

File

Access Matrix

Each *column* describes the **access list** for its subject: a complete list of users' privileges for this subject. F4, for instance, may be executed by U1, U2 and U3 and read by U4.

When a user attempts to access a file, the system checks the access matrix (or associated capability list or access list depending on how the information is stored) before deciding whether to grant or deny access. The access matrix itself must be protected from user access. Only the operating system may read and alter that information.

Permissions and Paths

Since many systems treat directories as files with associated privileges, directories may be used to control access. In a hierarchical file structure, access to a given file is controlled by checking a user's privileges for each directory in the pathname. A user is granted access to a nondirectory file only if he/she has appropriate permissions for every directory on the path to the file. For example, if access to /r/u is denied, then access to /r/u/b, /r/u/x, and /r/u/x/a is also denied.

Databases

Early in the history of data processing and computing, files and their manipulation was a major activity. Generally speaking, each unit within the larger organization was responsible for maintaining a given body of data. That data was normally of vital importance to the success of the unit. Each unit "owned" its own files.

It is easy to believe that a portion of each unit's data was also required by a different part of the organization. Thus, individual pieces of data were duplicated among several files owned by the different units. This **redundancy** of information gives rise to problems. **Data integrity** or **consistency,** for example, requires all occurrences of a given piece of data be identical. Accounts payable, accounts receivable and accounts overdue may have the name and address of the same individual: Hopefully, the address is the same in all three files. Multiple occurrences of data items requires multiple storage areas, an inefficient use of disk space.

When each organizational unit is responsible for its own files, the unit generally controls the application programs accessing those files. In fact, file structure is generally tied to the applications associated with it: Change the file structure and the programs accessing it must be rewritten. This tight coupling between files and application programs is known as **data dependence.** If each organizational entity has freedom to structure its own files, its files will probably be uniquely structured. As a result, data processing programs from one unit will not be able to access files from another. The data does not in any real sense belong to the organization. It is carved up among its constituents.

Databases
and Their
Advantages

A **database management system (DBMS)** consists of several parts: the data, a **query language** for making requests, a **data definition language (DDL)** for defining objects within the database, a **data manipulation language (DML)** for specifying the processing to be done, a **data dictionary** holding information about the database itself, and a **data administrator** to assume responsibility for the whole affair.

The data administrator tightly controls the data dictionary, a miniature database that maintains all important information relating to the actual database. In some respects the data dictionary is conceptually like an encyclopedia.

It is common for database systems to run as application programs. Every program wishing to access data calls the DBMS. This is in contrast to the file system approach where each application contained its own file-manipulating code. In a file system, application programs call the operating system for service. In a DBMS, the application programs call the DBMS which, in turn, calls the operating system for service. The DBMS acts as a layer of software added to the operating system. The user's view of data is the logical view supported by the DBMS.

The centralized database is geared to solving some of the problems discussed above. Primarily, use of a DBMS is an attempt by the organization to recapture ownership and control of data from its subunits. In the process, the organization should gain improved control over and better access to its information. While these two goals appear to be in conflict, they are both realizable in a database system.

Centralizing the storage of data should reduce data redundancy. Data integrity should improve and storage requirements should decrease.

Application programs make requests for data without regard to the physical storage structure. The database mechanism must translate the user's logical request to make a physical access, but the translation is transparent to the user. This is known as **data independence.** Data independence makes the data more easily sharable across the organizational boundaries.

Because a DBMS increases access to data, the DBMS design must balance the sometimes conflicting needs of various applications. Someone must have organizational authority to manage the database, enforce standards and arbitrate conflicting requirements. That same individual must be responsible for security mechanisms. Properly defined databases actually make security less a problem than when data is scattered all over the organization in a multitude of files.

Types of
Databases

There are several different approaches to the construction of a DBMS. The different types are categorized by their logical structure. Databases may be described in terms of the relationships between its data elements. The five general approaches are **hierarchical, networked, relational, text (or free form), and object-oriented.**

Hierarchical. In the hierarchical database, the relationship between data items takes the form of a tree structure. Every data element (except the top or **root** element) has a unique **parent.** Data items may have many **children.** (See Figure 4.23.) Fortunately, many collections of data may be represented by such a relationship. Unfortunately, many does not mean all.

Figure 4.23

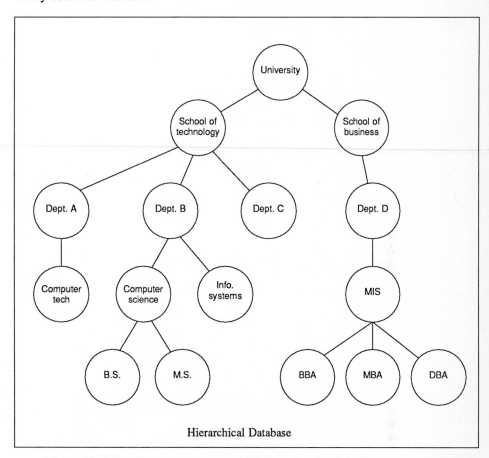

Hierarchical Database

Hierarchical databases are easy to establish and maintain and are easy to navigate from the root to any given data element. Easy, that is, if the user understands how tree structures work. As stated above, not all collections of data may be easily represented logically by a tree structure.

Networked. Networked databases remove the restriction of a data element having a single parent. Many parents are permitted. An example is shown in Figure 4.24. Networked databases may be navigated from root to leaf (top to bottom) or in almost any other pattern. It is possible to start from any data item and find any other. However, the relationships may get very complicated.

   While theoretically more flexible, networked databases are more difficult to maintain and navigate than hierarchical models. Networked databases work best with rela-

Figure 4.24

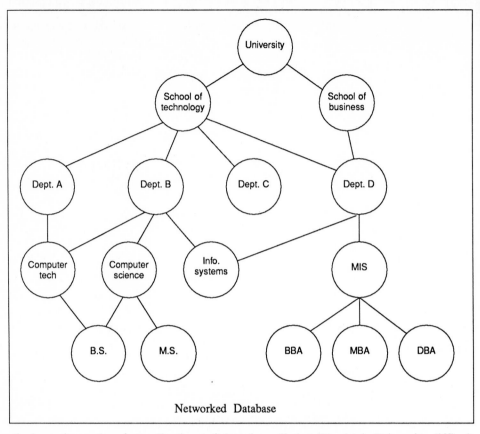

Networked Database

tively static, unchanging collections of data (so called **stable** data). It is quite difficult for the user to know how to navigate around in a networked database. The logical relationships are often very complicated for databases of any real size.

Relational. Users seem to love relational databases. The logical picture of the database is that of a table with rows and columns. Every user is able to represent data elements by describing the rows and columns that make up his/her view of the information. The user view (table) is called a **relation.**

Figure 4.25 shows the table for one relation. Each row is called a **tuple.** The

Figure 4.25

		Relation—Degree Advising		
School	Department	Program	Degree	Advisor
Technology	A	Cptr. Tech.	BS	Carpenter
Technolgoy	B	Cptr. Sci.	BS	Breshears
Technology	B	Info. Sci.	BBA	Sullivan
Business	D	MIS	MBA	Ford
Business	D	Info. Sci.	BBA	Solomon
Technology	B	Cptr. Tech.	BS	Hamel
Technology	B	Cptr. Sci.	MS	Ellis
Business	D	MIS	DBA	Richards
Technology	C	None	None	Swan
Business	D	MIS	BBA	Maier

Relational Database

Figure 4.26

School	Degree
Technology	BS
Technology	BBA
Business	MBA
Business	BBA
Technology	MS
Business	DBA
Technology	None

Projection
School/Degree

tuples making up a relation must be unique (that is, no two rows may be the same). The columns of the table are called **domains:** domains do not have to be unique (that is, two columns may be the same). The database itself is made up of many of these tables.

New relations or user views may be created by picking and choosing domains from an existing table to create a "smaller" relation. The new, smaller relation is called **a projection.** Larger relations may be created by forming one large table from several smaller ones. The larger table is called the **join** of the others. Figure 4.26 shows a projection of the table from Figure 4.25 onto the domains *School* and *Degree*. Figure 4.27 pictures the join of two relations. In this case, *tuples from R1 are concatenated with tuples of R2 which share the same D2 values.* Each resulting tuple is a row in the join table.

The beauty of relational databases is the fact that they are logical structures. Moreover, the user may create any logical structure deemed appropriate for the application at hand. Any structure used to actually store the data in a relational database is totally hidden and of no concern to the user. The idea of navigating through the data to

Figure 4.27

	Relation R1			Relation R2			Join of R1 and R2 on the condition (D2 values agree)		
	D1	D2		D3	D2		D1	D2	D2
T1	A	1	T6	S	3	T11	A	1	S
T2	A	2	T7	S	1	T12	A	1	H
T3	B	1	T8	Q	2	T13	A	2	Q
T4	B	2	T9	H	1	T14	A	2	H
T5	C	3	T10	H	2	T15	B	1	S
						T16	B	1	H
						T17	B	2	Q
						T18	B	2	H
						T19	C	3	S

The Join of Two Relations

find given data elements is unneeded. The tabular model helps the user define the important ingredients: the database does the navigating. See [10] for the original paper on relational databases.

Text/FreeForm.   Commercial text or free form databases are just starting to appear with HyperCard for the Macintosh being an early popular entry. The logical model is that of a shoebox: imagine data items written on a scrap of paper and tossed into the box. Each slip of paper is identified by a few **keywords** written on the back. Users retrieve information by simply using a keyword or two. All data associated with the keyword(s) will be delivered by the database.

Some liken a free form database to a wordprocessor with extremely good data retrieval capabilities. The various data items may be of any length. The text database is most powerful for generating reports and its value grows as the library of "text fragments" grows in size. (The term **hypertext** is also used for this notion. If the fragments may be graphic images, audio segments or other data items as well as text, the term **hypermedia** is applied.)

Object-Oriented.   **Object-oriented** databases are the most recent commercial development. Most database systems separate data from the functions that manipulate it. Object-oriented mechanisms, however, package functions (called **methods**) with the data (or object). There is no standard set of operations defined across all data as in most methods. Rather, the operations are defined for individual object types. The major value of object-oriented databases promises to be their power in dealing with very complex structures. Their history remains to be written.

Relationships of Database to Operating System

Operating systems are evolving so that database operations are migrating to operating system services. This is particularly true for the minicomputer market. The IBM System/38 is a commercially successful system of object-oriented design whose operating system controls database activity. The Pick operating system, implemented on a range of minicomputers from different manufacturers, is another example of a commercially successful operating system designed for database management. Each is a file-oriented operating system with a data retrieval language as part of the service.

For most systems, however, DBMS activity runs as an application called by programs requiring database action.

File Servers

A **file server** is a peripheral device dedicated to providing a file system. File servers are particularly favored among local area network (LAN) users where each user machine is a personal workstation without large local storage. Access to the files on a file server is designed to be transparent to the user. That is, users access the files from the server just as if their own machine held them. Three general implementations are found.

The central file server system may act as a remote disk for each workstation. In effect, the file server partitions its mass storage space into a collection of **virtual disks.** Each user is allocated his or her own "disk": Processing looks just like it does with a standalone personal computer. While being simple to implement and use, there is little or no capacity to *share* very large data collections when the file server is so partitioned.

The other extreme occurs when the file server acts as a single large file system. This allows file sharing and the construction of large files or databases. However, the sharing of files creates a security problem. Data must be protected by access control mechanisms. Moreover, file access must be synchronized to prevent file contamination by improper sequences of reads and writes by competing processes. Quite often **locks** are implemented in order to synchronize reading and writing. If the locking occurs at the record level, several noncompeting processes may work in a given file concurrently without concern for file contamination.

A third approach lies somewhere in between these two. The file server allocates and deallocates space for files and manages all physical activity concerning those files. The user, rather than the file server, maintains all directories. The server maintains an index of file identifiers that allow it to carry out its work. It reports the identifier for each newly created file to the user. The user must manage a personal directory mechanism that relates file names to file server identification numbers.

Since workstations accessing the data managed by a file server are remote to it, another problem must be considered. Changes to a file system must be considered **atomic.** That is, even though a file update may consist of several instructions, the file server cannot begin the update until it has all the instructions in hand and knows what the entire update is. The reason: One or more of the instructions may be lost or garbled in transmission. Executing some, but not all, of the instructions will result in contaminated data. Therefore, the server can do no instruction in an atomic set until it has the complete set. This is also known as **failure atomicity:** Do all the update activity or do none of it. This is particularly true for **transaction processing** so common to commercial database activity.

Exercises

1. Discuss each of the following notions:
   a. data redundancy
   b. data consistency
2. Discuss each of the following:
   a. data dependence
   b. data independence
3. Compare sequential and random access for files. When might each be the more appropriate?
4. What is the advantage in batching transactions on a sequentially organized file?
5. Describe why a read ahead mechanism might be helpful. When would it be a waste of time?
6. Describe why a delayed write mechanism might be helpful. What potential problems does it cause?
7. Compare/contrast the notion of file copying with file linking or aliasing.
8. Discuss the relative merits of an operating system that has facilities for many types of file structures versus one that allows only one or two.
9. UNIX has only one model of a file: a stream of bytes. Who is responsible for the logical organization of a file?

10. A file is to be read sequentially. Why might an indexed sequential format slow the activity over a simpler sequential structure? If the file system has a compaction/reorganization facility, how might it be used to help with the problem of slowness for the indexed sequential format?

11. A tape drive can be instructed to move forward and backward in records. Describe how direct access might be instituted on such a tape file. Is it a good idea?

12. Describe how a directly organized file might be processed (accessed) sequentially.

13. Describe what the psuedocode for updating the Customer file in the Billing Department example might look like.

14. Describe how the hashing of keys can be used to create a direct file organization using relative record numbers.

15. Describe the use/advantage of relative pathnames in a hierarchical directory scheme.

16. What is one advantage of a flat directory system for a low volume disk system?

17. Where in the file system is general information about each file stored?

18. Why are linking and indexing unnecessary in a contiguous allocation scheme?

19. In UNIX, the use of indirection slows the access for a given data block. Why might the designers of UNIX suspect that is not a significant problem?

20. How can the operating system know how to do a seek to byte B of a file?

21. File compaction routines often place files in contiguous or nearly contiguous regions. Why?

22. Why is file locking important in a multitasking environment?

23. If linking to files is allowed for nondirectory files only, why are cycles impossible in the directory's graph?

24. Why do most operating systems not allow a user to delete a nonempty directory?

25. Describe how one might delete data records from a sequentially organized file without rewriting the entire file? Deleted files can often be recovered by a utility routine. How do you suspect the "deletion" was accomplished?

26. Privileges may be associated with files or with the file entry in its parent directory. In the latter case, the linking of files presents a problem. Why?

27. What does each of the following show?
    a. access list
    b. capability list

28. Why is the hierarchical directory structure most popular?

29. Describe data ownership as contrasted in a file-oriented system versus a database system.

30. Describe data ownership in a network where data exists on a file server or in a distributed database.

31. Describe the frequency of backup as likely required by each of the following systems.
    a. a point of sale transaction system
    b. a batched sales transaction system processed nightly
    c. a desktop publishing network
    d. an inhouse software development system

32. Discuss the likely role for a *transaction log* in an online point of sale transaction system.

33. In some transaction-oriented systems, updating a record causes a new data block to be assigned. The block containing the record to be updated is copied into the new block with the update made. Why?
34. Why are relational databases so popular?
35. If the block size is 1K bytes and block numbers are 2 bytes in size, what is the maximum size for a UNIX file system?
36. Answer Exercise 35 for a block size of 512 bytes for ProDOS.
37. Give some pros and cons for: A call to *OPEN fileA* creates *fileA* if it does not already exist.
38. Describe how to establish each form of access for a sequentially organized file.
39. Stable storage is achieved by "shadow writing" that duplicates each record/file. Why would one bother?
40. Give an example of a serial file. Serial files are said to be ideal for archival purposes. Explain.
41. It is said that two-thirds of all file requests are READ. What are the implications?

5 Input/Output Management

Imagine a computer system with only a CPU and some memory—not much of a system, is it? To be of use in the real world, a computer system must have some way of rubbing elbows with users; generally that is accomplished through the use of peripheral I/O (input/output) devices. I/O devices, in fact, may represent the computer system to the nontechnical user.

Figure 5.1

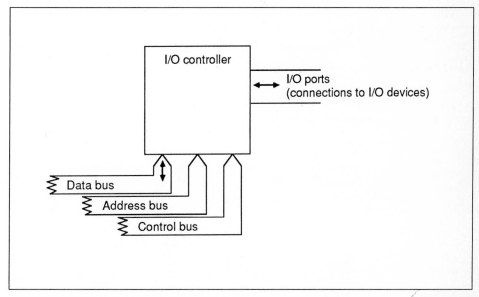

I/O devices must provide simple machine/user communication. Direct control of a peripheral device is difficult even for the most proficient system programmer. For that reason, most operational details are normally hidden from the user by the interface (controller) (Figure 5.1). The user should be able to use a printer, a file, or a terminal with uniform ease.

The actual work done by a device is accomplished through a **physical process** bearing little resemblance to the way a programmer thinks of the device. The programmer's **logical view** of the device should be all that is required for program control.

Application programs should be able to direct the activity of peripheral devices through a few very simple, mnemonic commands.

I/O is primarily concerned with **data movement** or **transfer** that takes place during a computing session. **Input** is the transfer of data (and device status information) from a device to the control of the CPU. **Output** is the transfer of data (and device control instructions) from CPU control to a peripheral unit. Since a system normally has several or even many attached devices, it is quite likely that various I/O actions will take place **concurrently** (for example, the printer is running, the disk drive is whirring, and the user is typing information at the keyboard). Synchronization of these concurrent activities is required.

Historically, I/O was the first class of activities managed by an operating system. Early on, the (comparatively) fast processor spent too much time waiting for I/O processes to complete. Intelligent I/O devices capable of **asynchronous** operation (relatively) independent of the CPU allowed for reduced processor waiting time. Any number of concurrent processes could be managed. Hardware interrupts provided the major key in untying the CPU from direct control over most I/O activity.

Devices and Their Management

The fundamental job of device management is making each device work with a particular computer. This can be a problem because of the many different I/O device types and manufacturers. Without standardization, each manufacturer's product tends to work differently from those of its competitors. In addition, each computer has its own preferred method of communicating with devices, a method it absolutely insists on using.

Kinds of Devices

Raw or **character devices** essentially transfer data byte by byte or word by word. The rate of data transfer may vary from a few characters to hundreds of thousands of characters per second. **Block devices,** on the other hand, move fixed-size *groups* of data with each transfer. While block devices generally transfer data much faster than raw devices, that rate of transfer is also variable (from several thousand bytes to several million bytes per second). If many bytes are transferred in a block move without CPU intervention, the device is a **DMA (direct memory access)** device. Device management must consider the amount of data in each transfer and the rate at which the transfer takes place.

Some peripherals require CPU oversight during the entire transfer of data; others do not. The transfer of data may need to be time-synchronized, or it may proceed asynchronously after being started by the processor. In the latter case, an interrupt or other mechanism signals completion. In other words, device management is affected by the type and amount of synchronization required.

Devices may be **dedicated** to a single user (as in an active terminal). Others are **shared** resources (for example, disk units on multiuser systems) and are only partially assigned to a user. The "partial" in partial assignment may imply: (1) partial capacity (wherein each user owns only a portion of the space on a disk) all the time, or (2) total capacity part of the time (for example, the entire printer is assigned but only temporarily). Most shareable devices are, in fact, **serially reusable** or **serially assignable:** The devices are shared among users but only one user is active at any moment. Device management is, therefore, affected by the private/public nature of the device.

Figure 5.2

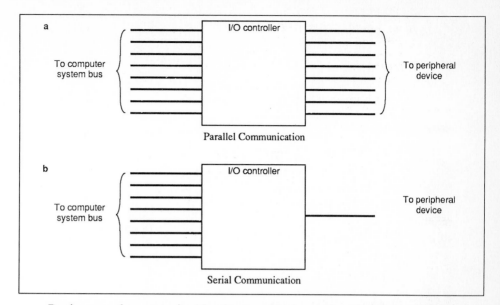

Devices are also categorized by the way data is transferred to them. If all bits in a byte or word are moved at the same time (see Figure 5.2a), the device is a **parallel device.** If each byte is transferred a **bit** at a time (one bit after another), the device is a **serial device** (see Figure 5.2b). Device management is affected by the data transfer technique.

Views of a Device

One goal of device management is to make all the different devices of a similar type "look" exactly the same to the user. For example, the user has one generic **logical view** of a printer: All printers are conceptually the same. If the system has six different printers, the individual differences between the printers must be hidden from the user. He or she wants to print characters or lines, tab, skip lines, go to the top of a new form, or some other function. Whether the printer is a serial or parallel device should not concern the user. Control information is passed to a printer by imbedding **escape codes** (metacharacters) within the data; however, if the user wants to tab, he or she calls for a tab, not an escape code. The kernel must translate "tab" into the correct escape code. How format control information is passed to the printer should also not concern the user.

All devices are mechanisms that receive instructions via electronic signals. The intelligence of the device transforms those signals into the appropriate electronic or physical actions. The signals required by the device are probably peculiar to it and its manufacturer, while bearing no resemblance to the memory and control signals that represent I/O activity to the processor (such as memory read, memory write, interrupt). Note that one can never expect the computer's processor/memory control signals to be the same as those needed by the peripheral device. A **device driver** (**device interface, device controller**) is a control program used to translate between these two entities.

In Figure 5.3 a layered approach is used to create the driver. The middle layer is the key: It presents a generic interface common to all peripheral devices on the one hand and allows application programmers to treat all devices in a consistent format and

Figure 5.3

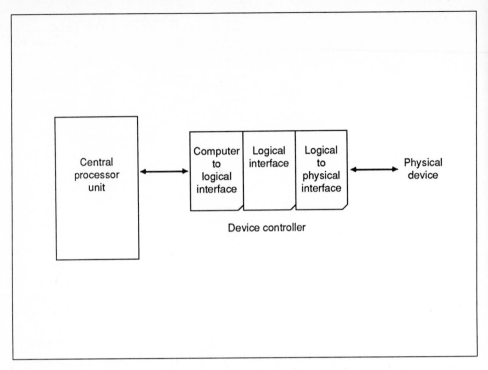

manner on the other. In a sense, the application programmer communicates with the generic layer to get the work done. The layer on the *computer side* translates the processor/memory signal requirements into those of the middle layer of the device controller. The layer on the *device side* translates the generic layer signals into those required by the device. The translation process, then, is bus to generic driver (logical) to device (physical), or vice versa—device to generic driver to bus.

The device driver may be written as a permanent part of the operating system's kernel; in this case, the manufacturers' peripherals are expected to match the system's requirements. More likely the driver is "installed" during system configuration or interactively created from a general driver by the selection of a few parameters. In the latter two cases, *the system is adjusted* to meet the peripheral's needs. As a marketing tool, device manufacturers often give drivers and parameter lists to purchasers of their devices.

Making all devices of the same type look the same to the system and user is one aspect, but a more general problem is that of making all different *kinds* of devices look the same to the system and user (for example, program control for printers is similar to program control for files). The goal is to follow the same format for program control of all devices, regardless of the type. Layered driver design is often used to meet this requirement. Generally, devices are treated very much like files. Peripheral devices are opened, closed, read from, written to, and so on. Status information and control information (in addition to the "data" transferred) are exchanged. Uniformity makes the application programmer's job much simpler: One generic set of I/O instructions applies to all devices. Each physical device may be a specific instance of one generic **virtual device.**

Figure 5.4

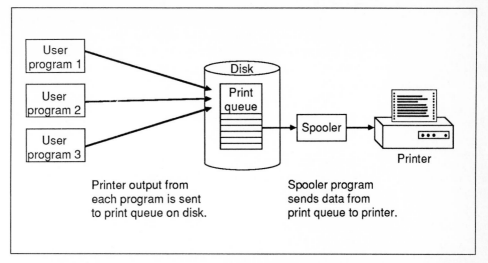

User program 1

User program 2

User program 3

Disk

Print queue

Spooler

Printer

Printer output from
each program is sent
to print queue on disk.

Spooler program
sends data from
print queue to printer.

A virtual device is a conceptual construct using software to simulate a (possibly) nonexistent physical device. The user imagines that he or she is manipulating a device, (say, a printer), when, in fact, a file is being written or read. SPOOLing (Figure 5.4) has this idea at its heart. Or a microcomputer communicating with a mainframe may use part of the mainframe's disk system as if it were a virtual floppy disk drive attached to the micro. Or a user workstation built around *microcomputer* X can appear to the mainframe computer as a brand Y *terminal* because of the communications software used.

The uniform treatment of peripherals allows for the notion of **device independence.** The user merely calls the device by a symbolic name and employs the uniform set of instructions for accomplishing I/O.

Device Management Functions

Physical devices are managed for efficiency and reliability; the responsibility for both lies with the intelligence and control within the device itself. Devices are also managed so their use is transparent to users; the responsibility for transparency lies primarily with the device drivers. The user should feel as though he or she has an easily used, direct channel to the peripheral device.

There is yet another concern for device management: Who has access to a given device at any point in time? And for what purposes? This is a question of **protection** and **security.** In a multitasking system, several programs may attempt to use a device concurrently. A user without authorization may try to access a peripheral. A user with restricted access privileges may attempt to use a device in a forbidden manner.

Data that is stored or transmitted is often stored or transmitted in some *coded form.* One purpose for changing the bit patterns representing the data is **security**, since stored and transmitted data is vulnerable to unauthorized reading and altering. **Encryption** (the encoding of data) is used to control any possible unauthorized access.

Encoding may also be used to add bits of information whose purpose is **error detection** and **correction.** Data is subjected to the introduction of errors as it is moved, and those errors need to be detected and corrected so that data transfer appears error free. Encryption for error detection and correction may be accomplished by software techniques or by hardware methods. In any event, encoding for such purposes *increases* the number of bits needed to represent the data.

Data compaction is another form of data encoding: Bit patterns representing the data are encoded in such a way that **fewer** bits are required. Data compaction saves storage space and transmission time at the cost of the translation process.

Where users buy access to another's computer power, I/O activities are often measured and charges levied. Before charges can be billed, some accounting must be done on behalf of both user and provider. Costs usually depend on the device used and the extent of use. Part of the management of I/O activities and devices, then, may involve the collection of journal-type information.

Another matter of concern to management is the productivity of each peripheral device. On large systems, several programs may request a given device at essentially the same time. Since most devices allow control by only one user at a time, some queueing mechanism must exist. The queueing strategy may be either **first come, first served (FCFS)** or some priority scheme. For instance, printer throughput may be enhanced by giving control to the **shortest job next (SJN).** A disk drive may be managed by the **shortest seek time first (SSTF)** scheme: Next service goes to the read or write request "closest" to the last read or write. Each device that is sharable probably has a queue of some sort.

Device Control

Device control by the CPU may take several forms. In the simplest case, the CPU oversees the entire data transfer itself. Since the I/O device is very slow with respect to the CPU, this is not very efficient. Intelligent peripherals that can oversee their own data transfer to and from main memory are more productive.

Where I/O devices operate autonomously (or nearly so), the usual pattern is as in the following. The CPU signals the need for a transfer of data and passes information about how much data is to be transferred, the location of the **buffer** (main memory region holding or receiving the data to be transferred), and so on. The CPU continues with other activities while the intelligent peripheral takes over. When the peripheral finishes the transfer, it signals the CPU by way of an interrupt.

There is at least one alternative to this interrupt scheme. The CPU can **poll** (check) peripheral devices on some scheduled basis to find out whether data transfers have been completed. This is more costly since CPU cycles are expended doing the checking. In an extreme case, the CPU may spend a lengthy time doing nothing but polling; this is called **busy waiting.**

Intelligent peripherals come in a variety of forms. A printer may, for instance, contain a very large buffer for holding data transferred at a fast rate, perhaps under CPU direction. The printer then retrieves the data from the buffer and prints it without further CPU intervention. On the other hand, there are more flexible devices known as **I/O channels** and **processors.**

I/O channels are complete, special-purpose computers capable of DMA activity. All that is required are signals and parameters from the processor. The channels are programmed to complete the data transfer task after initial CPU contact. It is common for a single I/O channel or processor to direct data transfer for several devices of the same kind.

The difference between an I/O channel and an I/O processor lies in the way instructions are received. Conceptually, they are very similar. A channel/processor used to manage data moves by interleaving data transfer streams for several (character) devices at once is called a **multiplexor,** while a channel/processor used for multiple block devices but without interleaving is called a **selector.**

Synchronization

Generally, the amount of concurrent I/O will be great enough to require more synchronization than interrupts can provide. Synchronization assumes that not everything should happen at once. At various times, some action or actions may need to be put on hold until other acts are completed. An **event signal** (or simply, **signal**) marks the completion of an event and is used to notify a waiting activity. The waiting activity may use its CPU time to regularly check for the event signal (busy waiting), or it may relinquish the right to the CPU (**sleep**) until the event signal directs the operating system to restore CPU rights (**wakeup**).

Producer/consumer problem.   One simple example of asynchronous activities requiring synchronization is the **producer/consumer problem.** One mechanism (the producer) is creating a product for use by the consumer. The producer and consumer act concurrently, and synchronization is required since nothing can be consumed unless it has first been produced.

As an example, suppose program P is producing data and writing it into a buffer B, while program Q is reading data from the buffer in the same order as produced (that is, the buffer is a first-in, first-out queue). Program Q cannot perform a read unless *unread* data has been placed in B. A signal *HasData* can be used to tell Q whether reading is permitted. If B has a finite size (that is, there is limited storage for produced items), P might fill the buffer and run the risk of overflow. To overcome the problem, employ a signal, say *HasRoom,* to tell P whether producing is allowed. Q is not permitted to read data from the buffer unless *HasData* is true, while P is not permitted to write data to the buffer unless *HasRoom* is true. (It is probably necessary to prohibit Q from reading while P is writing—and vice versa.)

Insuring that only one device or program is conducting a particular activity at any time is called **mutual exclusion.** Mutual exclusion is often at the heart of synchronization efforts. For example, only one actor (CPU or DMA device) can use the main memory bus at one time. To allow two devices to access the bus at the same instant can easily produce chaos. A similar problem occurs with files: It may be a mistake for two programs to write to the same file during the same time interval—or for one program to read a file during the time interval in which another is writing to it.

Concurrency concerns can be described in the following way: Suppose a set A_1, A_2, A_3, ... , A_n of activities *can* occur concurrently. Then assume the activities happen sequentially (one after the other) rather than concurrently. *If the order in which they execute and finish makes any difference to the outcome,* synchronization is required. Alternatively, if all possible sequences of completion yield the *same* outcome, syncronization is unnecessary.

Deadlock

Waiting for an event to occur when that event cannot possibly occur is **deadlock,** an issue related to synchronization. In essence, deadlock is waiting for the impossible.

Deadlock can occur whenever concurrent activity is permitted. The following example illustrates this concept. Suppose program A has been allocated control of the system's only magnetic tape drive, while B has been granted control of the only OCR (optical character recognition) scanner. Suppose further that A can continue processing only if it gathers input using the OCR device. Moreover, suppose B cannot proceed until it gains control of the magnetic tape device. Current device allocations prevent the operating system from making a further assignment. A standoff results: Neither program can advance. This deadlock illustrates **circular wait,** a condition in which each activity in a chain holds a resource needed by the next (see Figure 5.5).

Figure 5.5

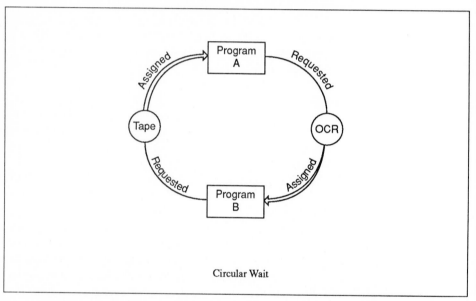

Circular Wait

Designers of operating systems know that the following four conditions must be present if deadlock is to occur:

- **mutual exclusion** (a maximum of one program using the resource at any given time)
- **hold-and-wait** (a program may request new resources while holding others)
- **no preemption** (no resource may be forceably removed from a program holding it)
- **circular wait** (there is a circular chain of programs, each holding at least one resource needed by the next program in the chain).

In the OCR/tape example, all four conditions are present. It is assumed that only one program can use each device at any time. Each program may hold its device while it waits for the other to be allocated. Neither device may be summarily removed from the program holding it. Circular wait has been shown.

Dealing with deadlock is painful and expensive. However, not dealing with it is also potentially expensive: Deadlock ties up resources and programs to no productive end. Moreover, a deadlock of some resources and programs almost always leads to deadlocks of other resources and programs, and thus the system can be quickly rendered inefficient or helpless.

There are several techniques for dealing with the problem. First, **deadlock prevention** makes deadlock impossible: "Simply" insure that at any point in time, one of the four conditions for deadlock (other than mutual exclusion, normally) cannot be true. The wait-and-hold condition is an easy one to choose. Allowing preemption of resources works but carries a heavy penalty in terms of overhead and restarting some actions.

Deadlock avoidance is a resource allocation policy that "looks ahead" and fills a request only if deadlock will not result. There are algorithms for doing this, but they too add dramatically to system overhead.

A third way of handling deadlock is the "not to worry" approach. This technique uses **deadlock detection/recovery** mechanisms. The plan looks easy: Let processing go on until such time as deadlock occurs. When deadlock happens, the operating system picks a **victim** program and stops its execution (**kill** or **roll-back**). The resources of the victim are assigned to another waiting program, allowing it to continue. When feasible, the operating system will restart the victim. Note that the difficult part is detecting the deadlock when it occurs.

There is likely much more concern and effort given to the theoretical considerations of deadlock than to the implementation of "anti-deadlock" routines. Only the most complex systems seem to implement serious measures. UNIX, for example, has little in the way of anti-deadlock mechanisms. Many smaller systems let the operator fix deadlocks manually. Massively parallel processor systems (systems with very large numbers of CPUs), however, are so complex that they create a need for more deadlock research. Networks for distributing computation among several computer systems create a similar need for deadlock handling.

Mass Storage Devices

Mass storage devices are used to create nonvolatile secondary memory, usually as an extension of main memory. Archived files often find their way onto magnetic tape. The swapping store used to improve multitasking capabilities is normally located on disk. Nonvolatile storage of files that are frequently referenced customarily relies on magnetic disk.

Disk Systems

Disks and disk systems come in a variety of sizes and capacities. For small applications, there are eight-inch floppy diskettes (decreasing in popularity), 5¼-inch diskettes, and 3½-inch microdiskettes. In each case, the disk is enclosed in a protective cover and is inserted into the disk drive when needed. Larger capacity harddisk systems for micro and minicomputers consist of one or more "platters," ranging from 3½ inches in diameter to over twelve inches in diameter. The hard disks are normally enclosed within the disk drive and are not removable (as in the case of the floppies). For larger machines, disk packs consist of several fairly large platters hermetically sealed in a package. These larger storage disk packs can be interchanged on disk drives as needed.

Capacities for floppy disks range from around 150K bytes to over 1 megabyte. For hard disks, the capacities start at around 10 megabytes and run to over 100 megabytes for microcomputers. Typical disk packs for large systems have capacities in the hundreds of megabytes. It is not unusual for mainframe systems to have a total online

Figure 5.6

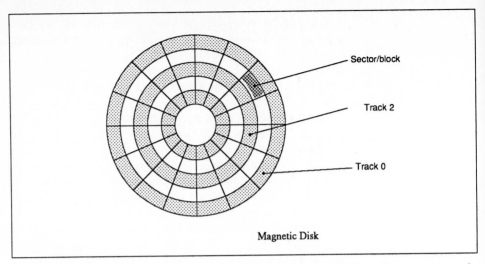

Magnetic Disk

storage capacity of 30 gigabytes or more. Terabyte capacities for online storage are in the works.

Note that rotational speeds for floppy disks start at about 300 RPM, and hard disks rotate faster. Disk units for mainframes rotate even faster than that. Note that rotational speed affects the rate at which data can be read from and written to a disk.

For all disks, the data is stored on either one or both sides of each platter; double-sided platters are the most common. A platter surface has an associated read/write head that must be positioned to physically locate a specific block of data on the disk or disk pack. The act of locating a particular block is called a **seek.** In most cases, all read/write heads will be connected to a single arm, which moves the heads across the disks between the outer edge and the center.

Each platter of any disk consists of concentric tracks, as shown in Figure 5.6. Tracks are partitioned into sectors, each of which holds a **block** of data—the amount of

Figure 5.7

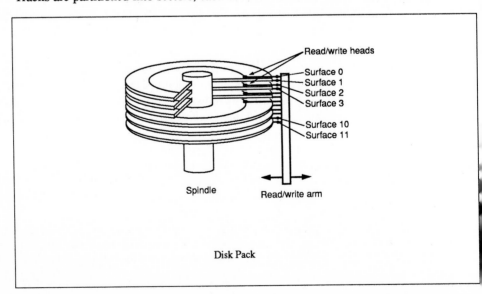

Disk Pack

data transferred with each read and each write. (Some systems differ slightly from this explanation.) For multiple-platter packs (Figure 5.7), a set of tracks that are vertically aligned are collectively known as a **cylinder.** The positioning of the single read/write arm places a read/write head over each track of some cylinder. The tracks and cylinders are routinely numbered from the outer edge to the center.

Blocks of data on a disk have an address that consists of a track number (cylinder and surface number for a multiple-platter unit) and a sector or block number within the track. Physically locating a particular block of data consists of two **latency** times: **seek time** (the time to move the read/write head over the correct track) and **rotational time** (the time for the disk to rotate the correct block underneath the head). The total read/ write times are also affected by the **transfer time** (the time it takes to complete the read/write transaction after the head is correctly positioned). On the average, the seek time is the greatest of all of these.

Multitasking systems often generate several seek requests at one time. A priority queueing mechanism is generally used to service them. The **shortest seek time first** (SSTF) strategy chooses to serve the seek that is in the track closest to the current head position. The goal is to minimize the average seek time. A **first come, first served** (FCFS) strategy can be used and will work reasonably well for light loads (short average queue lengths). An FCFS strategy is generally used for single-user multitasking systems.

Figure 5.8 displays a queued set of seek requests for a disk having tracks numbered from zero (outer track) to 815 (inner track). The job numbers indicate the order of arrival of the requests. As an example, suppose the head is currently at track 519. Since track 478 holds the request closest to track 519, the SSTF algorithm will service Job 2 next. From track 478, the heads will move to track 581 to service Job 8. SSTF will service the remaining requests in the following order: 671, 800, 346, 301, 209, 126, 19.

Figure 5.8

Job Number	Track Number for Seek
1	301
2	478
3	209
4	671
5	800
6	126
7	19
8	581
9	346

Under the same conditions, the FCFS strategy will service the requests in the order of arrival: 301, 478, 209, 671, 800, 126, 19, 581, 346. The total head movement as the requests are satisfied by the FCFS strategy is greater than that required for SSFT.

The **SCAN** strategy, also known as the **elevator algorithm,** is a popular disk scheduling strategy. The read/write heads sweep back and forth across the disk, servicing requests as the desired tracks are encountered. The direction of head movement is re-versed when the queue holds no further seek requests for tracks lying "in front of" the read/write heads (that is, all requests are "behind" the heads).

If the read/write heads are at track 519 and the current direction of head move-ment is toward track zero, the SCAN strategy will service the requests in Figure 5.8 in this order: 478, 346, 301, 209, 126, 19, 581, 671, 800.

C-SCAN (or circular SCAN) is much like the SCAN strategy except for one alter-ation: Seek requests are serviced in only one direction (usually as the heads sweep from the outer track to the inner). When there are no queued seek requests in front of the heads as they sweep the disk, *the read/write heads are reset to the beginning* and the process of sweeping and servicing is repeated.

If the read/write heads are positioned at track 519 and the C-SCAN seek direction is always from outer to inner tracks, the C-SCAN algorithm will service the requests from Figure 5.8 in the following order: 581, 671, 800, 19, 126, 209, 301, 346, 478.

Theoretical solutions for servicing disk seeks abound, and all kinds of priority queueing strategies have been proposed. However, those discussed in this chapter account for the majority of all implementations, with SCAN and C-SCAN being the most popular for moderate to heavy loading in multiuser systems.

Nonmagnetic disk systems are now making inroads into computer storage. **Optical disks** using lasers have a number of advantages in terms of huge storage capacities with extremely high reliability and good speed. The **compact audio disk** has entered the scene under the name **CD ROM.** The current limitations for these disk types lie with the difficulty in making them easily writable. They tend to be *read-only* or *write-once* media, although technological advances are quickly removing that restriction.

Magnetic Drums

Magnetic drums predate the widespread use of disks. Still, some large systems use magnetic drum storage for their swapping store. One advantage that the magnetic drum has is that is faster for information storage and retrieval than the disk. One disadvan-tage is that it has less storage capacity.

Magnetic drums have a cylindrical surface rather than the flat platter of the disk. Tracks are parallel paths around the cylinder, and each track has a fixed read/write head. That accounts for some of the speed, as there is no seek time with nonexistent head movement. (Some disk units also have fixed read/write heads but such is not the norm.)

Magnetic Tape

Magnetic tapes are used primarily for archival storage of vast quantities of data. Tapes range in size from a typical audiocassette tape (used in some microcomputer systems) to the large reel tapes of the mainframe machines. Currently gaining in popularity is the highspeed **streaming tape** used to make archival copies of large hard disks for small to medium systems and VHS-format video tape.

There are many reasons for archiving data contained on disk. Most generally, data is dumped from disk to tape for protection in case something goes wrong and disturbs the data's integrity. In information-sensitive settings, historical archives are used to create data processing histories and audit trails. In case of problems, corrupted informa-tion is reconstructed from the most recent archival copy by reprocessing those transac-tions occurring after the archival date.

System generation data and operating system updates are often shipped to computer sites on reels of magnetic tape. Magnetic tape is of very high capacity and relatively low cost, making it a convenient way to transfer data from one location to another.

The sequential nature of magnetic tape renders it unattractive as the major secondary storage medium. Disks and drums are **direct access devices;** that is, each block of data can be found and accessed about as quickly as any other. Magnetic tapes, however, are **sequential access devices.** While disk heads can be positioned directly over the desired block of data, a block of data on magnetic tape is found by reading each block of data between the read/write head and the desired block. Thus, even though tapes can be read forward or backward, access for any given data block is not direct.

Figure 5.9 shows that tracks on a tape are in the form of parallel lines, with nine tracks being fairly common. Bytes are stored *across tracks* and are strung together in records and/or blocks. The latency time for tape seeks is called **winding time.**

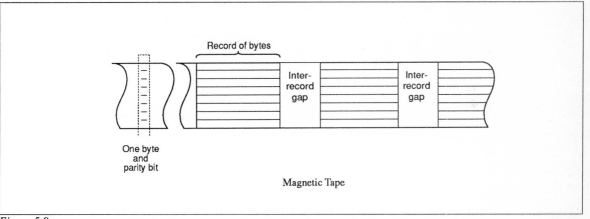

Figure 5.9

There is a second drawback for magnetic tape use: Blocks of data can normally be written only by appending them to the end of the existing data. Errors in the positioning of read/write heads and loose tolerances caused by stretching tapes do not allow very accurate writing. Overwriting data in the middle of a tape will almost surely lead to overwriting a portion of either the preceding or trailing block, thereby contaminating the data.

If, however, all data is to be entered/written at one time or if all additions of data are to be appended, tapes can serve well in data acquisition systems. The utility of magnetic tape is also enhanced if most data retrieval naturally requires reading all or nearly all of the stored data. Direct access devices excel when data reads and writes involve only a very small portion of the stored information.

A smaller problem of magnetic tape devices is shared with floppy disks: The read/write heads contact the magnetic surface during reading and writing. Wear factors are greater for these devices than for hard disk systems, where the read/write heads float on a cushion of air. Optical disks use light beams rather than the mechanical read/write heads and are, therefore, the least prone to such wear.

Other Secondary Storage Devices

A number of secondary storage devices are currently finding their way into the market. The optical disk and CD ROM mentioned earlier are of interest because of the potential for extremely high storage capacities (upwards of 500 megabytes per side or one gigabyte per platter if both sides can be read).

Removable cartridge devices are being developed, some as alternatives to fixed hard disk systems. In effect, they act as the equivalent of very high-capacity floppy disks. A **Bernoulli** box contains a floppy disk-like platter whose read/write heads float on a cushion of air rather than contacting the magnetic surface. The platters are removable (as with floppy disks) and have capacities of twenty megabytes and more. Magnetic tape cartridges which are only about four inches square have the storage capacity of the standard 10½-inch reel of magnetic tape (around 200 megabytes). Streaming tapes for microcomputers (as mentioned earlier) are small ¼-inch tapes that transfer data rapidly and hold up to 60 megabytes or so. Streaming tapes cannot be stopped and restarted accurately in the middle of the tape, so they are primarily suitable for archival dumps of hard disks.

"Jukeboxes" that play stacks of tape cartridges may do away with the need for multiple tape drives in the future, while reducing the mounting time and speed of access. Jukeboxes that play stacks of optical disks or CD ROM disks are also being introduced. Consider a jukebox that manages 100 optical disks, each of one gigabyte capacity—or imagine a tape jukebox using VHS video tapes having a capacity of ten gigabytes each.

Future systems combining main store extended by magnetic disk storage extended by optical disk storage extended by magnetic tape storage extended by.... In this future scenario, a terabyte of online storage presents no problem.

Exercises

1. Which of the following are most likely character devices?
   a. terminal
   b. modem
   c. disk
   d. magnetic tape
   e. cardreader
   f. magnetic drum
   g. light pen
   h. mouse
   i. printer
   j. local area network
2. Which of those in Exercise 1 are most likely to be serial devices? Parallel? DMA?
3. Which of those in Exercise 1 are most likely to be dedicated devices? Shared?
4. Which category (dedicated/private or shared/public) is the more natural for spooled devices? Why?
5. What is device independence? Why is it valuable to the user?

6. Suppose the disk system appears to be a system bottleneck. Why may adding another drive fail to help much? Why may multiple printers improve printing more than multiple disk drives improve disk access?

7. What is the primary value of DMA?

8. Microcomputer systems have historically lacked DMA capabilities for any peripherals. Why does this make large-capacity external buffers attractive?

9. Describe **virtual device** as it pertains to spooling.

10. Describe **virtual device** as it pertains to the simulation of a device. Couch your description in terms of having only a plotter for doing printing.

11. Discuss the advantages and disadvantages of using SJN for printer spooling.

12. What does a manufacturer mean when it says a certain printer is Epson-compatible?

13. What is an escape code? Suppose \ is the escape character for strings (for example, \n represents a new line). What does \\ likely mean?

14. Charging for computer use often includes charges for I/O. On what kinds of things are charges for I/O reasonably based?

15. One way to avoid deadlock over resources is to have each program specify all required resources. Execution does not begin until all those resources can be (and are) allocated to the program. Describe any disadvantages to this policy.

16. **Serialization of resources** (allowing a program to hold only one resource at a time) prevents deadlock on a single-processor system. Discuss some disadvantages of such an allocation scheme.

17. Suppose a deadlock occurs and is broken by removing one program. Describe any difficulties that may arise when restarting that program anew.

18. Suppose the design philosophy is, "Let the operator deal with deadlock." How can the operator deal with a deadlock when it occurs?

19. Some say spooling peripheral devices reduces the chances of deadlock. Why might they say this?

20. Compare/contrast indefinite postponement (see Exercise 21) and deadlock.

21. An event is treated to **indefinite postponement** or **starvation** when it fails to occur due to a priority mechanism that continually favors other events. How can starvation occur when SSTF disk scheduling is used? Which tracks on the disk are most prone to starvation? Why?

22. SCAN has been called **SSTF in the favored direction.** Why?

23. Why is SCAN called the **elevator algorithm?**

24. Which of SSTF and SCAN is likely to have the most predictable average seek time per service? Why?

25. SCAN places newly arriving requests in the active queue as they arrive. A version of SCAN (N-Step SCAN) holds all new arrivals until the current sweep has been completed. At that time, the accumulated arrivals are placed in the active queue. Give some advantages and some disadvantages of this approach. (The alteration can also be applied to C-SCAN.)

26. When might rotational latency be of interest?

27. Using the queue of seek requests from Figure 5.10, find the order in which each strategy services them. Assume that the read/write heads are at track 415 and the

Figure 5.10

Job Number	Track Number for Seek
1	811
2	121
3	52
4	614
5	400
6	486
7	519
8	211
9	15
10	721

last movement was in the direction of increasing track numbers. Which strategy gives the least disk head travel in servicing the requests?

a. FCFS

b. SSTF

c. SCAN

d. C-SCAN

e. N-Step SCAN (Exercise 25)

Figure 5.11

Job Number	Arrival Time	Track Number for Seek
1	0	450
2	0	1320
3	0	200
4	.1	23
5	1.0	750
6	2.0	1980
7	5.0	1700
8	5.5	1800
9	6.0	780
10	10.0	730
11	11.0	150
12	12.0	500

28. Use the stream of seek requests from Figure 5.11; assume the head starts at track 0, the time is 0, and the head movement rate is 100 tracks per unit of time. Assume no read/write or rotational delays, and find the order in which each strategy that follows services the requests. For which strategy is the head movement the least?

a. FCFS

b. SSTF

c. SCAN

d. C-SCAN

e. N-Step SCAN (Exercise 25)

29. Do Exercise 28 for the stream of seek requests from Figure 5.12.

Figure 5.12

Job Number	Arrival Time	Track Number for Seek
1	0	50
2	0	100
3	0	10
4	0	60
5	0.1	0
6	0.2	110
7	0.8	100
8	1.0	90
9	1.1	200
10	1.2	110
11	1.5	150
12	2.0	60
13	2.1	180
14	2.5	90
15	3.0	40
16	5.0	170
17	5.2	110
18	6.0	150
19	6.2	200
20	6.8	70

30. Write a program to simulate disk head scheduling. Assume that the disk tracks are numbered from 0 through 814, with the head positioned at track 0 to start. Disk head movement occurs at the rate of 100 tracks/unit of time. Assume no read/write or rotational delays. Interarrival times for seek requests are to be calculated by

$$t = -\ln(1 - RND)$$

where RND is a uniformly distributed random number, $0 <= RND < 1$ (Poisson distribution with mean $= 1$). The cylinder number for each seek is calculated by using two random numbers:

$$c = 75(-2*\ln RND1)^{0.5}(\sin(6.28*RND2)) + 500$$

(normal distribution with mean $= 500$ and standard deviation $= 75$). Let time run from 0 to 200.

Be sure the output displays all queueing activity and head movement. Average and maximum queue lengths and average head travel per seek should also be shown. Other information such as average and maximum wait times should also be included.

Run the simulation for each of the six strategies from Exercise 27.

6 Memory Management

To execute an instruction, the instruction must be in main memory. This statement may seem to be an oversimplification, but it does serve to introduce the notion of memory management. Memory management is a required activity of the operating system due to the following:

- For a user program to execute, at least a part of it and a part of the operating system must co-exist (co-reside) in the computer's main memory. Since program instructions normally change the contents of some memory cell(s), how can the operating system's cells be protected from change by the user program?
- What is the system to do if an application program is too large to fit in that part of main memory not used by the operating system?
- If multiple co-resident applications are to be used, which program goes where in memory? How does the system find a spot for each one? How is each application protected from alteration by the others? What does the operating system do if there are too many programs to fit in main memory simultaneously?
- How can memory-resident code be shared by several programs?
- How can these problems be solved so that the user is not even aware that he or she has created a problem?
- How are these concerns affected if the system is a multiuser one?

Storage

Chapter 2 discussed the hierarchy of memory types. This chapter focuses on **main memory (main store, physical store, real store, core memory)**—the storage generally associated with user program execution. Main memory is **random access memory (RAM)** which, on many machines, loses all data when powered down. (Memory which does not retain its data after power loss is said to be **volatile**.) The CPU does memory reads and writes over the data bus connecting it to main store. For most modern systems, main memory quantities run from half a megabyte to several gigabytes.

Most CPUs have a limited number of **hardware registers** (generally fewer than two dozen) that are effectively very fast memory (see Chapter 2). Some machines also have a small quantity of fast **cache** memory. Cache memory is generally reserved for operating system use, is quite expensive, and is usually restricted to just a few kilobytes.

Figure 6.1

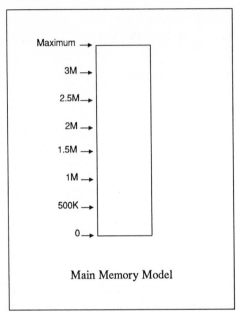

Main Memory Model

Main store is used for program execution, while cache is reserved for those items the operating system must reference very quickly or very often. Main store addresses are often described as the **physical address space** for the machine. Physical addresses start at zero and run consecutively through the maximum value. The projected image is seen in Figure 6.1.

Secondary memory or **backing store** is much less expensive, much slower, and generally (but not exclusively) installed with very large capacity through the use of magnetic media. Capacities on modern systems run from 360K (minimal microcomputer systems with one floppy disk drive) to multiple gigabytes. Even most microcomputer single-user systems will hold more than 20M bytes of secondary storage.

Backing store is not volatile and is used to hold files on a semipermanent basis. Backing store may also be used by the system as **swapping store,** a place to put programs and data that must be temporarily removed from main store during execution. Swapping is fundamentally (but not entirely) a process of copying images from main memory to swapping store, or vice versa.

The Fence

Figure 6.2 shows a typical, unsophisticated memory map: The operating system is loaded into and uses a contiguous set of memory addresses at "one end" of main memory. It is fairly customary for the lower addresses (that is, smaller address numbers) to be used for the operating system. The address that marks the boundary between the operating system and the rest of physical memory is often called a **fence.** This fence value is critical for protecting the operating system from any user routine that runs amok.

Before continuing with the memory allocation schemes, it is helpful to briefly examine how a program is prepared for loading into main memory prior to execution.

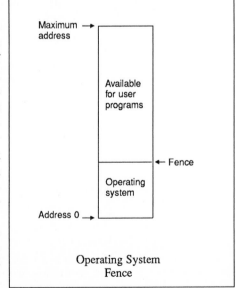

Operating System Fence

Figure 6.2

Addressing, Linking, and Loading

Application programs are written in a high-level language or assembly language to form a **source program.** The source program is translated (assembled or compiled usually) into a machine code **object program.** If the addresses in the object core represent actual physical addresses in main memory, **absolute addressing** has been used. The absolute addresses appearing in the code predetermine where the object program will be loaded for execution. Figure 6.3 illustrates a half-megabyte object module of contiguous code whose starting address is 1M. **Loading** is simply a matter of copying the object code image to the main memory addresses. The addresses in the object module are the same as the physical addresses when loaded.

Figure 6.3

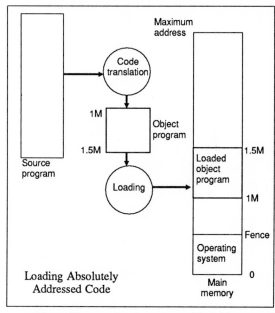

Loading Absolutely Addressed Code

Figure 6.4 illustrates the same object program but with a starting address of zero. When the starting address is zero and all other addresses are measured as offsets from zero, the object code addresses are said to be **relative** or **relocatable.** In Figure 6.4, the half-megabyte object module may be loaded anywhere the loader can find a vacant 0.5M bytes.

The addresses in the relocatable object module must be **translated** into physical addresses. In Figure 6.4 that translation is simply

physical address = 10M + relocatable address

This is called **base-plus-displacement** addressing with the base being the starting physical address and displacement being the relocatable address from the object module. The translation from relative to physical address must be done by the loader (static translation) or during execution by the hardware or operating system software (dynamic address translation). Note that the hardware is much faster at doing dynamic address translation.

Binding The act of assigning physical addresses to object code is called **binding.** In the case of absolute

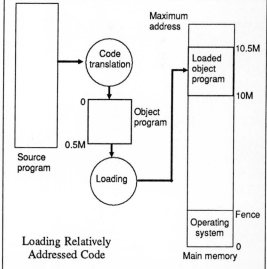

Loading Relatively Addressed Code

Figure 6.4

addressing, the binding takes place during writing, compilation, or assembly. This is called **early binding.** For relocatable code, binding can take place during loading or even later.

Linking   Applications are seldom written as a single large source program of contiguous code, however. It is more likely that several independently translated modules (for example, programs and functions from a program library) are combined to create the final program. This practice encourages the use of relocatable object modules.

Figure 6.5

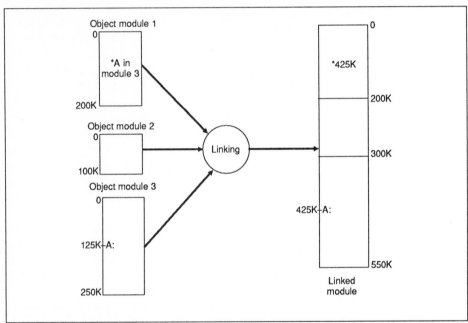

Figure 6.5 shows the process of **linking** several independent modules into a single object program. The diagram shows that putting the individual modules together is similar to loading them into memory, in that their starting addresses (all but the first module) change. This illustrates the value of using relocatable addresses. Note also that the linked module is relocatable code.

A more subtle problem faces the linker: If an instruction in one module refers to an instruction or data element (*A in Object module 1 from Figure 6.5) in another module (Object module 3 in our example), the compiler has no way of knowing what that address will be *after linking*. It is the linker that must find that address after the modules are put together. The linker then replaces the original address reference by the address in the linked module; this is called **address reference resolution.**

To this point, the discussions have been based on at least three assumptions:
- Once loaded, routines stay put until execution is complete.
- The code is loaded into a contiguous chunk of memory.
- When a routine is loaded, all its code is loaded.

As one might suspect, any given system may ignore all, some, or none of these conditions.

Dynamic loading implies that program code may be relocated one or more times during execution, requiring relocatable code, dynamic address translation, and a considerable amount of work every time the routine is moved. Routines may be moved for a variety of reasons, some of which will be discussed in the following sections. If much of this shuffling is to take place, one of the **noncontiguous** memory allocation schemes (to be discussed later) may become advantageous.

Swapping

One reason for relocating a program once execution has started may be due to the need for **swapping** of programs in and out of main memory. Should program execution be temporarily halted for some reason, the stalled program may be copied to a known location on backing store and another task copied from backing store to the vacated memory locations (in order to use the CPU during an otherwise idle time). At some later point, the original program can be reactivated after being reloaded from the swapping region. However, it might be reloaded in other than its original location.

Overlays and Chaining

Previously in this text the picture of an object program has been one "chunk" of code fit into contiguous memory locations. **Overlays** are one means of using a smaller physical address space than the source code's logical address space. When overlays are used, the program is subdivided into logical modules and subroutines. Only those subdivisions required for execution at any point in time are loaded (see Figure 6.6). Note that there is one **control module** that will be in memory at all times. Several other modules will alternate in and out of memory as required for execution. When execution requires that another subdivision be loaded from backing store, the operating system overwrites one or more of the nonessential subdivisions with the required one. If any outgoing subdivision has been altered during execution, it must be copied back to secondary storage before being overwritten.

Figure 6.6

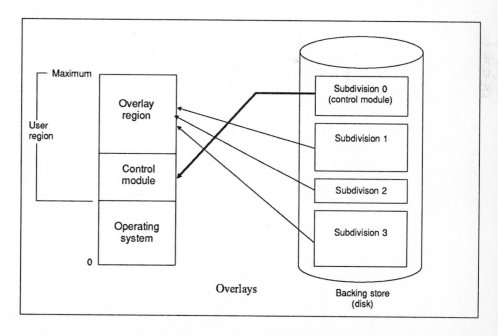

The management of overlays can be complicated and has mostly given way to the **virtual memory** allocation schemes shown later in this chapter. With overlays, the programmer is responsible for orchestrating memory management—which pieces are in main memory at any point in time, which pieces must not be in main memory at the same time, the sequence in which pieces are loaded, and the timing of each overlay action. Programmers would much rather leave these matters to the operating system.

Chaining accomplishes a similar end. The programmer divides the job into a sequence of independent subprograms. The first subprogram is loaded and executed; then the second subprogram replaces the first and executes *using the data provided by the first subprogram.* The data is usually stored in some well-understood place where subsequent loadings will not overwrite it. This cycle is repeated until the last subprogram is executed. The key to the cycle is the carrying forward of data from one subprogram to the next.

As seen earlier, overlaying requires the use of a single **control program** with additional segments being swapped as required. Chaining uses a sequence of independent segments (programs), each providing the data for the program that follows.

Contiguous Memory Allocation

Contiguous memory allocation schemes place entire programs in consecutive memory addresses. They are conceptually and historically important but their use today is limited to some microcomputer systems. The virtual memory techniques discussed later predominate in current operating systems.

Single Tasking

Single tasking systems (those designed to give service to one program at a time) are almost always found among less expensive microcomputers. Earlier discussions described how such systems do their memory allocation. Figure 6.7 shows a single program loaded into a contiguous portion of main memory safely isolated from the operat-

Figure 6.7

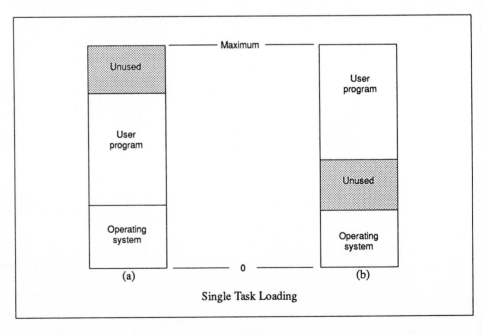

Single Task Loading

Figure 6.8

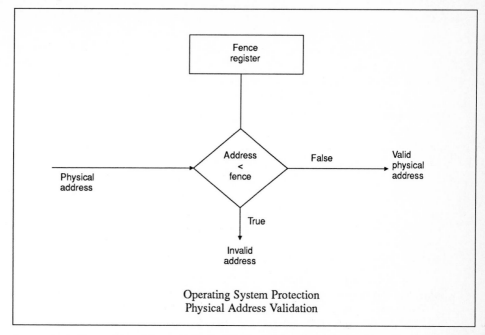

Operating System Protection
Physical Address Validation

ing system. Two reasonable ways to do this are: (1) to load the code at the first address available above the fence (as in Figure 6.7a) and (2) to load the program in the highest addresses available (as in Figure 6.7b). The second method is a less desirable design, for it is easier for programs to "grow" upward into unallocated memory. Addressing is simpler as well. Note that small programs waste memory while very large programs require overlays or chaining.

Operating system memory addresses must be protected from the application program. The application must never write data into operating system memory cells. Some systems not only protect against writing in any given chunk of memory but also against reading and executing code there.

The simplest protection compares each physical address reference against the fence value (Figure 6.8). It is preferred that the hardware make this comparison, since software checking drastically increases execution time. (Realistically, most inexpensive systems rely on the application programmer to not make any mistakes.)

There are alternative schemes for protecting the operating system space from another program. One involves the use of **hardware protection keys**, which are simply bit patterns assigned to blocks of contiguous memory. These keys can be set to one pattern for the operating system region and to a different pattern for the user space. The user program is assigned a **software key** that matches the hardware key assigned to the user region. Every memory reference is then checked by the hardware to see if the program's key matches the key for address referenced. The reference is allowed only if the keys match.

Loading can be either in an absolute or relocating fashion. If operating system revisions cause the fence to move, absolutely addressed application programs may have to be rewritten to accommodate the relocation. Relatively addressed code will require no alteration; it will simply be loaded into a new location by the loader. Physical

Figure 6.9

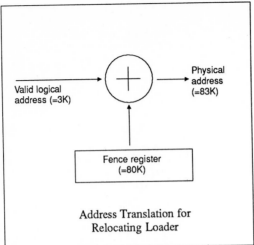

Address Translation for
Relocating Loader

addresses in this case are calculated easily as **fence address-plus-logical address** (Figure 6.9), much like the base-plus-displacement method discussed earlier.

Single task, contiguous memory allocation is uncomplicated: Simply give the single task full use of any memory not occupied by the operating system. Single tasking systems are inefficient in that the processor will likely sit idle most of the time. Only the greatly reduced cost of computer power now makes such systems cost effective (even though inefficient).

Multiprogramming

Multiprogramming, the act of loading more than one program into main memory at any time, is an attempt to use memory and CPU more efficiently. At least two general disciplines for contiguous memory allocation are known. The simplest has been called **MFT** (Multiprogramming with a Fixed number of Tasks) on some IBM systems, while the more complex and more flexible scheme was named **MVT** (Multiprogramming with a Variable number of Tasks).

Static Partitioning. For MFT, the scheme is simple: Partition the user memory space into a fixed number of contiguous **regions** and identify the partition addresses. (See Figure 6.10.) These partition addresses will become fences (or **bounds**) for any program loaded into that region. The lower address for each region will be the **lower bound** (or **base**) address. The base address for one region also serves as the **upper bound** for the region immediately below. The difference between the upper bound and lower bound is called the **limit** and indicates the size of the region.

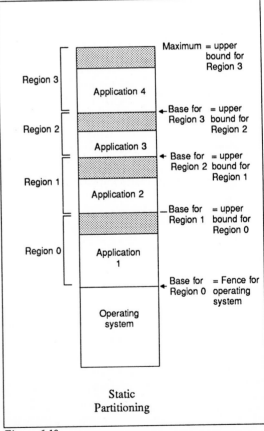

Static
Partitioning

Figure 6.10

Regions will usually be of varying sizes to efficiently handle programs of different lengths. By fitting programs into regions that just barely hold them, less main store will be wasted. Wasted space inside a partition is called **internal fragmentation.** The use of smaller regions decreases internal fragmentation, allowing more tasks in memory concurrently. Overlays and chaining allow large programs to utilize undersized regions if necessary. On many systems, the partitioning can be set to best match the job mix for the system.

The bounds for the regions hold the key to protection. Each address reference can be checked to see if the referenced cell lies within the partition; the physical address must fall between the lower and upper bound addresses. For relative addresses, only the upper bound needs checking. For example, suppose a partition has a lower bound of 11000, and an upper bound of 15000; a logical address of 3000 yields a physical address of 11000+3000=14000. Since 14000 is below 15000, it is a valid address for the specified region.

For relative addresses, correct address references can be verified by comparing against the **limit** value. In the example in the previous paragraph, the limit value is 4000 (= 15000−11000). Thus the logical address of 3000 is valid; the relative address must be smaller than the limit (3000<4000).

The hardware protection keys mentioned earlier can protect static partitions. Each key pattern is used for all memory cells in a given region, and the application program loaded there has a software key to match. Every memory reference is checked by the hardware to see if the program's key matches the hardware key. The reference is allowed only if the keys match (that is, only if the address lies in the assigned region for the program).

Jobs waiting for assignment to memory will be queued. There may be one queue for each region (Figure 6.11) or a single queue servicing all (Figure 6.12). If absolute addressing is used, the multiple queue system is preferred (as a program can only be

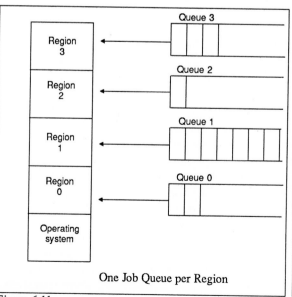

One Job Queue per Region

Figure 6.11

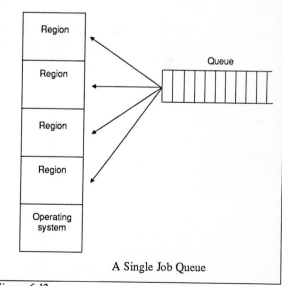

A Single Job Queue

Figure 6.12

loaded in one region because of its fixed addresses). With relative addressing, the program may be placed in any queue whose associated region is large enough to hold it. In this case, the operating system can make run-time placement choices and even out the workload among the various regions, increasing performance. However, the single queue mechanism does this more efficiently in most settings.

The single queue system requires a **placement strategy.** The most prevalent placement strategies are **first fit** and **best fit.** In each case, the list of currently unallocated (free or available) regions is maintained in a list. For a first fit strategy, this **free list** of available regions is searched until a sufficiently large region is found; the program is loaded into the region regardless of the resulting internal fragmentation. For the best fit strategy, the free list is searched for the *smallest* region that is large enough to hold the program. Generally, the lists of free regions are ordered by starting address (for first fit) or by size (best fit).

Figure 6.13

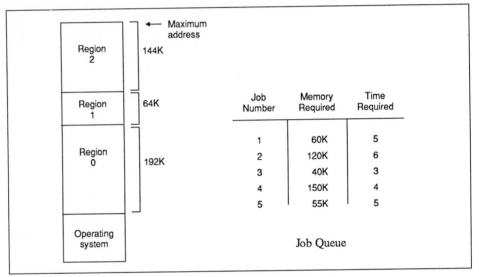

Job Queue

Figure 6.13 shows a single job queue (in job number order) with memory partitioned into three currently unallocated regions. If the first fit strategy is used (with free regions kept in order of increasing starting addresses), Job #1 is placed in Region 0, Job #2 in Region 2, and Job #3 in Region 1. Job #3 finishes first and vacates Region 1. However, Job #4 doesn't fit into Region 1 so it sits and waits for another region, blocking Job #5 that could use Region 1. As Job #1 finishes, Job #4 is loaded into Region 0, with Job #5 immediately loaded into Region 1.

Now reexamine Figure 6.13 with a best fit strategy (the free list containing the regions in order of increasing size) in mind. Job #1 is placed in Region 1, Job #2 in Region 2, and Job #3 in Region 0 (the only remaining region). As Job #3 completes, Job #4 is loaded into Region 0. Job #5 is loaded into Region 1 when Job #1 exits.

While static partitioning allows the CPU to split its time and attention between several memory resident programs (without expending time swapping programs in and out of memory), the number of memory resident programs is still limited. Swapping temporarily stalled programs out of memory in favor of one that can run effectively increases the number of programs that are "in process." However, the swapping overhead is high.

When swapping a program into memory, which program will be the **victim,** the process to be swapped out? When a swapped-out process is swapped in, will it be placed in the region from which it was swapped out or will it be swapped in to a different region? Swapping in to a different region requires a form of **dynamic loading** and creates extra work for the operating system.

Dynamic partitioning. MVT is a more complicated mechanism because memory is partitioned dynamically. There is no precondition on the *location* of any region to be established, nor is there any precondition on the *size* of a contiguous region. The number of regions that can be constructed may depend only on the amount of memory.

Relative addressing techniques are *required* for dynamic partitioning, since the memory to be assigned cannot be known in advance. In fact, each time the program is loaded, a different memory assignment is likely. Finding a region to hold an incoming program requires that the system maintain a list of available (free) regions. The strategies of first fit and best fit for placement are as valid for MVT as MFT. Other strategies such as **worst fit** (search for the largest free region that will work) can be used, although best fit and first fit are most widely used. Protection again uses the notion of bounds registers or base and limit registers.

Fragmentation exists in MVT but it is **external fragmentation.** There is no longer wasted memory *within* any region, since region sizes are allocated precisely to meet the needs of the job. Wasted space is unallocated space occurring in chunks too small to hold any waiting job (see Figure 6.14).

Figure 6.14

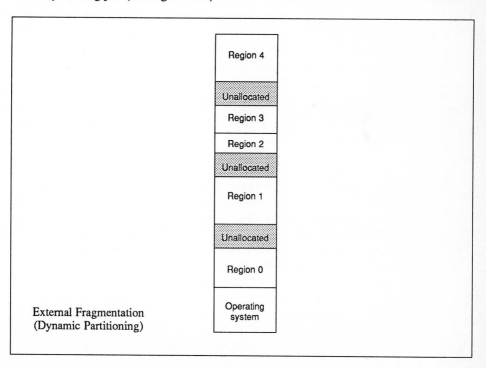

External Fragmentation
(Dynamic Partitioning)

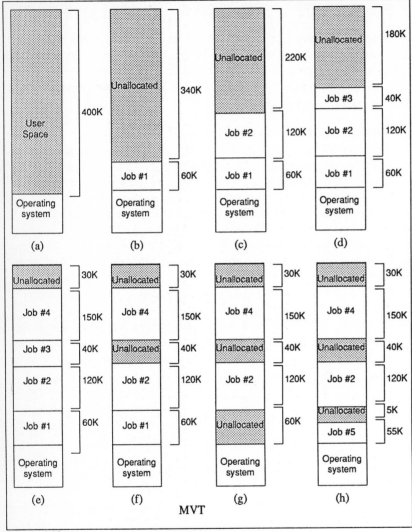

Reexamine Figure 6.13, but assume dynamic partitioning and no loaded user programs. Figure 6.15a shows such a memory map. Assume that a first fit placement is used with the free "hole" list maintained in order of starting addresses. In the beginning, there is just one unallocated chunk and Job #1 is loaded in its lower addresses just above the operating system (Figure 6.15b). Then Job #2 is loaded as in 6.15c, followed by Job #3 as shown in 6.15d. Job #4 fits in the remaining hole (6.15e) but Job #5 will not fit. When Job #3 finishes, there are two holes (6.15f), neither of which will hold Job #5. As Job #1 finishes, three free holes are on the list (6.15g), and one is large enough to hold Job #5. The loading of Job #5 creates a small hole (as seen in 6.15h).

In the example, Job #5 waited for 55K hole even when there were two holes (30K and 40K) whose combined size was large enough to hold the job. There are several ways to reclaim wasted space. If adjacent chunks are free, they may be **coalesced** into a single larger region. The larger region might then hold a waiting program.

If the unallocated chunks are not adjacent, the memory-resident programs can be *relocated* so that all unused memory appears in one large region (as in Figure 6.16). This act of **compaction** may create a region sufficiently large to hold another task. Compaction is not done indiscriminately. The work required to move the loaded programs is extensive and almost always comes when the system is already under severe pressure because of the heavy load. In point of fact, compaction occurs infrequently on those systems using it.

Swapping memory-resident tasks out to backing store to increase the level of multiprogramming can be useful in an MVT setting. However, since regions are not static as in MFT, a swapped out program is likely to be swapped in to a totally different

Figure 6.15

Figure 6.16

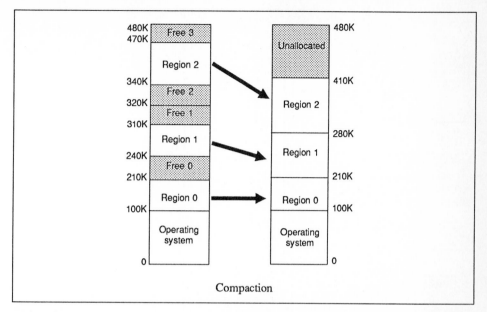

Compaction

region from the one it left. **Dynamic linking and loading** techniques are required, making the swap costly in terms of time. If the system must use a lot of swapping, one of the virtual memory schemes discussed in the following sections will prove superior.

Virtual Memory Techniques

Contiguous memory allocation, while relatively simple to implement, has a number of shortcomings, enough in fact that it is not widely used today. The **multiprogramming ratio** (the number of programs that can coexist in main store) is limited by the need to load entire programs into memory. Of course overlays, chaining, and swapping can be used to increase the level of multiprogramming but at a rather substantial cost to user and operating system alike. Furthermore, fragmentation represents a loss, either in terms of available memory at any given time or in terms of unproductive processor power used for coalescing or compaction.

Some Constraints

While it may not be clear now, base-plus-displacement address translation (as described earlier) is not suitable for the next step. A different address translation scheme using **tables** opens up new choices based on the idea that only a small portion of a program's code and data need be in memory at any time.

Overlays and chaining illustrate this fact. Their use is based on two notions:
- Programs can be subdivided into logically related pieces.
- At any time, continued execution requires only a small part of the program to be in main memory.

A New View

Picture the *logical* address space of a program as a chunk of contiguous memory. In fact, picture it as if it were the actual main memory address space with every part of the program linked together (Figure 6.17). In this view, even the operating system does not use any memory. Because this view is conceptual and not real, it is called a **virtual address space.** The virtual program image may exist only in the programmer's mind

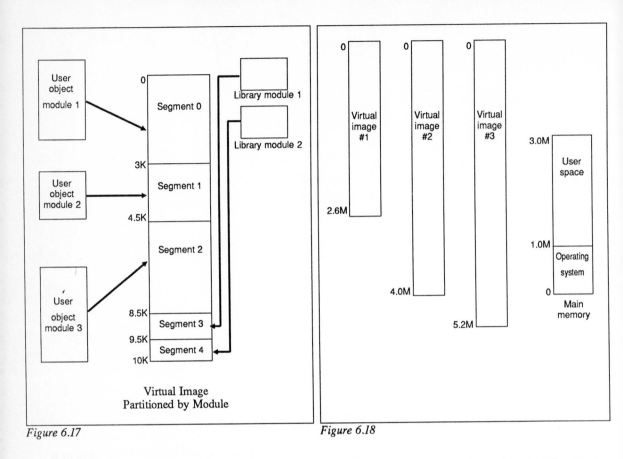

Figure 6.17   *Figure 6.18*

(his or her view of the program), or it may exist in the form of a **virtual memory** image in secondary store. In either case, the view allows the programmer to work not only as if he or she had all of main store for personal use but as much main store as required. The program is visualized as being loaded at starting address zero.

While this is great for the programmer, a multitasking operating system must find some way to squeeze several virtual images into one small main memory. In Figure 6.18, the problem is to load 11.8 megabytes of programs into 2 megabytes of user space. Since any virtual image may be larger than all of main memory, there may not be room for loading even one entire program, let alone several. The solution is to load only a small part of each image into main memory at any point in time.

In Figure 6.17, the virtual image is subdivided into contiguous blocks numbered from zero to four, each block holding one program submodule. The blocks, called **segments,** are of differing sizes. Figure 6.19 shows the same virtual image but with subdivisions of equal size. When the subdivisions are of equal size and have no logical relationship to the individual modules, the blocks are called **pages** rather than segments. In Figure 6.19, the pages are numbered from zero through nine, and the size of a page (determined by the system) is 1K. In both figures, each address in virtual memory can be described by a **block number** (segment or page number) and an offset into that block (as in Figure 6.20).

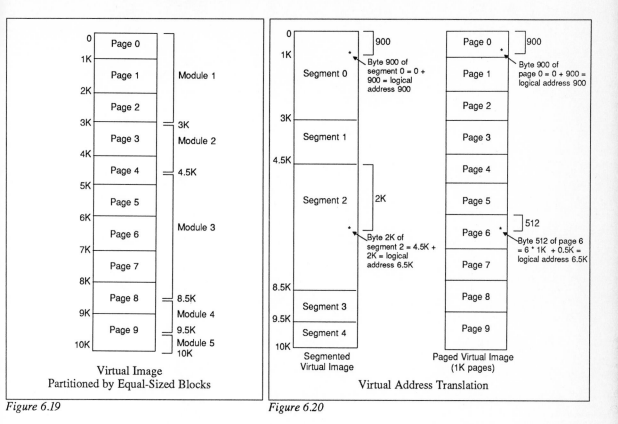

Figure 6.19

Figure 6.20

The concept behind virtual memory techniques is as follows: At any point in time, only a few blocks (those needed to continue execution) should be in memory. Not only does this reduce the amount of memory any program uses, it reduces waste due to fragmentation. Segments fit into smaller free holes in memory than programs, reducing external fragmentation. And pages are even smaller than most segments. Segments have no internal fragmentation; they are perfect fits. Where pages are used, every page except the last is used fully so that internal fragmentation is limited to a fraction of the last page for each program.

Virtual memory techniques have one major concern: how and when to move the proper segments or pages from virtual memory to main memory. Again, logical addresses from a virtual image can be translated into **pairs** of numbers (a segment or page number and an offset into that page or segment), as shown in Figure 6.20. The system maintains a table (Figure 6.21), showing all segments or pages for the virtual image, which segments or pages are currently in memory, where those in memory are located, and where the virtual image of each segment or page is located in secondary memory.

When a logical address is referenced, the system looks in the table to see whether the segment or page containing that virtual address is in main memory. If it is, the table tells where the *starting address* for the page or segment is located; the offset then gives the actual physical address. If the desired segment or page is not in memory, the system

Figure 6.21

Segment Number	Starting Virtual Address	In Main Memory	Starting Main Memory Address	Segment Size	Modified Since Loading
0	0	no	x	3K	x
1	3K	yes	2048K	1.5K	no
2	4.5K	yes	128K	4K	yes
3	8.5K	no	x	1K	x
4	9.5K	no	x	0.5K	x

Segment Table for Figure 6.20

Page Number	In Main Memory	Main Memory Frame Number	Modified Since Loading
0	yes	2132	no
1	no	x	x
2	no	x	x
3	no	x	x
4	no	x	x
5	yes	3197	no
6	yes	2062	yes
7	no	x	x
8	no	x	x
9	no	x	x

Page Table for Figure 6.20

locates it on disk, loads it into main store, and alters the table to show the change. Now the address reference can be completed as before.

The programmer doesn't worry about the actual size of the code, how the various parts will end up being pieced together, or how main memory will actually be apportioned to competing programs. He or she just thinks of the contiguous virtual memory image. It is the system's responsibility to keep track of which blocks are in memory, which need to be in memory, where all blocks (virtual or memory-resident) are located, and how to use the tables to do the address translation. Address translation still looks like base-plus-displacement: The base is the starting address for the page or segment, while the displacement is the offset into the segment or page.

Segmentation

Segmentation refers to memory management by subdividing virtual images into segments as described earlier. The key is that segments can be located anywhere in memory that space exists. Segments that are contiguous in the virtual image do not have to be contiguous in main memory. The addressing method allows the operating system to find the reference by knowing which segment holds it and where it is within that segment. Only a few segments need to be co-resident in memory. The placement of segments can be managed in an MVT-like manner, although a hybrid technique of segmentation and paging is more likely.

Paging **Paging** refers to memory management that divides the virtual image of a program into pages. The subdivision process is not based on logical or functional criteria related to the program as with segmentation. When the system has paging hardware, physical memory is statically partitioned into contiguous **page frames** of a fixed size (some power of two to make addressing easy), with page sizes of 512 bytes, or 1K, 2K or 4K bytes, being fairly common. The pages of virtual memory are the same size as the physical page frame. Memory allocation involves placing pages of virtual memory into page frames of main memory.

Only a few of the virtual pages will be in page frames concurrently, and page swaps will take place as address references require. Since pages are not large, each swap involves copying only small amounts between virtual and main memory. Address translation uses tables as described earlier.

Paged Segmentation In a hybrid combination of segmentation and paging (called **paged segmentation**), each segment of virtual memory is again subdivided into pages. (See Figure 6.22 and compare with Figure 6.19.) While internal fragmentation may increase (the last page of each segment being partially wasted), the paging means that only part of the segment need be in main memory when called. As before, tables are used for the dynamic address translation that must take place. Addresses are in triples: segment number, page number within the segment, and offset into that page (as in Figure 6.23).

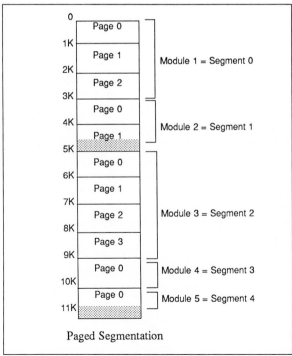

Paged Segmentation

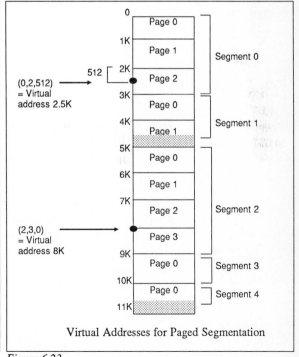

Virtual Addresses for Paged Segmentation

Figure 6.22 *Figure 6.23*

**More on
Segmentation**

Figure 6.24 shows a program divided logically or functionally into six segments. Each segment may represent a single procedure, a collection of closely related small procedures, a data storage area, a stack region, and so on. Note that addresses are two dimensional. Each location in virtual memory can be described by a pair of values (s,d), where s is the segment number holding the address and d is the displacement of that location from the start of segment s. Figure 6.24 shows that virtual address (2,0) is the starting address of Segment 2; (3,250) is the 250th byte (or word) of Segment 3, and (5,960) is the 960th byte (or word) of Segment 5.

Figure 6.24

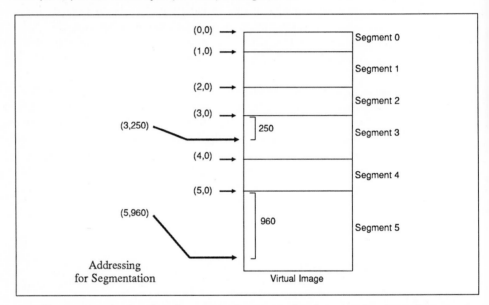

Segments exist in virtual memory but may also have copies in main memory. Keeping track of which segments are in memory and where the resident segments are located requires the operating system to maintain some tables of data. The system **Segment Table (ST)** is a global list telling where each program's individual **Segment Map (SM)** is located. The segment map has one entry for each virtual segment telling whether that segment is currently in main store, the starting memory location if it is resident, the segment size, its location in backing store, and whether the segment has been altered since loading. (Review Figure 6.21.) If a segment has been altered since loading, the memory-resident version differs from the backing store version. Any attempt to swap that segment out will require that its virtual version be overwritten with the memory-resident version.

**Address
Translation**

The two-dimensional virtual addresses can be translated to physical addresses by following pointers (as shown in Figure 6.25). The system table locates User n's segment map: The segment number s is then used as an offset into that map where the starting address for the physical copy of the segment is found. The offset d from the segment's starting address can be used to find the desired data element.

For example, the physical address holding data from User 4's virtual address (8,1250) can be found as follows. Since n = 4, look in the fifth slot (offset or jump over

Figure 6.25

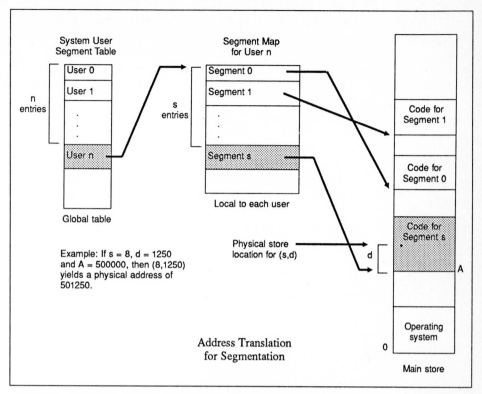

System User
Segment Table

User 0

User 1

.

.

.

User n

n
entries

Global table

Segment Map
for User n

Segment 0

Segment 1

.

.

.

Segment s

s
entries

Local to each user

Example: If s = 8, d = 1250
and A = 500000, then (8,1250)
yields a physical address of
501250.

Physical store
location for (s,d)

Code for
Segment 1

Code for
Segment 0

Code for
Segment s
.

Operating
system

d

A

0

Main store

Address Translation
for Segmentation

4 slots) in the system table to find the starting address for User 4's SM. For segment 8, jump over the first 8 SM slots to find the information about segment 8. The starting address for segment 8's memory-resident image is one data value found there: Suppose it is 500000. The desired address is then 500000 + 1250 = 501250.

Hardware does most of the translation for efficient systems. Depending solely on software translation exacts a time penalty of several CPU cycles for every address reference. Keeping a portion of the segment map in cache memory speeds up translation, since cache memory speeds may be ten times that of ordinary main memory. Note that address translation is a good application for **associative memory** where all cells are searched simultaneously for the desired value. Some hardware allows normal software translation activities to continue concurrently with cache lookup. The slower translation activities are aborted if a **hit** (successful cache lookup) occurs.

Referencing a segment not currently in memory causes a **segment fault**, and the required segment must be loaded. An MVT-like scheme can be used for selecting a contiguous region for the segment. If no available region is large enough, a victim segment must be swapped out before the desired segment is loaded. The victim being swapped out can be another segment of the same program or a segment from a different application program. Victim selection strategies are similar to those discussed later in regard to paging. Segment fault activity is **transparent** to the user. The operating system tables hold all data needed to manage the task.

Segment sharing among application programs is possible. Rather than loading a second and third copy of a segment, the segment maps for the second and third program simply point to the originally loaded segment. The code for a shared segment must be **pure** or **reentrant**, that is, the code and data within the segment must not be altered by use (**ROM—read only memory**—is an extreme example of reentrant code). This insures that the code is always the same every time it is used by a program. Where segment sharing is permitted, the operating system tables must identify the condition.

Fragmentation is lessened with segmentation because the segments are smaller contiguous chunks than are programs. Swapping is faster since smaller chunks of memory are being copied to and from backing store. Protection is built into the address translation scheme (only valid (s,d) pairs may be located). Overlays and chaining are not required since the system only loads as many of the segments as needed at any time. In effect, overlaying becomes an automatic function of the memory management system. When unneeded program parts are not kept in main memory, more programs can have a resident part concurrently.

More on Paging

Paging is different from segmentation, although the address translation process has some similarities. Virtual memory images are subdivided into pages and mainstore into (page) frames of the same size. Usually, several pages (a small part) of an active program occupy page frames. Even though pages may be contiguous in the virtual address space, the frames into which they are loaded will likely not be contiguous since the system likely chooses the first available frame. Keeping track of pages and page frames is very similar to managing segments.

The number of frames that should be allocated to a program so that it executes without too many page faults varies from one program to another. The number of frames assigned to a program may even vary during execution. Each program has a **working set,** the set of pages the program should currently have in memory to function efficiently. Not all systems use the working set, however.

A typical system maintains a global **Page Table (PT)** containing a pointer to *each user's* own **Page Map (PM)**. Each page map entry might indicate whether the page is memory resident, disclose the assigned frame number (if any), tell whether the page is **dirty** (has been altered from the backing store copy), and point to where the image of the page is located in the backing store.

Address translation for paging is a matter of following the pointers (See Figure 6.26). The value p from the virtual address pair (p,d) is used as an offset into the user's page map. It is desirable for paging hardware to take care of the translation. Without hardware assistance, the translation will be much slower, even if cache memory is available to the system. The value d is the offset from the start of the frame holding page p.

In Figure 6.26, for example, suppose the page and frame size is 1K. The users' virtual address 1536 = 1.5K lies 512 bytes into page 1 with address (1,512). Page 1 is stored in frame 1007, whose starting address is 1007K = 1.007M. The original virtual address 1536 is stored, then, in physical memory at 1.007M + 0.5K = 1.0075M.

Referencing a page not in memory yields a **page fault** and requires loading the appropriate page into some frame. Loading pages only after a page fault is called **demand paging.** The goal of the operating system is to strike a balance: Keep enough

Figure 6.26

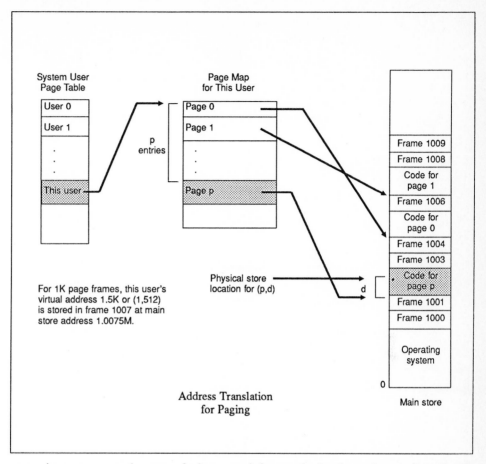

System User
Page Table

| User 0 |
| User 1 |
| . |
| This user |

p
entries

Page Map
for This User

| Page 0 |
| Page 1 |
| . |
| Page p |

| |
| Frame 1009 |
| Frame 1008 |
| Code for page 1 |
| Frame 1006 |
| Code for page 0 |
| Frame 1004 |
| Frame 1003 |
| Code for page p |
| Frame 1001 |
| Frame 1000 |
| Operating system |

For 1K page frames, this user's
virtual address 1.5K or (1,512)
is stored in frame 1007 at main
store address 1.0075M.

Physical store
location for (p,d)   d

0

Address Translation
for Paging

Main store

pages in memory so that page faults occur infrequently, but keep the number of resident pages low to increase the level of multiprogramming.

While it is desirable to keep the number of memory-resident pages low for each program, there is also a desire to keep the number of page faults low. Each change of pages takes valuable CPU time. The overhead grows even more burdensome when all frames are occupied and a victim page must be selected and swapped out. The victim can be a resident page from the same program (**local replacement**) or from a different program (**global replacement**). Users in a time-sharing system can actually see a severely slowed response time when excessive page faults occur.

Page replacement. A variety of **page replacement** (victim selection) policies are available. The simplest strategy is **First In, First-Out (FIFO)**, in which the number of frames allocated to a program is fixed. The selected victim is the page that has been resident for the longest time.

Figure 6.27 shows a string of page references for some program allowed to use only three frames. The example starts cold (no pages in memory). Thus, the first three different page references produce faults (each reference with an asterisk represents a page fault). The list of pages in memory is kept in FIFO order to make the tracking

Figure 6.27

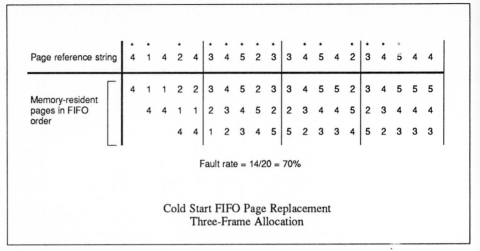

Fault rate = 14/20 = 70%

Cold Start FIFO Page Replacement
Three-Frame Allocation

simpler and the numbers for the actual frames used are not shown. After the initial three faults, eleven others occur, for a total of 14 faults in 20 references—a 70-percent fault rate.

In the **Least Recently Used (LRU)** policy, the page which has gone the longest without having one of its addresses referenced is the victim. LRU requires that the operating system somehow timestamp pages as they are referenced. Timestamping adds overhead, making LRU more costly than FIFO.

Figure 6.28

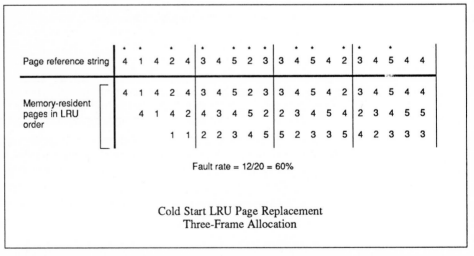

Fault rate = 12/20 = 60%

Cold Start LRU Page Replacement
Three-Frame Allocation

Figure 6.28 shows the same page reference string used in Figure 6.27 and the same limitation of three frames. The activity shown, however, illustrates the LRU strategy for page replacement. The fault rate is 12 faults in 20 references (or 60 percent).

The **Least Frequently Used (LFU)** policy selects as its victim the page with the lowest *number* of references. Counting the address references for each page adds to the operating system or hardware overhead. Note that LFU is more complicated than FIFO.

Figure 6.29

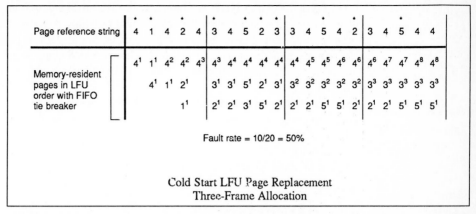

Fault rate = 10/20 = 50%

Cold Start LFU Page Replacement
Three-Frame Allocation

Figure 6.29 continues the previous examples showing LFU activity. Superscripts indicate the number of references since the last loading. FIFO is used to break ties. The page fault rate is 10/20 = 50 percent.

The **Not Used Recently (NUR)** strategy is a less expensive alternative to LRU. Each resident page has a bit that can be set when the page is referenced. The operating system periodically clears reference bits. Pages with cleared reference bits are most liable to be chosen as a not-used-recently victim. Along with a reference bit, many systems maintain a **dirty bit** that indicates whether the frame has been modified and differs from the virtual page that was loaded. Frames with dirty bit clear (not modified—the frame exactly matches the virtual memory page it represents) and reference bit clear are prime victim candidates, since they haven't been used recently and there is no need to copy an unmodified frame back to virtual memory.

Figure 6.30

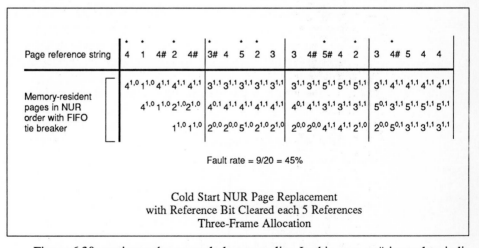

Fault rate = 9/20 = 45%

Cold Start NUR Page Replacement
with Reference Bit Cleared each 5 References
Three-Frame Allocation

Figure 6.30 continues the example begun earlier. In this case, a # is used to indicate that the page reference modifies the frame. Notice that having the dirty bit set reduces the likelihood that a frame will be swapped out. The superscript pairs show reference bits and dirty bits (1,0 means recently referenced but not dirty). All reference bits are cleared every five page references.

LRU, LFU and NUR are attempts to take advantage of the **principle of locality** that declares the next address references will probably be located in one of the most recently referenced pages. Address references do not in general jump across vast reaches of the logical address space. Researchers have created many other strategies intended to reduce page faulting by taking advantage of the principle of locality.

Working Sets.   The **working set** model offers another paging technique that tries to take advantage of locality. Unlike the previous strategies, the working set model allows the number of frames allocated to a program to vary during execution. The mechanism maintains a *window* of the most recently used page references (Figure 6.31). The window is of fixed length and highlights the last n (3 in Figure 6.31) page references made

Figure 6.31

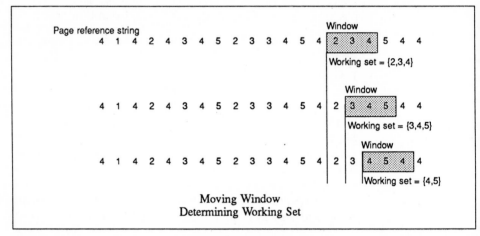

Moving Window
Determining Working Set

by the program. The pages referenced *inside the window* are those kept in main memory and make up the current working set for the program. As the window *moves* (the next reference is added and the oldest reference dropped), the number of *different* pages inside the window changes, along with the number of allocated frames of main memory.

The length of the window (the value of n) can be found by experimentation. As the length of the window increases, the working set tends to be larger and the number of page faults lower. At some point, however, a law of diminishing returns takes over, and increasing the window size makes little improvement in page fault rates. That point

Figure 6.32

Page reference string	4	1	4	2	4	3	4	5	2	3	3	4	5	4	2	3	4	5	4	4
Working Set Window size = 4	4	1	1	1	1	2	2	3	2	2	2	2	3	3	2	2	2	2	3	4
		4	4	2	2	3	3	4	3	3	3	3	4	4	4	3	3	3	4	5
				4	4	4	4	5	4	4	5	4	5	5	5	4	4	4	5	
									5	5						5		5		

Working Set Model

of diminishing returns gives the optimum window size. Figure 6.32 shows the working sets for a page reference string with a window size of four.

Note: These examples are not intended to indicate the relative value of any page replacement technique; simple treat them as exercises to show how each policy might work.

Prepaging, in contrast to demand paging, attempts to bring a page into memory *before* it is referenced. When the reference occurs, there will then be no fault since the page was loaded earlier. This allows the processor to do the page swapping at a time of its convenience (or by DMA activity), rather than under the pressure of a fault.

Like segmentation, paging activity is more complicated than contiguous memory allocation. Protection is the result of the address translation method (only valid (p,d) pairs may be located from the tables). Fragmentation is internal only and is very low. (A page of any virtual image can go into any of the page frames; there is no wasted frame. For each program, the average wasted space is half the last page.) Page swap-

Figure 6.33

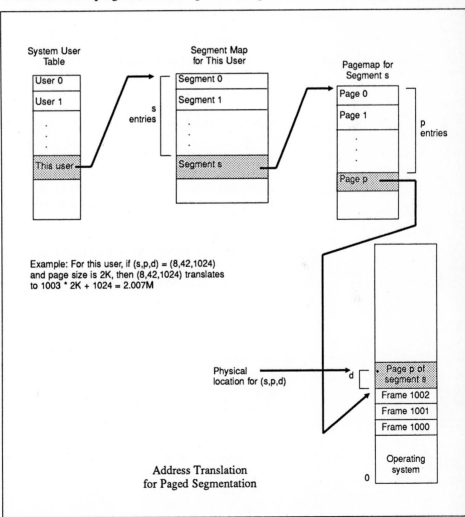

Example: For this user, if (s,p,d) = (8,42,1024) and page size is 2K, then (8,42,1024) translates to 1003 * 2K + 1024 = 2.007M

Address Translation
for Paged Segmentation

ping is faster than swapping entire programs, with overlays and chaining unnecessary. Paging, like segmentation, makes the sharing of code relatively simple because of the addressing techniques.

More on Paged Segmentation

As mentioned earlier, paging and segmentation can be used together. Each segment is broken into pages causing an average half-page per segment internal fragmentation (Figure 6.22). The operating system manages the segment- and page-related tables associated with each individual technique (Figure 6.33). Virtual addresses are now three-dimensional, consisting of triples of the form (s,p,d). S is the segment number and the offset into the user's segment map, p the page number and offset into the page map for segment s, and d is the displacement into the frame holding page p of segment s. The address translation process is shown in Figure 6.33. For efficiency, hardware should provide most of the address translation process. In spite of its complexity, paged segmention is the most popular form of memory management for noncontiguous allocation schemes.

Exercises

Note: All addresses below are given as decimal values.

1. A salesman states that, while his single-user system is not a multitasking system, there are many utility programs that can be loaded in a co-resident fashion. Simple keystrokes, he says, bring any utility to life instantly. He wants you to believe that is as good as multitasking. What are the disadvantages of such a system in relation to multitasking?

2. What value does a single-user multitasking system have over a single-user system without multitasking? What disadvantages?

3. A sales representative says that Model X is a multitasking system. What questions (relative to memory management) need to be asked when contemplating a corporate purchase? Why?

4. A sales representative says that Model Y can support multiple users (terminals). What questions (relative to memory management) need to be asked when contemplating a corporate purchase? Why?

5. Why should a user care about cache memory and "hit ratios" for address translation?

6. What is meant by virtual memory management and how can it make a user's life easier? At what price?

7. If you are buying a paged virtual-memory system, what should you ask about hardware frames and paging hardware?

8. If system A uses static partitioning, what information would help decide whether/how to repartition main store? Why would you care about the ability to dynamically alter the partitioning?

9. For a contiguous memory allocation scheme, under what conditions might static partitioning work better than dynamic partitioning? And vice versa?

10. How is memory management for segmentation similar to memory management for dynamic partitioning? How is it different?

11. Which would appear to be simpler to implement for virtual memory management: paging or segmentation? Why?

12. What is the advantage of increased main memory in each of the following cases?
    a. single-user/single tasking
    b. single-user/multitasking
    c. multi-user/partitioning
    d. multi-user/paging
13. A user program is too large to fit in any possible memory allocation. Describe the user's choices in each of the following cases.
    a. contiguous memory allocation
    b. paging/virtual memory
14. Which memory management schemes require the maintenance of a "free list"? Explain.
15. When a segment or page is removed from main store in a virtual memory system, what determines whether it must be rewritten to backing store?
16. What is the advantage of having the operating system in a contiguous chunk of memory starting at address zero?
17. a. Describe internal fragmentation with each memory management scheme.
    b. Do part (a) above for external fragmentation.
18. A relocating loader is to load program B in a contiguous allocation scheme. The relocation register holds value 10752. Convert the following stream of logical addresses to physical addresses.
    15,0,915,614,2162,1948
19. For a partitioning allocation scheme, the base register value is 10752, and the limit register value is 2048. Using the logical address stream from Exercise 18, convert each to a physical address.

Figure 6.34

Job Number	Length in K's	Arrival Time	In Memory Time for Execution
1	30	0	6.5
2	5	1	2
3	60	2	7
4	20	3	3
5	10	4	3.5
6	20	5	3
7	40	6	4
8	5	7	1.5
9	10	8	2.5
10	40	9	8
11	5	10	1
12	5	11	1.5
13	15	12	2
14	25	13	3
15	30	14	3

20. System C has 131072 (128K) of real memory and implements contiguous allocation with dynamic partitioning. The operating system occupies addresses zero through 10239, the fence being at 10240 (10K). The free chunks are maintained in a time-ordered list (top of list = first in). When a program is assigned to a region, the lower addresses of the chosen free chunk are used, and the left-over fragment is placed at the bottom of the free list. Assuming a cold start from time zero, trace

through the allocation process for the table of Figure 6.34 for each of the placement strategies. Assume that no program is swapped out during execution. Determine when each job is permitted into memory, where it is placed, and when it completes its run. Assume also that jobs are placed into memory in a first come, first served (FCFS) manner.

a. First fit

b. Best fit

c. Worst fit (Why would anyone think this scheme is good?)

d. Next fit (The list of free chunks is circular. The search always starts from the free region following the last chosen chunk—"circular first fit.")

21. Redo Exercise 20 where FCFS is replaced by "the earliest arrival that will fit in an existing free chunk."

22. System D uses 512 byte pages and frames for its virtual memory scheme.

   a. Program Q's logical address space is 20 pages long. Convert each one-dimensional logical address in the following stream to the (p,d) format.
      12,52,2322,528,5280,1550,943,862,10002,9999,
      4693,5000,7500,400,9850,1741,899,2400,1329,1540

   b. Assuming that the program from a above is allocated five frames during execution and that demand paging with local replacement is used, decide which page references from the stream cause page faults under each replacement strategy below.

      i. FIFO

      ii. LRU

      iii. LFU

   c. Redo b where only 3 frames are allocated to program Q.

23. Using the page stream generated in Exercise 22 and a window size of 5, show the working set at each reference. With a cold start, how many page faults occurred?

24. The page table for system TX and the page map for program E are shown in Figure 6.35. Convert the following stream of E's virtual addresses to physical addresses.
      (4,200),(1,25),(10,144),(3,293),(19,2),(8,128)

25. Write a program to (1) generate a random sequence of 200 page references from a 20-page virtual address space; (2) process the stream using each of FIFO, NUR, and LRU (assuming that five frames are allocated on a demand-paging, local-replacement basis, with a cold start); and (3) calculate the **page fault rate** (percentage of the 200 references that result in a fault).

26. Exercise 25 quietly assumes that the page references are distributed in the same manner as your random number generator (probably **uniform distribution** with each of the 200 pages equally likely to be the next referenced page). Redo Exercise 25 under the assumption that 75 percent of the time, the next page reference will come from a page already occupying a frame (that is, assume some locality). Compare the results.

27. Redo Exercise 26 for a working set model using a window of length 5.

Figure 6.35

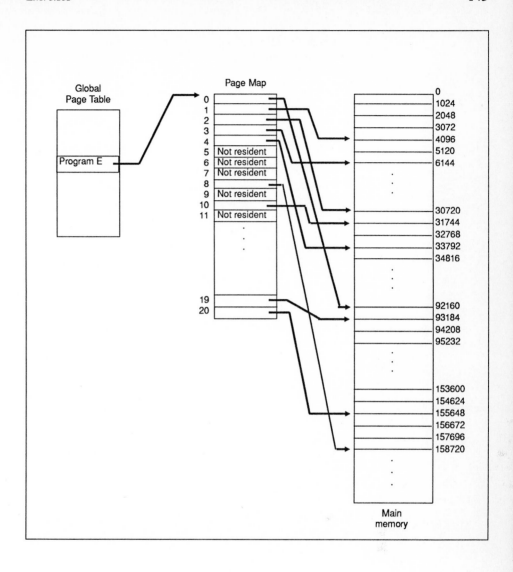

7 Process and Processor Management

Processor power has typically been the least plentiful resource for a computer system and thus needs careful management. Management of the CPU is a form of time management—time during which actual computation or management overhead takes place. Scheduling generally involves a very small part of the operating system's code.

For single-user, single-tasking microcomputers, managing the CPU is relatively easy; the processor is assigned to the only program running. For multitasking systems, however, sharing the processor among competing programs (or competing users) becomes a major activity. For multiuser systems, one common goal is to make each user feel that a complete machine is at his or her disposal.

A processor management scheme **schedules** processor time among the various users and programs. Think of the CPU as a **server** with the various programs queued up and awaiting service (see Figure 7.1). Maintenance of this queue is a major CPU scheduling activity.

Figure 7.1

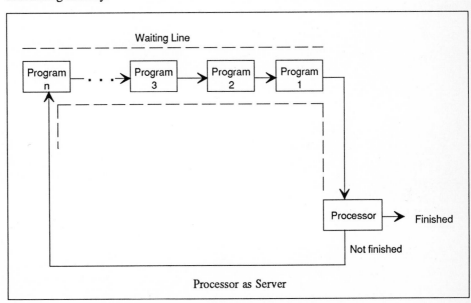

Processor as Server

The processor serves an executing program for some period of time and then turns its attention to the program next in line. Switching service from one program to another requires a significant amount of activity, particularly if the interrupted program has not completed its execution. There are many reasons for turning processor service away from one program and toward another. A currently executing program (the one receiving CPU attention) may voluntarily relinquish control of the processor (for example, for an I/O wait), or the operating system may **preempt** the program by removing CPU control from it and reassigning control to some other activity.

Processes

A program is basically a set of instructions (an **executable file**) for carrying out some computing activity. A **process** is an instance of an active program. Note that a process is more than a program: It is a copy of the program that has been assigned computer resources.

Some operating systems create one process per user, and that process carries out all the steps requested by the user. This is characteristic of batch systems and early interactive environments. In **process-rich** systems such as UNIX, each user can create as many processes as desired (within reasonable bounds). Each job **step** may create its own process to carry out the work. A user may concurrently invoke individual processes to copy an object code file, run a batch program to update the account payables file, send a message to another user, and update a text file from the keyboard. In such systems, programs tend to be composed of smaller modules, each of which invokes its own process.

Process States

Each process is created and eventually dies; during its lifetime, it exists in various **states**. Processes in multitasking systems change states frequently, passing through most states at one time or another. Figure 7.2 shows a "typical" state diagram.

Figure 7.2

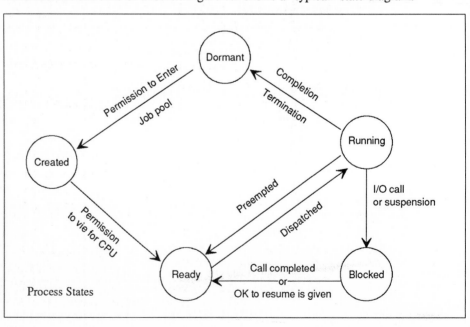

Process States

The **dormant state** is a state of nonexistence as far as processor scheduling is concerned. Programs normally reside in files on disk during the dormant state. As a job enters the system, it becomes **active** (is created). Processes in the **created state** have been recognized by the operating system but for some reason not given permission to compete for system resources.

Eventually, the process is placed in the **ready state,** enqueued awaiting its turn to control the CPU. At this point, a process is competing for the processor and other resources. Other processes in the ready queue may have already passed through the running state.

In the **running state,** the process has control of the CPU and is moving toward completion; those in the **blocked state,** while they were running at some point, are not currently vying for processor control. The CPU may have been voluntarily relinquished to wait for the completion of an I/O activity, or the operating system may have chosen to suspend the process. In any event, an interrupt occurred and some event must be completed before a return to the ready state is allowed. The blocked state is characteristic of multitasking systems in general and multiuser systems in particular.

In each case (created state, ready state, and blocked state) the state is often decomposed into two separate states for commercial multiuser systems (see Figure 7.3). If a swapping mechanism is used, processes in the created state may be assigned main memory or may reside entirely on disk. Any time a process is not running, the operating system may move it out to a swap space on disk. This is quite likely to happen with blocked processes but may even happen to ready processes.

Figure 7.3

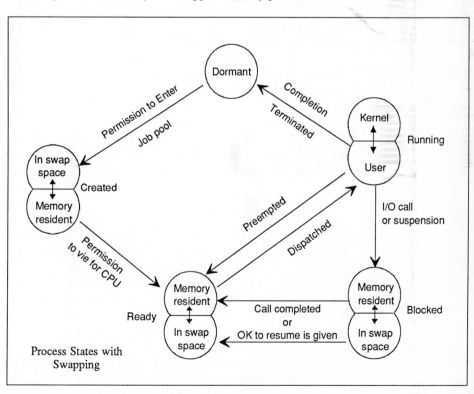

Process States with
Swapping

Many systems also divide the running state into two separate states. A running process normally executes in the **user mode.** A process enters the **kernel mode** by issuing a system service call to request some operating system service. A **system service call** is essentially an interrupt requesting that the operating system perform some activity on behalf of the user process.

The magnitude of the scheduling problem should now begin to appear to the reader. Scheduling algorithms can get sufficiently complicated that management overhead dominates the processor's time. Complicated queue maintenance, priority calculations, process switching, and swapping can become expensive activities, swallowing machine cycles at an alarming rate. It is interesting to note, however, that on uniprocessor computers, the code for process scheduling represents only a very small part of the operating system's code.

Goals and Measures

A variety of simple measures is used to indicate system efficiency. **Utilization** is the percent of system time during which the CPU is busy (that is, is not idle). Being busy, however, is not necessarily being productive (for example, the CPU may be performing some overhead activity). **Throughput** is the number of completed jobs per unit of time, a measure of how much work is being turned out. **Turnaround time** is the time differential between submission and completion for batch jobs, while **response time** is a similar measure for interactive tasks (that is, how long job steps take). **Reaction time** measures the delay between the issuing of a request and the first action taken; reaction time is of importance to real time control systems and to interrupt handling where any delay in taking action may be destructive.

Elapsed time is the total time a process spends on the system. It is the sum of **service time** (the amount of CPU time allocated to complete the job) and **wait time** (time in states other than the running state). Of course, most people consider wait time to be wasted time. Ratios of wait time to elapsed time, CPU time to elapsed time, and wait time to CPU time are also used as measures of efficiency. More complicated indicators of efficiency can be found.

Consistency and **predictability** are important factors in evaluating computer systems. A wide variation in the throughput of a system from week to week may signal a wide swing in system workloads or the need for system tuning. A response time that varies widely will distract users as they may interfere with the user's view of the system as a personal system. Widely varying wait times may signal uneven loading of the system or occasional thrashing, indicating excessive overhead. Statistical **variances** are, therefore, valuable measures of system efficiency.

Questions of efficiency fall into two categories: the efficiency of the machine (including its peripherals) and the productivity of the users. Machine efficiency is measured in terms of the actual work completed or the work done in relation to how much the machine is capable of doing. Human productivity factors involve measures of time (for example, the length and variability of response times). Machine efficiency may be measured in terms of how evenly the various I/O devices are used: Are some underutilized, while others cause scheduling bottlenecks? Another issue is **availability:** Is access to the computer's power available when needed?

Why are efficiency concerns an issue related to scheduling? A major purpose of scheduling is to make the CPU more productive: Eliminate idle time and give the processor something to do virtually all the time. The goals are to gain increased through-put and more satisfied users. The two can be at odds with one another, as you will see in Chapter 11. The system administrator must have some means of measuring system behavior and customer satisfaction in order to know what, if any, tuning needs to be done.

Levels of Scheduling

The scheduling of jobs is not a single-step activity. Figure 7.3 illustrated the various states of process existence. Each **movement between states** (state change) represented a scheduling action. Those events are generally divided into the following three levels.

High level (or **long term**) scheduling involves job initiation and termination. **Low level** (**short term**) scheduling manages all transitions between the running and ready states. Transitions out of the running state are due to either process completion or an interrupt. Assigning the CPU to a ready process is often called **dispatching. Intermediate level (medium term)** scheduling describes movement into and out of the blocked state, together with the swapping of ready and blocked processes between main and secondary memory. Figure 7.4 summarizes the relationships between the levels.

Figure 7.4

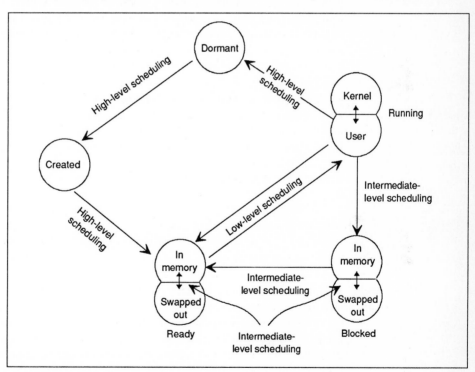

Types of Dispatching

All scheduling strategies involve **priority scheduling,** even if the priority is first come, first served (FCFS). Priority schemes other than FCFS run the risk of indefinitely postponing service to low priority processes. Nevertheless, priority scheduling other than FCFS is predominant.

In priority scheduling, each process is assigned a **priority value** that may be static or (more likely) dynamic. Static priority values may be assigned by the time of arrival onto the system or may be externally determined by the user or system administrator. Dynamic priorities change as execution progresses, in order to meet **fairness and efficiency goals** governing the system management policies.

Various strategies for managing priority queues of ready processes are available, and the decision to choose a particular strategy is based on the kind of multitasking system involved. Scheduling may be **nonpreemptive:** Once a process has control of the CPU, it keeps control until completion, an I/O call, an error condition, or other interrupt. **Preemptive** strategies also exist: If process R has the CPU and process H of higher priority arrives, R is involuntarily removed to the ready state in favor of H. Preemptive strategies are most common among commercial systems and are implemented through interrupts. It is not far fetched to say that multitasking scheduling activities are interrupt-driven.

Timesharing systems use the hardware clock to generate interrupts for preempting running processes. The purpose is to allow another ready process to enter the running state. This exchange (running process to ready state and ready process to running state) is called a **process switch.** The length of time a process has control of the CPU between clock interrupts is called a **quantum** or **time slice.** Time slice length (**quantum size**) is variable: The length used can be determined by the system manager in order to give the best performance. Time slices may be of uniform length for all processes or may differ depending on process characteristics.

The quantum size has a direct bearing on system performance. If the quantum is small in comparison to process switching time, the overhead for process switching is too high. For example, a 15 msec quantum with a 6 msec switching time uses almost 29% of the CPU time for this one overhead activity alone. A 300 msec quantum results in only a 2% overhead. However, if 20 users rotate ownership of the CPU, each using a full 300 msec quantum each pass, users wait over six seconds between successive services. As the quantum size increases beyond some optimal value, response time becomes unacceptable for interactive users. For an extremely long time slice, service more nearly resembles nonpreemptive scheduling.

Timesharing systems almost always preempt a process that requests an I/O action, since the process cannot use the CPU until the action is complete. In fact, processes are normally put in a blocked state while the I/O activity takes place. Otherwise, the CPU would sit idle unnecessarily.

FCFS and
Round Robin

The simplest scheduling strategy uses a **first come, first served (FCFS)** approach. It uses the simplest queueing mechanism, the FIFO (first in, first out) queue, which requires no computation of priority values. Processes arrive at the back of the ready queue and are dispatched to the running state from the front. Both preemptive and nonpreemptive scheduling policies use FCFS as all or part of their mechanisms. FCFS, by itself, is a **nonpreemptive** scheduling strategy.

FCFS is simple to implement but there are problems: Short processes are penalized most heavily by the unpredictability of wait times. The **penalty ratio** for a process is defined to be

(elapsed time)/(service time)

where elapsed time is the total time spent from creation to termination and service time is the amount of CPU time given to the process. Elapsed times for a given job may vary widely depending on the job mix. Penalty ratios can become large in two different ways—big elapsed times and very short service times. Short processes waiting in the ready queue behind long jobs experience high penalty ratios since both factors work against them: The wait time is large *and* the required service time is short.

For **preemptive systems** (timesharing systems in particular), FCFS has a cousin known as the **round robin (RR)** strategy. When an unfinished process is preempted from the running state by a timer interrupt, it enters the back of the FIFO-managed ready queue and the front process is dispatched. Processes on a timesharing system are continuously shuffled in and out of the running state with each clock interrupt. Because of this cycling action, long processes do not penalize short processes as heavily as with the nonpreemptible FCFS strategy.

Figure 7.5 shows a FIFO queue of five jobs and their respective times to completion. An FCFS policy will complete the processes in the order 1, 2, 3, 4, and 5, assuming the higher job number means a later arrival. The respective completion times (starting at t=0) will be 5, 6, 9, 11, and 15.

Figure 7.5

Job Number	Time to Completion
1	5
2	1
3	3
4	2
5	4

If the quantum is one unit of time, and if dispatching uses the RR strategy, then the order of dispatching will be 1, 2 (completed at t=2), 3, 4, 5, 1, 3, 4 (completed at t=8), 5, 1, 3 (completed at t=11), 5, 1, 5 (completed at t=14), and 1 (completed at t=15). Each process (except Job #2) had multiple running states. Observe that the total time to completion is still 15: No scheduling strategy can reduce the total service time required to complete all processes. Only the order of completion is affected. Note, however, that the number of context switches is higher with RR, resulting in more CPU overhead (zero overhead was artificially used in this example).

SJN and SRT

Giving high priority to short processes is a widespread scheduling practice. Two policies accomplishing this are the nonpreemptive **Shortest Job Next (SJN)** and the preemptive **Shortest Remaining Time (SRT)**. In each case, processes are positioned in the ready queue according to the amount of CPU time required for completion (least first, greatest last). The shorter the time to completion, the higher the priority.

The idea is simple: Dispatch to the running state that process in the queue requiring the least CPU time to complete. The "required CPU time to complete" is used as a priority value, and a priority queue implements the policy. How are those CPU times determined?

For a given process, the required CPU time will not, in general, be known. However, application programmers can be required to estimate that value and supply it to the system. With SJF and SRT, such estimates are often used. After a program has executed several times, the operating system will have gathered enough "accounting information" to create its own estimate of the time required for completion; that estimate may then replace the user's estimate. The operating system overhead for these strategies is significantly more than required for FCFS and RR.

Of course, users quickly learn that projecting very short times for completion results in priority service. The area of **countermeasures** is a study in how users may attempt to manipulate the system in a selfish way and what can be done to prevent it. (For example, removing any process that exceeds its time estimate is a powerful tool. Charging very high rates for CPU time in excess of the estimate is also effective.) While priority scheduling is desirable, it always increases the complexity (and cost) of scheduling. Good priority scheduling policies must pay dividends with higher value than the cost incurred by the extra overhead.

Note that SJN and SRT have their detractors. Long processes tend to remain at the back of the ready queue when shorter jobs elbow their way to the front. In extreme cases, long process may suffer from **indefinite postponement** (also known as **starvation**) by a steady stream of shorter jobs.

While time slicing and RR show improved performance over FCFS (in terms of the penalty ratios for short processes), SRT does not create the same advantage over SJN. Indefinite postponement is still possible, and unpredictable response time has a negative impact on an interactive user. SRT is more likely be used for preemptive scheduling in a single user, non-timeshared, multitasking setting. As a new process N enters the ready queue, its time to completion is checked against the remaining time to completion for the running process R; process switching takes place if N's time is less than R's. Otherwise, N takes its priority-determined place in the ready queue as with SJN. SRT has more overhead than SJN (times to completion must be recalculated after each period in the running state) and may or may not improve performance.

Figure 7.6 shows a job stream. SJN starts Job 2 first and completes it at t=2. By then Job 3 has arrived and is chosen over Job 1, completing at t=5. The jobs follow in the order 4, 5, and 1, with respective completion times of 6, 10, and 15.

Figure 7.6

Job Number	Arrival Time	Time to Completion
1	0	5
2	0	2
3	1	3
4	3	1
5	3	4

For SRT (without time slicing), Job 2 still finishes at t=2 and Job 3 begins. At t=3, however, Job 3 is preempted (with 2 units of service time still needed) by Job 4, which finishes at t=4. Then Job 3 is dispatched and finishes at t=6. Jobs 5 and 1 finish at t=10 and t=15, respectively.

HPRN

Note that SJN and SRT are not widely used in the form described earlier. There are any number of variations that are as easy to manage and that also perform well. The **Highest Penalty Ratio Next (HPRN)** strategy is an example of such a policy in a non-preemptive setting. HPRN is also known as **Highest Response Ratio Next** (or **HRN**), the response ratio being the *inverse* of the penalty ratio. The current priority for a process is calculated as its current penalty ratio:

$$(W + R)/R$$

where R is the estimate of the job's total service requirement and W is the currently accumulated time spent waiting for service. The higher the penalty ratio, the higher the priority. Observe that all jobs start with a penalty ratio of 1 since, initially, wait time is zero.

While no guess work is needed to calculate the priority value if the service time is predictable, much calculation is required. The elapsed times must be calculated every time a process completes, and the penalty ratios must then be recomputed. Positions on the ready queue can change with great frequency: Queue management is far more complicated than with the FIFO mechanism. In fact, the queue might be implemented as an ordinary table (array) and the highest penalty ratio determined during the recalculation.

The HPRN improvement? It accounts for the **age** of a process (current elapsed time on the system) in determining priority. Priority increases as elapsed time increases. While short jobs are favored (small denominators mean large priorities), aging without service increases the priority, allowing long jobs to eventually get past the line of short jobs. Starvation will not occur.

For the job stream of Figure 7.6, HPRN dispatches either Job 1 or 2 first (both initially have a penalty ration of 1.0). Suppose the tie-breaking feature of the implementation dispatches Job 1 first. At t=5 Job 1 completes, and Jobs 2 through 5 have respective penalty ratios of 3.5, 2.33, 3.0, and 1.75. Job 2 is dispatched and completed at t=7. The penalty ratios at that time for Jobs 3 through 5 are 3.0, 5.0, and 2.0, respectively. Job 4 is dispatched and finished at t=8. The penalty ratios are then 3.33 and 2.25: Job 3 finishes at t=11 and Job 5 at t=15.

It is interesting to note that changing the penalty ratio formula to

(current elapsed time)/(accumulated service time)

takes into account aging and level of service. No guesswork is required (actual times are used, not estimates). The calculation requirements carry a somewhat higher overhead, however. Notice also that a ratio of **one** must be used until the first service increment is received.

Multilevel Feedback Queues

For timesharing systems, multilevel feedback queueing mechanisms allow the participation in scheduling of static **external priorities** (nonsystem-set priorities with which processes enter the job stream) and dynamic **internal priorities** (for example, upward priority adjustments because of aging or downward adjustments for previously allocated CPU time).

Figure 7.7

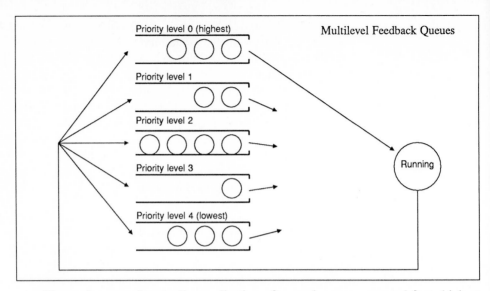

The ready queue is actually a collection of several queues arranged from highest priority to lowest (see Figure 7.7). Each individual queue can use any queueing discipline, with FIFO (RR) the most popular. The scheduler always dispatches a process from the nonempty queue of highest priority. Generally speaking, processes move among the various queues during their lifetimes, often moving to a lower priority queue after CPU service and to a higher priority queue during longer waits without CPU service.

Real CPU Scheduling

Systems seldom use these algorithms as illustrated. In fact, scheduling usually involves more than the single consideration of dispatching by priority. In particular, intermediate and high level scheduling can have an effect on dispatching. It is common to see FCFS used as one piece in a complex scheduling picture.

For example, swapping normally involves two choices: a process to be swapped in and a victim to be swapped out. FCFS may be used to select a (ready state) process from swapping store and there may be no regard for priorities. Priorities might be used, however, in the scheme for selecting a victim to remove from main store: Choose the blocked process with lowest priority or, if there is no blocked process in main memory, choose the ready process with lowest priority. There seems to be no compelling reason to use priorities for both swapping in and swapping out. (UNIX has historically used a mechanism like this.)

One simple version of a multiple queueing system uses RR for each queue but moves processes to lower priority queues as CPU service time is accumulated. Longer jobs, then, move to a lower priority status as they continue to use the CPU.

Some multiple feedback queueing mechanisms use variable length time slices, with longer slices going to processes in lower priority queues (that is, tasks in the lower queues get service less often but get more service when it does come available. IBM's MVS operating system uses a version of this technique.

If a process ages in a lower level queue without being dispatched, the queueing system may move it upward to a queue with higher priority. UNIX uses this approach: It also moves processes to lower level queues when service time is received.

Each of the multiple queueing techniques attempts to be **adaptive**: that is, the scheduling mechanisms attempt to alter scheduling behavior based on the current load and mix of processes. Adaptations to load patterns can take the form of altering the average quantum size according to the number of ready tasks. Lengthening the time slices for older (aged) processes is also adaptive. Reducing the frequency of dispatching for CPU-bound processes is yet another adaptive technique. These measures can be used with any scheduling policy, whether single or multiple queues are involved.

RR is easily modified by the use of aging as just discussed. New arrivals can be required to age for awhile until their priority is high enough to compete on a round robin basis with older jobs.

While there are hundreds of priority schemes for dispatching, RR with dynamic priority adjustment for aging seems most popular. Dynamic priority adjustments normally take the form of lowering the priority because of received CPU time and raising the priority as the process ages without service.

Managing the Process

The focus to this point has been on the scheduling stragegy without regard for how the kernel manages to identify and track each process. Neither has there been any concern for what must take place to switch processes into and out of the running state. This section examines the data that represents a process to the operating system, the general action of context switching, and the actions performed on processes by the operating system.

Process Control Information

A multitasking system must have a portion of its memory space devoted to data structures containing information about each process. The actual form of the data structures varies among the different operating systems. In this discussion, a single, generic structure called the **process control block** (**PCB**) will be used. Each process will have an assigned PCB.

The PCB must contain enough information so that the kernel knows the state of the process, which memory locations (if any) have been assigned, scheduling statistics involved in priority determination, privileges to which the process is entitled, devices being held, files that remain open, and accounting information collected by the system. There must be indicators as to the owner of the process and whether the process is in memory or swapped out. There must be space for storing context information used to switch the process into and out of the running state. There will likely be memory allocated for the receipt of signals or messages for synchronizing with other processes (**interprocess communication**). Space for storing service call parameters is often found in the PCB. If the PCBs exist as nodes in a linked list, each PCB will hold pointers to other PCBs.

Context Switching

Every process has a **context**, which describes its environment at any point in time. The context may be considered to be a snapshot of the process in execution. The context is saved when the process is removed from the running state and is precisely the information which must be known in order to restart execution at some time in the future.

The context includes the information in the PCB as mentioned above. The program counter, processor status register, and general register values at the time of a context switch are part of the context as well.

Context switches take place under several different situations. The first case is the **mode switch**, which occurs when the user makes a service call, invoking the kernel to perform some function on its behalf. The context of the user process is saved and the operating system kernel is restored to the running state. Restoring the kernel involves using its saved context to reset the register values and so on. The reverse situation (the kernel takes itself out of the running state and dispatches an application process) is also a mode switch. Here, the kernel context is saved and the dispatched process's context is restored.

The second case of a context switch involves one application process being replaced (in the running state) by another. In this case, there is a context switch from the currently active process to kernel mode (a mode switch) and then from kernel mode to new user process (a second mode switch). This kind of double mode switch is called a **process switch.**

The third instance of a context switch occurs with an interrupt. When the CPU receives an interrupt, the context of the running process is saved and the kernel mode is activated (mode switch) to deal with the interrupt. The kernel decides which kind of interrupt has been signaled and starts the execution of the appropriate interrupt handling routine. When the interrupt has been successfully handled, the kernel does another mode change to restart some application process (perhaps the one interrupted, perhaps some other process).

Most computer systems have several levels of interrupts. When an interrupt is being handled, it may not be itself interrupted except by an interrupt with a higher level of priority. For example, an I/O interrupt-handling routine may be interrupted by a hardware malfunction interrupt but not by a timeout condition.

Process
Management
Actions

The actions that typically define process control include **process creation, process termination, block, wakeup, change priority, check status**, and **synchronization.** They live under various names and in several combinations, but essentially these activities take place.

Process creation is the means by which a program becomes a process. The process is identified (by name or number) and tied to an owner (likely an owner process that is already running). Memory and other resource allocations must be made. The PCB must be established and filled with initial information. Often, a dummy context is generated so that the startup environment will be established when the new process is dispatched. The PCB for the new process is placed in the correct list awaiting the dispatcher's action.

Each process is typically attached in the **process hierarchy** as a child of some parent. The parent process is the process responsible for creating the child. The child process is usually created to perform some task for the parent. Generally, there is message passing from child to parent to indicate progress toward the goal for which the child was created.

Termination of a process is the reverse of the creation activity and removes all traces of the process from the kernel. Memory must be returned to the system, resources must be deallocated and files closed and generally cleaned up. The PCB must be dismantled (or more likely, returned to a list of free PCB nodes). If the process being terminated has children, the children processes must be handled. Two approaches are used: all children are terminated with their parent, or children of a terminating parent are assigned to another process (often a kernel process) and continue running until their normal termination. The latter is the case with UNIX process management.

A process may block itself (by issuing an I/O call, for example) or may be blocked by the system (an interrupt, perhaps). Blocking temporarily removes a process from the ready to run state so that it does not vie for the CPU. When a process blocks itself, it does so because it cannot use the CPU until some event is completed. When the operating system blocks a process it may do so to alleviate congestion from overloading: This type of blocking is often called **suspension.** Suspension generally takes the process out of the ready state for longer periods of time.

Wakeup activity is the reverse of blocking: The process is returned to the ready-to-run state. Wakeup occurs when an awaited event takes place. The awaited event is often announced by a **signal** recognized by the operating system. If the blocked state were a suspension, **resume** is used in place of wakeup.

Change priority and check status are clear. The owner of a process may change the priority of a process, generally by lowering the priority to allow other processes to take precedence. A user might do this for a background or batch activity where time is not a major concern. The system administrator can usually alter process priorities (raise or lower) to change the way the system is currently performing. The goal is usually to speed one or two processes to completion to meet some demand or deadline. However, the administrator may do the same in order to deal with a sudden degradation in performance.

Synchronization is a major consideration of the next section.

Event Management and Concurrency

Concurrent activities take place in a computer system, as a given. On single processor machines, individual instructions from concurrent activities are more interleaved in execution than simultaneous. When the order of interleaving has no effect on the results generated, the concurrent processes are said to be **disjoint.** If the order of the interleaving does affect the outcome, a **race condition** exists and the interleaving must be controlled or **synchronized**.

One need for synchronization was seen in Chapter 5—the competition for I/O resources. Interrupts acted as timing signals to coordinate the use of I/O devices, insuring that **mutual exclusion** (a limit of one process accessing the device at a time) was enforced. Problems caused by concurrency in the use of shared resources is more complex than this I/O example, however.

For instance, consider the use of shared memory. If variables (memory cells) are shared among cooperating processes, concurrent efforts to manipulate those variables may create race conditions. The hardware arbitrates simultaneous attempts to access any given memory cell and mutually exclusive access is guaranteed. A problem arises, however, when some *series of instructions* involving a memory cell is interrupted. The following sequences illustrate:

Process A	**Process B**
Table[Counter] := AValue;	*Table[Counter] := BValue;*
Counter := Counter + 1;	*Counter :=Counter + 1;*

Suppose that *Counter* and *Table* are variables shared by processes A and B and that *Counter* currently has value 23. Suppose further that *AValue* is 12, *BValue* is 76 and process A has the CPU. The first instruction sets *Table*[23] to 12. If A is preempted in favor of B before executing the second instruction, B overwrites *Table*[23] with the value 76, increments *Counter* to 24 and goes on about some other business. As process A recovers the CPU, it continues by incrementing Counter to 25 and exiting this section of code. The intent of process A was to place a 12 in one slot (23) of *Table,* B intended to put a 76 in a different cell (24) and *Counter's* purpose was to make sure *Table's* cells were filled in order with no overwriting and no gaps. That, of course, is not what happened: execution of the two sections of code produced a race condition with undesirable consequences.

A section of code that manipulates shared memory (such as each of the two above) is called a **critical section.** The problem here is different from the I/O example in that access to *two different entities* (the two critical sections) must be synchronized. For the code to work as intended, only one process may be in its critical section during any interval of time. In the above example, when process A executed the first instruction from its critical section, *process B should have been prevented from entering its critical section* until A completed the second instruction and exited its critical section. **Serialized access** to critical sections is the normal solution for race conditions.

Mutual exclusion can be enforced by a number of software and hardware techniques, each requiring some form of signaling. Processes are delayed and released by the signaling activities. The next chapter looks at devices such as switches, locks, special hardware instructions, abstract data structures and message passing. They all create some form of interprocess communication for purposes of synchronization.

Chapter 5 also showed that enforcing mutual exclusion can lead to the problem of **deadlock.** A deadlock occurs when one or more processes are waiting for an event that cannot possibly happen. The involved process or processes cannot progress toward completion and tie up needed resources while they wait. Improper handling of critical sections can easily lead to deadlock. Chapter 8 takes a more in depth look.

Exercises

1. What kinds of processes must have the very highest priorities?
2. The terms scheduling and dispatching are sometimes used synonymously. Compare/contrast the two. Describe the term *scheduling mechanism* as it has been used.
3. Some say that a time slice should be about 100 times as great as the time needed for a context switch. What problems arise if the time slice is very much smaller? Very much larger?
4. What are the greatest potential problems for preemptive, priority-based scheduling mechanisms?
5. Why are batch jobs given lower priorities than interactive jobs?
6. Why should a system give higher priority to a process holding important resources? What are some problems in doing this?
7. Some scheduling objectives conflict.
   a. A system manager desires to have maximum throughput and to serve a maximum number of interactive users. How do the two goals conflict?
   b. The manager wishes to enforce a policy based on priorities but wishes to have fair treatment for all users. Describe the conflict between the two.
   c. What are some conflicts between the desire for high utilization and fast response times?

     d. Describe the problems in achieving maximum throughput with high levels of predictability (low levels of variance).

8. What might the term *graceful degradation* mean in relation to scheduling policies, considerations, and choices?

9. In each case, describe whether the scheduling decision is a high, intermediate or low level activity.
     a. Which process is the next to enter the running state?
     b. Which swapped-out process is the next to be swapped in?
     c. Which memory-resident process is the next victim to be swapped out?
     d. Which suspended process is to be given the next wakeup call?
     e. Which process is to be the next suspended process?
     f. Which program is the next to be activated?

10. Describe the behavior of a round robin strategy as the time slice is increased to a large value.

11. An **I/O-bound process** is characterized as one that customarily gives up the CPU (for an I/O service call) before its time slice expires. Most priority systems favor (give higher priority to) such processes. Describe the rationale for such a scheme.

12. A **CPU-bound process** is one which seldom gives up the CPU before timer-out takes it away. Such processes are often given lower priorities. Discuss the pros and cons. CPU-bound processes also tend to be given longer time slices to go with the lowered priorities. What are the advantages and disadvantages?

13. A process has been preempted frequently. On what basis should it receive an increased priority? On what basis should it not?

14. Describe a process that might be considered to have very good behavior traits so far as scheduling is concerned. What kinds of behavior, relative to paging, might be considered good behavior by the scheduling mechanism?

15. Deadline scheduling is based on two pieces of information: the CPU time needed for completion and the time and date by which the process must complete its work. Describe general ideas and problems for such a preemptive scheduling algorithm.

16. Suppose deadlock has occurred and a process has been terminated so that others may continue to a timely completion. What problems can arise when restarting the terminated process?

17. Use the job stream from Figure 7.8. Determine the job completion times for each job under each dispatching strategy. For each job also calculate the wait time, elapsed time and penalty ratio. If ties occur for any dispatching situation, use FCFS as a tie-breaker.

     a. FCFS
     b. SJN
     c. HPRN

Job Number	Arrival Time	CPU Service Time
1	0	6
2	0	2
3	0	1
4	0	4
5	.5	3
6	1.5	2
7	4.5	3
8	6.5	1

Figure 7.8

18. Follow the instructions of Exercise 17 for the job stream of Figure 7.9 and the preemptive strategies that follow. Use a time slice of 3 units.

   a. RR
   b. SRT (assume a running process must give up the CPU at timer out unless no other process is ready)

19. Redo Exercise 18 with a time slice of one unit.

20. Follow the instructions of Exercise 17 for the job stream of Figure 7.10, assuming a two queue system. One queue is for **foreground** (interactive) processes and the other is for **background** (batch) processes. Foreground processes always have priority for dispatching. Use a time slice of 3 units.

21. Some UNIX systems calculate a priority value from two values: *priority value = base value + CPU count.* Base value is an external priority. The CPU count starts at zero and is increased immediately after a running state (new CPU count = old CPU count + CPU count for this slice). Aging of the CPU count takes place at the end of each time slice when it is cut in half for *all* ready processes. The lower the priority value, the higher the priority. Thus, the priority level decreases for any process using the CPU and increases for any process not getting CPU attention. Suppose the time slice is one unit and the CPU count is 100 for each one unit of time in the running state. Follow the instructions for Exercise 17 and the processes of Figure 7.11. Assume that processes do not give up the CPU except at timer-out and completion.

22. Write a program to simulate dispatching for a computer system having one CPU. Use a random number generator and the formula

$$t = [-\ln(1-RND)]/a$$

to generate the time t between successive arrivals of processes into the system (a is the average interarrival rate). The same formula is used to generate the total CPU

Job Number	Arrival Time	CPU Service Time
1	0	5
2	0	4
3	0	2
4	0	5
5	2	2
6	3	1
7	4	7
8	8	2
9	9	2

Figure 7.9

Job Number	Arrival Time	CPU Service Time	Process Type/ Queue
1	0	5	f
2	0	2	b
3	0	3	b
4	0	2	b
5	1	1	f
6	3	4	b
7	7	2	f
8	9	1	b

Figure 7.10

Job Number	Arrival Time	CPU Service Time	Base Priority Value
1	0	5	100
2	0	4	100
3	0	2	75
4	0	5	100
5	2	2	50
6	3	1	50
7	4	7	100
8	8	2	50
9	9	2	50

Figure 7.11

(service) times required for each process. Assume that context switching takes no time and that there are no I/O interrupts or waits. Run the simulation for time starting at t=0 and running through t=100. The output should show queueing activity, job sequencing and appropriate summary information such as average wait times, turnaround times, penalty ratios, queue lengths, and so forth. Do the simulation for each strategy using an average service rate of one job per unit of time and each of the three average interarrival rates of 0.5, 1, and 2.

a. FCFS
b. RR with time slice = 0.1 (Note: FCFS can be gotten "free" if RR is done correctly.)
c. SJN
d. SRT (no time slicing)
e. HPRN

8 Multiple Processors and Concurrency

Multiple processor systems are created to offer increased computing power or to offer power more economically. Because of their complexity, however, the change from a single CPU to three CPUs will not triple the throughput. Until recently, three CPUs were likely to deliver slightly over double the performance of a single processor. Multiple processor operating systems have to be more efficient than their uniprocessor cousins to allow better productivity gains. A few of today's multiple CPU systems come close to realizing the full power gain for each added processor (when the number of processors is less than ten). The promise of increased reliability also contributes to the increasing popularity of multiprocessor systems. Moreover, multiprocessor systems are changing the way people think about computer solutions to problems.

Concurrency occurs in uniprocessor systems having intelligent I/O devices; concurrency also occurs in single CPU multitasking systems. The nature and complexity of concurrency increases for systems with more than one processor, but many synchronization considerations are similar regardless of the number of CPUs. Solutions, however, grow more complex in multiple processor systems.

Concurrency on uniprocessor multitasking systems involves **pseudoparallel** instruction processing: Only one instruction is executed at a time, with instructions from several processes interleaved. This interleaving gives the appearance of simultaneous process execution. With multiple CPUs, it is possible to execute several instructions (one per CPU) simultaneously.

Multiple CPU systems are categorized in a number of ways, one general distinction coming in memory-related architecture. Multiple processors sharing a common main memory are **tightly coupled.** If each processor has its own main memory, the system is **loosely coupled.** Tightly coupled CPUs have a bus mechanism for connecting them to the shared memory, while loosely coupled processors are connected by a communication device (as in Figure 8.1). Tightly coupled systems are called **multiprocessors,** while the loosely coupled systems are said to be **distributed.**

The synchronizing tools that work on multiple CPU systems can be (and are) used with uniprocessor systems as well. These tools include interrupts, locks, switches, and hardware instructions, as well as certain abstract data structures using shared memory. In the case of distributed systems, shared variables (shared memory) won't work;

Figure 8.1

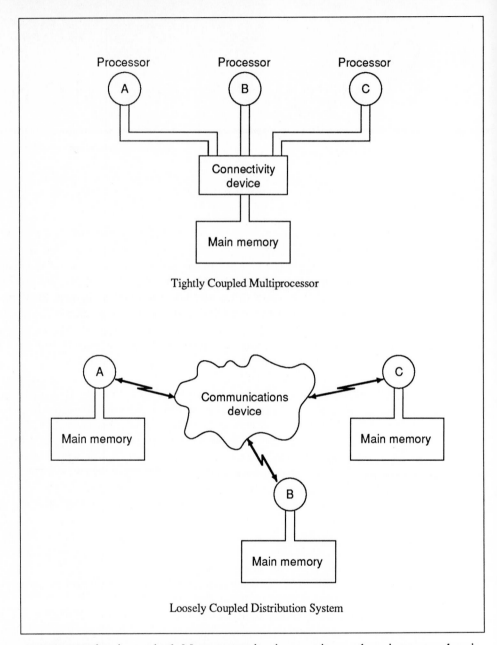

Processor   Processor   Processor

A   B   C

Connectivity
device

Main memory

Tightly Coupled Multiprocessor

A   C

Communications
device

Main memory   Main memory

B

Main memory

Loosely Coupled Distribution System

message passing is required. Message passing is emerging as the primary synchronizing tool for uniprocessor and multiprocessor systems.

The likelihood of deadlock increases with the number of CPUs and the level of
simultaneous processing. While the concept of deadlock is the same for all systems,
anti-deadlock mechanisms are more difficult to build for those that are loosely coupled.

The subject of loosely coupled multiple CPU systems is closely connected with
two other significant topics. **Computer networks** (as discussed in Chapter 9) create

loosely coupled systems. In some networks of complete, standalone computer systems, a job may be subdivided and the pieces farmed out to several processors, which cooperate to complete the task. Sharing the computational load in this manner is known as **distributed processing.**

　　　Parallel processing goes beyond concurrency and job sharing (as discussed earlier). Parallel processing does include the simultaneous execution of instructions and the distribution of subtasks among various processors. However, pure parallel processing involves more finely grained load sharing: A single instruction in a high-level language usually generates several machine language instructions, which may be executed by several processors. True parallel processing changes the way programmers think about problems and their computer solutions.

Tightly Coupled Multiprocessors

Systems with multiple processors are, for the most part, created to increase processing power. However, when several processors share memory, memory access can become a point of contention. The bus may become a bottleneck limiting the processing gains afforded by extra CPUs, but alternatives to single bus memory alleviate the problem.

　　　There are several ways to organize the interrelationships of tightly coupled processors. Each arrangement or structure has its specific advantages and disadvantages, as discussed in the following sections.

Shared Memory Bus Arrangements

As mentioned earlier, the single, common bus can become a bottleneck in multiprocessor systems. A **bus** is a path connecting processors, main memory, and more (see Figure 8.2). With several processors attempting to address memory at the same time, contention for the single path increases. One solution to the bus contention problem is to have more than one bus (or path to memory). This is normally accomplished by constructing main memory from independent submodules, each capable of being accessed independent of the others. Since there are several such modules, a number of simultaneous, nonconflicting memory accesses (one per module) are possible. To do so requires a mechanism whose job it is to connect each CPU to the correct memory module *every time a memory access is required.*

Figure 8.2

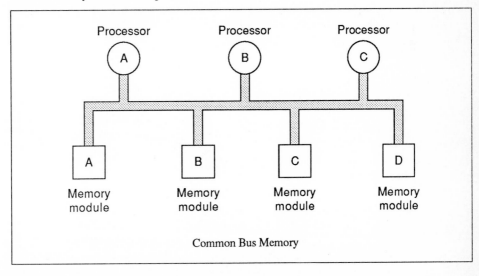

Common Bus Memory

Figure 8.3

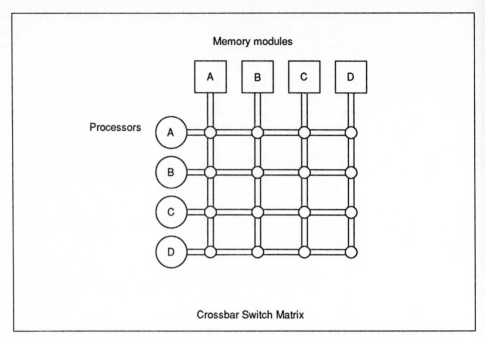

Crossbar Switch Matrix

Crossbar switch.   The **crossbar switch** is one common solution. In effect, *each memory module has its own bus.* Conceptually, the processors and memory modules form a table or matrix, as shown in Figure 8.3. Each circle in the matrix is a decision or switching point. By deciding which points to close and which to open, the crossbar switch creates paths between processors and memory modules. The simplest case: Only

Figure 8.4

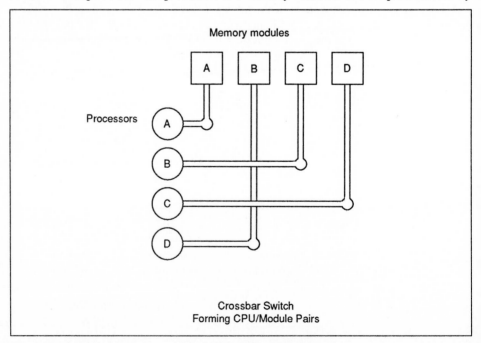

Crossbar Switch
Forming CPU/Module Pairs

one CPU has a path to any memory module at any point in time (see Figure 8.4). Some variants allow other switching patterns (several CPUs matched simultaneously with one or more memory modules). The crossbar switch and its variants, then, match CPUs with memory modules and arbitrate conflicting access requests.

Crossbar switches generate multibus main memory and decrease bus contention levels for multiprocessors. Primary drawbacks to the crossbar switch include its cost (as a complex piece of hardware) and the limitation on the number of modules and CPUs that can be serviced. Crossbar switches customarily serve a maximum of fewer than 35 CPUs. Systems with a massive number of processors (hundreds or thousands) pose serious problems for this approach. Note that recent developments have produced fiber optic switches that are faster and can service a greater number of memory modules and CPUs.

Multiport memory. An alternative to the crossbar switch is **multiport memory.** Conceptually, the multiport memory scheme creates *a private bus for each processor* rather than for each memory module. Each memory module has several ports to which processors may be attached (as in Figure 8.5). The hardware of the memory module selects one access request at a time from among its ports; that is, the memory module itself arbitrates contention for access to its addresses.

Figure 8.5

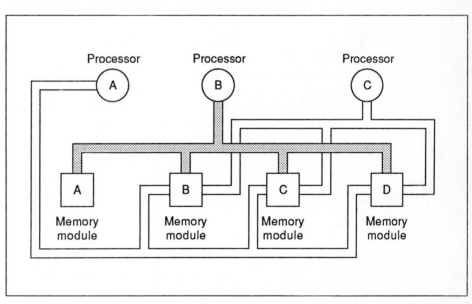

Figure 8.5 shows how multiport memory allows both shared memory and private memory. Memory module A is private to processor B, while all other modules are shared among the three processors. As one might suspect, multiport memory is more expensive than single port memory.

CPU Interconnection

Relationships between the several processors of a multiprocessor system can be established in a number of ways: The two most prevalent are the **master/slave** and **peer** architectures. Again, each has its own set of advantages and disadvantages.

Master/slave organization.   Typical personal computers use a master/slave organization. The single CPU does computation and runs the operating system, while a number of other processors perform special tasks for the (master) CPU. Such tasks include CRT management, keyboard management, math coprocessing, disk controlling, and peripheral interfacing.

Figure 8.6 shows a simple master/slave system. In that diagram, processor M is the master processor: M runs the operating system and does the computation, farming out I/O to processor S. Such arrangements are simple and allow increased throughput by offloading all I/O activity from the master.

Figure 8.6

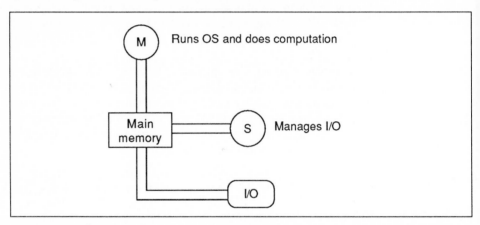

In this setting, it is entirely likely that the master and slave are different kinds of processors designed for different types of responsibilities. Actual gains from this master/slave system depend on the job mix: If the mix is not properly balanced between I/O and computation, one of the two processors will be idle too often. Load balancing is not easy to accomplish unless the job mix can be controlled. Moreover, if the master becomes inoperative, the slave cannot take over its role and the system must crash.

Figure 8.7

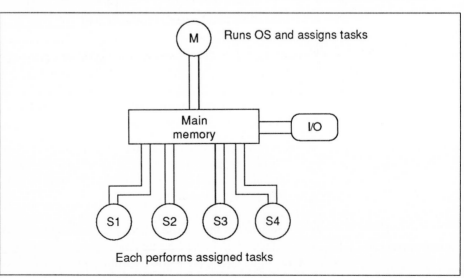

It is possible, of course, for the master to control several identical slave processors. In such an arrangement (Figure 8.7), the master essentially runs the operating system and schedules the computation and I/O among the slave processors, although the master likely handles all I/O. Load balancing among the slave processors is possible. If one slave becomes inoperative, redistribution of work among the remaining processors allows the system to continue to function, although at some lower level of service.

Note that if the master malfunctions, the system stops. However, if the master and slave CPUs are *identical,* it may be possible to designate one of the slaves as the new master and continue processing. In such a case, the *reliability* of the system is improved over its single CPU competitors. This is important as system availability and system reliability are often goals of multiple processor systems.

Peer organization. Figure 8.8 illustrates a second organization for multiprocessors. In this case, all CPUs are **peers,** with no processor dominant. Several identical processors are hooked in such a way that each has access to main memory and I/O capabilities. In addition, each is capable of executing the *single copy* of the operating system. The operating system is a shared resource and must be designed accordingly (that is, it must be reentrant).

Figure 8.8

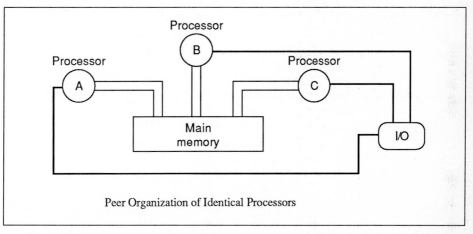

Peer Organization of Identical Processors

Since the operating system is a shared resource, it becomes a source of contention. Even with reentrant code, having several processors executing operating system commands concurrently can lead to race conditions involving the system's global data structures used to manage processes and resources. A usual synchronizing technique is to designate one CPU as the **controller** or **executive:** Only the processor assigned controller status is allowed to maintain global system data structures. Such an arrangement enforces a kind of mutually exclusive access (by processors) to those structures. This is not a master/slave relationship for two reasons:

- The controller does not actually control any other processor.
- Any processor can be designated controller, but only one at any time.

The operating system may assign complete jobs to individual processors. When the job is scheduled, some available processor is assigned and runs the job through to completion. On the other hand, the operating system may be designed so that processors cooperate in the completion of any given job, a format similar to distributed computing. Indeed, the differences between multiprocessor systems and distributed systems can be blurred by implementation patterns.

The peer model (also called the **symmetric model** or **democratic model**) can be more efficient than other models because of the flexible load distribution and sharing capabilities. In addition, the demise of one processor need not bring the system down. Reliability can be greater than that for uniprocessor systems and some master/slave architectures. However, the operating system is significantly more complex for peer-organized multiprocessors.

Adding processors to peer systems can increase system horsepower without changing the user interface. The operating system incorporates the added power, but the user sees no difference except for improved service. The physical installation of an added processor can be simpler than installing a different (but larger) machine.

Distributed Systems

CPU power is relatively inexpensive with microcomputers making it economically possible to create systems with a massive number of processors. Multiprocessors consisting of many tightly coupled MPUs (microprocessor units) have been used to create commercial micro-supercomputers and mini-supercomputers of extraordinary processing power.

This same microcomputer technology removes the need for users to share processors. One or more processors per user is economically reasonable in many cases. A problem with time sharing systems is that they deliver essentially the same system to each user, despite their different system requirements. Asymmetric private processor power can be delivered to the user where he/she is, but there are many resources (data, programs, expensive peripherals, secondary storage) that must be **shared** for operational reasons or for economic purposes. Isolated microcomputer systems make some kinds of sharing quite inefficient at best and impossible at worst. Distributed systems composed of complete, standalone computers (perhaps one per user), connected by comunications facilities, offer an alternative multiple processor organization that allows personal computing, increased power, and resource sharing.

Distributed systems have become increasingly attractive for a number of reasons, one being the growing acceptance of international standards for communication protocols (as discussed in Chapter 9). Communication technology makes high speed links between computers available and economically feasible. The popularity of distributed systems is fueling research in parallel processing, distributed databases, and distributed operating systems.

Loosely coupled systems of multiple processors may be similar to multiprocessors in a number of ways but quite different in others. Because of the general lack of shared memory among the independent machines making up a distributed system, interprocess and intermachine communication is more difficult to achieve. Shared variable techniques for concurrency control do not work and message passing becomes necessary. In addition, scheduling is more complicated and error handling more difficult. In spite of the difficulties, distributed systems hold the promise of increased power and new computing environments and techniques.

Distributed Architectures

Many of the simplest distributed systems "just happen." An organization in need of more computing power decides to add a new machine while retaining the old system.

By doing so, the existing applications continue to run on the old machine without change. New applications can be developed on the new machine. By connecting the two through a communications link, users may access either machine from a single terminal or workstation, and data transfer between the two is possible. Each machine runs its own operating system: If the operating systems are different, users must know both operating systems in order to use both machines. Of course, users must also learn any control language used with the communications system.

Each machine has its own set of jobs to run. Jobs are always run on the same machine; there is no sharing of loads between the two. It is common for each system to have its own complete set of peripheral devices. **VAX clusters** are systems of this type (although the CPUs generally run the same operating system).

The sharing of resources is made possible by interconnecting the standalone machines through communications facilities. Sharing is made reasonable when operating systems render the use of interconnected resources **transparent** (when the user can't see it). While operating systems for distributed architectures must deliver the same services that uniprocessor operating systems offer, that is not enough.

Requests for access to a resource should not require the location of the resource as a parameter. That is, resource use should be transparent as to location. Some file system data may be replicated in various places, but access to replicated data should not require any user knowledge of the replication and data requests should be transparent with respect to replication. In general, all communications (network) activity should be transparent. Processing should appear to the user to be happening on an isolated, standalone system. Note that communications-related errors create special problems and require special handling.

In order to achieve these goals, all processors should run the "same" operating system, even though the processors may not be identical. The single operating system run by all processors is called a **distributed operating system.** Distributed operating systems, which are larger and more complex than their standalone cousins, must manage communication among the various processors and the use of local resources. The ability to share resources depends on how the communications routines are implemented.

If the communications layer sits atop the local operating system, the access of remote resources is difficult to make transparent. The communications package is merely an applications package running on top of the local operating system. In fact, there is no requirement that the underlying operating system be the same at all sites. The communications layer simply translates network instructions into the correct set of operating system commands. Such application programs are often called **network operating systems.** It is more difficult to achieve transparency with network operating systems, but the underlying machines and operating system need not be the same. Thus these systems are reasonable choices for creating a heterogeneous network of machines.

The other extreme, one quite useful for distributed systems, places the communications layer below the process management, memory management, and file management layers. (See Figure 8.9.) For example, the file manager can designate a particular data element without regard for its location, pass it on to the communications layer, and expect the communications layer to find the data element wherever it may be. Similarly, the process manager can order the creation of a process without regard

Figure 8.9

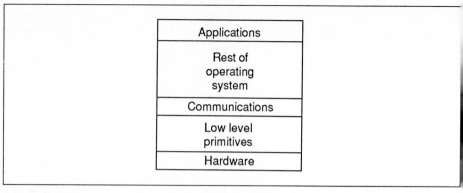

for the machine on which it will reside—the information is simply passed to the communications layer.

The physical network connecting the units in a distributed system can have many forms. Some of these possible structures are examined in Chapter 9, along with general networking concepts and concerns.

Message Passing

When processors have no shared memory, communication and synchronization take place in the form of **message passing**. Message passing requires a **protocol** (set of rules) for transmitting information over the communication links and another protocol for the construction of the messages themselves. Message passing is nothing more than a means of direct data movement between processors or processes, the actual handling of messages being the responsibility of the operating system. Users or processes issue **send** and **receive** instructions, which are translated into operating system service calls requesting message service.

For **direct** process-to-process communication, the send and receive instructions must be addressed (that is, the sending and receiving processes must be identified). For **indirect** process-to-process communication, senders address messages to predesignated **ports** or **mailboxes** (memory locations). Processes pick up the messages from these repositories. Ports that have a single writer (sender) and a single reader (receiver), and are managed in a FIFO manner, are often called **pipes**. Other ports may have multiple readers and/or multiple writers.

Messages may be of fixed length (the easiest to manage) or of variable length. Most messages for communication purposes are very short, generally just a few bytes or words. Messages are used to pass data between machines (operating systems) or between user processes. They may also be used as convenient and powerful tools for synchronization or for transfer of other forms of data.

In some systems, messages are treated as remote procedure calls, complete with returned values (messages of acknowledgment).

Message passing between local processes looks just like message passing between processes on different machines, except that there is no need to pass the message over a communications link. This makes message passing within a distributed system transparent as to location. In addition, this symmetry illustrates that message passing is also easily usable in both tightly coupled systems and uniprocessor systems.

Message passing between machines poses another problem—the uncertainty of perfect message transfer over the communications link. Error detection and correction techniques must be used to insure that the correct receiver indeed receives the correct message. Moreover, the sender must know that this has occurred. A typical protocol requires the receiver to acknowledge receipt of a valid message, the acknowledgment being a message subject to the same vagaries as the original. Note that retransmission of lost and garbled messages may be required. Refer to Chapter 9 for a further look at the specific problems involved.

Parallel Processing

The value of multiple processor systems is their ability to do **parallel processing,** the simultaneous execution of multiple instructions. Parallel processing on most commercial systems, however, is rather coarse-grained. Each job is generally assigned to a processor that runs it to completion. Optionally, each job is functionally decomposed into several subtasks, each of which is assigned to one processor. Fine-grained parallel processing goes so far as to subdivide at the *individual instruction* level for multiple CPU assignment. The major problem with typical parallel processing systems is how to find and express parallelism in programs. Alternatively, there is the difficulty of how to find parallelism in the solution to problems. Is the programmer or the system best at finding parallelism and doing the synchronization?

Some parallelism is easy to find in a system. One classic example is loop activity, such as:

```
FOR I := 1 To 100 DO
   A[I] := A[I] + 1;
```

One hundred processors, each incrementing one array cell, could perform all the loop cycles simultaneously. Another well-worn example involves arithmetic:

```
A := B + C + D + E;
```

The addition can consist of two parallel operations (B + C and D + E), followed by a final action as indicated by:

```
A := (B + C) + (D + E).
```

With two processors, the problem is done more quickly than with a single CPU performing three sequential actions, as in:

```
A := (((B + C) + D) + E).
```

The two examples above indicate that intelligent compilers can detect and prepare for some **implicit** parallel activity. Some languages (Ada, Occam, Modula-2) have constructs that allow the programmer to designate **explicit** parallel actions.

Refer to Figure 8.10, a bubble chart showing a collection of activities and the relationships between them. The arrows indicate dependency: A2 and A3 are dependent on A1 but are independent of each other, while A4 is dependent on both A3 and A4. The

Figure 8.10

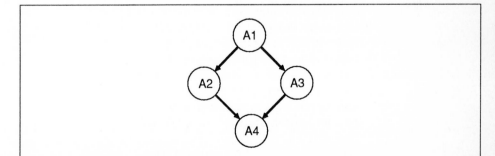

phrase *A2 is dependent on A1* simply means that activity A2 may not begin until activity A1 is completed.

For Figure 8.10, a suitable "program" might look like that in Figure 8.11; cobegin/coend indicate parallel activity. However, not all combinations of sequential and parallel activity can be programmed so clearly, as Figure 8.12 illustrates. The "solution" given in Figure 8.13 accomplishes all the required tasks but requires activity A5 to wait for the completion of A2. The bubble diagram's structure, however, allows A5 to begin at the completion of A3, regardless of whether A2 has finished.

```
BEGIN
  A1;
  COBEGIN
    A2;
    A3
  COEND
  A4
END
```

Solution to Figure 8.10

Figure 8.11

Figure 8.12

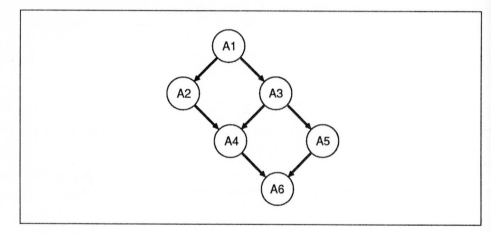

In the case of Figure 8.12, a different construct, **fork/join,** does a better job. The forks and joins are explicitly shown in Figure 8.14, along with a proposed solution. The execution is sequential until a fork instruction is encountered. A fork initiates parallel activity: The sequence of instructions located at the fork's **label** begins and the sequence of instructions **immediately following** the fork statement itself is also started. A join statement is a **signal,** with the variable (here, C1 or C2) being a counter. Each time the join instruction is called, the variable is decremented. Execu-

```
BEGIN
  A1;
  COBEGIN
    A2;
    A3;
  COEND
  COBEGIN
    A4;
    A5
  COEND
  A6
END
```

Solution to Figure 8.12

Figure 8.13

Figure 8.14

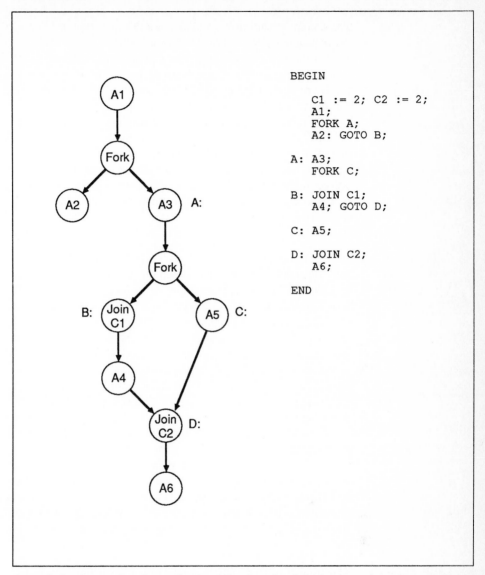

```
BEGIN

    C1 := 2; C2 := 2;
    A1;
    FORK A;
    A2: GOTO B;

A:  A3;
    FORK C;

B:  JOIN C1;
    A4; GOTO D;

C:  A5;

D:  JOIN C2;
    A6;

END
```

tion of the instruction immediately following the join begins when the variable is decremented to zero.

These language constructs allow explicit parallelism to be stated and exploited. However, the levels of parallelism indicated by these means tend to be low, normally involving fewer than a dozen processors in actual practice. To effectively use massive parallelism, designers must find other means.

Alternative Architectures

Users are now studying alternatives to the Von Neumann architecture, and some models have already been produced. Von Neumann architectures look at instructions in some control order and fetch data for use by the instructions. The **data flow** or **data driven** architecture allows instructions to be executed *whenever the input required is available.*

The output is then made available to any instruction needing it. Data flow models look at the data available and fetch the required instructions. With the data flow architecture, finding the inherent parallelism in a program is automatically done by the system if an applicative or functional programming language (as opposed to a procedural language) has been used. (The Japanese fifth-generation effort is an example of data flow architecture.)

Demand driven architecture is another alternative under study. Demand driven systems fire an instruction (assign an instruction to a CPU and execute it) whenever the output of the instruction is demanded by another instruction. This is akin to a backwards process: The firing of a needed instruction may itself require the execution of one or more instructions, each of which may require . . . , and so on. Like the data flow model, demand driven systems automatically find the inherent parallelism in a program or problem solution.

Transputers

A recent entrant into the commercial field of parallel processing is the **transputer,** a self-contained microcomputer based on Von Neumann architecture. The transputer chip includes a CPU, a limited amount of memory, a clock, a facility for connecting additional external memory, and four direct links for communicating with other transputers. (These transputers are high-speed microcomputers.)

The four communications links mentioned here are of particular interest, since they allow many transputers to be networked in a distributed fashion to create a very powerful system with processing speeds of 100 MIPs and more. The links are high-speed links used for very low overhead message passing. One interesting application of transputers is to attach a network of transputers to a personal computer as if the network were an I/O device. Then the CPU of the personal computer becomes the controller, farming out jobs to the transputers, with personal micro-supercomputers as a possible result.

Occam has been a favored parallel processing language of transputers during the early phases of development. Since the underlying design is Von Neumann, gaining the full power of the network of transputers still depends on finding the parallelism in the application. To date, most applications of transputers have been very specialized, with the interconnection of the transputers being based on the nature of the problem itself.

Concurrency and Synchronization

The need for synchronizing concurrent (and parallel) activities has been described in Chapters 5 and 7 in terms of enforcing mutual exclusion between competing processes or between cooperating processes. As discussed earlier, most peripheral devices admit only one activity at a time, with main memory admitting only one memory access on a bus at a time.

The access to critical sections of process code must be mutually exclusive to prevent race conditions. Furthermore, execution of critical code must appear atomic with respect to competing and cooperating processes, since race conditions are the natural result of interrupts that occur during the execution of critical section code. Once process P begins execution of a critical section, no competing or cooperating process is allowed to enter that critical section until P completes its work there, *even if P is interrupted.*

Solutions to the problem of mutual exclusion for critical sections must have the following characteristics:

- If process P is outside its critical section, it cannot block another process from entering.
- No process can be kept from its critical section indefinitely.
- Solutions must not depend on the speed and relative timing of instructions from the concurrent processes.

Attempts to enforce mutual exclusion can be categorized in a number of ways: Solutions may be *purely software solutions* or use *special hardware features*; they may use *busy waiting* or invoke some form of *blocking* (sleep/wakeup). Solutions may use *shared variables* (shared memory) or depend on *message passing*. Shared data structures may be managed (and protected) by the operating system or function as special language constructs established by compilers. These devices may automatically enforce mutual exclusion or may place the burden of proper use on the applications programmer.

Disabling Interrupts

Mutual exclusion can be enforced on uniprocessor systems by disabling interrupts. If interrupts are disabled as process P enters a critical section, P will continue execution until it once again enables the interrupts. While interrupts are disabled by P, no other process may do anything, let alone enter the critical section. P must, then, enable the interrupts just as it exits the critical section. This technique is restricted to uniprocessor systems since an interrupt on one processor has no effect on the activity of another. Disabling interrupts does *not* protect shared memory and code for multiprocessor systems.

Note that there are other drawbacks, even on uniprocessor systems. When interrupts are disabled by a user process, the operating system has no way of regaining control of the machine until the user enables the interrupts. Even timer-out interrupts are disabled. Time sharing systems, in particular, cannot tolerate such a level of user control and the resulting unpredictability.

The operating system may disable interrupts for its own critical activities that require very short processing time, but that capability is not normally granted to user processes. (The UNIX kernel effectively disables interrupts for some of its activities by temporarily raising the priority level so high that no interrupt can override.) The disabling of interrupts is often used to create other operating system primitives for enforcing mutual exclusion.

Hardware Locks and Instructions

Hardware locks represent another technique for managing mutual exclusion. A hardware lock can be as simple as a single bit boolean flag (for example, 0 = unlocked and 1 = locked). To perform a protected activity, a process waits until an unlocked condition is found, sets the lock, performs the activity, and then resets the lock to zero. In addition, some vendors employ atomic hardware instructions in this situation.

The hardware facilities do not prevent race conditions directly but are used to create **software switches**, which govern entrance to critical activities and enforce mutual exclusion. Their use employs busy waiting (which is not good) but works for multiprocessor systems with shared memory (which is good). These locks and atomic

Figure 8.15

```
        stalled := TRUE;
        WHILE stalled DO TestAndSet(stalled,busy);
        (* Enter critical activity here. *)
        busy := FALSE;
```

Mutual Exclusion Using TestAndSet

instructions are also used by operating systems and compilers to create other primitives for enforcing mutual exclusion.

Figure 8.15 illustrates one use of the **TestAndSet** hardware instruction. The variables *stalled* and *busy* are boolean variables shared by all processes competing for the critical section. As an undivisible (atomic) action, TestAndSet reads the value of *busy*, sets *stalled=busy*, and resets *busy* to *TRUE*. The *while* loop represents busy waiting: The process cycles within the loop until *stalled* is set to *FALSE* (*busy* is initialized to *FALSE*, becomes *TRUE* when TestAndSet is invoked, and is returned to *FALSE* when a process leaves its critical section). Each cooperating process must have this code surrounding its entrance to the critical activity. This simple solution, however, does allow for starvation. (See the exercises at the end of this chapter.)

Software
Switches

Software techniques for synchronizing access are conceptually simple, but they were quite difficult to develop. Software switches, as they are known, have a common trait: They employ *busy waiting* and depend on shared variables. While busy waiting uses CPU resources without completing any processing, software switches do implement mutual exclusion without concern for hardware attributes. While locks and atomic instructions (as described earlier) may be used to create software switches, they are not required. Software switches work well for multiprocessor systems with shared memory. Figure 8.16 illustrates one solution attributed to G. L. Petersen—a solution involving only two cooperating processes.

The shared variables in this example are *wait* and the array *stalled*. When process i wishes to begin the critical activity, it states its intention by declaring itself *stalled* and then graciously defers to the other process, pointing the *wait* finger at itself. Process i cycles within the null WHILE loop until either the other process (which has a similar segment of code) is not stalled or the wait finger points to the other process. (This mechanism is extendable to any number of cooperating processes.)

Figure 8.16

```
            Code for Process i

        stalled := TRUE;
        wait := i;
        WHILE (stalled[(i+1) MOD 2] AND wait = i) do;
        (* Enter critical activity here. *)
        stalled[i] := FALSE;
```

Mutual Exclusion Using A Software Switch

Semaphores

The **semaphore** is one of a collection of specialized data structures developed for use in synchronization. The semaphore is shared among the competing/cooperating processes and is encapsulated in a module that hides its implementation from the user. Actually, the module is implemented within the operating system and includes the variable semaphore value, the procedures that manipulate it, and a waiting queue. Semaphore solutions to enforcing mutual exclusion avoid busy waiting on the part of application processes by blocking any process in a waiting queue.

Each semaphore is managed by the operating system. To users, a semaphore S is a variable manipulated by the three primitive operations **Init, P,** and **V.** Each of the three operations generates an operating system call, with no direct access to S for the user. Init(S,V) is a request to initialize S to the value V, usually a positive integer and often V = 1.

P and V are atomic operations used to achieve synchronization. A process issues the instruction P(S) *before beginning* the critical activity protected by S. P(S) checks to see if S is positive: If S is positive, S is *decremented* by one and the process continues execution. Otherwise, the process enters the wait queue managed for S and sleeps (that is, the process is blocked). The instruction V(S), used by a process *exiting* the critical activity, *releases* a sleeping process from the wait queue if the queue is nonempty. Otherwise, V(S) causes the value of S to be *incremented* by one.

This example of semaphore use is quite simple, but in most real settings, several semaphores are required. The applications programmer is responsible for the orderly use of the P and V instructions. The exercises at the end of this chapter illustrate more complex applications.

Monitors

The **monitor** is a language-based data structure that enforces mutual exclusion by its design, rather than relying on the applications programmer's skill. The monitor is designed so that only one process may be active within it at any time. Synchronization is conceptually simple: To execute a critical section of code or acquire a resource, place access to the critical section or resource inside the monitor. The process must first gain access to the monitor and then request access to the critical section or resource. The programmer's only responsibility is to request entrance to that monitor managing the critical item; the monitor created by the language compiler does the rest.

Encapsulated with the monitor are an initializing routine, local variables, two kinds of waiting queues, and all procedures for manipulating the local variables. Access to any monitor variable is achieved through calls to its **entry procedures.** Each monitor has a waiting queue associated with entry; processes making a call to an entry procedure when the monitor is already occupied will be placed in the queue. Processes sleep while in the queue (no busy waiting). When a process exits the monitor, one process from the waiting queue is permitted to continue with its entry procedure.

A process active inside a monitor can encounter a condition that temporarily blocks it. For each condition that might block the process, there is a monitor variable of type **condition.** A condition variable allows the process to check for the blocking condition through a **wait** instruction. The atomic wait instruction blocks the process (that is, places the process in an associated **condition queue** where it sleeps until released by a **signal**) or allows it to continue execution. Since a process in a condition queue is

Figure 8.17

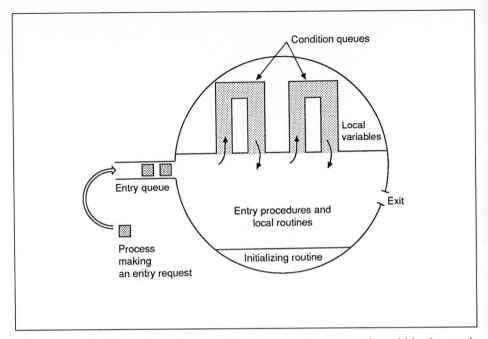

inactive, the blocking action allows another process to become active within the monitor. Figure 8.17 shows the general nature of a monitor with two condition queues.

Monitors are easy to use, but few languages have a monitor type available. (Ada and Modula-2 include a monitor type in their structure.) Some feel that the way monitors enforce mutual exclusion is too restrictive for general applications requiring synchronization without full-time mutual exclusion. (However, it has been shown that monitors can be used to implement the "more flexible" semaphores and locks.) On the other hand, semaphores can be used by compilers to implement monitors where the language does not make them available.

Other Tools   Message passing, as mentioned earlier, is used for distributed systems. However, the technique can be used effectively with shared memory systems as well (for example, to establish mailboxes, ports, or other depositories for messages).

In addition, research has revealed many data structures that can be used to achieve synchronization and mutual exclusion. Some of these structures are *critical region*, *conditional critical region*, *sequencers*, *serializers*, *path expressions*, and *invariant expressions*. (Further information on this subject can be found in the resources listed in the Bibliography.)

Deadlock   Recall from Chapter 5 that **deadlock** (waiting for an event that cannot occur) is an issue related to synchronization and resource sharing. Deadlock is possible whenever concurrent activity exists. Four conditions must be present if deadlock is to occur:

- **mutual exclusion** (a maximum of one process may use the resource at any given time)
- **hold-and-wait** (a process may hold allocated resources while awaiting assignment of others)

- **no preemption** (no resource may be forcibly removed from a process)
- **circular wait** (there is a circular chain of processes, each holding at least one resource needed by the next process in the chain, as in Figure 8.18)

There are several techniques for dealing with deadlock (also known as a **deadly embrace**): deadlock prevention, deadlock avoidance, and deadlock recovery.

Figure 8.18

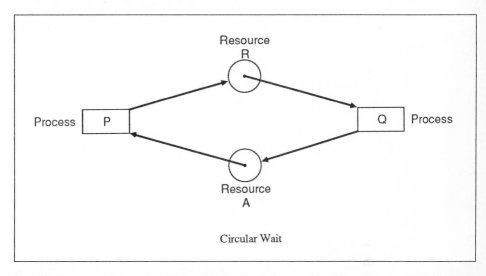

Circular Wait

Deadlock Prevention

Deadlock prevention strategies make deadlock impossible. To guarantee that deadlock cannot happen, a system "simply" prohibits one or more of the four necessary conditions for deadlock. Generally, mutual exclusion is *not* the condition prevented, since most resources do require access by only a single process at a time.

Hold-and-wait. The simplest means of prohibiting the hold-and-wait condition is to **serialize** resource use, that is, allow a process to hold (have allocated) at most one shared resource at a time. To gain a new resource, the process must first release the held resource. While this is simple, it is too restrictive to be favored by most systems.

Another relatively simple solution to the hold-and-wait problem requires that each process declare all resource needs at the time of creation. Execution is not begun until all resources are assigned. When the resources are assigned, each resource is held until execution is complete or until the resource is no longer needed; therefore, no executing process is blocked because it lacks resources. However, holding resources in this manner is a form of static resource allocation that prevents use by other processes of assigned-but-idle resources. Inefficient resource use is likely to occur. Thus dynamic resource sharing is a preferable solution.

A variant for breaking the hold-and-wait condition is to allow processes to begin execution *without having all resources allocated in advance*. This executing process requests resources as need arises. However, any time a resource request cannot be met, the process must release all resources being held (a form of forced preemption). To resume, the process makes requests to reacquire the released resources in addition to those in the unmet request. Note that the overhead for this approach can be high, with process starvation theoretically possible. A variation of this approach requires a waiting process to give up a held resource *only if it is required* by another process. Thus, only released resources must be reacquired. In this case, the overhead is still high and starvation still possible.

Preemption.   In breaking the hold-and-wait condition, the resources of blocked processes are preempted. Such preemption not only makes it more difficult for a process to restart, but it also leads to added expense as the process may need to be rolled back to an earlier point in its execution with some actions restarted. Preempting a resource from a running process in order to assign it to another (probably of higher priority) is seldom used due to the guaranteed heavy overhead cost for rolling back and restarting the interrupted process. (Preemption of the CPU for multitasking and time-sliced multiuser systems is the best known exception.)

Circular wait.   The circular wait condition can be prevented by an allocation scheme known as *hierarchical resource allocation.* The resource hierarchy consists of a number of levels, each resource in the system being assigned to a level. Processes are then constrained in the way they may request resources: At any time, process P may request resource R only *if every resource held by P lies in some level below that of R* (see Figure 8.19). If P holds a resource A with level higher than that of R, A must be released, R acquired, and then A reacquired. IBM's flagship operating system MVS uses a variant of this hierarchical resource allocation scheme.

Earlier, Figure 8.18 gave a simple example of a **resource allocation graph** with a circular wait condition. Process P is requesting resource R, which is assigned to process Q. Process Q is requesting resource A which is assigned to process P. Deadlock exists if neither can continue without having its request met.

To show that hierarchical resource allocation prevents circular wait, suppose hierarchical resource allocation leads to the condition in Figure 8.18. Since P is holding A and requesting R, A's level is *lower* than R's. However, Q's request for A means that A's level is *higher* than R's. Both conditions *cannot* be true; therefore, circular wait and hierarchical resource allocation cannot coexist.

Figure 8.19

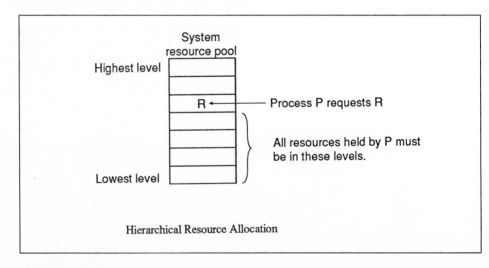

Hierarchical Resource Allocation

Deadlock Avoidance

Deadlock avoidance allows all four conditions for deadlock to exist. Avoidance is, rather, a resource allocation policy that "looks ahead" and fills a request only if doing so is "safe" (that is, deadlock will not result). *To look ahead requires that all resource needs for a process be known in advance of execution.* The algorithms for doing this (such as the Banker's Algorithm) add dramatically to system overhead.

Banker's algorithm. The **Banker's Algorithm** looks like the following:

Suppose process P makes a request for resources. Assume that the request is made, adjust the resource pool accordingly, and perform the following analysis:

S:
- If there are no uncompleted processes, the situation is *safe*. Otherwise, continue.
- If there is an unfinished process but the slack (unallocated) resources are not sufficient to complete any unfinished process, the situation is *unsafe*. Otherwise, continue.
- Pick a process P that can be completed with the current slack resources and mark P as completed; return P's held resources to the pool.
- Reenter at S: above and continue.

Eventually, a safe or unsafe verdict is determined. If the verdict is safe, the allocation may be made. Otherwise, the process should be blocked and the allocation withheld until it is safe.

Figure 8.20 shows a system with four processes and three resources, some allocated and some not. The current allocations and slack resource columns indicate that the system has 9 instances of resource R1, 3 instances of R2, and 6 instances of R3. Suppose P2 makes a request for a single R1 and a single R3. Should the request be made?

Figure 8.20

	Maximum Requirement			Current Allocation			Current Slack Resources		
	R1	R2	R3	R1	R2	R3	R1	R2	R3
P_1	3	2	2	1	0	0	1	1	2
P_2	6	1	3	5	1	1			
P_3	3	1	4	2	1	1			
P_4	4	2	2	0	0	2			

Figure 8.21

	Maximum Requirement			Current Allocation			Current Slack Resources		
	R1	R2	R3	R1	R2	R3	R1	R2	R3
P_1	3	2	2	1	0	0	0	1	1
P_2	6	1	3	6	1	2			
P_3	3	1	4	2	1	1			
P_4	4	2	2	0	0	2			

Figure 8.22

	Maximum Requirement			Current Allocation			Current Slack Resources		
	R1	R2	R3	R1	R2	R3	R1	R2	R3
P_1	3	2	2	1	0	0	6	2	3
P_3	3	1	4	2	1	1			
P_4	4	2	2	0	0	2			

Figure 8.23

	Maximum Requirement			Current Allocation			Current Slack Resources		
	R1	R2	R3	R1	R2	R3	R1	R2	R3
P_3	3	1	4	2	1	1	7	2	3
P_4	4	2	2	0	0	2			

Figure 8.24

	Maximum Requirement			Current Allocation			Current Slack Resources		
	R1	R2	R3	R1	R2	R3	R1	R2	R3
P_4	4	2	2	0	0	2	9	3	4

If the request were made, the resource situation would be as in Figure 8.21 with four unfinished processes. Can any of the four be completed with the meager slack resources? That is, can the *difference* between the maximum requirement and current allocation be met from the resource pool *for any process?* Certainly not for P1, as there are not enough of any resource. However, by assigning one R3 from the pool to P2, P2 would have its maximum resource requirement met and could finish. Assume that is accomplished and the resources of P2 returned, as pictured in Figure 8.22. Can any of P1, P3, and P4 be completed? Yes, each *can* be completed. Completing P1 produces Figure 8.23. Following with P3 gives Figure 8.24 and finally, finishing P4 returns all resources to the pool with no unfinished processes remaining. The condition is *safe*, so go ahead and make the allocation requested by P2.

Now return to Figure 8.20 and start all over again. Suppose P1, rather than P2, makes the request for one instance of each of R1 and R3. Should that request be granted? Figure 8.25 shows the state if this request were granted. Now observe that

Figure 8.25

	Maximum Requirement			Current Allocation			Current Slack Resources		
	R1	R2	R3	R1	R2	R3	R1	R2	R3
P_1	3	2	2	2	0	1	0	1	1
P_2	6	1	3	5	1	1			
P_3	3	1	4	2	1	1			
P_4	4	2	2	0	0	2			

none of the four processes can be completed (each needs an R1 but the pool has none). The system would be deadlocked (assuming resources are not preempted or voluntarily relinquished); the state is *unsafe.* Thus the allocation to P1 should not be made.

Deadlock Detection

A third way of handling deadlock is the "not to worry" approach. This technique uses **deadlock detection/recovery** mechanisms. The plan looks easy: Let processing go on until such a time as deadlock occurs. When deadlock happens, the operating system picks a **victim** process and stops its execution (**kill** or **roll-back**). The resources of the victim are assigned to one or more waiting processes, allowing them to continue. Of course, it is possible that *more than one process* will have to be killed or rolled back in order to break the deadlock and continue processing others. When feasible, the operating system will restart the victim(s). However, some operating systems are so primitive in these matters that operator intervention is required. The difficult part is detecting deadlock when it occurs.

If processes have their total resources declared before execution starts, deadlock detection can look like part of the Banker's Algorithm:

S:
- If there are no uncompleted processes, the situation is *safe.* Otherwise, continue.
- If there is an unfinished process but the slack (unallocated) resources are not sufficient to complete any unfinished process, the situation is *unsafe.* Otherwise, continue.
- Pick a process P that can be completed with the current slack resources and mark P as completed; return P's held resources to the pool.
- Reenter at S: above and continue.

An unsafe verdict implies that *deadlock is imminent:* Even though processing may be continuing, no process will be able to finish.

This process, however, looks at total system deadlock. There may also exist deadlocks of processes within the system, even though the entire system is not currently in danger of deadlocking. An alternative method of detecting deadlocks (one not requiring foreknowledge of total resource needs) uses **resource allocation graphs** such as seen in Figure 8.18. Cycles (parts of the graph where starting at point P and "following the

Figure 8.26

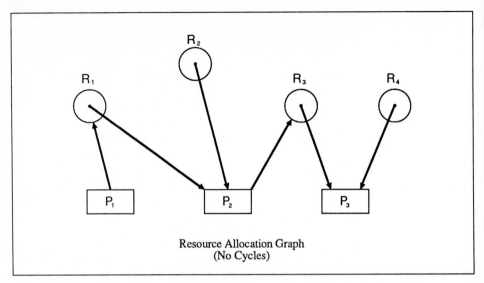

Resource Allocation Graph
(No Cycles)

arrows" returns to point P) in the graph indicate either deadlock or the potential for it. In Figure 8.26, there is no deadlock, while Figure 8.27 contains at least one cycle.

Operating systems that maintain resource allocation graphs can study them to detect cycles and deadlock, but managing and studying these graphs creates quite a bit of overhead. System designers must determine whether the resource allocation graph will be updated and checked *continuously* (expensive but most responsive) or *periodically* (less expensive and less responsive). Some designers consider both approaches to be too expensive and thus only update and check graphs *when one or more processes has been inactive for an extended period.* (This is also an effective way to deal with indefinite postponement or starvation.)

Deadlock detection in distributed systems is even more difficult. A decision must be made as to whether each local system is to maintain its own resource allocation

Figure 8.27

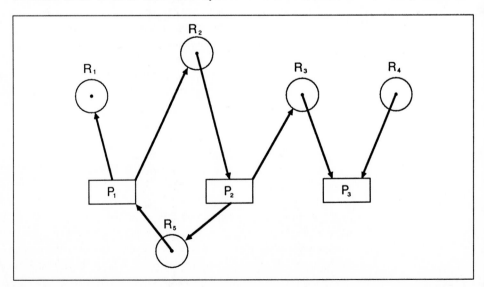

graph. If so, how does one generate a picture of the resource allocation condition for the entire network? This can be done but it is a difficult proposition. An alternative is to have the graph for the entire system maintained centrally.

Distributed systems have yet another problem worth discussing: Because of the physical separation between processors, there is generally no common system clock available. Each local system maintains its own physical clock, with system time measured as **virtual time.**

Common Synchronization Problems

In addition to the problem of producers and consumers given in Chapter 5, several other synchronization problems can be used to illustrate the difficulties in dealing with deadlock, indefinite postponement, and general synchronization of resources among processes. Each of these problems has a number of solutions using the various tools available. (The purpose here is to show the nature of the problem, so note that no solutions are given.)

Readers and Writers Problem

The Readers and Writers Problem (introduced in [5]) confronts two kinds of processes (readers/writers) attempting to use a common resource. Since writers alter the resource (a memory cell, a disk file, and so on), no process may use the resource concurrently with a writer. Multiple readers may have concurrent access, however. The problem is to coordinate access for the many readers and writers without allowing deadlock or starvation.

Giving priority to either readers or writers could cause indefinite postponement of the lower priority group. Hoare [8] suggested the following: Readers' requests are queued (placed on hold) behind a waiting writer, but after the waiting writer has completed, waiting readers have top priority. His solution uses a monitor with entry procedures that might be named *request_read, request_write, done_reading,* and *done_writing.*

Dining Philosophers Problem

The Dining Philosophers Problem (described in [7]) assumes that five philosophers (processes) are seated at a round table as in Figure 8.34. Five forks (resources) are distributed as shown; each philosopher alternates between eating and thinking. In order to eat, a philosopher must have possession of two forks, the fork on his or her immediate left and the one on the immediate right.

The problem is to synchronize the philosophers' acquisition of the forks to prevent deadlock (possible if each philosopher has one) and indefinite starvation. A number of solutions have been given, including the use of semaphores and of monitors.

Smokers Problem

The (Cigarette) Smokers Problem was introduced in [12] and, like the Readers and Writers Problem, involves two kinds of processes. Unlike that problem, there are three different classes of resources. To make and smoke a cigarette requires that a smoker have possession of three ingredients: tobacco, paper, and a match. Each of *three smokers* has two ingredients in ample supply (one lacks tobacco, one paper, and one matches). Each smoker has a continual desire to make and smoke a cigarette. The *one agent* process has an infinite supply of all three. The agent process places one ingredient on a table and signals the smokers. When the appropriate smoker completes the

Figure 8.28

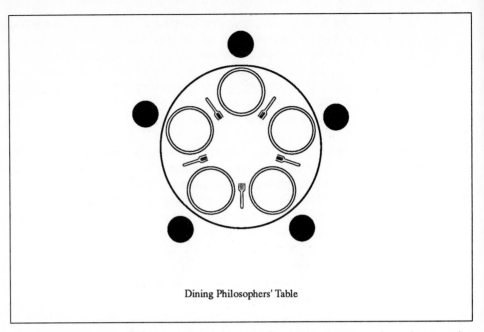

Dining Philosophers' Table

making and smoking activity, he or she signals the agent; the agent then places an ingredient on the table, and the infinite loop starts over. The coordination of the smokers and agent to avoid indefinite postponement has several known solutions, including the use of semaphores and monitors.

Sleepy Barber Problem

The Sleepy Barber Problem, like the Dining Philosophers Problem comes from Dijkstra and is found in [5]. In this case, processes play the role of customers who need a haircut, while the resource may be considered a process performing an activity (cutting the hair).

The barber's shop consists of a fixed number of chairs in a waiting room and a separate room holding the barber chair. The barber sleeps when no customers are present. An entering customer acts in the following manner:

- If all chairs are full, the customer leaves.
- Otherwise, if the barber is busy, the customer takes a chair.
- Otherwise, the customer wakes up the barber and sits in the barber chair for a haircut.

The goal is to write a program to synchronize the actions of the barber and the customers.

Exercises

1. Engineers seem to be able to continue to develop more powerful CPUs. Why, then, are multiprocessor systems attractive?
2. What are at least three significant questions to ask about any tightly coupled multiple processor system?
3. From an operating system point of view, give at least three fundamental choices that must be made in developing a distributed multiple processor system.
4. Suppose a UNIX system is given the following *pipeline* of instructions:

   Instr_1 | Instr_2 | Instr_3

   (The output of Instr_1 becomes the input to Instr_2, whose output becomes the input to Instr_3.) In UNIX the three instructions will operate concurrently. If the system is a multiprocessor system capable of assigning each instruction to its own CPU and if each instruction requires N milliseconds of CPU time, what range of execution times would you expect for the pipeline?
5. In Exercise 4, it is possible for the pipeline's elapsed time on a three processor system to be *less than* one-third the elapsed time on a uniprocessor system. How do you think that can be?
6. Write a fork/join solution for Figure 8.10.
7. Write a fork/join solution for Figure 8.29.
8. Write a cobegin/coend solution for Figure 8.12 using a single semaphore. Figure 8.30 shows a partitioning of the diagram showing some parallelism. An arrow crossing the vertical partition dictates the need for a semaphore: A2/A4 can be done in parallel with A3/A5 if A3 signals its completion by a V call and A4 waits on a P call.
9. Use a single semaphore in a cobegin/coend solution to Figure 8.29. Use the discussion from Exercise 8 as a guide.

Figure 8.29

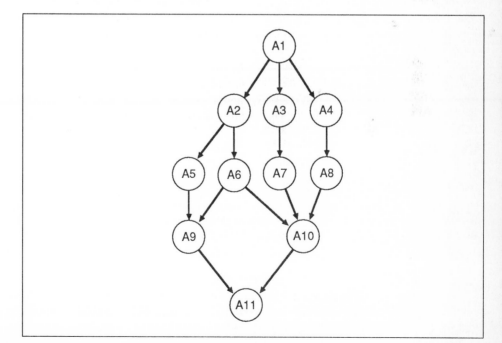

Figure 8.30

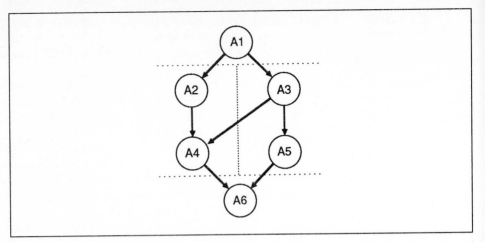

10. Describe how starvation is possible in the concurrent execution of the code in Figure 8.15.
11. In Figure 8.31, *Busy[]* is a shared variable with *Busy[i]* initialized to *FALSE* for i = 1,2. Describe how two processes can violate mutual exclusion (for the critical section) while executing the code concurrently. (Hint: Where must the interrupts occur and what must be true at that time?)

Figure 8.31

```
         Code for Process i

         While Busy[(i+1) MOD 2] do;
         Busy[i]  :=TRUE;
         (* Enter the critical section here. *)
         Busy[i] := FALSE;
```

12. In Figure 8.32, *Ready[]* is a shared variable with *Ready[i]* initialized to *FALSE* for i = 1,2. Describe how two processes can deadlock while each is trying to execute the code concurrently. (Hint: Where is each process interrupted?)

Figure 8.32

```
         Code for Process i

         Ready[i]  :=TRUE;
         WHILE Ready[(i+1) MOD 2] do;
         (* Enter the critical section here. *)
         Ready[i] := FALSE;
```

13. Redo the Peterson algorithm to handle three cooperating processes.
14. Why is static resource allocation inefficient for multitasking (particularly multi-user) systems?

Figure 8.33

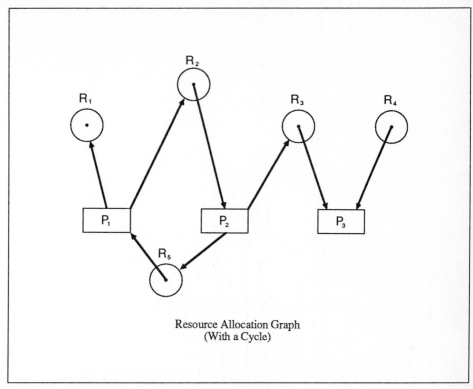

Resource Allocation Graph
(With a Cycle)

15. Compare/contrast the three general approaches to dealing with deadlock.
16. Suppose the resource allocation graph of Figure 8.33 shows the state of a system using a hierarchical resource allocation scheme. What can be said about the relative levels of the various resources? What cannot be said?
17. Is the current state in Figure 8.34 safe or unsafe? Does deadlock appear imminent?

Figure 8.34

	Maximum Requirement	Current Allocation	Current Slack Resources
	R1	R1	R1
P_1	5	1	2
P_2	6	1	
P_3	1	0	
P_4	5	1	
P_5	3	1	

Figure 8.35

	Maximum Requirement	Current Allocation	Current Slack Resources
	R1	R1	R1
P_1	5	1	4
P_2	6	1	
P_3	1	0	
P_4	5	1	
P_5	3	1	

18. In Figure 8.35, can three instances of resource R1 be safely allocated to P4?
19. Is the current state in Figure 8.36 safe or unsafe?
20. Can one instance of each of R1, R2, and R3 be safely allocated to P2 in Figure 8.36?

Figure 8.36

	Maximum Requirement			Current Allocation			Current Slack Resources		
	R1	R2	R3	R1	R2	R3	R1	R2	R3
P_1	3	2	3	1	0	0	1	2	3
P_2	6	3	3	4	1	2			
P_3	3	1	4	2	1	1			
P_4	4	2	2	0	0	2			

21. Figure 8.37 shows a bubble chart for an arithmetic calculation. What is that calculation? Write cobegin/coend pseudocode for this calculation.
22. Draw a bubble diagram to show the sequential and parallel constructs inherent in the calculation of
$$(a + f) ** (d + e) / (5 * b * c - 7)$$
Then write a cobegin/coend solution. (See Exercise 21 for background information.)
23. Suppose *SV* is a shared variable and each of two processes has the following code segment (*TV* is local to each):
$$TV := SV;$$
$$TV := TV + 1;$$
$$SV := TV;$$
If the two execute concurrently, each executing the code five times, what range of values may SV have at the end?

Figure 8.37

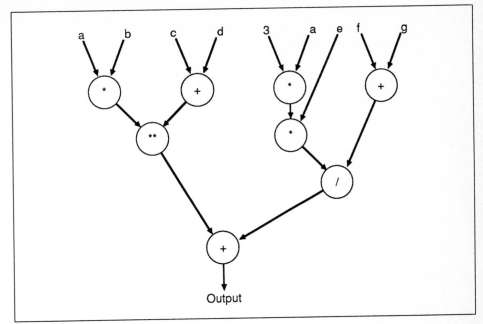

24. Why is transparency of commands so important in a distributed system of computers?
25. In a layered distributed operating system, describe the implications of placing the communications above the scheduler memory manager and device drivers but below the file handler.
26. What import does the buffering capacity of a mailbox have?
27. In a message passing system where messages exist in pairs (transmitted *message* and returned *acknowledgment*), what problems may occur if the *acknowledgment* is lost?
28. Write a semaphore-based solution to each of the following:
    a. Producers and Consumers Problem
    b. Readers and Writers Problem
    c. Dining Philosophers Problem
    d. Smokers Problem
    e. Sleepy Barber Problem
29. Redo Exercise 28 using a monitor solution.

9 Networking and Communications

Networking is not a new area of concern to the computer industry. Quite early on the concept of a **remote job entry (RJE)** station allowed batch jobs to be submitted from remote sites. Early time-sharing systems were networks of terminals used to share the resources of a single CPU among a number of interactive users at several locations. When the number of peripherals became too large for a single room, they were relocated and networked to the mainframe. In each of these cases, however, a single CPU controlled all computing. Today, a network is most often taken to mean a set of two or more *computers* interconnected by some communication medium.

The networking of computers has been growing in popularity, particularly with the development of local area networks (**LANs**). The maturing of personal computers and intelligent workstations generated that interest and nurtured the desire to use multiple computers in synergistic ways. Some networks of computers are interconnected through one or more controlling computers. Other networks (**peer networks**) consist of autonomous machines having equal rank and priority with no one machine acting as the network server/controller. Resources may also be centralized and managed by a **server** (for example, a file server), or they may be distributed throughout the network. Some networks even consist of groups of interconnected networks.

Many networks are constructed as alternatives to time-sharing systems. Rather than sharing the CPU and memory of a single large system, networks are designed for sharing peripherals that may be scattered about, data that may be centralized or scattered about, and even computational loads. These (generally peer) networks allow any CPU in the system to communicate with any other CPU.

While a PC on every desk solves the problem of getting computing capability in the hands of more people in organizations, standalone islands of computing power have proved limiting even if there are many islands. For example, the sharing of programs and data are difficult for standalone computer users. Thus came the evolution of networking, with its major intent being to get data *and* computing power out in the workplace where it is under the control of those most likely to use it. Much distributed computing done at workstations is for personal service and support, rather than what might be called transaction data processing. As power, versatility, and accessibility increase, new uses will be found. Some of these visionary uses will certainly require enhancement of the tool, which in turn will lead to new expectations—a cycle of growth.

Even now, discussions concerning diskless workstations are creating new attitudes about networking. With the very large RAM sizes common in today's personal computers and workstations, some are predicting that workstation processing will consist of loading data from a file server, processing that data as required, and returning output back to the file server. Accordingly, there will be no need for massive local secondary storage. If data security is important, not having a diskette or other removable secondary storage device at a workstation makes it difficult for anyone to remove classified information.

However, networking involves more than meets the eye. Even though a communication medium connects two computer systems, that does not mean that the systems will understand each other. These systems are liable to be different mechanically, electrically, and logically, so **protocols** (sets of rules) for interaction are required.

When two users are connected for network computing, the time period of the connection is called a **session.** Each session consists of **messages** that are transmitted between users. A message is a variable length logical entity that has significance in the mind of the user. Normally the hardware is concerned with the physical signals to be transmitted. Data transmitted is often placed by the network software and hardware into bit patterns called **frames** or **packets.** While it is transparent to the user, a message may be divided into several packets for transmission and then reassembled at the destination. Alternatively, several messages may be blocked together into a packet, transmitted, and subdivided back into the original messages at the destination.

Networks establish communication paths between users. How a particular route is chosen for moving a package of data from the source to the destination is a major topic of concern. (With deregulation, even the routing of telephone calls can be of interest because of the various rates charged by different carriers. Intelligent phone systems route calls to accomplish minimal cost.) In some systems, the same route between a given pair of users will always be used, while in others each session can use a different route. In fact, some networks dynamically alter the routes from packet to packet during a single session.

The transmission media for a network may be of two different types. **Baseband** signaling transmits a stream of bits and utilizes the full capacity of the physical path for each data item transmitted. **Broadband** signaling uses radio frequencies to transmit several streams of data simultaneously over a single physical carrier. Broadband carriers can send baseband data, voice, and video data simultaneously. The transmitters and receivers make broadband signaling more complex and expensive than baseband— and also more flexible. Broadband carriers are sometimes used as bridges between networks.

Purposes for Computer Networks

Generally speaking, there are three purposes for creating computer networks: for remote logon, resource sharing, and distributed computation.

Remote Logon   The purpose for remote logon systems is to provide access to computing facilities that are not local to the site. The model is that of a large, centralized time-sharing computer system with any number of peripheral data terminal devices.

Remote Job Entry (RJE) workstations offer one example: Batch jobs are forwarded from a remote site to the central system site, processed, and then returned to the RJE site. Such an arrangement makes the full batch processing capability of the system available at geographically remote sites. A typical application involves retail chain stores with little or no local computing power. Each store collects its transaction data during the day, week, or month and forms a batch job. During some period of light loading (late night or weekend), the batch job is forwarded to the chain's central computer for processing.

Online data bases offered as a commercial service give an interactive example of remote logon communication systems. The **bulletin board** offers a relatively new use of remote logon systems. Computer conferencing and electronic mail are also emerging as very important uses of these kinds of systems.

The major characteristic of remote logon systems has been the inability to use the intelligence of the device hooked to the remote end of the communication channel. PCs and intelligent workstations essentially act as terminals accessing the resources and power of the mainframe. Data and file transfer are the most complex communication operations generally available. Peer communications between active users is generally supported poorly (if at all). Figure 9.1 shows an IBM 3270 network of this variety.

Figure 9.1

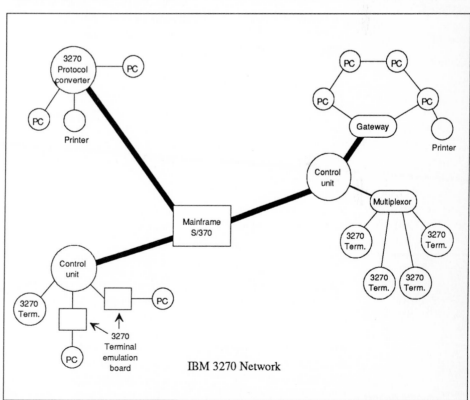

IBM 3270 Network

Resource
Sharing

Networks of workstations or other standalone computer systems are often created for the purpose of resource sharing. (Remote logon systems and time-sharing systems do permit resource sharing, but CPU sharing is the main interest.) The shared resources for multiple computer networks tend to be databases, libraries of programs, and peripheral equipment that is too expensive to duplicate for every station. Resource sharing networks are not normally time-sharing systems but are, in fact, often deliberately chosen as alternatives to these systems.

In resource sharing networks, the CPU and memory are not shared as primary resources as in time-sharing systems. Each local computer will likely have data and programs not available to others on the network; thus the problems of fairness common to time-sharing systems are minimized for these networks. However, because resources are being shared, priority setting and access control are concerns just as with any time-sharing system.

Distributed
Computation

Distributed computation can come in various forms, even a form as simple as **load sharing**, in which tasks required at one site are shipped over the network to another station for processing. In effect, the second computer's CPU is borrowed to perform a job for the first. Work that is the normal responsibility of a disabled processor may *migrate* to some other functioning machine. In this case, the network is being used to improve the reliability of the standalone systems.

Distributed computation can be as complex as parallel processing where, in effect, the network is used as a multiprocessing (multiple CPU) computer. In such cases, a job at one site may be partitioned into several subtasks to be distributed for processing (as in the compilation of a massive system of programs). Eventually, this kind of computer network will become the norm.

A variant of this idea allows a single user at one workstation to designate tasks to be done at other workstations. The user may invoke several workstations to perform a massive compilation, one to direct a DBMS activity, and another to perform an extensive spreadsheet calculation. At the same time, the user's own workstation manages two data transfer communication sessions with mainframes, while the user works with a CAD (Computer Assisted Design) package to update an engineering drawing.

**Types of
Operating
Systems for
Networks**

Chapter 8 explored the two general types of operating systems used to manage networks: **network operating systems** and **distributed operating systems**. As you may recall, the differences were quite pronounced.

Network
Operating
Systems

A **network operating system** allows each station to run a local operating system native to its hardware. The network operating system itself sits on top of the local operating system and runs as an application program interfacing to the network.

Such an arrangement allows existing local application programs to continue to run unaltered. The network may be created from a variety of different systems, since homogeneity is not required. However, this flexibility has its price: A user at one site does local processing on a familiar system and remote processing with an entirely different and unfamiliar system. Confusion (or at least, reduced productivity) is a natural consequence. The portable operating system UNIX is often found as the underlying host operating system, particularly for engineering and manufacturing applications due to its ability to span a wide variety of disparate machines.

Distributed
Operating
Systems

Distributed operating systems present the other choice. A **distributed operating system** is the resident operating system at every site, with every station in the network using the same operating system. Thus, local and remote processing take place on "look alike" systems. However, application programs existing prior to installation of the distributed operating system cannot be expected to run without significant alteration. Therefore, the cost of conversion to a distributed operating system can be much higher than that for network operating systems.

Note that distributed operating systems often require that all nodes have essentially the same hardware. There are a few operating systems that can function as either a network operating system or as a distributed operating system; that is, they can run on top of native operating systems or replace them.

Topologies

The stations (CPUs, servers, printers, and so on) in a network are called **nodes**. Nodes may be physically and logically interconnected in a variety of patterns called **topologies**. Two general categories of network topologies are **multiple drop** and **point-to-point**.

Multiple Drop
Topologies

Multiple drop topologies are sometimes known as **broadcast** topologies, since messages sent from one node are transmitted almost simultaneously to every other node. The visual image of a radio transmitter sending simultaneous signals to all radio receivers is a fitting parallel. No node may block the signal (message) from reaching another node, nor is an intermediate node required to relay a message from one node to another. Figure 9.2 illustrates three broadcast topologies: the **linear bus, the ring bus,** and the **star network.**

Figure 9.2

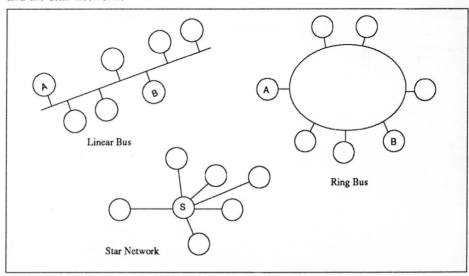

Linear Bus

Ring Bus

Star Network

The two bus topologies have no central machine to control the network (an advantage). All the nodes are directly connected to a single pathway that carries all communications. The communications do not "pass through" any node but arrive at every node. Since only one node can transmit on the bus at a time, competition for the right to transmit over the single pathway is a primary concern and a limiting factor on the amount of communication that can take place. The bus itself limits the nodes to being geographically close. A break (failure) on the bus may cause the entire network to fail.

The star topology has one machine (see Figure 9.2) whose welfare affects the entire network (a disadvantage). If the central controller node (Node S in the figure), malfunctions, the entire network becomes inoperative. The star does give central network control; the hub node may also manage the network file system. Since there is no contention for the pathways in a star, the volume of communication may be higher than with the bus topologies. Moreover, if one link or a (noncontroller) node fails, the remaining links and nodes are still operative.

The star is different from the bus topologies in that any two noncontroller nodes must communicate through the controller. For this reason, and since the controller node could transmit over a single path to one node only, some do not consider the star a true broadcast topology. However, it is common for the physically wired star to function electronically and logically as a bus.

The use of satellites or other transmitting devices as the communicating medium naturally generates multiple drop topologies, although they may also be used in point-to-point systems such as the **interconnected star** of Figure 9.3.

Figure 9.3

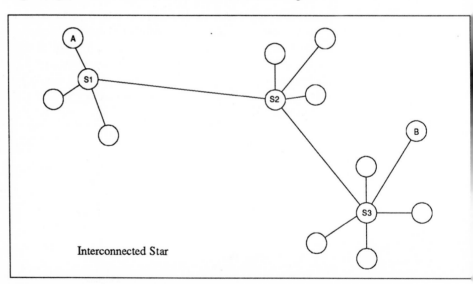

Interconnected Star

Point-to-point Topologies

Point-to-point topologies are quite different from the multiple drop versions, particularly in the physical nature of the interconnections. Point-to-point topologies may send messages between two nodes over a physical **link** directly connecting the two, or messages may be sent over pathways made up of several links. In Figure 9.3, for instance, Node A and Node S1 are connected by a link, but Node A is connected to Node B by a pathway of four links (A to S1, S1 to S2, S2 to S3, and S3 to B).

Figure 9.4 shows several kinds of point-to-point topologies. **A fully connected topology** is one in which the network media directly connect every pair of nodes: Each node has a direct link to every other node. Paths other than direct links also exist. In the fully connected network of Figure 9.4, Node A can send a message directly to Node B or over any of several multiple link paths. For instance, A could send the message to D, which retransmits it to E, which in turn transmits the package to B. This use of paths is known as **store-and-forward** communication, since each node must examine the message to know how to forward it. The existence of multiple paths implies that the failure of any given link or node may cause relatively little slowing of network service.

Figure 9.4

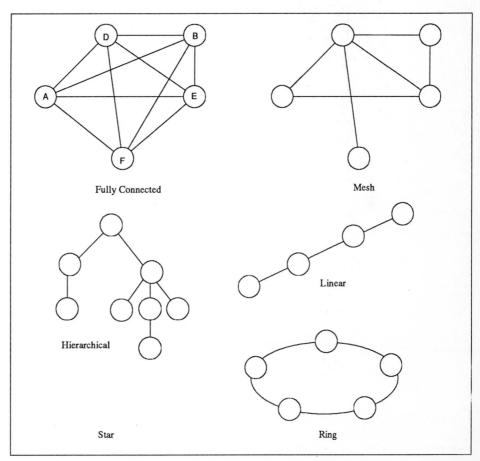

Fully Connected

Mesh

Hierarchical

Linear

Star

Ring

The **mesh** (partially connected) **topology** does not directly link every pair of nodes. Some pairs of nodes may communicate only through one or more intermediate nodes via the store-and-forward mechanism. The same is true for the other variants shown in Figure 9.4.

For communication to take place between Nodes A and B in a network using point-to-point topology and store-and-forward communication, there must be at least one **circuit** (set of links forming a path) between the two nodes. (Note that the terms circuit, path, and route can be used interchangeably.) The originating node sends a package of data over a link to an intermediate node that captures the data (stores it), examines the address and network information included in the package, and then forwards the package over the designated link to a next node in the path on the way to the destination. This is repeated until the destination node receives the data.

For networks that span a geographical region measured in miles, hundreds of miles, or thousands of miles (known as **medium haul** or **long haul** networks), a collection of interconnected, locally clustered systems may be used. A typical pattern is to use one of the topologies from Figures 9.2 or 9.4 at each location and interconnect them via phone lines, microwave links, satellite links, and so on. (See the interconnected star of Figure 9.3.) Each local cluster may represent a different network operating under its own protocol. If different protocols are used for the various clusters, a **gateway (protocol converter)** must be employed to perform the internetwork conversion required (Figure 9.5).

Figure 9.5

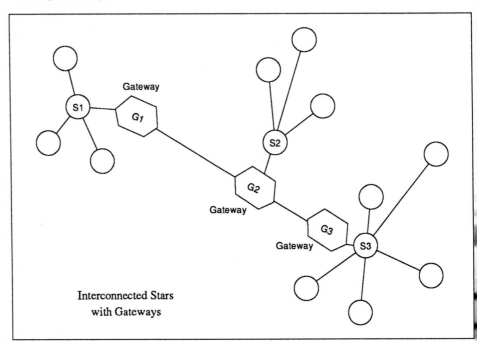

Interconnected Stars
with Gateways

Transmission Media

The medium used to move messages/data from one node to another determines, to a great extent, the maximum link length, the rate of transmission, and the cost of installation. The maximum separation of nodes may be measured in meters, kilometers, or thousands of kilometers. The data transfer rate is usually measured in thousands, hundreds of thousands, or millions of bits per second (**bps**).

Links are also categorized as **simplex** (one-way traffic only) or **duplex** (bidirectional traffic). A duplexed link may be **half duplex**, in which transmission may take place in either direction, but in only one direction at a time—that is, only one node may transmit a message at a time. In **full duplex** links, however, both nodes may transmit at the same time.

Twisted Pair Cable **Twisted pair cable** consists of two wires twisted together to form one link between nodes. The cable may be shielded to isolate electromagnetic interference. It is the simplest and cheapest means of connecting closely positioned nodes.

Where shielding is not required, ordinary telephone wire can be used; if a building is wired for telephone service, that wiring can be used for some networking purposes. Cables holding several twisted pairs can make installation simpler. However, the length of any given link is usually measured in a very few hundred meters. **Repeaters** may be used to amplify signals and connect two segments to increase the geographical span, as in Figure 9.6.

Figure 9.6

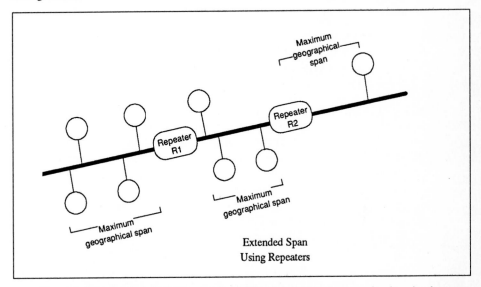

Extended Span
Using Repeaters

The maximum transmission rate over twisted pairs has been quite low in the past, but recent advances have pushed the maximum rate to over 10 million bps (10 Mbps). These features (short geographical span, lower transmission rates, low cost, ease of installation) are making twisted pair cable the popular standard for **departmental computing.** For networks confined to a single floor of a building, for instance, the telephone-wire twisted pair cable is often used.

Coaxial Cable **Coaxial cable** consists of a single conductor surrounded by a nonconducting material, which is in turn covered by a mesh-like conductor acting as a shield from electromagnetic interference. While coaxial cable is more expensive than twisted pair and is limited to short geographical spans, its maximum data transfer rate can be 20 times as great as for twisted pair cable.

There is a **thin coax** that is used for shorter spans of two or three hundred meters, a **thick coax** with a span of over 1000 meters without repeaters, and a **CATV coax** with very high transfer rates. The cost increases from thin to thick to CATV coax. As with twisted pair cable, repeaters can be used to extend the geographical span. Coaxial cable is quite popular for installations that span several floors of a building. In general, coax is used for larger networks (in geographical span and number of nodes) than twisted pair cable.

Fiber Optic Cable

Fiber optic (optical fiber) cable promises to be a popular transmission media in the future. Optical fiber cables are smaller and lighter than twisted pair cables and coaxial cables. Fiber optic cables can service links up to tens of kilometers in length with very high data transmission rates (as much as 400 times the transfer rate for a twisted pair).

Fiber optic cable tends to be more secure than twisted pair or coaxial cable, since it creates no electromagnetic signal and is not easily tapped. Its costs are currently higher than the others but those costs are declining rapidly. Fiber optic cable is growing in popularity for networks that span greater geographical areas and encompass more than one building.

Lasers

Lasers are used in some fiber optic systems to generate the light-based bit stream of data. In state-of-the-art systems, lasers are being used as line-of-sight transmitting devices where the use of cables is inconvenient or impossible.

Phone Lines

For some applications, telephone lines offer suitable transmission of bit streams. The data may be transported as a digital signal over more expensive, dedicated **digital quality** lines or as an analog signal over ordinary **voice quality** phone lines.

Modems are devices that translate digital signals to analog, and vice versa. Modem is short for **modulate** (digital to analog translation by modulating a carrier signal) and **demodulate** (translation from modulated carrier signal to digital bit pattern). Technological advances have increased the rates of data transmission from a few hundred bps to more than 90,000 bps in just a few years. Modems are often used for intermittent connection to remote databases, bulletin boards, and time-sharing systems, but they may also be dedicated, permanent parts of a computer network.

Note that phone lines offer one reasonable means of interconnecting small local networks into larger systems spanning great geographical regions.

Microwave/ Satellite Transmission

Ground-based microwave transmission of signals is a type of line-of-sight transmission. Microwave, therefore, can be used to interconnect individual nodes of a point-to-point network or local networks within a larger system. Microwave transmission is particularly useful for medium and long haul networks where distances make cable impossible or unattractive. Much movement of telephone signals is, in fact, accomplished by microwave transmission.

Like ground-based microwave, satellite transmission of signals is a radio transmission. Satellites, however, cover a fixed portion (typically thirty percent) of the earth's surface. This huge coverage holds whether the satellite is acting as a receiver or as a transmitter. The satellite is, in fact, a high-flying relay device that accepts a signal from any point within its "footprint" and relays that signal to *all* points within the same footprint. See Figure 9.7.

Satellites have very large capacities in terms of the number of channels of communication they control. The distance between the originator of a message and the recipient of that message has no bearing on the cost of transmission. Therefore, any two nodes within the footprint may participate in a broadcast topology network, regardless of the distance between them.

Figure 9.7

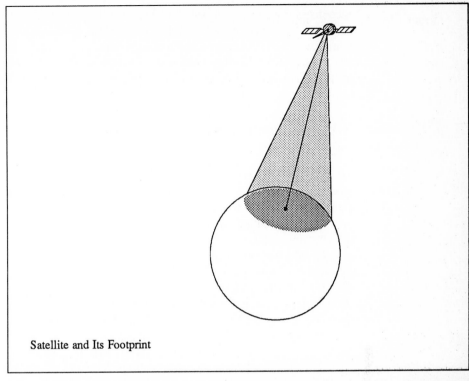

Satellite and Its Footprint

Routing and Switching

The network's responsibility is to get each package of data successfully routed from the source node to the destination. In many point-to-point networks, there will be more than one available route between two given nodes. The network must, then, select some particular path. Three methods of routing are generally used.

Fixed Routing

With **fixed routing,** the path between any pair of nodes is prespecified. Communication between the two nodes *always takes place over the same path,* unless there is a failure of some link or intermediate node along the designated path.

If the network is busy, one or more links in a required path may not be available. Thus contention for network services is a particular concern for fixed routing, since sessions will be delayed while the nodes wait for the prescribed route to become available. The problem is compounded because users transmit messages only over a very small percentage of their "connect" time; that is, a dedicated circuit lies idle much of the time even when assigned. On the plus side, messages do arrive at the destination node in the same order in which they were sent, making message processing relatively uncomplicated.

Virtual Circuit Routing

In **virtual circuit routing,** a path between the communicating pair of nodes is chosen *at the time the session is established.* The path is then used for the entire session. The next session between the same two nodes may use a different virtual circuit.

Virtual circuits tend to adapt to loading conditions better than fixed routes. Since the network has a choice of routes for transmitting the session, the likelihood of encountering waits is lessened. Still, the virtual circuit is dedicated to a single pair of nodes for the entire session, and the circuit lies idle when users are not actually transmitting. As with fixed routes, the messages for a session arrive in the order of transmission. The network hardware and software must be able to examine network activity in order to find and select an available circuit. The overhead is higher than with fixed routing.

Dynamic
Routing

If **dynamic routing** is used for communication between two nodes, the route chosen may *vary with each package of data* sent during the session. The established communication path is valid for sending one package of data only. Each transmission of a new package of data invokes the circuit selection process. While the same path may be used more than once, the choice is made individually for the packages of data being exchanged.

Dynamic routing adapts best to loading conditions, since a route is dedicated for only the time it takes to forward one package of data. The theory is that the shorter the time for which a circuit is established, the less idle time the links incur and the greater the number of transmissions that can take place. However, since different routes may be used for different packages, the messages can arrive at the destination in a far different order than they were sent. Not only must the network make more routing decisions, it must help piece packages together into comprehensible messages.

A package of data may represent a complete individual message, several messages, or only a partial message. Dynamic routing uses **message switching** if each package of data represents an entire message. While messages are logical units of communication that generally vary in length, most networks transmit fixed-length units of data known as **frames** or **packets** (Figure 9.8). A long message may be broken into several packets with each packet sent individually; or messages shorter than a packet may be combined or blocked into a single packet. In cases where routes are established for *individual packets* rather than messages, the dynamic routing is said to use **packet switching.** Fixed routing and virtual circuit routing are said to use **circuit switching.** Note that message switching and packet switching incur more overhead than circuit switching.

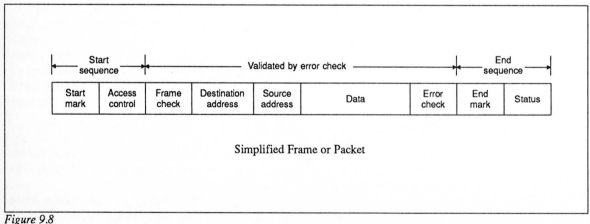

Simplified Frame or Packet

Figure 9.8

Protocols

A **protocol** is simply an agreement on how things will be done—a set of rules. For computer networks, protocols describe how communication between users will take place, how communication between a system and a user will occur, how one node will be permitted to access data from another node, how data will flow from one node to another, how one node may utilize the CPU from another node for purposes of distributed computation, and how the resources of the network will be allocated and synchronized. A number of common protocols exist and have received varying degrees of acceptance. Several representative protocols are discussed in the following sections.

ISO/OSI Layered Protocol

One proposed standard for a network protocol comes from the **International Standards Organization (ISO)**. The proposal is called the **Open Systems Interconnection (OSI)** protocol and represents a layered approach to design. In a layered design, each layer represents some level of abstraction and may communicate only with those layers that are contiguous. Figure 9.9 illustrates the ISO/OSI model.

Figure 9.9

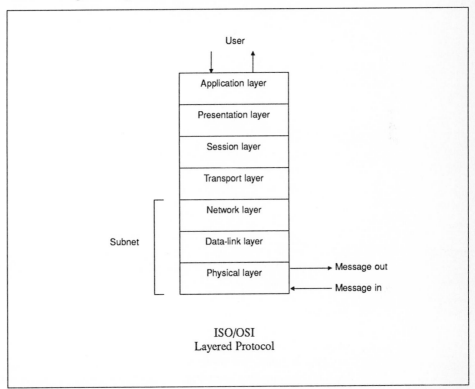

ISO/OSI
Layered Protocol

Each of the seven layers is relatively independent from the others, and each layer has its own function to perform. A well defined interface between adjacent layers allows this independence. Such a design technique permits the implementation of any particular layer to be altered without having any effect on the others, so long as the interface is maintained.

The bottom three layers (physical, data-link, network) comprise the **subnet**, which is conceptually a part of the network rather than a part of the node's computer system.

Figure 9.10

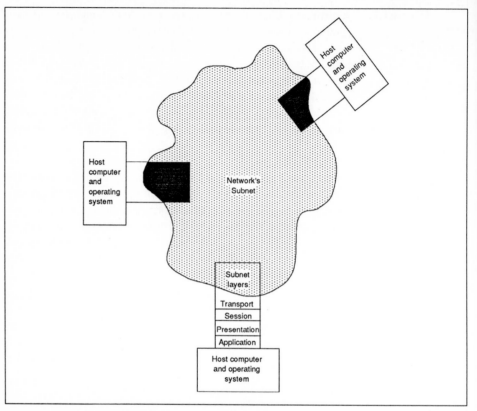

However, the subnet will usually be implemented as an application program at the local site. Figure 9.10 offers one picture describing this arrangement.

Physical layer.   The **physical layer** interfaces to the physical network link. It is responsible for sending the bits that make up the message. In particular, this layer manages the physical connections between the communicating nodes and creates the form of the signal transmitted.

Data-link layer.   The **data-link layer** attempts to make the physical link look error free; that is, each layer above the data-link layer may assume that the package of data received is exactly the same as the package of data sent.

Before sending a package of data, the data-link layer will append some error-checking information (as in Figure 9.8). Conversely, when receiving a package of data, the data-link layer will examine the error-checking information to validate the received package. **Flow control** is an additional factor in presenting the error-free picture: The data-link layer insures that senders and receivers are synchronized so that receivers are able to keep up with senders and do, in fact, receive all information sent.

In preparing a package of data, the data-link layer may encrypt the *address information* identifying the sender and receiver. The purpose is to thwart **traffic analysis—** the act of trying to determine information based only on knowledge of the identity of the sender and receiver.

Network layer. The **network layer** has knowledge about the network that permits it to establish routes or circuits for transmitting the package of data to the destination node. This layer has the responsibility for dealing with congestion in the network. It also controls the user interface to the network. All layers above the network layer belong to the host computer system physically and conceptually.

Transport layer. The transport layer interfaces the host machine to the network and transforms the user's messages into frames or packets where appropriate. Because communication is usually sent in several parts and not in one burst, there may be problems. As mentioned earlier, if dynamic routing allows each packet to be routed over a different circuit (a process known as **datagram service**), it is possible that the arrival order for frames differs from the transmission order. The transport layer must sort out the correct order and identify frames that are never received and require retransmission. It must also deal with frames that are received more than once. While the data-link layer provides error-free *frames* (physical data transmission) for layers above it, the transport layer provides error-free *messages* for the layers above.

Session layer. The **session layer** manages the user-to-user connection. It negotiates the beginning of a session between two users (remote logon, for example), maintains that connection during the communication session, and terminates the session when it is over (logout).

Some network activities, while they consist of several operations or instructions, must appear as **atomic events** (events that must not be interrupted once begun). Suppose the destination node is asked to do a database update requiring several instructions. Performing any of those instructions without completing *all* of them will corrupt the database contents. Because individual instructions might be lost or garbled and split among several packets, the receiving node must collect and assemble the instructions without performing any until all have been correctly reassembled. To identify atomic events, the sender's session layer **brackets** the instruction set by marking the first and last instructions with starting and ending brackets respectively. The session layer of the receiving node senses the opening bracket, holds all subsequent operations until the closing bracket is found, and then and only then performs the entire set of instructions.

Presentation layer. The **presentation layer** performs data compression, data compaction, and data encryption (remember that the data-link layer did *address* encryption). In short, the layer performs data formatting. Other formatting activities involve the reconciliation of data among differing file systems and databases, differing computers, and differing languages.

The presentation layer also bridges the gap between the **virtual terminal protocol** required by the network and the physical terminal actually used by the host. It is this layer that goes a long way toward making the use of the network relatively transparent to the user.

Application layer. The **application layer** contains the network's application programs. It is here that one expects to find a network operating system or distributed operating system, distributed database components, and distributed computational facilities.

Systems Network Architecture

IBM's **Systems Network Architecture** (SNA) differs somewhat from the ISO/OSI model, but it is another layered architecture. Its popularity is growing, at least partially because of the level of IBM's equipment and influence. SNA is not a standard in the same sense as the ISO/OSI model, which is a standard hammered out by an international cast of players. Yet SNA is becoming a defacto standard, since it is used for distributed data processing by many owners of IBM hardware. SNA is intended to be IBM's evolving and expanding answer to all networking needs for their customers and is moving toward compatibility with the ISO/OSI model.

The layers of SNA are seen in Figure 9.11. NAU refers to Network Addressable Unit, which may be thought of as being the node device. FMD is the Function Manager layer.

Figure 9.11

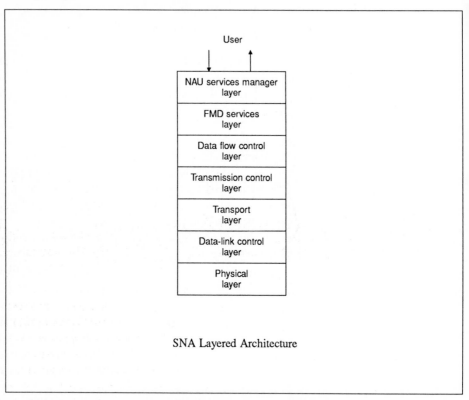

SNA Layered Architecture

As with the ISO/OSI model, the bottom three layers manage most network affairs, while the upper layers primarily manage host activities and needs. The two models do not correspond precisely layer-for-layer but they are similar.

SNA does not use the packet concept (network layer), but its path control layer does do segmentation and blocking of messages. To use SNA in a packet-switching network, added equipment using the X.25 packet interfacing standard (see following sections) is employed.

Digital
Network
Architecture

Digital Equipment Corporation's **Digital Network Architecture (DNA)** is DEC's layered architecture for networking. Figure 9.12 illustrates the six-layered approach taken in this case. As with the ISO/OSI and SNA models, each layer has a very specific function to perform.

Figure 9.12

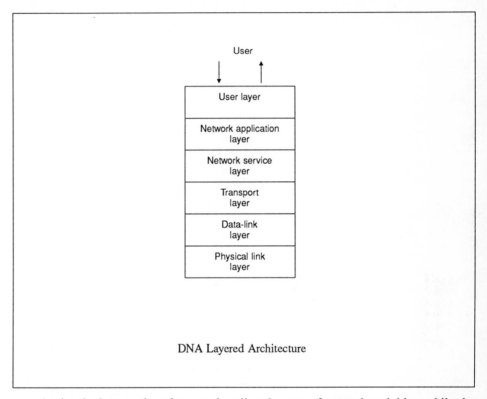

DNA Layered Architecture

Again, the bottom three layers primarily take care of network activities, while the upper layers cooperate to achieve essentially the same functions as the upper four layers in the ISO/OSI model. DEC is moving DNA toward compatibility with the ISO/OSI model.

X.25 Protocol

What has become known as the **X.25 protocol** is actually a collection of standards that has grown up since the mid-1970s. It was the brainchild of the **Consultative Committee for International Telegraphy and Telephony (CCITT)** and was intended to create standards for interfacing to networks. The X.25 standard is not a complete layered architecture and should not be considered in the same context as the layered models described earlier. It is, however, a three-layered design, including a physical layer, a data-link layer, and a top layer.

The committee's work, as intended, gave life to packet-switched public information networks by establishing standard formats for packets and procedures for their use. The packet interface is used to implement the network layer of the ISO/OSI model. The major drawback to the X.25 protocol has been its use of virtual circuit switching rather than dynamic routing.

Contention Handling

In a network where all nodes have equal rights and equal access, **contention** for a particular route will occur as a natural consequence of use. Generally an idle link is used on a first-come, first-served basis. Simultaneous transmission on a link is possible, particularly with heavy network loading. The likelihood of contention is highest for bus topologies and rings where everyone must use the same media segment for all transmission and communication.

A standard control mechanism for contention simply involves listening to see if data is being transmitted. If so, the data is captured, stored, and the destination address checked. If the address is that of another node, the captured message is discarded in broadcast topologies and forwarded for point-to-point. Otherwise, the message is processed. If no data is currently being transmitted, then transmission may be attempted.

Even at that point, there is a potential for the collision of messages. Two nodes may try to transmit on a silent link simultaneously. The result is an intermixing of the two individual transmissions with distortion to each. Nodes must be able to detect collisions and deal with them according to some predetermined scheme. The alternative is to develop a means whereby no collisions occur.

Collision Control by Detection/ Retransmission

One listen-and-wait scheme for dealing with collisions is simple: When a collision occurs, each transmitting node simply waits a *random* amount of time and tries to retransmit. The mechanism is quite common and is called **Carrier Sense Multiple Access/Collision Detection (CSMA/CD)**. Carrier sensing refers to the act of listening for and finding the carrier signal (free link) or a modulated signal (occupied link). Since CSMA/CD expects collisions to occur, it is a contention protocol that determines how collisions will be detected and corrected.

Note that the random waits for contending nodes tend to be different lengths, and one node will gain use of the link first. Under very heavy loading, such **try-wait-try** schemes may lead to seriously degraded service. CSMA/CD is most often used with a bus network having lighter loading and relatively short average data transfers. In contrast to this collision detection scheme, the techniques that are described in the following sections are more accurately characterized as **collision avoidance**, rather than collision detection.

Time Slots

One easily implemented contention avoidance scheme is the use of **time slots**; it is similar to timesharing on a computer except that transmission time on the network media, rather than CPU time, is being shared. Each node has a time slot in which to transmit, and the time slots are managed in a round-robin manner. Collisions are not a problem, but time slots often go unused much of the time, thereby wasting valuable link capacity.

Token Passing

Token passing offers an attractive alternative for networks, particularly those that are physical ring networks or other topologies **logically managed** as rings. That is, the network does not have to be a physical ring but may be one in which the protocol requires messages to be transmitted from one node to another until all nodes have traversed in a

Figure 9.13

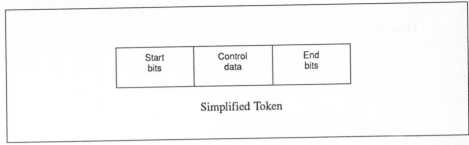

Start bits	Control data	End bits

Simplified Token

ring pattern. A special message called a **token** (Figure 9.13) is passed from one node to another.

A node wishing to transmit a message waits until the token (a special, nondata message) arrives, captures the token, sends whatever messages it wishes, and then restarts (retransmits) the token. The token systematically offers each node a "turn" that it may use or pass up. Token-passing rings are, in effect, store-and-forward mechanisms with a (perhaps logical) point-to-point topology.

Physical or logical rings using token passing are called **token rings.** The primary problem that must be considered is how to detect and replace a lost token. Much overhead and complexity is involved in initializing a ring and restarting tokens. However, token-passing rings can be quite fault tolerant in the face of broken links and failing nodes. They are valued where reliability, heavy loading, and high-volume average data transfers are the rule.

Message Slots

A variation on the token-passing scheme for rings uses **message slots,** which are fixed-length messages having a space into which data may be placed. The network has a collection of these slots that are transmitted around the ring from node to node. When a message slot arrives at a node, the node examines the slot to see if it contains a message or is empty. If the slot is empty, the node may insert a message and send the slot on to the next node, or it may forward the empty slot.

If an arriving slot contains a message and is addressed to this node, the node withdraws the message. The slot is now empty, and the node has the choice of inserting a message before forwarding the slot. If the packet is addressed to another node, the message slot is forwarded immediately. Collisions don't occur, but there is a great deal of store-and-forward activity.

Local Area Networks

Local Area Networks (LANs) are comprised of a set of geographically close nodes often consisting of a mixed bag of personal computers and/or workstations. While minicomputers are sometimes used as LAN controllers, LANs often involve no mini- or mainframe machine. In fact, the growth in networking reflects a tendency to shift away from mainframe-centered computing. When a mainframe is involved, it is typical to find individual LANs connected to it via gateways.

In a kind of arrogance, some users of LANs connected to mainframes consider the mainframe a wonderful peripheral to their PC or workstation. The ability to use great amounts of the mainframe's secondary storage (perhaps as a virtual floppy disk), to execute mainframe library routines as calls from programs running on their PC, and to accomplish remote execution of mainframe programs is attractive. In addition, mainframe data backup and security measures usually far outstrip those of the workstation and enhance local processing.

LANs are currently popular as an alternative to a large time-sharing system and generally involve peer-to-peer communication rather than the slave-to-host communication characteristic of mainframe timesharing (and IBM's SNA protocol). Since the sharing of data and peripheral devices are usual goals, LANs are frequently implemented in an office setting. The use of LANs for connecting engineering workstations, however, has caused some of the more dramatic advances in LAN technology.

The (linear) bus and ring are the most popular logical and physical topologies for LANs, with CSMA/CD and token-passing access methods employed most often. Linking small departmental LANs together into larger networks (as in Figure 9.14) by the use of bridges (gateways or repeaters) is a rapidly growing phenomenon. Most LANs are created to allow direct peer-to-peer communication among machines of equal priority and standing. The development of relatively low-cost, powerful, 32-bit workstations having high-quality graphic capabilities, at least 4 Mbytes of main memory, and 80 Mbytes of local secondary storage has fueled the growth of LANs. The interLAN link system is often called a **backbone.**

Figure 9.14

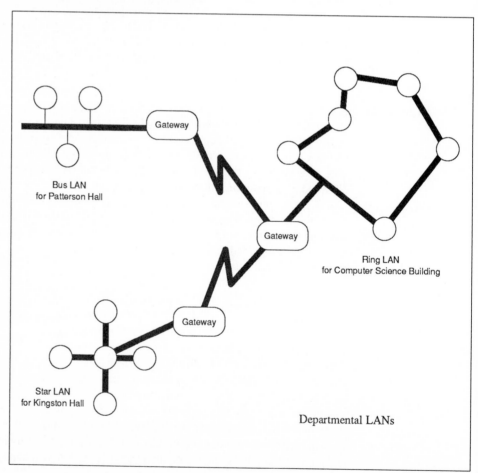

As with every network, the selection of LAN equipment involves choices for geographical span, transmission rates, cabling, topology, contention handling, and number and types of nodes. Most current LANs use baseband signaling. A number of IEEE LAN standards attempt to mesh LAN protocols with the lower two layers of the ISO/OSI model (Figure 9.9), so that general network software can be built as layers on top of the LAN software.

EtherNet EtherNet, designed by Xerox, has been one of the favorite LAN systems; it dates back to the 1970s. This system is a CSMA/CD device with rates of transmission (under light loading) in excess of 10 Mbps. EtherNet uses a multiple drop coaxial bus for the most part, although some twisted pair and fiber optic implementations exist. Messages are sent in packets of EtherNet design. There is no need for a central controller, but each workstation must be outfitted with a hardware device (transceiver) to prepare, transmit, and receive the packets. The transceiver typically takes the form of a board inserted into a workstation expansion slot or a "black box" positioned between the bus and workstation (Figure 9.15). EtherNet is a **baseband** system, because it places the data signal directly onto the cable and the entire capacity of the link is utilized for each transmission of data. Note, however, that baseband transmission can be implemented as a single channel of a broadband medium.

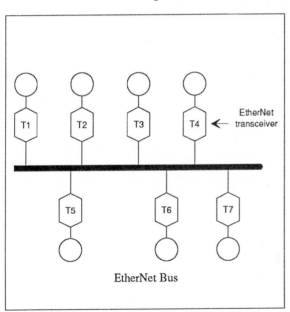

EtherNet Bus

Figure 9.15

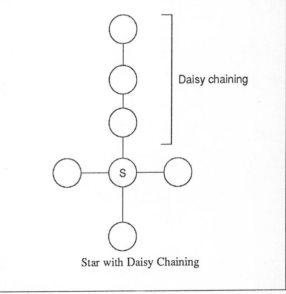

Daisy chaining

Star with Daisy Chaining

Figure 9.16

StarLAN For small LANs (geographically and in number of nodes), AT&T's StarLAN has been popular. StarLAN is physically wired into a star (or interconnected star) by twisted pair cable. Logically and electronically, StarLAN is a bus using the CSMA/CD access method at a relatively slow 1 Mbps. The physical topology can deviate from the star pattern by the use of **daisy chaining** (serial extension), as shown in Figure 9.16. Most StarLan installations hold 10 or fewer nodes with a geographical span of 200 meters or less. Like most commercial networking systems, these capacities can be extended by the equivalent of repeaters and interconnected star patterns. The low transmission rate, however, does not allow large numbers of nodes to participate effectively.

MAP and ARCnet

MAP (Manufacturing Automation Protocol), developed through General Motors and ARCnet (a liaison among several manufacturers) are made up of **token bus** LANs. The logical topology is that of a token (passing) ring. MAP uses a bus over which the token is passed from node to node in a logical ring order (Figure 9.17). This bus is generally some form of coaxial cable with transmission rates of up to 15 Mbps. Broadband versions of MAP can be found.

Figure 9.17

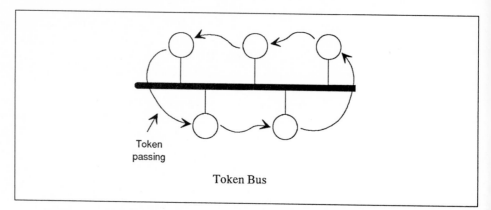

Token passing

Token Bus

ARCnet uses a form of interconnected star for the bus topology whose cabling is coax. Transmission rates extend beyond 2 Mbps, while the geometric span can extend to several thousand meters under the appropriate configuration. The hubs of each star are passive or active: Active hubs have characteristics similar to repeaters and extend the geographical span and number of LAN nodes.

Token Rings

A number of computer manufacturers (Prime, Apollo, and IBM among others) have developed token ring LANs. IBM's token ring is interesting in that it is logically a token (passing) ring but physically an interconnected star whose hubs are physically connected as a ring (as in Figure 9.18).

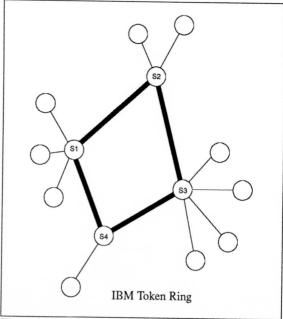

IBM Token Ring

Figure 9.18

Private Branch Exchange | A **Private Branch Exchange (PBX)** scheme may be used to construct a LAN. Unlike the EtherNet scheme, the PBX system is a central controller that routes all "calls" to the appropriate destinations. Data communications are as capable of being routed as are telephone voice communications. Special wires or cables are not needed, since most office buildings are already sufficiently wired for telephone service. Some recent systems allow voice and data to be transmitted simultaneously so that phone lines can serve concurrent purposes.

Broadband | **Broadband** LANs are growing in popularity because they seem to reach into the future. A broadband system sends a carrier signal over a cable (CATV coax typically) like those used by cable television. The cable is able to carry radio signals, television signals, voice, video of various sorts, data signals, and several baseband LAN signals simultaneously. While being more complex and expensive than other systems, broadband does give the capability of managing all the currently important forms of communication with a single integrated system.

Exercises

1. What can networking accomplish for an organization?
2. Describe what is likely meant by the term **virtual conference table** in relation to computer conferencing.
3. Compare long haul networks with LANs. Which is more likely to use a bus topology and why?
4. How do you suspect that each node in a bus network knows which messages belong to it?
5. A node transmits a message. Is it important that the sending node know that the message was received in readable form? If so, how might that knowledge be acquired?
6. How might it be possible for a packet to be received at a node more than once?
7. Long haul networks often use point-to-point topologies. Why might it be sound practice to use an interconnected star rather than some general mesh pattern? Why are bus topologies not a good choice for long haul networks?
8. A pair of nodes have been connected, but communication is impossible: nothing is intelligible. Where is a likely first place to look for a solution to this problem?
9. What is the importance of protocol standards for networks?
10. Compare/contrast collision detection and collision avoidance.
11. In a ring, the use of time slots is sometimes called **decentralized polling.** Why?
12. For a ring, is polling a form of collision detection or avoidance? Explain.
13. In a token ring, it is customary for a node to transmit a message and for the receiving node to mark the message and pass it on. Why? When will the transmitting node likely forward the token?
14. In a **slotted ring,** several packets are circulating simultaneously. A node receiving an empty packet may use it to forward a message. What did the chapter call this scheme?
15. Ring networks were discussed as unidirectional relative to data transmission. What might the pros and cons of bidirectional data transmission be?

16. In a token ring, how might the loss of a token be detected? If a token is lost, someone must recreate it and start it circulating. Think of ways to accomplish this task. Or do a literature search for further answers.

17. In a logical ring, it is possible to detect a nonfunctioning node and reconfigure the logical ring around that node. Think of how this might be accomplished. Or search in literature for possible solutions.

18. Describe how it is possible to have deadlock in a CSMA/CD scheme.

19. Compare/contrast the various topologies in terms of:
    a. cost
    b. reliability
    c. security

20. Describe the merits of layering in a protocol.

21. Examine the literature for information about multiplexor concentrators. What is a communications frontend?

22. A firm is going to install a LAN. Why is it important to have answers to each of the following questions?
    a. How many networks has this vendor installed?
    b. How many and what kinds of nodes can be connected?
    c. What network functions does this system offer?
    d. What do performance statistics look like with various levels of loading?
    e. What other vendors' equipment will interface to this system?
    f. What kinds of cable, what data transfer rates, and what node separations are allowed?

THREE

Management Issues

10 System Management Concerns

The management of a computer system has one major goal: to make all resources available upon demand in order to meet organizational needs. Hardware must run, software must do its job, and data must be complete and accurate. The system must be both reliable and cost effective. But management of a computer system involves much more than just keeping a piece of machinery running with relatively bug-free software. It entails management of the complete information system of the organization. This **information management** normally drives the choice of computer and software.

Information systems development is a field unto itself, although it bears some resemblance to software systems development and hardware systems development. Management of computer systems also involves operational management, where day-to-day concerns include security and control, efficiency, costing, and generally keeping users happy. Somewhere between the *systems development* and *systems operations* comes the *systems evaluation* activities used for both purposes.

Information System Development

Information system development and management follows a cyclic pattern. Figure 10.1 illustrates the cycle: Determine the feasibility of developing a (new) system, determine the users' requirements, list the alternative solutions and choose one as the target solution, design a system around that choice, develop and test the system, and install the system. The dashed lines from the figure indicate that the process does not always immediately move forward from one step to the next, but that cycles exist within the larger picture.

Feasibility

The first step in the information management and development cycle is to determine whether a problem exists with the current information system. Each problem must be identified and *defined* to the satisfaction of the user community.

A feasibility study is undertaken to determine whether to press on with the development of a new system. For example, is it even *possible* to solve the problem (a technological consideration)? If so, is it *cost effective* to solve the problem (an economic consideration) through change? Will change save or generate more money than it costs? Can a solution to the problem be created *in time* to solve the problem? If the answer to each of the above is yes, then management's permission to continue should be sought.

Figure 10.1

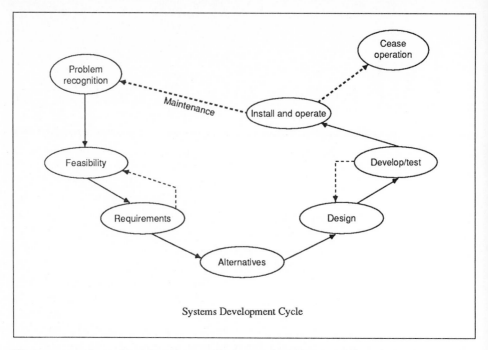

Systems Development Cycle

Requirements

The next step is to document the **requirements** for all users. What kinds of user inter-faces are required? Just exactly what is it that each user will require of the system if the problem is to be solved? What kinds of things must the system do? The accumulation of this information into a single document becomes the basis for all work that follows. It spells out all of the functions the system must perform in order to solve the perceived problem.

The dashed line from the requirements phase back to the feasibility phase (Figure 10.1) indicates a need to return to the initial study, probably because the users are not satisfied with the requirements document. If the users are dissatisfied, the information-gathering phase needs to be returned to and the requirements document rethought. While Figure 10.1 shows only a few instances of "doubling back" to an earlier stage, there may, in fact, be many places where difficulties arise to indicate a need to back up a step or to rethink earlier work.

Choosing a Solution

The next phase involves three separate but related activities. At this point all recognized solutions to the problem must be *developed* (including any possible solution using the existing system). Each solution should specify the hardware and software to be used. However, each solution must also clearly illustrate the *data, personnel, and procedures* that will be needed. Technical people often tend to slight these categories.

Next, each alternative solution is *evaluated*. Generally this evaluation is based on **cost-benefit ratios.** The "payback on investment" drives most decisions at this point if all other matters are relatively equal. While it is possible for subjective issues to be assigned dollar values, you can be sure the real dollars-and-cents issues will be difficult to override. The final step of this phase is to *make the actual choice* among the alternatives, specifying the direction for the rest of the cycle.

Design *Each of hardware, software, data, personnel, and procedures required by the chosen solution must be designed.* To design is to write **specifications.** Specifications communicate what it takes to meet all the requirements using the chosen solution.

The hardware specifications indicate the characteristics a machine must have in order to be considered. The specifications can be delivered to vendors for their use in bidding. That is, vendors submit proposals (with costs) for meeting the specifications with their products.

Hardware acquisitions will almost always be purchased "off the shelf." Seldom is an untried piece of hardware custom designed for use in a business setting. Software specifications, however, can lead down several different paths. Commercially available ("canned") software might be available. On the other hand, specifications often dictate that custom programs be developed to meet the need. Somewhere in the middle is the custom tailoring of canned software.

Of significant concern to an organization are the *changes in operation* required by the specifications for data and procedures. Changing the way business is done can be traumatic and costly. In the simplest case, forms may need alteration to capture different data or to capture the same data in different format. In more dramatic situations, the organization may need to install new operational procedures. Organizations become especially concerned when specifications indicate the need to retrain existing personnel or to change personnel, particularly if the specifications require an increased workforce or a more costly workforce.

Development and Testing When new hardware and software are available, testing can begin. Test data is constructed artificially or from historical data and run on the system. The prospective users must be given a chance to test out the proposed system and procedures. (Actually, users should have the opportunity to try prototypes before the hardware and software are acquired if at all possible.) Training becomes a major factor at this point. (Some training should have been taking place steadily after the "go" decision was made.) When everything is ready, a complete shakedown of the entire system is run. The dashed line of Figure 10.1 shows some possible backtracking from the test stage to the design stage if all does not go well with the tests. Designs don't always work the first time out.

Installation and Operation Once the shakedown, testing, and training are complete, the system may be placed into service. Several installation methods are used in the industry:

- (cold turkey) Switch entirely to the new system
- Run the new system in parallel with the old until everyone is satisfied.
- Run the new system on a partial basis:
  - Install one or two of the new system's procedures at a time until every part is up and running.
  - Install all the procedures at once but in a limited setting.

The last two cases may be described as installing part of the procedures for all the data or all the procedures for part of the data.

The cold turkey method can be the least expensive method since it requires the minimum amount of work. It is dangerous, though, if a thorough shakedown has not been performed. Remaining bugs will affect the organization's data processing in perhaps catastrophic ways. The parallel operation is the safest since it tests the new system under actual conditions without risking devastating errors to the data. It is much more expensive. The piecemeal implementations attempt to compromise on the cost and safety of the cold turkey and parallel operation styles.

Even after the system is installed, the development activity is not finished. **Maintenance** is required to keep the system up and running and make modifications as required. The only time the continuing cycle is broken is when a decision to halt operations is made.

Protection/ Security

Several protection and security issues have been discussed in other chapters but are mentioned here again. With any information system, management must be concerned with the security of its equipment, software, data, and personnel. The goal is to have all resources continually available for use in solving organizational problems and to avoid the misuse of those resources. While equipment and software are occasionally misused, it is data that stands the greatest risk of corruption, destruction, and misuse. Don't overlook the simple fact that one of the best information safety assurance devices is the periodic backup to archive all systems at fixed points in time.

Some Concerns

As mentioned earlier, the physical wellbeing and operation of the equipment and software is a major concern. The mechanisms involved in the protection of equipment (and to a lesser extent, software) primarily deal with natural catastrophe and vandalism.

Software security also focuses on intrusion by unauthorized users of the system and on destructive user errors.

Data security is a more difficult issue. Data may be lost by user error, software error, or by hardware error and failure. Data may be corrupted rather than lost. Corruption may result from errors in data collection, data entry, or data processing. Corruption and loss of data may occur because of error or failure. Data may also be damaged by intent.

The misuse of data, even though data is not lost or corrupted, may have negative consequences for an organization, as in the leaking of confidential data to unauthorized persons. These misuses occur primarily with data that is of a sensitive nature and may lead to embarrassment, loss of competitive edge, and so on.

External Factors

External factors in security and protection deal with "nonexecuting" activities and generally have nothing to do with the actual operation of the hardware and software. They can be subdivided into two classifications: those factors dealing with physical considerations and those dealing with policy or operational matters.

External physical factors. The external physical factors involve such things as fire, flood, and vandalism (that is, natural and man-made disasters). Included in this same category is physical intrusion into the system area. Obvious countermeasures include detection devices such as fire extinguishers and sprinkler or halon systems. Less obvious measures include the acquisition of uninterruptible power supplies and backup copies of system files stored in fireproof locations separate from the system hardware. Physically secure equipment and storage space (that is, locks, etc.) combat intrusion.

Some larger data processing organizations improve their security by locating their operations in an unidentified building and maintaining a low profile.

External operational factors.   Operational concerns include the restriction of authorization for system use. Closely related is the careful choice of system personnel themselves and this general rule: No one person should be the *only* person doing any particular activity, having access to any particular data, or maintaining knowledge of any given process. Each activity, piece of data, and bit of knowledge should involve at least two people. The flip side of this rule is **division of labor:** No one person should be able to perform every activity, have access to every piece of data, and have all knowledge. No sole access and no total access should be permitted.

System reliability has a goal of uninterrupted service. Survivability in the face of hardware or software failure requires that the system continue to be available, functioning properly, and without data corruption. The systems that meet this criteria are said to **degrade gracefully,** which means that failure normally allows continued processing at a reduced level rather than causing total work stoppage. Such systems are generally characterized by **redundancy** of major components. TANDEM Corporation pioneered redundant commercial systems by providing machines with a spare CPU, a spare bus for each bus type, spare peripheral devices of each type, and a spare device driver of each type. Part of the challenge, however, is to design the system so that it can spot difficulty, dynamically switch to a redundant item, and continue processing without missing a beat. This obviously makes the job of the operating system more complex.

Another concern arises from the growth in microcomputer and personal workstation use. Anyone working at a floppy-based workstation has the potential for capturing the system's data and programs on a diskette and walking out the door with them. While standalone micro-based workstations do concentrate computing power where it is needed, they also increase the need and concern for security. In addition, most micro-based systems operating as standalone units have almost no security built into the hardware or software. As the microcomputer industry matures, these issues are being addressed. Some, however, have proposed that diskless workstations will become increasingly popular because of this security concern (and because of the reduced cost).

Internal Factors

Internal factors are those that are carried out by the hardware and software of the system during execution. Authentication (placed in the external category by some) is an attempt to restrict access to the system. A related effort is the restriction of access to programs, data, and other system parts through the use of internal checks. The maintenance of security audits as a means of monitoring users and activities is a part of this picture.

Authentication.   Authentication of the user by means of identification numbers, passwords, or smart cards is an example of controlling access. Of course, technology is offering new means of authentication such as digital signatures, digital keys and locks, fingerprint verification and the scanning of various parts of the body (for example, the eye) for identification. Authentication of individuals is usually based on something the user **has** (such as smart card or key), something the user **knows** (such as identification number, password) or something the user **is** (such as finger, voice, or eye prints).

Monitoring.   An operating system that continually monitors critical activities can be a very useful security component. The concept is relatively simple: Access to any resource (or critical resource) is performed only by the operating system. Each user wishing access must make a request of the operating system, which decides to allow or deny the request. An access matrix, access list, capability list, or locks/keys can be used to make the access decision. In addition, operating systems can easily create an audit or log of these activities as requests are made. Such records are valuable tools in managing the security of system resources.

Encryption.   Data can be protected even when it is physically accessed by unauthorized persons. Data can be encrypted (encoded) in such a way that makes it extremely difficult for an unauthorized person in physical possession of the data to decipher. That makes the misuse and leaking of information hidden in the encrypted data nearly impossible. Of course, one with physical access can corrupt or destroy the data, but interpretation or falsification of the data is a less likely occurrence.

A number of encryption schemes are used—some for data compaction, some for error detection and correction, and some for data security. The most powerful encryption schemes available for data security are known as **public key systems**, involving the use of two numeric keys—one used by the encoder and the other by the decoder. The controller of the system makes the encoding key public knowledge. Any one can encode data or a message. By keeping the decoding key secret, however, the controller is the only one who can decode data. Knowing the public (encoding) key is of no practical value in determining the private (decoding) key (at least until mathematicians figure out how to calculate the decoding key from the encoding key).

The use of encryption gains importance when networking is involved, since data moving through the network is susceptible to interception and alteration by intruders. But there are purely economic reasons for encryption: The time it takes to transmit data is related to the number of bits being transmitted. Encoding data to reduce the number of bits required saves storage space and transmission time. Shorter transmission times allow for increased data flow over the network and, often, reduced transmission costs. Transmitted data is vulnerable to corruption by the system itself during transmission, raising the need to encode for error detection and correction to guarantee error-free movement of data.

System Control

Management concerns extend to control of the resources held and the jobs performed on the system. Uneven loading of the peripheral devices may require alteration to the priority queueing mechanisms or the acquisition of duplicate resources. Excessive paging may require some tuning of the paging parameters or additional main memory. Excessive seek times may signal the need to reorganize file systems or disk packs. Some reorganization and fine tuning requires shutting down the system. Routine maintenance also requires shutting down the system. Shutting down the system interrupts system availability. System startup and shutdown range from very simple user-driven activities to quite elaborate schemes involving specially trained operations people.

Jobs submitted to the system must be initialized, must have resources allocated as needed, and must be terminated appropriately. Resource accounting and costing are part of the resource control activity, as is the logging of information for security purposes.

If the system includes a network, the technical expertise required to keep it running increases. The balance between mainframe, minicomputer, PC, and workstation resources complicates the system design considerations. Transparency of resource use in a network is not automatic but must be planned. There are copyright and other legal questions involved with the distribution of software among multiple users, particularly with microcomputer software.

A sometimes-overlooked requirement of daily operation of a computer or information system is the collection of utilities available to make the users' jobs easier. There is a constant need to stay aware of what utilities are available. In addition, user training for the operating system, application, and utilities represents a necessary ongoing effort (and cost).

Job Control

Early in the history of digital computers, users directly controlled the machine and, hence, were responsible for job setup and teardown, as well as controlling the availability and use of peripherals. That is still fundamentally true of most single-user systems. On large multiuser systems, however, the use of an operator to oversee the transitions from one job to the next has remained firmly entrenched since automated (batch) job sequencing was developed. The need to do job startup, termination, and resource management still hangs over those who do batch processing.

Batch processing precludes interactive job control: Users must specify all needed system commands in advance and in the proper order. Such jobs normally have an identification (number) and are separated from other batch jobs by operating system statements. A job may consist of any number of smaller tasks, each of which must be sequenced and identified. Job setup usually describes any need for compilers, linkers, peripheral devices, and so forth. Systems have a specially created programming language for these purposes. Such languages have historically been called **job control languages (JCL)**, particularly by IBM. JCL programming is an art unto itself.

Most control languages have been modified to include control statements for interactive programming. Of course, interactive job control is simpler, since the user can intervene as needed to indicate the next step and to smooth over any difficulties. A good example of such a control language is Digital Equipment's DEC Control Language (DCL).

System Configuration and Generation

Almost no one simply buys a brand X machine, plugs it in and begins computing. Virtually all systems offer choices; most require the system manager (who may be the user on a small system) to make choices. The amount of main memory is one choice. The amount and kind of secondary storage require a choice. The kinds and numbers of peripheral devices offer choices. Even the number of CPUs and their interconnection may be selected. This is all part of the hardware configuration process.

There are also operating system choices. Each operating system must be configured to match the hardware and choice of peripherals. The operating system likely offers choices to optimize performance for the local job mix: What is the mix of interactive and batch jobs, what is the mix of novice and technical users, and what is the range of applications? Answers to those and other questions lead to the selection of parameters affecting the scheduling mechanism, the level of multiprogramming, the amount of I/O buffering, and other factors.

The operating system for a larger multiuser system normally resides on magnetic tape. Built into the hardware are short ROM routines for **loading** the operating system from tape to main store. **System generation** routines then allow the operator to configure the operating system to fit the peripherals available and the job mix anticipated. Most of the system generation is done by menu and/or parameter selection: The system guides the operator through the setup. System generation aims at maximizing the effectiveness of the organization's investment.

Finally, the operating system initializes itself by establishing the required data structures, validating initial values, and checking the resources. Then and only then is the operating system ready to deal with jobs.

Costing

There are two general perspectives associated with costing: a desire to know what computing activities cost and the need for a process for charging computer services to its users (whether customers of the organization or members of it). If the user is a member of the organization itself, this charge is often called a **chargeback.** Whether the purpose is to create revenue or to identify levels of usage, the primary goal of costing computer services is to insure that computing activities are cost effective in meeting organizational needs.

Whatever the mechanism used, the costing of computer services should be simple enough that every user understands the basis on which charges or chargebacks are made. If no charging mechanism is used, the costing process must give decision makers a clear picture of what organizational computing dollars are accomplishing.

Moreover, the costing mechanism should be able to **reproduce** its values. Users should know that the same activity will incur the same cost each time. Costs for updating a given file system should be roughly the same next week that they were yesterday. Connected with this idea is the desire that the costing scheme should adequately explain the assessments made.

The costing process should be **equitable** to users. Users taking advantage of similar services should receive similar charges. A related notion: Costing should be able to adjust for priority service. If a user wishes better or faster service, the cost should be higher. Similarly, if a user is willing to accept slower service or service during lull periods, lower costs should follow.

Costing can be used in a carrot-and-stick mode. Heavy loading during a certain time period can be managed somewhat by charging higher rates for processing during that time. Likewise, charging quite high rates for scarce resources encourages the use of alternative resources or, at least, diminished use of the critical resource. That is, costing can be adjusted to encourage a better resource usage profile. In effect, these are priority charges.

Resource Use Accounting

Costing is normally tied to resource-use accounting. It does seem reasonable to charge users essentially for the actual computing services delivered. A modification to this attitude would allow the use of some minimal charge based on fixed computing costs incurred by the system: a fixed charge plus a variable cost. The first decision in fixing a costing practice, then, is to determine what kind of resources are fair game for charges.

Time as a resource.   Time is probably the most widely used commodity for figuring charges. The categories of time used are generally the following: **connect time** and **CPU service time.**

Connect time is a timesharing term referring to the length of a terminal session. Charges based on connect time are easy to figure and justify, as a connected terminal uses resources just by being connected (even though no useful computing is being accomplished). The terminal ties up a communications access point so that others may not use it. This probably attracts the attention of the CPU or communication front-end long enough to determine if it needs service. In many systems, a login process is created and run just to manage a terminal, whether or not any useful computing is being accomplished.

CPU time generally carries a cost for users, as the CPU time generates most useful computing and users believe it equitable to pay for. The charge for CPU time is a charge for "real" computing service. Such charges imply that the operating system accurately logs the CPU time associated with each job and/or user.

Main store as a resource.   Charges may be made for mainstore in a large multitasking system, and these charges are generally based on the amount used and, perhaps, the length of time held. In a paged environment, the number of pages used or the number of page faults encountered may be a part of the costing formula. A system manager must remember that any charges of this type require significant overhead for monitoring and logging. A secondary problem with paging can arise: The number of page faults is often as related to the amount of system loading as to the program's own activity. Thus the user may see uneven billing based on circumstances beyond his or her control.

Secondary storage as a resource.   The amount of space allocated to and used by any given individual account in a multiuser system is relatively easy to audit and verify. What is more difficult to monitor is the amount of backing store used for swapping programs during execution. Even more costly to monitor is the number of accesses made to the secondary storage system on behalf of an active user. Each of these may be considered legitimate targets for costing, provided adequate logging is in place.

I/O as a resource.   The use of peripheral devices also carries a cost to the system. Costs for conducting I/O may be based on the type of device, the length of service time for an I/O request, the number of I/O requests, or some combination of these items. Accounting for I/O device usage can be a sophisticated exercise, and accumulation of the needed information is often an extensive undertaking.

Systems programs as a resource.   Most multiuser, multitasking systems have an extensive collection of system programs available. Applications programs may invoke system programs to do searching, sorting, editing, compiling, or linking. Users may take advantage of spreadsheets, wordprocessors, text formatting, and database facilities. Each of these services can be charged to the user.

Other points.   There is usually a miscellaneous category for any costing mechanism. For example, charges may be levied for time spent in consultation with computer personnel—or for paper and paper clips. Generally, it is better to bill for very minor items through a fixed minimum cost or as an overhead percentage based on the user's other charges.

Note that single user microcomputers and intelligent workstations create yet another world in terms of costing. For standalone operation, users may be billed as if they used the full capacity of the machine for the duration of the session (as no one else has simultaneous access). Alternatively, they may be billed for the actual kinds of work done (that is, for the software used). Networked microcomputer users may be billed in a similar way to those in timeshared systems.

Exercises

1. Why should every development/acquisition cycle begin with a definition of the perceived problem(s)?
2. Some say that acquiring a microcomputer system should proceed as in the following pattern: Define the problem, find software to get the job done, and then find hardware to run the software. Comment on this approach.
3. From what you have seen to this point, describe why it is useful to have the users involved in the development cycle.
4. List the potential advantages and disadvantages of choosing canned software as part of a problem's solution.
5. Do Exercise 4 for custom software.
6. Discuss the advantages and disadvantages of installing a new system in parallel with the old during "shakedown."
7. Do Exercise 6 for a "cold turkey" installation where the old system is removed and the new system is on its own from the start.
8. Describe the nature and role of the requirements document.
9. Do Exercise 8 for the system specifications document.
10. Many say that the testing procedure for a new system should be developed at the design phase or earlier. Why not wait until the system has been implemented?
11. Some say the creator of the testing procedure for a new system should have little or nothing to do with the system's design. Why?
12. Many claim that user training should be formulated during the design phase. Why might this be so?
13. Make a list of the kinds of activities/changes that might characterize maintenance as it occurs after installation and before the next development cycle.
14. Describe graceful degradation and its importance to a user or organization.
15. How does redundancy contribute to reliability?
16. What values might an organization attach to user satisfaction? To timeliness?
17. Describe the value of user confidence. List the aspects that contribute to it. Then describe the kinds of things that lower it.
18. Give examples of the kinds of things a user knows that might be useful for authentication.
19. Do Exercise 18 for things a user has.
20. Do Exercise 18 for things a user "is."
21. Why might data falsification be harder to spot than other forms of data corruption?
22. Why might division of labor be considered a security measure?

23. Why might it be good security practice for each part of the system to be accessible by two or more persons?

24. Make a list of ways an organization's hardware and software can be misused. Describe the costs to the organization in each case.

25. Do Exercise 24 for data.

26. Do Exercise 24 for manmade catastrophes. In addition, describe the detection and security devices and techniques that might lower susceptibility to such loss.

27. Discuss the advantages and disadvantages of diskless workstations.

28. How might intelligent workstations increase the possibility for security violations (in comparison with dumb terminal use)?

11 System Evaluation

The computer system or information system exists to serve, and most system managers are concerned with the quality of the service being rendered. They must find ways to measure how well their community of users is being served.

Performance is one key to service. Administrators must consider the efficiency of the system as a resource manager. The hardware, operating system, applications programs, and users must cooperate to the benefit of all. This illustrates the kinds of things that must be monitored and evaluated in order to make judgments about system performance. Most impressions of system performance are based on hardware and operating system evaluation.

Performance evaluation takes place at three different times in the life of a system: **during design** and before construction, after construction but **before acquisition**, and **after acquisition.** Evaluation takes place before system construction in order to predict performance characteristics and capabilities, as measured against the uses for which it was designed. Modeling and simulation are widely used at this point. Evaluation of an existing machine or system is used in the system selection process to answer questions such as: Will this system meet the needs for which it is being acquired? An installed system is monitored to collect data about its current operation and make decisions about its level of efficiency.

Performance evaluation for existing systems may be viewed in terms of three different activities: new system **configuration,** system **reconfiguration,** and system **tuning.** Initial system configuration and reconfiguration have long-term effects and do not occur often. System tuning is a dynamic activity performed relatively often with short-term effects. Initial system configuration and system reconfiguration are rather significant activities involving decisions about CPUs, memory size, and numbers and types of I/O channels and peripherals. Tuning is, by comparison, a minor adjustment to the system involving the alteration of parameters (for example, time slice length, priorities for categories of processes, queue lengths, working set sizes, and so on).

Performance evaluation is grounded in a desire to better serve the organization. Organizational needs compared against system capabilities and performance drive the evaluation. Comparisons are made by the use of **measures** whose values are determined by data acquisition. In the discussion that follows, the term **system** refers to multiuser systems or networks. Performance evaluation for single user machines is not the objective here.

Some Measures

Measures relate to **time, work,** or **rate of occurrence.** While most measures give a single numeric value summarizing information about a particular idea, the **variance** for a measure indicates something of its dynamic nature. Of course, there are some ideas that are difficult to express in terms of numbers (such as how user friendly this system is).

Measures Relating to Time

User concern for the time it takes to do a job relates to the type of job being done. Batch users are concerned with **turnaround time,** the elapsed time from the submission of a job until its return. Interactive users are concerned with **response time,** the time between the issuing of a command and the generation of output in response. For real-time systems, the **reaction time** is the chief issue—the delay between the issuance of a command and the *commencement* of processing. It is clear that reaction times will be shorter than response times, which will in turn be shorter than turnaround times. A reasonable goal is to keep these times as short as other constraints allow.

Variance.   When a single number is attached to one of these measures, it represents an average. To say that the average response time is one second, for example, is not to say that every interactive effort will have a one-second response time. Response times vary between processes and according to system loading. If the variation in response times is too great, however, the system will appear to be unpredictable. Users expect consistently similar response times for similar activities. The **variance** of a measure indicates the **predictability** of the associated event. The variance for each measure should be reasonably low in order to enhance predictability.

Availability.   Another time-related measure is **availability**—the likelihood with which system resources are accessible at any given moment. If a user can't find an open terminal, the system isn't available. If the computer is down because of error, malfunction, or maintenance, it isn't available. If the system makes a simple task difficult, it will not be considered available for such applications. If the likelihood of user error is high, the system will not be considered available.

Reliability.   **Reliability** is an associated idea, since an unreliable system generally has a lower availability rating. Unreliability also generates a lowered degree of user confidence. Lowered confidence portends lowered productivity. Reliability can be measured in terms such as **mean time between failures, mean time to repair,** and **mean number of records lost** with each failure—that is, how often does a failure occur, what is the downtime for a failure, and what information contamination results from failure?

It is clear that each of the **metrics** (measures) discussed above requires data collection through monitoring and auditing devices. In some cases, user-registered complaints may be the source of data. In other cases the operating system may be able to log the needed information.

Measures of Work

System performance may be monitored in terms of the work required and the work performed. **Workload** represents the work requirements for the organization and may include the numbers of jobs, the mix of applications, and the amount of processing time anticipated. **Throughput** is the term most often used to describe the actual work processed by the system. Both workload and throughput may be expressed in terms of units of work per unit of time (number of jobs per hour or per day, for example). **Capacity** refers to the system's maximum theoretical ability to produce work. **Utilization** describes the percentage of the system's capacity being used for meaningful work.

If used correctly, these measures indicate the state of the system. For instance, if workload exceeds capacity, the system can't handle the load. If throughput is lower than capacity, then either the workload is below the system threshold (a safe state) or there may be a **bottleneck** preventing the best system performance. If throughput seems peaked out but utilization is low, system overhead may be eroding the ability to do meaningful work.

Again, data must be collected in order to assess performance, and system tuning is a likely outcome of the process. Occasionally, system reconfiguration may be dictated when the measures present a very bad picture of performance. Very rarely, an evaluation of these figures will dictate the need for a new system.

Measures Relating to Rates

Today, CPU cycles are relatively inexpensive. In most system design and acquisition processes, the admonition is to buy plenty of CPU cycles. The most expensive part of efficient operation has to do with I/O. **I/O waits** and the CPU cycles tied up in their management (such as extra swapping) are often the first place to look when evaluating performance or when trying to find bottlenecks to efficient processing. I/O bottlenecks may indicate the need to add I/O channels and peripherals.

A related measure is the **page fault rate.** High page fault rates may indicate a need to alter some parameters involved with paging or the level of multitasking. If fine tuning doesn't have the desired effect, increased main memory and reconfiguration may be in order.

Keep in mind that inefficient applications software may contribute to both types of problems. There have been many examples where organizations extended the life of an existing system by improving the efficiency of their applications software. Inefficient use of the best system in the world will eventually lead to poor performance.

Performance Measurement

There are two general methods for measuring the performance of a system. The first method involves analyzing data gathered by **monitoring** the system while it runs and works. The data-collecting monitors may be either hardware or software in design. The data collected usually relates to system loading, job distribution, and resource scheduling efficiency. The second technique involves the use of **modeling,** either analytic or by simulation.

Monitoring for Measurement

Monitoring system activity for performance evaluation is common. By nature, data-gathering devices are artificial intrusions into the work being done. A serious concern with any data-gathering device is the kind and amount of error caused by its intrusion.

Monitoring is an overhead-generating activity: the more data collected, the greate. the overhead. Some monitors collect data for an activity every time the activity occurs Some sample the activities on a time-controlled basis. The former give accurate meas ures of the data. The latter generate less overhead but are less accurate, since actua system values must be extrapolated from the sample data.

Software monitors are programs that utilize computer resources to gather dat about normal system activities. Because they are programs, software monitors are rela tively inexpensive to create and quite flexible in the monitoring they may accomplish To function, software monitors must interrupt program execution. Because they utilize the same resources needed by user applications and the operating system's resource management activities, software monitors can impair performance to some degree and worse, introduce error by their intrusion. They are, however, capable of identifying the system activity each program and module generates.

Hardware monitors, while much more costly and much less flexible than soft ware monitors, do not compete for system resources, at least not significantly. Hard ware monitors are sensing devices attached to signal lines. They sense state changes i the CPU, peripheral, or memory unit by measuring electronic pulses in the line. The introduction of error in the monitoring process is lessened when hardware monitor: gather the data. The reduced flexibility is a concern: If the kinds of data being moni tored are changed, significant costs will be incurred. Moreover, hardware monitors can not normally identify individual programs or modules with the activity they cause.

Monitors may also be classed as **real-time (short-term)** or **long-term** monitors Real-time monitors gather data primarily for dynamic tuning of system parameters dur ing operation. Generally, such monitors maintain overviews of system operation an detailed views of parts that are likely targets for dynamic change. Long-term monitor: tend to collect much more data than they display. This data is ordinarily used to create system logs that are useful in nondynamic tuning and system reconfiguration.

In any event, monitors collect huge quantities of data that must be analyzed i meaningful use is to be made of it. Data is collected on job profiles, CPU usage queueing activity, disk activity, paging activity, I/O channel activity, and a hundred o more items. Real-time monitors concentrate on data relating to the current job mix i order to improve immediate performance. Long-term monitors tend to focus on system problems and trends that have long-range implications.

Models

The use of models is an alternative to data gathering during system operation. Model. are quite often used for new or proposed systems where such data gathering is not eas or even possible. There are two general types of modeling: analytic modeling and sim ulation. While models avoid operational data gathering and allow the evaluation o nonexistent or nonavailable systems, models are not as accurate in their descriptions.

Analytic models. **Analytic models** are models created using a variety of mathemati cal methods. This mathematical nature requires a certain sophistication on the part o the investigator, thereby limiting the use of analytic models. Moreover, mathematically precise descriptions of a system are usually limited to its less complex aspects. Error in any description render the model inaccurate.

Analytic modeling is a technique used primarily by system designers and vendors. Relatively few data processing organizations rely on analytic modeling to any great extent.

Simulations.   **Simulations** are programs written to mimic the behavior of a system. Though the execution of a simulation, data is artificially created, gathered, and analyzed as if it were generated by the actual system. As with analytic models, simulations can be constructed for nonexistent and nonavailable systems. In contrast to analytic models, however, simulations need not be mathematically sophisticated. Accordingly, the use of simulations is more widespread than the use of analytic models.

Simulation, like monitoring, can create huge amounts of data to be analyzed. The data is handled in exactly the same way monitor-gathered data is treated. In addition, an error in any assumption about the system will lead to erroneous output and false conclusions.

Simulations are "driven" in one of two general ways. **Script-driven** simulations are those controlled by data (the script) created to mimic anticipated system conditions and parameters. The accuracy of the data is critical to the value of the results. It is possible to use magnetic tape files of actual historical data to control a script-driven simulation. **Event-driven** simulations are ones in which probability theory is used to mimic the natural occurrence of system events. Events are generated according to some probability distribution that adequately describes the real world. The accuracy of the probability distribution in describing the real situation is critical.

Other Evaluation Mechanisms

An article by Caroll and Rosson, [7], discusses a number of mechanisms that can be used to evaluate system performance. Performance monitoring, analytic modeling, and simulation (as discussed earlier) are included in that study. This section is devoted to other, perhaps simpler, techniques.

Timings

Timings are relatively simple measurements of machine capacity (such as the number of millions of instructions per second the CPU can execute). While they are of some value in showing the hardware's abilities, timings are of very limited value. However, timings might be of use when, for instance, comparing several IBM PC-AT compatible machines. Where machines are very similar in architecture, increased capabilities may be evident when timings are compared.

Mixes

Instruction mixes are statistically weighted combinations of instructions executed in order to give a better picture of system capability than afforded by timings. Mixes are relatively simple mechanisms, although not as simple as timings.

Instruction mixes are best tailored for individual sites. By evaluating the workload and job mix for a given system, a profile can be drawn to show the relative frequency of use for each machine instruction. An instruction mix can be chosen to best mimic that profile. Mixes, like timings, are best used to compare hardware capabilities.

Kernels

Kernels are programs written to look like typical applications for the target system. However, they are designed for conceptual execution by using hardware specifications:

Kernel programs are not executed on a real system. The goal is to create a timing for a typical program.

One attractive feature of kernel programs is that they give some estimate of performance for nonexistent and nonavailable systems just as timings and mixes do. They do it better, although at a greater cost. The method of executing kernel programs offers the first technique we've discussed in this section that can be used to evaluate and predict software performance.

Benchmarks

Benchmarks take the notion of a kernel program one step further: Benchmarks are actual programs run on the target system using that system's data-gathering capabilities. Benchmark programs are most valuable when they represent actual application and utility programs to be used on the system. In order to get a good idea of performance, the benchmark programs should represent a wide spectrum of the actual programs to be used. Benchmarks are often chosen for comparing systems under given applications. Benchmark programs are widely available as commercial or public-domain offerings. They must be chosen carefully to reflect the proposed use of the system. Benchmark programs should be as close to the actual application programs as possible.

Synthetic Programs

Synthetic programs are programs written specifically for testing and evaluation. They have the flavor of benchmarks in that they are intended for execution on a machine. They also resemble kernels, since they are artificial programs rather than normal user routines.

A well-written synthetic program makes the gathering of performance data easier than it might otherwise be. Only one program or series of programs needs to be run in order to develop the database for evaluation. Such an advantage might show itself in the system selection process where the actual users' jobs cannot be run. On the other hand, a synthetic program is an artificial program whose costs are incurred for the evaluation of one system and job mix only.

Other Factors

The measures discussed above are all related to the speed and efficiency of hardware and software systems. For the most part, they give reproducible measures of performance. System tests, though, should include far more than simple performance evaluations. Reliability, ease of maintenance, ease of use, ease of learning, and levels of user comfort are just a few other considerations. How safe is the system's use in terms of data integrity? Does the system correctly do what it claims to do? How much of the job to be done can actually be done by the system? What kind of support can be expected from the vendor(s)? How compatible is the system with the way business is being done? How well integrated are the various components of the application programs?

To measure the quality and appropriateness of the system requires a specification to measure against. What needs to be done by the system? Who will use the system? How will the various players use the system to do their jobs? What kind of documentation, training, and support is expected? How does the organization measure usefulness and useability?

These considerations and questions imply that software correctness, application completeness, consistency of user interfaces, readability of manuals and help screens, ease of doing routine activities, and ease in handling exceptions all need to be thought about. The ability of the system to do the job and the above-mentioned human considerations are important in making business decisions.

How can a decision-maker fortify himself or herself to get on with the task of deciding? Trade magazines and journals have a constant stream of reviews of hardware and software products. Colleagues in the business are another good source of information: Use the experience of others. Find reputable dealers with reputations for quality products and support. Acquire written guarantees about what the system will do. Design the evaluation process to check as many of the specifications as possible with the checks being carried out as often as possible by the people who will ultimately use the system.

System Acquisition

The acquisition of a new hardware/software system is a painful process for any organization. Besides the significant dollar cost in acquiring the new system, there may be considerable interruption to the current way of doing business, and the users must readjust to all the newness. Learning a new system does not usually rank at the top of employees' favorite activities. The development cycle discussed in Chapter 10 is useful in formalizing the acquisition process and creating built-in safeguards. Mistakes in acquisition can be devastating.

The feasibility study should survey the organization's information and processing needs as they currently exist *and* as they are likely to evolve over the next four to six years. Additionally, a specially designated team should evaluate the present system's performance and make judgments about its ability to continue meeting organizational needs. Decision possibilities include the status quo, expansion/reconfiguration, and replacement by a new system. The feasibility study should yield a system-requirements document. If the decision seems to be "go" on acquisition, cost/benefit estimates should be provided.

The requirements document can be used as the basis for preparing system specifications, which are in turn used to prepare an **RFQ** (Request for Quote) or **RFP** (Request for Proposal) to be distributed to vendors. Widespread practice seems to favor the solicitation of proposals from four or five vendors.

Each vendor's response should include a proposed equipment configuration and associated costs, a proposed software solution and costs, a list of vendor support services and costs, the terms of delivery and payment, a performance evaluation for the proposed system, a list of any changes from the original specifications, and other information deemed appropriate. Proposals can be ranked by the team using a predetermined point assignment scheme.

In some cases, vendors make provision for performance testing of hardware/software systems so that the proposed system may be evaluated. In other cases, testing occurs after delivery. In any case, replacement of the existing system should be postponed until after sufficient testing and shakedown have been accomplished. That may require the parallel operation of the old and new systems for a time.

Exercises

1. Give a list of advantages and disadvantages of performance monitoring for performance evaluation.
2. Do Exercise 1 for modeling.
3. Describe the general differences between hardware and software monitors.
4. Why would anyone care about identifying the specific user process that causes any system activity?
5. Why are system managers concerned with the variances of performance measures?
6. Why are the performance characteristics of single user systems generally of limited interest?
7. Compare/contrast the user's view of "useful CPU work" with the view of the system manager.
8. Answer each of the following:
   a. In what way are instruction mixes better than timings?
   b. Compare/contrast kernel programs with instruction mixes.
   c. How are synthetic programs like instruction mixes? What kinds of information does the writer of a synthetic program need?
   d. What information do benchmarks provide? What are their limitations?
9. Which evaluation techniques can be applied to a hardware system in the design phase (not yet constructed)?
10. Do Exercise 9 for a computer system sitting in the vendor's warehouse.
11. Describe the general differences between system tuning and system reconfiguration.
12. Describe the general process of system generation.
13. Compare/contrast the nature and use of real-time monitors and long-term monitors.
14. What kinds of users are concerned about each of the following:
   a. turnaround time
   b. response time
   c. reaction time
15. Do Exercise 14 for the following:
   a. workload
   b. throughput
   c. capacity
   d. utilization
16. Do Exercise 14 for the following:
   a. I/O call rate
   b. interrupt rate
   c. I/O waits
   d. page fault rate
   e. channel busy rate
   f. device busy rate
17. Make a list of conditions that adversely affect the availability of a system. Include psychological aspects since availability may be as much a perceived measure as a real one. In each case, think of at least one cure.
18. Make a list of conditions that improve system availability. Include psychological aspects.
19. Redo Exercises 17 and 18 for reliability.

20. How has the term **bottleneck** been used? Make a list of possible bottlenecks in a computer system and the situations likely to cause them. Think of at least one solution in each case.

21. Suppose a system manager added two new disk units to a disk system that already had sufficient storage capacity to meet the requirements. However, disk access continued to be a bottleneck. How might this be?

22. The amount of main memory is increased to accommodate a higher level of multi-programming. What might account for an actual drop in performance?

23. If the paging rate is extremely low, a system manager might view that as undesirable. Why?

24. Discuss the pros and cons of increasing working set sizes.

25. Do Exercise 23 for low device busy rates.

26. If an analysis shows unusually high seek times, what possible cures exist?

27. If the rate of interrupt occurrence is low, what kind of job mix might be suspected?

28. How may device busy and I/O channel busy differ?

29. Simulation might be the most widely usable performance evaluation technique. What are some of the disadvantages that keep it from being used more frequently?

30. List some advantages of script-driven simulations over event-driven ones. And vice versa.

FOUR

Operating Systems Applications

12 MS-DOS, Windows, and OS/2

MS-DOS (Microsoft Disk Operating System) evolved from a Seattle Computer project whose initial goal was to develop a single-user, single-tasking, CP/M-80 compatible operating system for the 16-bit Intel family of microprocessors, such as the 8086. The Microsoft Corporation bought the rights to Seattle Computer's product and developed MS-DOS. A major event leading to MS-DOS popularity came when Microsoft entered into an agreement with IBM for the development of PC-DOS. PC-DOS/MS-DOS has been the dominant operating system for microcomputers since the early 1980s.

The roots in CP/M have been obscured as MS-DOS has evolved toward a more UNIX/XENIX-like operating system. (XENIX was Microsoft's one and only operating system when the MS-DOS project was started.) Since version 2.0, MS-DOS has had some upward compatibility with UNIX. In fact, the command language now looks like a subset of UNIX, and the system service calls are handled in a UNIX-like manner. The file system has also taken on a UNIX look. MS-DOS has been upgraded continually and is used on a variety of 8086/8088, 80286, and 80386 systems.

Microsoft Windows added an object-oriented, icon-based graphics interface to MS-DOS and, for specific machines, introduced a first generation multitasking capability. For most purposes, Windows afforded a Macintosh-like user interface, allowing data transfer between windows, some background processing, and easy context switching between memory-resident or pop-up applications.

Like CP/M, which faces a challenge in stepping up from the 8-bit machines, MS-DOS faces the challenge of adapting to the newer 32-bit machines, particularly the Intel 80386, which is capable of multiuser, multitasking operations of seemingly mainframe proportions. Microsoft has taken a series of steps to maintain its market position. Version 2.0 introduced the hierarchical file system to handle the hard disks of the PC XT. Version 3.0 adapted MS-DOS to the PC AT, while version 3.1 added some network-handling capabilities. Version 4.0 of MS-DOS, used extensively in Europe and Australia, provides multitasking for single user systems under some restricted conditions. Rumors of version 5.0 supporting multitasking with an address space of 16M bytes for 80286 machines and version 6.0 supporting multiuser multitasking on 80386 systems have abounded.

The creation of OS/2 as the multitasking successor to MS-DOS for 32-bit machines (80286, 80386, 80486, and so on) is no longer a rumor. Some declare that OS/2 is simply the new title given to version 5.0 MS-DOS. OS/2 is the operating system designed for the IBM PS/2 family of microcomputers. These machines and OS/2 are designed to move ahead in the growing office automation, networking, and workstation markets. OS/2 has been designed to be as compatible with MS-DOS as possible (the PS/2 family can run MS-DOS), while at the same time attempting to allow OS/2 applications to run under MS-DOS as well. OS/2 incorporates a user interface similar to the Windows interface.

Figure 12.1

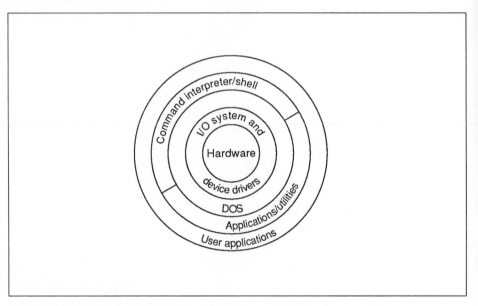

MS-DOS

Figure 12.1 illustrates the layered design of MS-DOS for single tasking systems. The I/O system is machine dependent just like its forerunner CP/M. One of the major improvements of version 2.0 was an improvement in the ease with which I/O drivers could be installed as a part of the BIOS. The rest of the operating system is machine independent, again in the mode of CP/M. **DOS** is the heart of the resource allocator. Sitting above DOS is the **command interpreter.**

Version 3.1 included specific networking features. Up to that time, networks of MS-DOS machines were based solely on the products of other vendors. Currently, virtually all LANs for PCs support the use of MS-DOS. Identifying network resources requires only a very slight modification of the MS-DOS identification for local resources, so that network use is relatively transparent.

One of MS-DOS's greatest strengths has been the tremendous number of software tools and applications programs available from independent vendors. (Almost any kind of utility and applications program imaginable is available from someone.) Multitasking and multiuser programs can be set on top of MS-DOS if one wishes—editors, debuggers, language compilers, spreadsheets, database managers, graphics programs, and on and on. It is primarily because of this huge marketplace of software that the IBM PCs and compatibles dominate serious business and industrial use of small machines.

However, that market has not escaped the eyes of makers of operating systems for larger systems. UNIX has migrated from the minicomputer arena to the microcomputer world. Such movement is likely to accelerate with the increasing popularity of the very powerful 32-bit microprocessors. Operating systems for minicomputers were designed as multitasking, multiuser systems and can naturally take advantage of the capabilities of the newer chips (whose designs were inspired by successful minis). For traditional single-tasking, single-user operating systems, however, the step upward requires a major redesign and rethinking. Keep in mind, also, that designers typically want to keep backward compatibility with each new system; that is, they want programs designed under older versions to run on the newer ones. This, of course, makes it easier for them to keep their existing system users. Note that this is a primary goal of OS/2.

The User Interface

MS-DOS is a command-driven operating system. The command interpreter, often called the **shell,** is the user's normal interface. It is a simple interface with roots in mainframe computing. The command line offers a prompt and expects the user to react by typing in a command. The commands are essentially UNIX-like in all but the earliest versions of MS-DOS. Error messages are used to inform the user of any problem that has arisen.

Some of the MS-DOS commands are encoded as part of the operating system. More, however, are disk resident and are loaded when called. Applications programs may be executed in the form of a command, thereby extending and customizing the interface to suit the individual user. A program is executed by simply typing its name on the command line.

Redirection.   One of the major attractions of MS-DOS is its facility for the **redirection** of I/O. Commands normally have a standard input and standard output device: For most commands, the console (keyboard and video display unit) acts as this device. Input and output from a command can be sent to other devices or files by the use of redirection. For example,

    DIR >TEMP

places a listing of the contents of the active directory into the file TEMP instead of printing the listing on the screen. Similarly,

    SORT <TEMP

feeds the information from TEMP as input to the SORT routine: The contents of the directory are displayed on the screen in sorted order.

A similar result can be achieved by the use of a **pipe.** A pipe is a mechanism for channeling the output from one command as input to another. In essence, a pipe is a file written by one process and read in FIFO order by a second process. Thus

    DIR | SORT

mimics the output of the pair of instructions above, displaying the contents of the active directory on the video screen. The pipe automatically manages the reading and writing of a temporary file. There is another potential advantage: The pipe can be read anytime there is unread data. That is, the two commands can (theoretically) operate concurrently rather than sequentially. The use of redirection via > and < must occur sequentially, but pipes make concurrency possible. Some UNIX implementations do take advantage of concurrency.

Redirection in general and pipes in particular encourage the building of programs through the use of **filters.** A filter is a program that accepts a stream of data as input, performs some simple transformation on that data, and passes it on as output. Complex results can be generated by "piping" several simple filters together. For one example, using the filters SORT and MORE, creates a useful command.

DIR | SORT | MORE

displays the contents of the active directory of the default drive in sorted order, one screenful at a time (because of MORE).

Batch files.   **Batch files** (also known as shell scripts in UNIX and command files in a variety of operating systems) consist of lists of MS-DOS commands. Such files are often created to automatically perform a series of activities in a noninteractive way or to create a program through the use of MS-DOS commands and redirection. Automating startup procedures for some software packages is a popular way of utilizing batch files.

Since the user interface for MS-DOS is dated, many vendors have supplied alternatives in the form of menus and iconic interfaces using pointing devices. Windowing mechanisms abound as add-ons: Microsoft Windows has been one of the most popular and will be discussed later in this chapter.

Memory Management

Memory management is uncomplicated in this single-tasking, single-user system. Figure 12.2 shows a typical memory map. MS-DOS is a real memory system: Virtual memory techniques are not used in versions prior to 4.0. The major difficulty has been the limited memory management capability of the 8086/8088 and the 80286 running in real mode; the 80286 running in the real mode is essentially a fast 8086.

Lower memory addresses consist of system interrupt vectors with the I/O system just above and DOS just above that. Recall that DOS is machine independent. The segment in next higher memory is the memory-resident part of the command interpreter. A transient part of the command interpreter is given a chunk of memory at the highest addresses. In between the two parts of the command interpreter lies the user area (**Transient Program Area**). The transient part of the command interpreter may be overwritten by application programs (and restored after execution). Otherwise, large programs must use overlay techniques.

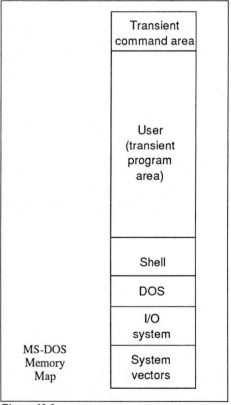

MS-DOS Memory Map

| Transient command area |
| User (transient program area) |
| Shell |
| DOS |
| I/O system |
| System vectors |

Figure 12.2

For the IBM PC AT and clones using Intel's 80286 chip (24-bit addressing), multitasking is quite possible. The 80286 has a fairly sophisticated onboard memory-management unit allowing for virtual-memory techniques. While MS-DOS has not taken direct advantage of this feature except in a limited way (version 4.0 supports memory partitioning with no swapping in the 640K RAM), OS/2 does.

The 8086/8088 chips are capable of addressing one megabyte of RAM. Since the IBM PC was built to address only 640K directly, MS-DOS was designed accordingly. Many PCs and clones are equipped with additional memory, but software tricks must be used to benefit from anything beyond 640K.

The added memory is generally categorized as either **extended** or **expanded** memory. Extended memory (up to 15 Mbytes) can be used only as a RAM disk from within MS-DOS. Expanded memory (up to 8 Mbytes) can be used by MS-DOS programs designed for its use. One standard for its use (EMS or LIM, for Lotus/Intel/Microsoft) involves the use of a 64K byte window in the lower 640K address space: Data from the expanded memory is swapped into and out of that 64K byte window in 16K byte pages as needed by the program. While not as efficient as having 8M bytes of directly addressable RAM, the mechanism does greatly enhance the processing capability of certain programs demanding large quantities of main memory.

I/O Management

All peripherals are managed through the combination of DOS and the I/O system. Logical device names passed to DOS are translated to physical device information and sent on to the I/O system. Logical device names reserved by MS-DOS include CON: (console), AUX: or COM1: (serial port), LPT1: or PRN: (parallel printer), and NUL: (dummy device). Note that the colon is a part of each device name. Disk drives are named A:, B:, C:, and so on.

The I/O system and installed device drivers are specific to the MPU and devices attached to it. In the IBM PC, the I/O system actually consists of the MS-DOS BIOS together with a ROM BIOS installed in the machine. DOS, on the other hand, is system independent and uniform across all MS-DOS systems.

Almost every imaginable peripheral device has been connected to an MS-DOS machine. Vendors have devised controller cards and device drivers for a wide range of devices. One of the most popular peripherals is the high-capacity memory board that makes memory available for RAM disks. These **logical disk units** consist of RAM connected to the I/O system via device drivers that simulate disk I/O activities while actually making memory reads and writes. They are treated by the user as if they were actually physical disk drives. RAM disks, while normally volatile, offer much faster access times than physical disk systems, speeding up many kinds of processing. Regardless of the peripheral device, a primary concern to purchasers is the inclusion of an *installable device* driver as part of any delivered package.

CPU Scheduling

There is little CPU scheduling by MS-DOS since it is effectively a single tasking operating system. However, MS-DOS does support background activity in the form of a print spooler.

In addition, there is a service call that terminates a process but leaves it memory resident. Subsequent programs can be loaded without disturbing the memory allocated to the terminated process. The terminated process is effectively a user-defined interrupt handler. Since keyboard use generates interrupts, it is possible to have special keystroke sequences trigger the user-define interrupt routine whenever desired. At that time, the context of the executing process is saved and a terminated-but-resident program becomes active. This is the way a number of *desktop accessory* programs (so-called **pop-up** programs) are designed.

Version 4.0 does make some multitasking available using preemptive scheduling for very special environments. Version 4.0 has seen very limited use and is preempted by OS/2.

PC Networks

In any discussion about networking PCs, it should be remembered that until very recently, IBM saw the mainframe as the center of all networks, where nodes communicate through mainframes rather than communicating directly as peers. Most early uses of PCs in networks came in the form of PCs as slaves to the mainframes, with the PC running generally as a terminal. Recently, however, IBM has changed its stance.

IBM PCs and compatibles have been the target of many vendors developing LANs. IBM itself jumped into the fray with its **Cluster Control Program** in early 1984, followed later in that year by **PC Network** and in 1985 by its **IBM token ring**.

The Cluster Control Program was not advertised as a LAN, primarily because of its low-end capabilities (375K bits/second), and it has not been widely received as a network alternative. PC Network, operating at 2M bits/second has been more popular. Both systems utilize carrier sensing with collision detection and packet switching.

The IBM token ring allows transfer rates to 16M bits/second with fiber optic cable, although the current maximum is 4M bits/second. Lower rates are available with less expensive media, such as coaxial cable and twisted pair cable.

The major problem with many LAN products for PCs (and there are many) is their proprietary nature, effectively making the systems **closed.** Incompatibility among the various third party LANs is well-known. However, systems based on some well-understood standard tend to be more nearly **open.** EtherNet LANs have been successfully constructed in the 10M bit/second range. ARCnet LANs are also available.

Nodes in PC networks are of two types—the **user** and the **server.** The server may be a PC of some flavor, particularly if it is well-endowed with generous RAM, a hard-disk system of reasonable volume, and other peripherals that can be shared but not maintained at each PC location. However, other kinds of servers are found. Some are specialized network servers designed for that purpose, while others are minicomputers such as the VAX. Network servers tend to be dedicated to network activities and lose their identity as a local workstation.

LAN users have two conflicting goals in mind: maintain the standalone capability of the PC and partake of the benefits of networking. PC networks have been established to allow peripheral sharing, to improve information access, and to establish electronic mail as a personal-communication mechanism. One special class of peripheral sharing involves the use of **gateways** to (IBM) mainframe computers.

The File System

All files in MS-DOS are, as far as MS-DOS is concerned, simply streams of bytes of data. This is also the case with UNIX. However, in contrast to the flat directory system of CP/M, MS-DOS (starting with version 2.0) manages a hierarchical file system. Files are accessed by name or, more accurately, by **pathname.** The file names are similar to

Figure 12.3

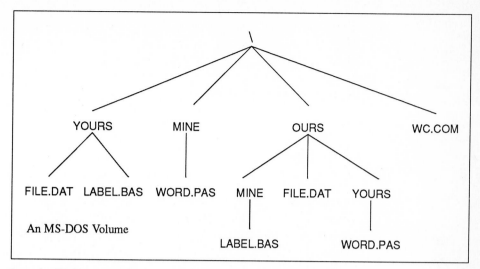

An MS-DOS Volume

those in CP/M, consisting of a primary part with up to eight characters and an extension of up to three characters.

When a disk (or volume) is initialized (formatted), a **root directory** is created. Other directories, called **subdirectories** (named without extension), can be created to organize the files within a volume. Figure 12.3 shows a disk organized with four files (three directories and one .COM file) as children of the root. Each subdirectory has children of its own, some of which are also directories. Files that are not directories must be leaf nodes in the volume tree.

This tree structure is a valuable organizational tool for larger-volume disk packages. MS-DOS systems are known to utilize 360K and 1.2M floppy disk units as well as hard-disk systems running 40 megabytes and more. Until version 4.0, hard-disk systems of more than 33 megabytes had to be partitioned into two or more smaller units (logical disks).

Pathnames are used to locate files. For example, \YOURS\LABEL.BAS finds one file whose individual file name is LABEL.BAS, while \OURS\MINE\LABEL.BAS locates the other. Each pathname starting with a \ indicates an **absolute pathname** starting from the root: Each subsequent \ separates directory names and file names encountered along the way. (Identifying a file at a remote PC in a LAN can be as simple as prefacing the file path name with an extra \.)

At any given time, one directory is designated as the **current directory** or **working directory**. Any path name *not* starting with a \ is a **partial pathname** beginning at the current directory. Thus, MINE\LABEL.BAS locates the file \OURS\MINE\LABEL.BAS if \OURS is the working directory. Similarly, if \OURS\MINE is the working directory, the partial path name LABEL.BAS is all that is required. The choice of working directory is set by the user through the CHDIR command.

Files may be created, opened, closed, deleted, renamed, read from, written to, and so on. These actions may be directed from user application programs, utilities, or by MS-DOS calls directly. Files are time stamped by MS-DOS when they are created or modified. The directory entries for a file hold the name, extension, attributes, date/time

Figure 12.4

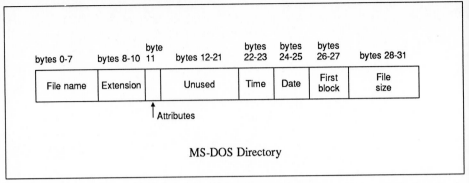

MS-DOS Directory

for creation or last modification, number of the first cluster, and the file size (as in Figure 12.4). A **sector** consists of 512 bytes and a **cluster** consists of several adjacent sectors. Clusters of two sectors each are typical for 360K floppy disks, but clusters may be composed of eight sectors for large-volume hard disks. A cluster is the minimal assignable unit.

The clusters that make up each file are chained together in the **File Allocation Table (FAT)**. Figure 12.5 shows the chaining process: The directory entry points to the first assigned cluster, and that pointer is also the offset into the FAT slot for that cluster.

Figure 12.5

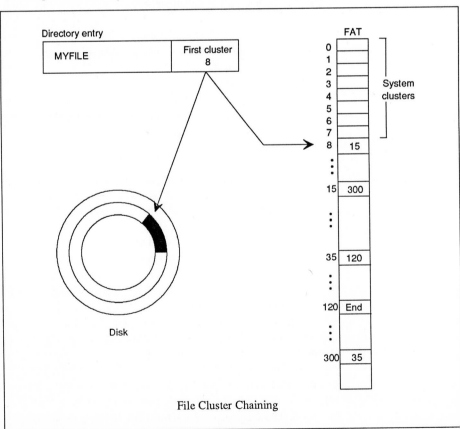

File Cluster Chaining

The entry in the FAT gives the pointer to the next cluster assigned to the file—and, hence, to the offset in the FAT for the next pointer. By following the pointers in the FAT, all clusters assigned to the file can be found (in this case, 8, 15, 300, 35, and 120). Noncontiguous cluster allocation is the rule. Free clusters are maintained as a list in the FAT.

The outer track of the disk contains two copies of the FAT for the volume: One copy is the backup for security purposes. When booted, a copy of the FAT is placed in RAM. The FAT varies in size with the particular disk system (FAT slots are 12 bits long for under 20M systems and 16 bits long for those over 20M). In any case, the FAT absorbs a sizeable chunk of main memory.

The outer tracks also contain the boot sector, the root directory, and other system information. The arrangement of information on these tracks is fixed so that MS-DOS will be assured of finding everything it needs to boot and maintain the disk system.

Session with the Command Language

To boot the system, place a system disk in drive **A:** (the : is part of the drive's logical name) and turn on the power to all components. Figure 12.6 illustrates the message that appears. The references to the date and time require inputs from the user as shown. The prompt indicates which drive is the default drive and tells the user that the system is ready.

Figure 12.6

```
Current date is Tue 1-01-1980
Enter new date (mm-dd-yy): 8-25-88
Current time is 0:00:53.55
Enter new time: 10:15

The IBM Personal Computer DOS
Version 3.10 (C) Copyright International Business Machines Corp. 1981,1985
                (C) Copyright Microsoft Corp 1981, 1985

   A>




                              Boot Screen
```

Typing **B:** in response to the prompt will change the prompt to **B>** . Drive B: is now the default drive. Typing **A:** again will return **A:** as the default drive. What follows is a session on an MS-DOS machine.

```
A>B:
B>A:
A>GOTCHA
Bad command or file name
A>DIR
```

```
Volume in Drive A is PCDOS V310
Directory of A:\

COMMAND   COM   23210   3-07-85   1:43p
ASSIGN    COM    1509   3-07-85   1:43p
ATTRIB    EXE   15091   3-07-85   1:43p
CHKDSK    COM    9435   3-07-85   1:43p
COMP      COM    3664   3-07-85   1:43p
DISKCOMP  COM    4073   3-07-85   1:43p
DISKCOPY  COM    4329   3-07-85   1:43p
EDLIN     COM    7261   3-07-85   1:43p
FDISK     COM    8173   3-07-85   1:43p
FIND      EXE    6403   3-07-85   1:43p
FORMAT    COM    9398   3-07-85   1:43p
GRAFTABL  COM    1169   3-07-85   1:43p
GRAPHICS  COM    3111   3-07-85   1:43p
JOIN      EXE   15971   3-07-85   1:43p
KEYBFR    COM    2289   3-07-85   1:43p
KEYBGR    COM    2234   3-07-85   1:43p
KEYBIT    COM    2177   3-07-85   1:43p
KEYBSP    COM    2267   3-07-85   1:43p
KEYBUK    COM    2164   3-07-85   1:43p
LABEL     COM    1826   3-07-85   1:43p
MODE      COM    5295   3-07-85   1:43p
MORE      COM     282   3-07-85   1:43p
SELECT    COM    2084   3-07-85   1:43p
SORT      EXE    1664   3-07-85   1:43p
SYS       COM    3727   3-07-85   1:43p
TREE      COM    2831   3-07-85   1:43p
        26 File(s)    165888 bytes free

          System Disk Directory
```

Figure 12.7

```
        28 File(s)    163840 bytes free
   Directory of  A:\
   Volume in drive A is PCDOS V310
   06123333          0   1-04-80   6:18a
   06123521          0   1-04-80   6:18a
   ASSIGN    COM    1509   3-07-85   1:43p
   ATTRIB    EXE   15091   3-07-85   1:43p
   CHKDSK    COM    9435   3-07-85   1:43p
   COMMAND   COM   25210   3-07-85   1:43p
   COMP      COM    3664   3-07-85   1:43p
   DISKCOMP  COM    4073   3-07-85   1:43p
   DISKCOPY  COM    4329   3-07-85   1:43p
   EDLIN     COM    7261   3-07-85   1:43p
   FDISK     COM    8173   3-07-85   1:43p
   FIND      EXE    6403   3-07-85   1:43p
   FORMAT    COM    9398   3-07-85   1:43p
   GRAFTABL  COM    1169   3-07-85   1:43p
   GRAPHICS  COM    3111   3-07-85   1:43p
   JOIN      EXE   15971   3-07-85   1:43p
   KEYBFR    COM    2289   3-07-85   1:43p
   KEYBGR    COM    2234   3-07-85   1:43p
   KEYBIT    COM    2177   3-07-85   1:43p
   KEYBSP    COM    2267   3-07-85   1:43p
   KEYBUK    COM    2164   3-07-85   1:43p
   LABEL     COM    1826   3-07-85   1:43p
   MODE      COM    5295   3-07-85   1:43p
   MORE      COM     282   3-07-85   1:43p
   SELECT    COM    2084   3-07-85   1:43p
   SORT      EXE    1664   3-07-85   1:43p
   SYS       COM    3727   3-07-85   1:43p
   TREE      COM    2831   3-07-85   1:43p
```

Figure 12.8

Figure 12.7 shows the response to A>DIR. Typing DIR A: will result in the same screen output. Continue with the session.

          A>DIR | SORT

(See Figure 12.8 for the output: Why the first two file entries?)

          A>DIR >TEMP
          A>COPY TEMP CON:

(See Figure 12.9 for the output: Where did the first two files from Figure 12.8 go?)

          A>ERASE TEMP
          A>DISKCOPY A: B:
          Insert SOURCE diskette in drive A:
          Insert TARGET diskette in drive B:
                Press any key when ready . . .

```
Volume in Drive A is PCDOS V310
Directory of A:\

COMMAND   COM   23210   3-07-85   1:43p
TEMP                0   1-04-80   6:21a
ASSIGN    COM    1509   3-07-85   1:43p
ATTRIB    EXE   15091   3-07-85   1:43p
CHKDSK    COM    9435   3-07-85   1:43p
COMP      COM    3664   3-07-85   1:43p
DISKCOMP  COM    4073   3-07-85   1:43p
DISKCOPY  COM    4329   3-07-85   1:43p
EDLIN     COM    7261   3-07-85   1:43p
FDISK     COM    8173   3-07-85   1:43p
FIND      EXE    6403   3-07-85   1:43p
FORMAT    COM    9398   3-07-85   1:43p
GRAFTABL  COM    1169   3-07-85   1:43p
GRAPHICS  COM    3111   3-07-85   1:43p
JOIN      EXE   15971   3-07-85   1:43p
KEYBFR    COM    2289   3-07-85   1:43p
KEYBGR    COM    2234   3-07-85   1:43p
KEYBIT    COM    2177   3-07-85   1:43p
KEYBSP    COM    2267   3-07-85   1:43p
KEYBUK    COM    2164   3-07-85   1:43p
LABEL     COM    1826   3-07-85   1:43p
MODE      COM    5295   3-07-85   1:43p
MORE      COM     282   3-07-85   1:43p
SELECT    COM    2084   3-07-85   1:43p
SORT      EXE    1664   3-07-85   1:43p
SYS       COM    3727   3-07-85   1:43p
TREE      COM    2831   3-07-85   1:43p
      27 File(s)    163840 bytes free
       1 File(s) copied
```

Figure 12.9

and after a keypress the screen shows:

```
Copying 40 tracks
9 Sectors/Track, 2 Side(s)
Formatting while copying
Copy another diskette (Y/N)?
```

Responding with N discontinues the disk-copying routine. The diskette in drive B: is an exact duplicate of the disk in drive A:. DISKCOMP can be used to verify the duplication. Return to the session.

```
A>FORMAT B: /S
Insert new diskette for drive B:
and strike ENTER when ready
Formatting...Format complete
System transferred
  362496 bytes total disk space
   62464 bytes used by system
  300032 bytes available on disk
Format another (Y/N)?
```

An N will end the formatting process. The disk in drive B: has been initialized for use with MS-DOS. It has a directory, a FAT, the loader block, and has been verified. Because the /S option was used, certain system information was also added. If the /S option is not used, the disk is a data disk and cannot be used to boot the system. Continue with the session.

```
A>CHKDSK B:
  362496 bytes total disk space
   38912 bytes in two hidden files
   23552 bytes in 1 user files
   30032 bytes available on disk
  381952 bytes total memory
  345056 bytes free
A>MKDIR B:USR
A>B:
B>MKDIR \USR\JIM
B>MKDIR \USR\SALLY
B>MKDIR \USR\JIM\SCHOOL
```

The disk in B: now contains four directories. Use of COPY will create another file.

```
B>COPY CON: \USR\JIM\FILE1
THIS IS LINE 1
THIS IS LINE 2
THIS IS LINE 3
^Z
   1 File(s) copied
```

Figure 12.10

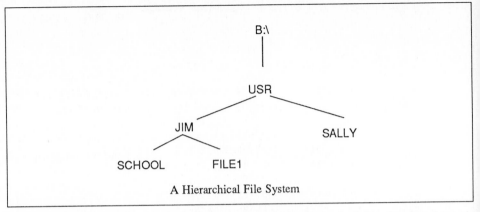

A Hierarchical File System

A three-line file has been created. The ^Z (<ctrl>-Z) is the end-of-file signal and terminates the console-to-file copy. The hierarchical structure for the volume in drive B: is shown in Figure 12.10. Continue with the session.

```
B>CHDIR \USR\JIM
B>DIR
    Volume in drive B has no label
    Directory of B:\USR\JIM
    .           <DIR>        8-25-88      10:20a
    ..          <DIR>        8-25-88      10:19a
    SCHOOL      <DIR>        8-25-88      10:21a
    FILE1                48  8-25-88      10:22a
        4 File(s)   294912 bytes free
```

The entries . and .. stand for the working directory itself (\USR\JIM) and the parent directory (\USR). Return to the session.

```
B>COPY FILE1 \USR\SALLY\FILE1
    1 File(s) copied
B>CHDIR ..
```

The current directory should be the parent of JIM. DIR without an argument gives the listing for the current directory.

```
B>DIR
    Volume in drive B has no label
    Directory of B:\USER
    .           <DIR>        8-25-88      10:19a
    ..          <DIR>        8-25-88      10:19a
    JIM         <DIR>        8-25-88      10:20a
    SALLY       <DIR>        8-25-88      10:20a
        4 File(s)   293888 bytes free
```

Now use DIR with a partial path name.

```
B>DIR SALLY
    Volume in drive B has no label
    Directory of B:\USR\SALLY
    .           <DIR>        8-25-88      10:20a
    ..          <DIR>        8-25-88      10:19a
    FILE1                48  8-25-88      10:22a
        3 File(s)   293888 bytes
```

Now COPY from a file to the console.

```
B>COPY JIM\FILE1 CON:
THIS IS LINE 1
THIS IS LINE 2
THIS IS LINE 3
   1 File(s) copied
B>A:
A>COMP  B:\USR\JIM\SCHOOL\FILE1  B:\USR\SALLY\FILE1
B:\USR\JIM\SCHOOL\FILE1 - File not found
Compare more files (Y/N)? Y
Enter primary file name
B:\USR\JIM\FILE1
Enter 2nd file name or drive id
B:\USR\SALLY\FILE1
Eof mark not found
Files compare ok
Compare more files (Y/N)? N
A>RENAME  B:\USR\JIM\FILE1  B:\USR\JIM\FILE2
A>ERASE  B:\USR\SALLY\FILE1
```

MS-DOS has a way of showing the tree structure for any disk volume.

```
A>TREE B: /F
```

Check Figure 12.11 for the results of the TREE command. The /F option merely adds nondirectory files to the list. Without /F, only directories are given. Continue with the session as a batch (**.BAT**) file is created.

```
A>COPY CON: B:\USR\JIM\SCHOOL\SCHOOLFILE.BAT
ECHO SCHOOL FILE BATCH PROGRAM
VERIFY
TYPE B:\USR\JIM\FILE2
```

Figure 12.11

```
DIRECTORY PATH LISTING FOR VOLUME BOOKDISK

Files:                    COMMAND.COM


Path: \USR
Sub-directories:          JIM
                          SALLY
Files:                    None


Path: \USR\JIM
Sub-directories:          SCHOOL
Files:                    FILE2


Path: \USR\JIM\SCHOOL
Sub-directories:          None
Files:                    None


Path: \USR\SALLY
Subdirectories:           None
Files:                    None
```

```
                     DATE
                     TIME
                     REM REMARKS CAUSE NO ACTION
                     PAUSE A DELAY MOMENTARILY
                     DIR B:\USR\SALLY
                     ^Z
                       1 File(s) copied
```
ECHO merely prints to the screen the message string attached. TYPE prints the contents of the text file given as input. DATE and TIME request date and time values. REM simply prints the associated message. PAUSE halts execution after printing the attached message and *asks for a keystroke* to allow execution to resume.

```
                     A>B:
                     B>CHDIR \USR\JIM\SCHOOL
```
Now execute the batch file by calling it.

```
                     B>SCHOOLFILE.BAT
```
Check Figure 12.12 for the result. The lines of the batch file were executed just as if

Figure 12.12

```
              B>ECHO SCHOOLFILE BATCH PROGRAM
              SCHOOLFILE BATCH PROGRAM


              B>VERIFY
              VERIFY is off


              B>TYPE B:\USR\JIM\FILE2
              This is line 1
              This is line 2
              This is line 3


              B>DATE
              Current date is Tue  1-01-1980
              Enter new date (mm-dd-yy): 8-25-88


              B>TIME
              Current time is  0:08:35.31
              Enter new time: 10:21


              B>REM ISN'T THIS FUN?


              B>PAUSE DO SOMETHING
              Strike a key when ready . . .


              B>DIR B:\USR\SALLY

               Volume in drive B has no label
               Directory of  B:\USR\SALLY


               .        <DIR>        3-25-87 10:20a
               ..       <DIR>        3-25-87 10:20a
                    2 File(s)   292864 bytes free
```

they were typed at the keyboard one instruction at a time. Startup files that execute upon booting the system are built in this manner and installed by naming the batch file AUTOEXEC.BAT. The full programming power of MS-DOS goes far beyond what has been shown here (as its FOR, IF, and GOTO instructions might imply).

The annoying message about drive B: having no label can be fixed.

```
B>A:
A>LABEL B:
Volume in drive B has no label
Volume label (11 characters, ENTER for none)? MYDISK
```

Typing the MYDISK in response to the question labels the disk in drive B: with the name MYDISK.

Microsoft Windows

In late 1985 Microsoft released **Windows,** an operating environment running under MS-DOS and providing a visual user interface. While Windows runs as an application program and is not an operating system as such, it does manage most resources, with the exception of the MS-DOS file system. Because it does run on top of MS-DOS, Windows runs very slowly on 8086/8088-based machines and requires an 80286- or 80386-based system to be of practical value. That system should also have a minimum of 640K bytes of RAM and a hard disk.

Windows was at least partly designed to answer the challenge of the Macintosh. In fact, Microsoft has a number of license agreements with Apple allowing it to use some "look and feel" characteristics of the Macintosh interface. The interface is graphical, iconic, and object-oriented. Version 1 releases of Windows used tiling techniques. Version 2 allowed overlapping windows. Version 2 was released in late 1987 after the announcement of OS/2 and its Presentation Manager. While all Windows-based applications present the user with a common interface and similar command structure, the version 2 interface and command structure was chosen to be consistent with that of the proposed Presentation Manager. That single fact seemed to guarantee the popularity of Windows.

The appearance of Windows screens shares much with the Macintosh. Scroll bars, caption bars, menus, and dialog boxes are used. Windows have a style, size, and position on the screen and are identified by icons. One screen at a time is the "hot" or interactive screen. Inter-window communications take place. A mouse is a valuable input tool.

While applications should be specifically designed for Windows to best use its features, older MS-DOS applications may run in a window. The key to an MS-DOS application running successfully is tied to whether it is a "well-behaved" or "badly behaved" application. Well-behaved applications use BIOS calls to manage all I/O. (The ideal is shown in Figure 12.13.) Badly managed

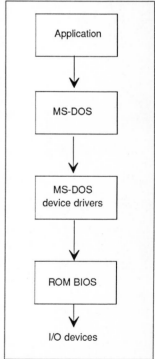

Figure 12.13

Figure 12.14

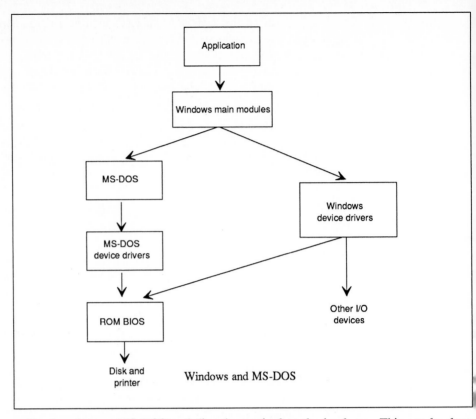

applications bypass MS-DOS and directly manipulate the hardware. This can be done because single-tasking operating systems do not isolate the user from any part of the system. Any application that "cheats" and fails to use MS-DOS facilities will invariably find that it is not portable across various PC clones running MS-DOS. Portability comes from letting MS-DOS do all resource management. Interestingly, Windows could be called a badly behaved application (Figure 12.14).

Each "running" process has its own window and is, in effect, a RAM-resident **pop-up** routine (also known as **TSR,** Terminate but Stay Resident). While Windows provides multitasking by some definitions, preemptive scheduling is not supported. Data may be transferred between applications (windows) through a **clipboard** or via an interprocess communication device known as **DDE** (Dynamic Data Exchange). Windows does the memory management and scheduling associated with its form of "multitasking."

Windows are objects, which means that as data structures they are packaged with the operations performed on them. Actions that take place do so as the result of **messages** sent to individual windows. Windows maintains a central system message queue and an individual message queue for each window. Each window represents a running process. Scheduling is fairly simple: The running process/window tends to run until it blocks on an empty message queue. Another window with a nonempty message queue is then allowed to run. There is no preemptive scheduling. In short, a process runs as long as it is able to run.

Memory management by Windows is somewhat more complicated. The MS-DOS user space in Figure 12.2 is used for Windows itself (roughly 300K bytes) and the applications. The scheme uses segmentation with segments running to 64K bytes maximum. Segments are classified as **fixed, moveable,** and **discardable** (which are also moveable). Fixed segments are generally required for older MS-DOS programs not specifically designed to run under Windows. Discardable segments are those that can be removed from memory when extra space is needed (program code segments are typically discardable), and the victims are chosen according to a global replacement LRU algorithm. Moveable (but not discardable) segments may not be removed before a process has completed and often represent data segments for programs. Windows essentially does no segment swapping in the sense that it does not write segments to a swap space: When a segment is discarded before its owner has completed, the segment will be reloaded from the owner's executable file rather than from a swap space. A form of garbage collection is used when the loading of a fixed or removable segment requires it: Moveable segments are relocated to accomplish the task. Segment sharing, particularly for code segments, is supported by Windows.

I/O is accomplished through Windows' own device drivers (Figure 12.14) except in two cases. Disk system accesses and printer commands pass through the ROM BIOS. It is the ROM BIOS that gives MS-DOS compatibility across machines that use differing I/O hardware. Windows directly manages the keyboard, video display, mouse, and other hardware.

OS/2

OS/2, Microsoft's single-user, multitasking operating system for the IBM PS/2 Family was designed to provide MS-DOS compatibility (upward and downward) in a system having several other design goals. The PS/2-OS/2 systems were designed to support office automation and networking. A graphical interface using object-oriented techniques was required. Memory management techniques were to take advantage of the hardware capabilities of the 80286, 80386, and other chips in this 32-bit family (OS/2 will not run under the 8086/8088-based PCs.) Preemptive scheduling was designed with response to user needs taking priority over throughput. I/O was to be device independent and virtual. OS/2 was to be expandable and upgradable for years to come, while maintaining upward and downward compatibility with new versions.

An overriding goal was to preserve as much software compatibility as possible with software designed for PCs, XTs, and ATs and allowing that software to run on hardware that is significantly incompatible with those machines. PS/2 machines are hardware incompatible with the earlier 8086/8088 and AT machines.

The User Interface

The primary user interface under OS/2 is the graphical, icon-based, object-oriented interface managed by the **Presentation Manager.** The interface operates as a subsystem under OS/2, providing all applications and users with a uniform interface. With the older command-line interface, each application had to create its own user interface, making it difficult to transfer data and activity between different applications. Many feel that the Presentation Manager will define the uniform-user interface across all IBM systems under SAA (Systems Application Architecture), their proposed portability standard. Under MS-DOS, the user interface of each software package played a major marketing role.

The interface provided by the Presentation Manager is fundamentally Microsoft Windows in an OS/2 setting. The Windows environment becomes even more valuable in the multitasking arena provided by OS/2. Developers may install their own user interfaces through an alternative called VIO.

Another useful feature of OS/2 is not so much a user interface as it is an added facility. The **3x Box** provides emulation for an 8086-based PC running MS-DOS (version 3.3 initially). That is, users can run MS-DOS applications in a window under OS/2. That feature has been considered important in the first days of OS/2.

Another feature of value to the user and developer is called **Family API** (Applications Program Interface). Family API is really an execution environment which allows programs to be written in such a way that their executable files will run under OS/2 and MS-DOS alike, even though the MS-DOS machine is 8086-based. When run under MS-DOS, some OS/2 functions not available in MS-DOS are made available, essentially enhancing MS-DOS. In a sense, this provides a measure of downward compatibility. While runnable on 8086-based machines, programs written to conform to Family API are able to take advantage of the special hardware features of the 80286 machines when run under OS/2.

Memory Management

One of the major features of OS/2 is that it was designed to take advantage of the memory-management and protection capabilities of the 80286 running in its **protected mode**. (Recall that in its real mode, the 80286 runs as a fast 8086.) OS/2 memory management incorporates segmentation and swapping to create a virtual-memory environment. A crude memory map is shown in Figure 12.15.

The 80286 hardware manages a real address space of 16M bytes and a virtual memory space of 1G byte using memory segments whose sizes may range up to 64K bytes. The 80286 provides address translation support, protection of a segment from processes other than its owner, and segment swapping support. OS/2 allows programs to use **huge segments** by using software control to convert those huge segments into a collection of 64K byte segments and a last segment, possibly smaller than 64K bytes. (For example, a 200K byte huge segment consists of three 64K byte segments and an 8K

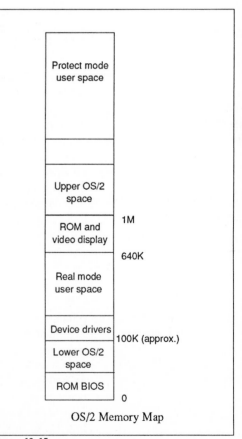

Figure 12.15

byte final segment.) OS/2 uses **LDTs** and **GDTs** (Local and Global Descriptor Tables), which maintain **segment selectors** describing starting addresses and lengths for each allocated segment. Future versions of OS/2 will take advantage of the larger address space and paging capabilities of the 80386 and its successors to provide virtual-memory techniques using 4K byte pages.

Currently, OS/2 uses a working set model for selecting which segments are to be in memory at any given time. Programs always require 384K bytes or less of RAM in order to execute under its management scheme. The operating system will not start a process unless there is sufficient space in swapping space to hold it. Swapping space is defined as the swapping file on disk together with all but 384K bytes of the RAM that is eligible for swapping. (Not all system-used RAM segments can be swapped.) In this way, OS/2 does not overcommit resources and cause deadlock. Moreover, OS/2 will not start a process unless there is enough "freeable" memory to run it.

When a segment must be swapped out to make room for a new segment (for example, a segment fault has occurred), a global LRU algorithm is used: Process and thread priorities make no difference. A program written as a collection of small segments incurs a higher overhead and higher fault rate, while one written as a collection of large or even huge segments makes the segment-replacement activity inefficient. Writing programs for OS/2 execution requires careful planning so that the right segmentation mix results.

OS/2 memory management is more complicated than this brief description shows. There is a suballocation mechanism for treating a segment as a heap for internal management by the process owning it. There are two types of shared memory, named shared memory and giveaway shared memory, used respectively for (public) communications between processes and threads and for fast, private-data transfer between processes. In fact, OS/2 has fairly sophisticated interprocess communication capabilities using semaphores and other shared-memory devices.

I/O Management

In a manner reminiscent of UNIX, each process does its output through STDIN and STDOUT, the standard input and output. The BIOS routines in OS/2 deliver services very much like those of MS-DOS, with the addition of some locking services and other features that support multitasking. Logical device names are used to create device-independent output.

In an unusual arrangement, some processes are allowed direct control of some I/O devices by what is called the **I/O Privilege Mechanism.** Under this mode, processes bypass the device driver and manipulate the device ports and memory locations. Most multitasking operating systems consider such action too risky and force all I/O through the operating system. Realization of the full implementation of the privilege mechanism depends on having an 80386-specific version of OS/2.

I/O devices are of two general types: **character mode** and **block mode.** Character mode devices and drivers operate in a FIFO manner. Block mode devices and drivers are not required to follow a FIFO strategy. I/O in OS/2 is asynchronous in that control of the CPU may be returned to the caller before the I/O activity is completed (with a message that I/O is incomplete). I/O requests are queued and managed by the device drivers.

The bus mechanism for IBM's PS/2 machines represents a different, patented element. The **Micro Channel** architecture features a 32-bit wide bus that is incompatible with the bus structure of PCs and ATs. The full 32-bit width is realized with 80386-based machines. The term **channel** implies that IBM intends to bring the I/O structure and capabilities of their microcomputers into line with their mini- and mainframe efforts. Data transfer over the channels is asynchronous DMA. Sixteen levels of interrupts are supported.

CPU Scheduling

OS/2 uses a priority dispatching mechanism. While processes are instances of executing programs, OS/2 has another entity called a **thread.** Each thread is an instance of a *path of execution through a process.* Multiple threads within a process accomplish multitasking within that process. (Process-rich operating systems spawn new processes to accomplish the multitasking, but threads cost less to create than processes.) Threads belong to the process that created them and share the resources allocated to the process. Threads are the entities that are dispatched by the OS/2 scheduler.

Each process and thread has an assigned priority. The scheduler simply runs the thread with the highest priority as long as the thread can make use of the CPU. If two or more ready-to-run threads have the same priority value and that value is the highest among the ready-to-run threads, timeslicing is used to move the CPU between them. The arrival of a ready-to-run thread with a higher priority causes preemption of the executing thread.

Threads fall into one of three priority categories: **time critical** (highest priority), **general,** and **low.** Each of these has three subcategories: **interactive, noninteractive foreground,** and **background.** The terms foreground and background are used here to refer to the characteristic of the "screen group." Priorities are a mixture of user-set, inherited, and dynamic. General-priority threads have their actual priority values incremented by I/O-bound behavior and decremented by CPU-bound behavior.

Processes begin life with three files that are similar to those in UNIX: STDIN, STDOUT, and STDERR. Processes may spawn child processes, to create a hierarchy of processes. When processes spawn children, the children are instances of different programs. When a process creates a thread, it is conceptually like creating a process identical to itself—one that will have a particular path of execution. Threads are an OS/2 technique for making this kind of activity faster and less costly than the spawning of processes. In addition, threads can become parents by creating other threads.

Interprocess communications is fairly sophisticated. RAM semaphores, system semaphores, shared memory segments, and pipes represent agents for synchronization. Interprocess communication between process can take place even if the processes are resident on different machines within a network.

Networking

OS/2 is designed to incorporate a **LAN Manager** as a part of the operating system. Under OS/2's multitasking, LAN Manager will run network communications in the background with little user interaction or interruption. Consequently, OS/2 is being designed with inherent LAN access, whereas PCs and ATs require some significant add-on capability. The primary reason for the inclusion of the LAN Manager is the belief that the days of the standalone personal computer are numbered.

The LAN Manager is designed to incorporate the functionality of the first four layers of the ISO/OSI model. OS/2 machines are well-designed to be OSI engines. TCP/IP (Transport Control Protocol/Internet Protocol) is supported as the most popular connectivity mechanism for multi-vendor networks, allowing OS/2 systems to interface to virtually any OSI-based network. Of course, OS/2 is intended to work well with PC Net and IBM's Token Ring networks.

The LAN manager works best with networks of a client/server architecture. Added security features will appear throughout the life of OS/2 as its use in multiuser systems (networks) grows and the distributed applications become more sophisticated. An **Extended Edition** incorporates the LAN Manager, a relational DBMS, some terminal emulation capability (IBM and DEC), and data import facilities.

The File System

The file system packaged with the early release of OS/2 looks like an MS-DOS file system and is FAT-based. Much of the concern over performance of PS/2 systems and OS/2 has been related to the relative slowness of file accesses for large-volume secondary-storage media. It is the FAT that causes most of the problem. To make access faster, larger cluster sizes can be used, but these do increase the internal fragmentation for the file system. OS/2 does allow large-volume storage media to be partitioned into several smaller file systems, each with its own FAT. This compromise increases access efficiency and allows smaller cluster sizes for manageable fragmentation. The partitioning does rule out system applications requiring very large files.

OS/2 designers do not feel the above problem will be around very long. The reason? OS/2 itself does not include a file system but was designed to require that a file system be attached to it in much the same way that a device driver is attached. The facility is called **IFS** (Installable File System) and provides an interface for installing file systems of the developer's design. All releases but the first expect to provide IFS.

In any event, file systems will use pathnames similar to those constructed in MS-DOS (except that the eight-character limitation on file names will be removed). Pathnames will be used for file systems and other I/O devices. Networking will take advantage of the pathname concept: Remote devices can be accessed by simply including some network names in the pathname.

OS/2 does provide a very important feature for multitasking by making asynchronous reads and writes to I/O. That is, control may be returned to the calling thread after an I/O request is made but before it is *complete*. MS-DOS required that the CPU either participate in the I/O or sit idle until the I/O completed.

Since OS/2 is a single-user system physically, little file protection was built in. File locking and record locking are used to provide some mutual exclusion capabilities for dealing with synchronization in the multitasking environment. Since, however, OS/2 systems in a network are part of a logical multiuser system, OS/2 will have to deal with access-protection mechanisms for the file system in the near future. There is some suspicion that access lists will be the major technique provided.

Exercises

1. Give at least two contributing factors that made MS-DOS the standard for 16-bit operating systems.
2. Why is MS-DOS easily portable?

3. The shell may be overwritten by an MS-DOS application. What does this imply about the construction of such an application?

4. If you owned Microsoft, what would you be looking to do with MS-DOS?

5. Describe the MS-DOS user interface in one sentence.

6. One MS-DOS system presents a user interface with windows. Redraw Figure 12.1 to show at least two approaches to its design.

7. Where is MS-DOS's boot information likely to be stored?

8. How is an MS-DOS disk volume's list of free blocks managed?

9. How are the directory entries for a disk volume managed in MS-DOS?

10. When a file is opened in MS-DOS, its directory entry is loaded into memory. Alterations to the FCB are not copied back to disk until the file is closed. Why can this be a problem? Why do it this way?

11. In MS-DOS, how are a given file's data blocks known and managed?

12. Most hard-disk systems have the capability of partitioning the disk into several logical subsystems. Why might this be not be as important for an MS-DOS user as for a CP/M user?

13. Interpret each field from the listing for a DIR command, such as in Figure 12.7. Do the same for DIRS.

14. Describe the results from each of the following.
    a. A>COPY *.PAS B:
    b. B>COPY *.* A:
    c. A>COPY *.?AS B:
    d. A>COPY ABC GHI
    e. A>SYS B:
    f. B>CHDIR \
    g. A>CHDIR
    h. A>RMDIR SAM
    i. B>DIR ..
    j. A>DIR | SORT /R | MORE
    k. A>DIR >B: \TEMP
    l. A>DIR | SORT | FIND ".COM"

15. Create an MS-DOS startup batch file that sets the date to Sunday, January 1, 2000, and the time to 12:00:00 am automatically upon bootup.

16. Create an MS-DOS batch file that removes all Pascal source files from the disk in drive B:.

17. Find a text discussing MS-DOS, and then write a batch file that mimics that of Exercise 16, except that each Pascal source file is presented to the user for a "thumbs up or thumbs down."

18. How can a user interrupt a running MS-DOS program?

19. Some have said that Windows and the Presentation Manager have made it more difficult for applications programs to be distinguishable. Why? On what basis will applications under Windows or OS/2 be distinguishable?

20. List at least 10 advantages of OS/2 over MS-DOS.

21. What will happen to MS-DOS?

13 Macintosh Operating Systems with Finder/MultiFinder

Apple Computer's Macintosh system introduced the computing public to a different world of user interfacing. The Macintosh interface can be described in various terms: graphic, iconic, metaphorical, object-oriented. The system's roots are found in the **Smalltalk** research activities conducted at Xerox's Palo Alto Research Center. A number of Xerox's employees carried their experiences to Apple. The technology was used for the short-lived Lisa project. The Macintosh system gained much from the **Lisa** activities and not only survived but flourished.

The use of a graphic interface allows users to think in terms of pictures and concepts rather than the traditional command line. Users indicate their requests by manipulating icons instead of offering a command in response to a prompt. (For example, the user may "click" on the icon representing a given file and "drag" it to the trashcan icon, thereby disposing of the file in a such a way that it is still recoverable if needed. At some later point in time, the simultaneous selection of the trashcan icon and the "empty" menu selection empties the trashcan, completing the file deletion process. The file is now essentially irretrievable. All of this may be done with the mouse device.) The visual presentation of icons and menus means that the user need not memorize command names, parameters, and formats. **Finder** is the facility (not technically part of the Macintosh operating system kernel) used to open and execute applications from the "desktop."

The graphic/iconic interface makes sense to users because of the **metaphorical** imagery. The screen and icons are designed to remind the user of a desktop and other familiar office fixtures. Users draw on their knowledge of ordinary activities to direct the Macintosh to carry out requests. By using earlier experiences as the base for computing activities, the learning time is drastically shortened and the process "seems natural."

Users think in terms of objects and actions. **Object-oriented design** has been incorporated into the Macintosh operating system as a natural means of implementing the metaphorical approach. In one extremely simple view, an **object** is a data structure which includes not only the storage mechanism for the data but the operations that are used to manipulate the object. Object-oriented design considers everything to be an object. From a programming point of view, manipulating the object sends the object a message, telling it what to do (such as send the *file* a *delete* message). The Macintosh operating system is of object-oriented design.

The heart of the Macintosh machines is the Motorola 68000 (68020 or 68030 for some newer systems), which is a 32-bit chip. The 68000 has 24-bit addressing while the 68020 and 68030 have full 32-bit addresses. In either case, directly addressable memory space is larger than the one-megabyte limit for most 16-bit machines.

Although the Macintosh represented a revolutionary step for personal computing, it gained acceptance slowly within the business and industrial community, primarily because of the lack of MS-DOS compatibility. Third-party vendors did make some level of compatibility possible, but not enough to make a significant impact. Application programs taking advantage of the Macintosh capabilities were relatively slow in arriving, the major breakthrough coming in desktop publishing where the Macintosh's user-friendliness and graphics capabilities could be readily utilized.

The state of user interfaces offered by the computer industry was altered dramatically by the introduction and success of the Macintosh. Virtually all operating systems, regardless of age, are now supported by software making "point and poke" iconic interfaces available. User interfaces now tend to be metaphorically designed to adapt computing to the user rather than forcing the user to learn unnatural commands. So strong has the impact of the Macintosh interface been that many consider the machine to have no "real" operating system.

The Macintosh does have an operating system, of course, one not designed to be easily ported across a wide variety of machines but designed to appear on Apple systems alone. Macintosh clones have not appeared; hence, software written for the Macintosh is essentially designed for the Macintosh owners alone.

Macintosh networks exist, particularly within the desktop-publishing industry and office settings. The Macintosh is gaining some acceptance as a low-cost, intelligent workstation for connecting to mainframe resources. Apple's philosophy puts the personal computer at the center of the computing universe and positions mainframes as magnificent peripheral devices at the beck and call of those personal computers. Apple's intent is for the Macintosh to succeed in peer-to-peer networks where nodes communicate directly with each other rather than through a mainframe.

The main evolution for Macintosh operating systems lies in increased processing speeds, greater RAM capacities, and multitasking. Later Macintosh entries (SE and Mac II) now incorporate the use of "slots" into which peripheral device cards can be installed. This increases the potential of the machine, particularly where compatibility and coprocessing are of concern. The move to color graphics from black-and-white enhances the machine as well.

Continued evolutionary change will be required if the Macintosh is to be competitive, since other microcomputer offerings have moved to 32-bit chips, powerful graphics, iconic interfaces, multitasking, and multiuser environments. All these capabilities are appearing on machines that are already well-entrenched in the business/industrial applications market or that are compatible with some of those machines.

The User Interface

As mentioned earlier, the user interface is metaphorical and graphics-based. Users manipulate objects, some of which are represented by icons. **Windows** are objects defined for purposes of communication between user and process. **Menus** are objects used for selection from among a list of possible activities. Icons, windows, and menus, like all objects, can be manipulated. Most manipulation takes place by using a mouse to **point, drag** and **select** or **click**. Figure 13.1 shows some icons, windows, and menus.

Figure 13.1

Figure 13.2

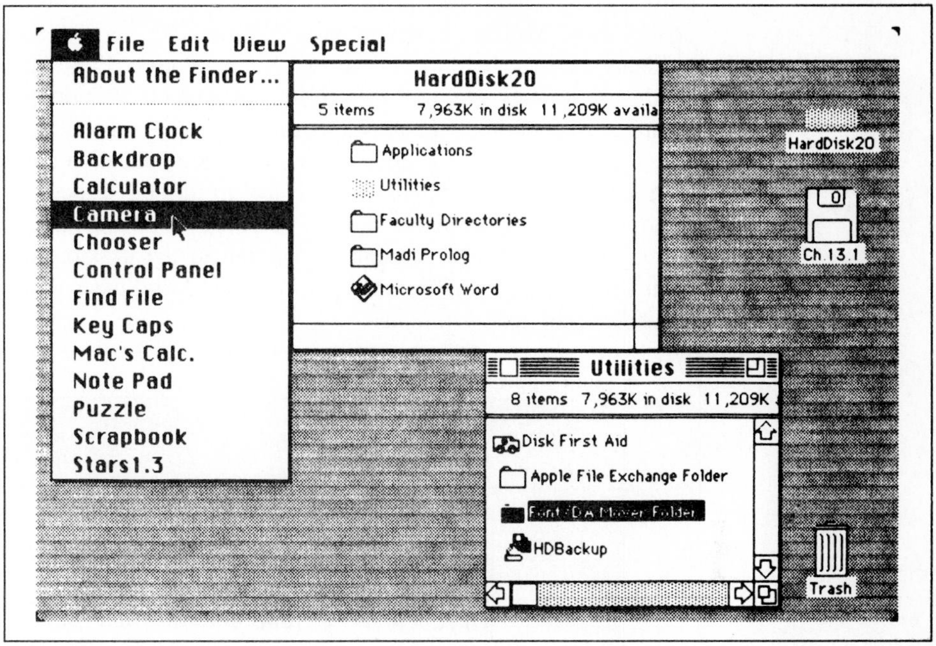

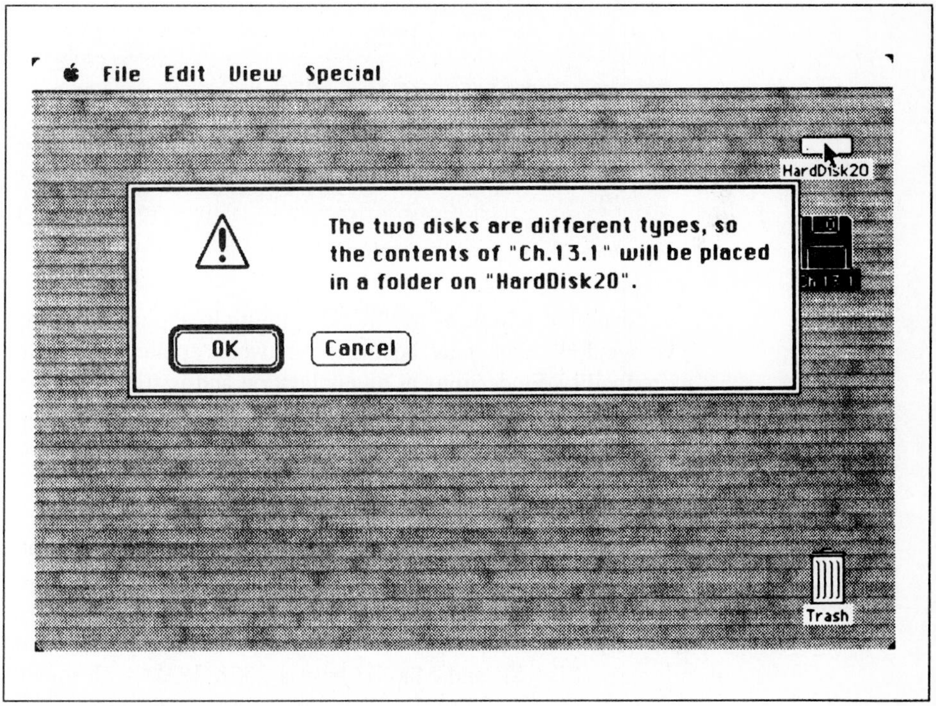

Boxes (windows that serve special communications purposes) are objects that come in several varieties. **Alerts** involve warnings to the user, warnings that the user must acknowledge before proceeding (as in Figure 13.2). **Dialogs** may be either modal or modeless. **Modal dialogs** interrupt the user and require selection from one of the available options before work may resume. Figure 13.3 illustrates a modal dialog. **Modeless dialogs** are used to inform of some condition while allowing the user complete freedom to continue without immediately responding to the message.

Until the advent of **MultiFinder,** only one application could be open at any given time. Finder, the first application to come up running at boot time, manages the opening of applications available from the desktop. To change applications with Finder requires moving from the current application to the desktop and then using Finder to open a new application. A newer utility called MiniFinder now makes the process easier under restricted conditions.

Figure 13.3

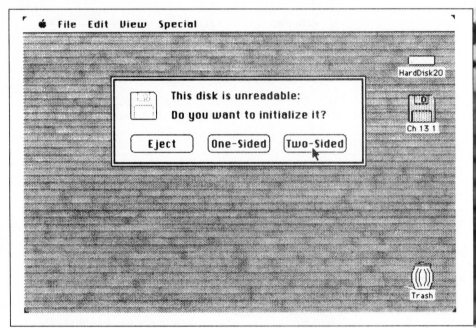

Since the advent of MultiFinder, multiple applications may be open, each with its own window. Data may be moved between applications (windows), giving the user more facility. Finder runs as an application and is still used to open new applications in the MultiFinder environment. With MultiFinder, the user may switch between applications without going through the desktop. The user can interact only with the current application, while all others operate as background processes.

Memory Management

The original "Mac" memory consisted of 64K ROM for operating-system routines and 128K RAM. Macintoshes became "Fat Macs" when stuffed with 512K of RAM. The Mac Plus involved an upgraded ROM (128K) and a base RAM of 512K. Of course, each version has been able to use RAM in excess of 512K in some useful ways. Newer offerings (Mac SE and Mac II) have a 256K ROM with much larger RAM, generally between one and two megabytes—but up to 8 megabytes is possible. The address space for the 68020-based Mac II is a whopping four gigabytes. Use of larger quantities of RAM in a Macintosh normally involves the creation of RAM disks.

The ROM holds about 500 routines that drive the Macintosh. About one-third of the routines belong to the operating system, while the rest are considered to be part of the **toolbox** which manages the user interface. Half the interface routines belong to **QuickDraw,** the graphic-management facility borrowed from the Lisa project.

The 68000 chip has no memory-management capabilities on board, and the early Macintosh systems made no attempt to do multitasking. Context switching was available, but switching from one resident routine (such as a *desk accessory*) to another was the responsibility of the application program, not the operating system. Finder allowed only one application to be open at a time, but since late 1987, MultiFinder allows multiple windows to be open on a variety of processes and offers some multitasking capability.

The Mac II, utilizing the 68020 chip, is coupled with the Motorola 68851 paged memory management unit (**pmmu**) to make multitasking with paged virtual memory effective. The 68851 allows page sizes from 256 bytes to 32K bytes. It has a 64 entry translation look-aside buffer as an associative cache for page table use. When MultiFinder appeared it made multitasking possible. UNIX for the Mac II (to include Apple's A/UX) takes advantage of the 68851 pmmu, to provide more efficient multitasking.

Figure 13.4 illustrates a memory map for the early Macintosh (before Multi-Finder). Note the **screen buffer** region. Maintaining the complicated Macintosh bit-mapped screen with all its graphics takes a considerable amount of memory and a major portion of the processor energy. In early systems, managing the screen could

Figure 13.4

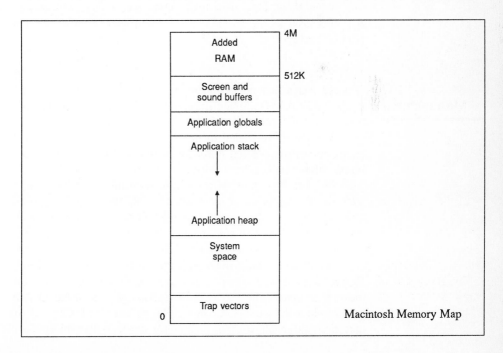

Macintosh Memory Map

easily take most of the CPU time. The SE and II reduce that overhead considerably and result in significantly faster machines.

In spite of the single-tasking nature in preMultiFinder times, the Macintosh has always come equipped with a memory manager, whose major function is to manage the heap space. There are two heap spaces—the **system heap zone** and the **application heap zone.** Heap zones consist of variable-sized chunks of contiguous memory called **blocks.** A block may or may not be **relocatable.** If relocatable, it may be **locked** (to prevent movement) or not. If locked, it may be **purgeable** (to allow for reclaiming) or not.

Requests for dynamic memory allocation from the heap space are met in a **circular, first fit** fashion beginning from the end of the last allocated block. If no sufficiently large block is found, **compaction** is attempted by rearranging the unlocked, relocatable blocks until a sufficiently large block becomes available. If compaction does not produce a sufficiently large block, purgeable blocks are reclaimed and compaction is used as needed to produce the required space. If all that fails, a **grow zone function** takes more drastic action: It attempts to move and purge other blocks and retry compaction. Should that fail, an error message is returned.

On the early Macintosh systems, the application heap was very small. Consequently, many programs required segmenting for the use of overlays. The operating system provides a **segment loader** to assist in this matter.

MultiFinder required some changes to facilitate multitasking. Each application that is open under MultiFinder is assigned a contiguous segment of memory. That is, MultiFinder uses dynamic partitioning and contiguous memory allocation with no swapping. External fragmentation is a serious problem as applications are opened and closed: The only way to reduce fragmentation once it occurs is to close all applications and reopen them. Only the current application (active window) allows user interaction: All other tasks as background tasks. (MultiFinder comes with a printer spooler, a most popular background task.)

I/O Management

Original Macs had no peripheral slots and therefore had limited expandability. The internal disk drive (3.5-inch floppy) held 400K bytes and was notoriously slow at data transfer. An external disk drive could be accommodated. Early in the Macintosh story, disk drives were upgraded to the 880K double-sided floppies. Original systems were equipped with two serial ports for connecting peripheral devices other than the keyboard, mouse, and external floppy drive.

The hard-disk units on early systems were somewhat slow. They were serial devices, and the hardware of the Macintosh did not support interrupt-driven data transfer. The Mac II, by contrast, has a parallel SCSI port for high-speed data transfer that is interrupt-managed. The amount of RAM available for disk caching has grown as the amount of RAM itself has grown. Disk access speeds up under such circumstances.

Expansion of early Macintosh machines had the aura of major surgery. The Mac II, by comparison, has six slots into which peripherals or peripheral controller cards may be installed. The bus (**Apple NuBus**) is established in such a way that a CPU installed in a slot can operate in parallel with the 68020. In fact, such a CPU can opt to take over the machine. That means, for instance, that an 80286 CPU can be installed and make the Mac II operate as an MS-DOS machine. The SE has one such expansion slot.

Input devices generate interrupts and create **events** that are placed in a FIFO event queue. Events are the major element in the scheduling scheme.

CPU Scheduling

Early Macs were single-user, single-tasking machines. However, the complex nature of the graphic interface and the operating system itself required forms of control bordering on scheduling in the traditional sense. MultiFinder, declared by Apple to be a Macintosh operating system, manages a time-slicing arrangement to create multitasking capability. Interestingly, this "operating system" can be turned on and off at will: With MultiFinder turned off, Finder becomes the operative method for opening applications (running one application in memory at a time). Some applications written for the Macintosh do not run in the MultiFinder environment, necessitating this unusual feature.

It is interesting to note that many applications for microcomputers have run afoul of multitasking when introduced. Until recently, microcomputer applications assumed single tasking as the normal mode of operation and simply took over the entire machine. Adding to some users' woes is the fact that a Macintosh with MultiFinder loaded and operating "eats up" a significant amount of RAM, leaving very little room for applications unless the machine is populated with several megabytes of main store.

"Scheduling" in the early Macintosh sense meant intercepting events as they happen, placing them on an event queue and allowing the application program to do any actual scheduling. In effect, these events are interrupts that are queued by the operating system and then handled by the application. The interrupt-handling routines invoked by the application are conceptually much like the terminate-but-stay-resident programs in MS-DOS. The user has the ability to switch from the execution of one task to another. The context switch is managed by the interrupt mechanism. While not true multitasking, it does give users a lot of flexibility in a single-user setting. Recall, however, that MultiFinder does add time-sliced multitasking.

Events fall into several categories determined by their origin and meaning. Mouse events (mouse key up/down), keyboard events (key up/down and auto-key), and disk events (insert) are three. There are also events associated with peripheral devices and networks, and the event manager reports a null event when there is nothing to report. Application programs may define event types of their own. The **event manager** does the monitoring and enqueueing required for all events. However, it is up to the application program to handle the events as it sees fit.

There are events that do not go onto the event queue and are handled with a higher or lower priority than those in the queue. The activation/deactivation and update of the windows are examples. The window manager is the responsible routine.

Macintosh Networks

As mentioned earlier, the Macintosh is becoming a popular LAN-based intelligent workstation. **AppleTalk** is a software protocol for small, low-speed, low-cost LANs of Macintosh computers and intelligent peripherals, such as file servers and laser printers. AppleTalk is a bus topology handling 30 or more stations, using as much as 1,000 feet of shielded, twisted-pair cable. A transmission rate of 230.4 Kbps is used. AppleTalk incorporates packet-switching, the functionality of the ISO/OSI model, and CSMA/CA (collision avoidance using random delays). AppleTalk LANs can be bridged together and linked to other networks via gateways.

Macintosh systems have been successfully incorporated into EtherNet LANs, such as EtherMac, which uses a special hardware network server. Mac to PC communications has become popular, as in the TOPS system, where any Mac or PC can act as a server, and PC MacBridge, which uses Appletalk boards in the PCs. Apple and DEC have announced networks linking Macs with VAX computers. Apple has also announced products to incorporate Macs into IBM's SNA-based networks, allowing Macintosh users to take full advantage of IBM's connectivity efforts. Macs have also been integrated into Unix-based networks. These communications capabilities are crucial to the Macintosh's success in the workstation market.

The File System

Early Macintosh systems used the Macintosh File System (**MFS**), a flat directory system. Of course, as the move to larger volume hard disk systems took place, flat directory systems became unwieldy, even unworkable. The Macintosh Plus used an upgrade to a Hierarchical File System (**HFS**) with **folders** being the metaphorical (sub)directories. Since folders may contain other folders, the hierarchical arrangement is possible. Some HyperDrive hard-disk systems extend this arrangement to provide for **drawers,** which are conceptually a lot like file systems in UNIX, volume directories, or disk partitions. This is not, however, a Macintosh feature. Most hard-disk systems provide for partitioning into logical subsystems.

The typical file operations of create, open, close, read from, and write to are supported by operating system routines. Toolbox routines also allow for file deletion, duplicating, copying, renaming, and so on. The user seldom sees pathnames for files since most user manipulation is accomplished through the iconic interface.

A file, to the Macintosh system, is merely a named sequence of bytes, usually stored on disk. A disk sector holds 512 bytes, while an assignable block is normally two sectors (1K). The first pair of logical blocks contain the boot information.

Logical blocks two and three constitute a master directory. That directory contains volume information about dates and times of initialization and last backup, volume attributes, volume name, counts on files contained and blocks used, pointers of various kinds, and other information. A volume-allocation block map is also present: It marks blocks (starting with logical block 2) as used or unused and maintains linked lists of blocks allocated for each file, much in the manner of the FAT from MS-DOS.

The file directory containing entries for each file on the volume follows the block map. (This description is for the MFS. Some differences for the HFS will be found.) A typical floppy-disk setup and file-directory entry is shown in Figure 13.5.

The arrival of **HyperCard** has been hailed as a major event in the Macintosh story. HyperCard affords a hypermedia data-storage mechanism that handles video, graphics, text, and audio forms of data in a free-form manner. Some liken it to a book-like database system that fits the way users naturally think. It is, in fact, a high-level, somewhat natural programming language as well as a database system. Regardless of the description, HyperCard is expected to provide increased sales and popularity for the Macintosh and will spawn comparable software for MS-DOS and OS/2 systems. Whether HyperCard changes the way users interact with and program their machines remains to be seen.

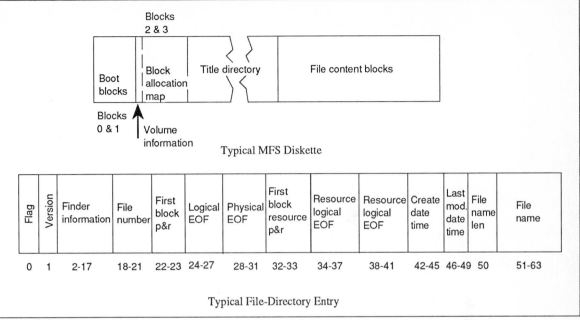

Typical MFS Diskette

Flag	Version	Finder information	File number	First block p&r	Logical EOF	Physical EOF	First block resource p&r	Resource logical EOF	Resource logical EOF	Create date time	Last mod. date time	File name len	File name
0	1	2-17	18-21	22-23	24-27	28-31	32-33	34-37	38-41	42-45	46-49	50	51-63

Typical File-Directory Entry

Figure 13.5

A Command Language Session	To boot the system, turn on the Macintosh, wait for a beep. After some time and a message or so, the system disk's icon will be visible at the upper right (Figure 13.6). In this case, the system disk is a hard-disk; there may or may not be a window open for the

Figure 13.6

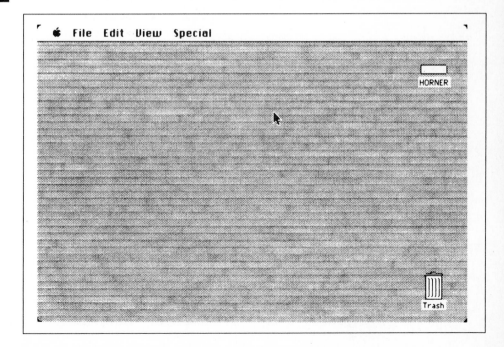

Figure 13.7

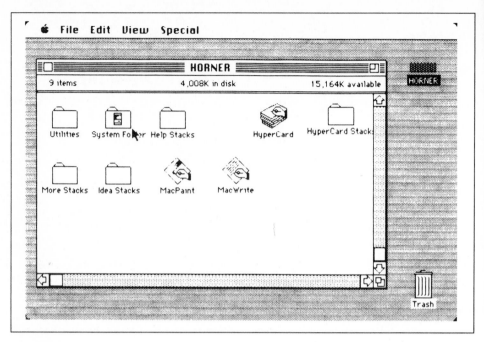

disk. If not, move the mouse pointer until the point is within the system disk's icon and **double click** (depress and release the mouse button twice in succession without altering the mouse's location). A window showing the contents of the system disk will be drawn (Figure 13.7). System information is contained in the **system folder.** In what follows, a system having one floppy disk and a hard-disk is assumed. (Note: to start a

Figure 13.8

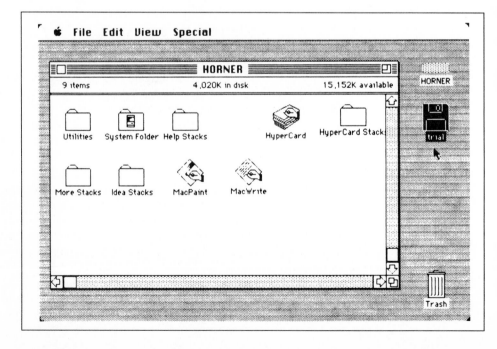

Figure 13.9

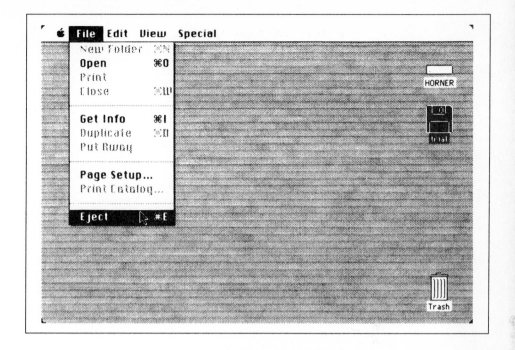

dual floppy system, place a system disk in the internal drive and continue as above.)

Insert a blank disk in the floppy drive. A dialog box will appear (as in Figure 13.3). Follow the directions (move the pointer to the appropriate response box and click) for formatting the diskette. After the formatting is complete, another dialog box will ask you to type the name of the formatted disk. Follow the directions and type in *trial*. A look at the icon for the new disk will show that it is the **selected** icon. (It is the dark icon. See Figure 13.8.) Move the pointer to the top row of menu titles until it is over the *File* menu. Depress and hold the button to display the menu entries (Figure 13.9). With the button depressed, move the pointer to the *Eject* entry. Release the button. The newly formatted *trial* will be ejected from the drive. Place another blank disk in the external drive and format it using the name *book*.

Opening a window on a disk or a folder essentially displays the directory of files it contains. Close the system-disk window by moving the pointer to the small box in the extreme upper left corner and clicking.

Now, move the pointer to the disk icon for the *trial* disk. Depress and hold the button. **Drag** the *trial* icon by moving the mouse until the arrow is pointing to *book's* icon. An outline of the system disk icon will appear superimposed over *book* (Figure 13.10). Release the button. Follow the instructions in the dialog box to copy the entire contents of *trial* onto *book*. That's all there is to making a copy of a disk.

It should now be clear what the terms "click on" and "drag to" mean in the context of the Macintosh user interface. To select an icon, click on it once. Clicking on an icon twice in quick succession is called **double clicking.** Double clicking starts some kind of action. For example, double clicking on a disk icon or a folder icon opens a window displaying the contents, while double clicking on a program starts its execu-

Figure 13.10

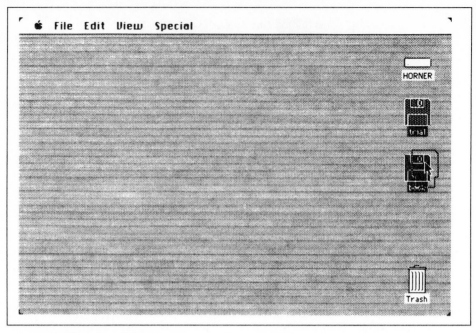

tion in a window. Double clicking on a file created by an application begins execution of that application using the "clicked-on" file as input.

Eject the disk named *book* by depressing simultaneously the "daisy" key, the shift key, and the 1 key. (The daisy key is the key immediately to the left of the space bar. Typing daisy-shift-2 ejects the disk in an external floppy drive.) Reinsert *trial* into the

Figure 13.11a

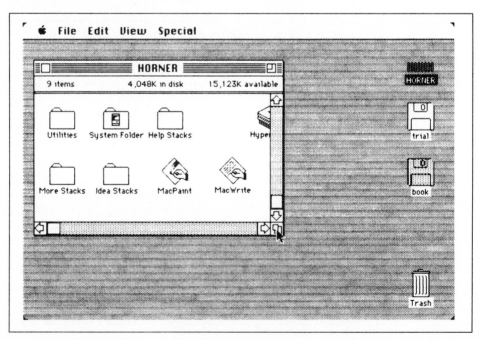

Figure 13.11b

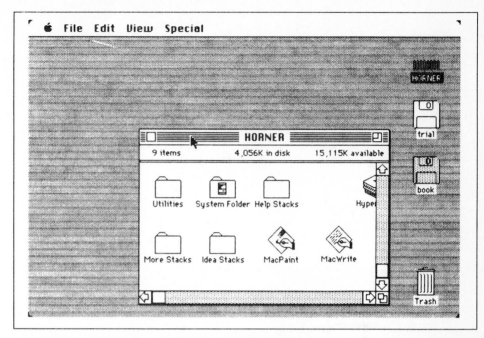

floppy drive and then double click on the system disk to open a window. Find the **sizing box** at the lower-right corner of the window. Click on it, keep the button depressed, and move the mouse (Figure 13.11a). Release the button and observe that the size and shape of the window is altered. Do a similar activity for the **title bar** at the top of the window. Observe that the window's location is changed while the size remains fixed (Figure 13.11b). Windows can be positioned and sized to suit the user.

Click on the MacWrite icon (or any file icon within the window) and drag it to the icon for *trial*. Release the button, open a window for *trial* and see that MacWrite (or whatever) has been copied to this disk (Figure 13.12). Now, adjust the size and position

Figure 13.12

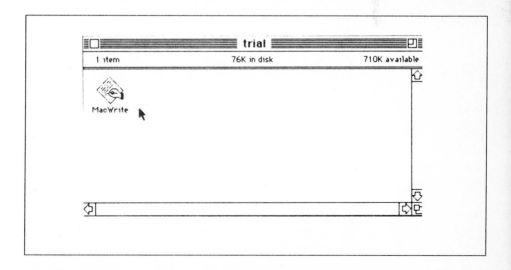

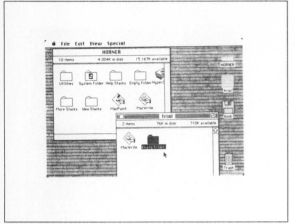

Figure 13.13a

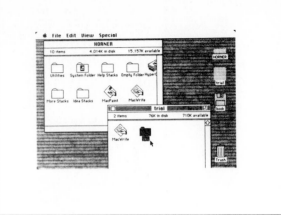

Figure 13.13b

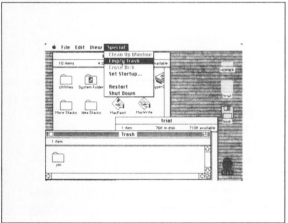

Figure 13.13c

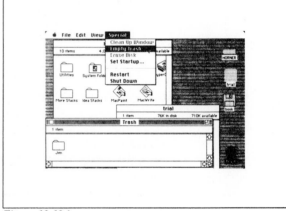

Figure 13.13d

of both windows so that the contents of each are visible. Click somewhere inside *trial's* window to make it the active window. Pop open the *File* menu, and select *New Folder.* A copy of the folder has been created inside *trial,* as shown in Figure 13.13a. Since the empty folder is selected, by typing in *Jim,* the copy of the empty folder is automatically renamed *Jim* (Figure 13.13b). Click on *Jim* and drag the icon to the *Trash.* Double click on *Trash* to open a window for *Trash* and find *Jim* still hiding there (Figure 13.13c). At this point in time, *Jim* can be returned to *trial* if desired. However, select the *Special* menu and *Empty Trash* (Figure 13.13d). See *Jim* disappear. *Jim* may no longer be recovered. Close the *Trash* window.

Create another *Empty Folder* for *trial.* With *Empty Folder* selected, pop open the *File* menu and choose *Duplicate.* Observe that the copy appears in *trial's* window (Figure 13.14a). Rename *Copy of Empty Folder* as *Jim* (Figure 13.14). Select *Empty Folder* in *trial* and rename it *Sally.* Make a copy of *Sally* and name it *School* (Figure

Figure 13.14a

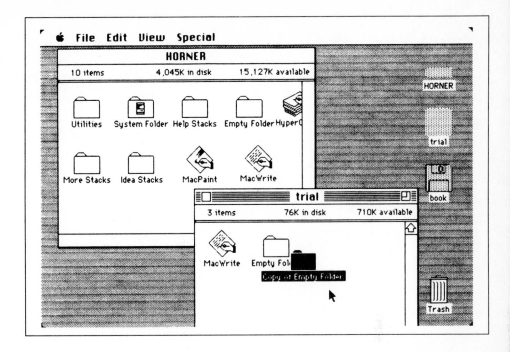

Figure 13.14b

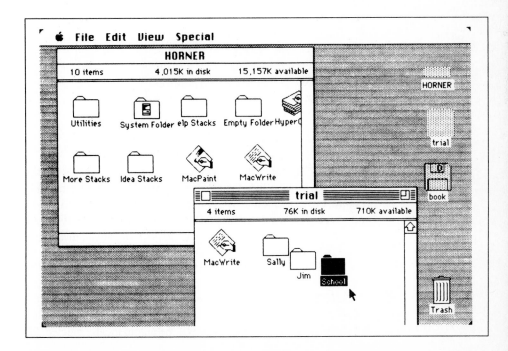

Figure 13.14c

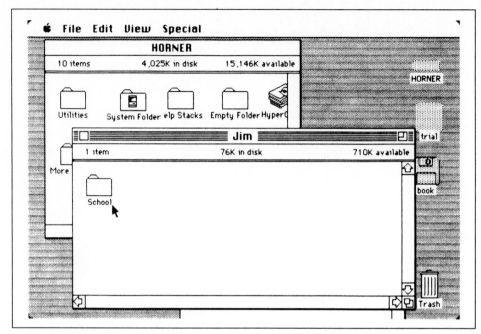

13.14b). Drag *School* to *Jim*. This action makes *School* a folder (subdirectory) within *Jim*. (Figure 13.14c shows a window opened for *Jim*.) Figure 13.15 shows the hierarchical nature of *trial* at this point.

Next, use MacWrite to create a document. Double click on *MacWrite* to execute it. Figure 13.16(a) shows a blank MacWrite document. Start typing as with any word processor, entering three lines:

Line 1
Line 2
Line 3

Figure 13.15

Go to the *File menu* and select *Save As* (Figure 13.16b). Follow the directions in the dialog box to save the document as *File1*. Use the *File* menu again to exit *MacWrite* (Figure 13.16c). Open a window for *Jim* and drag *File1* to *School*. (Some repositioning and resizing of windows may be needed.) *File1* now exists as a file in *School*. (A window for school is shown in Figure 13.17.) If path names were being used, this path would be something like */trial/Jim/School/File1*.

Make a copy of *File1* and drag the copy to the folder *Sally*. Open *Sally*, select the *Copy of File1*, and rename the copy *File1* by typing in the name as shown in Figure 13.18. (Why was the renaming delayed until the repositioning?)

Close all windows. Choose *Special* from the menu line and *Shutdown* from *Special* (Figure 13.19). All disks will be automatically ejected. Turn off the machine.

Figure 13.16a

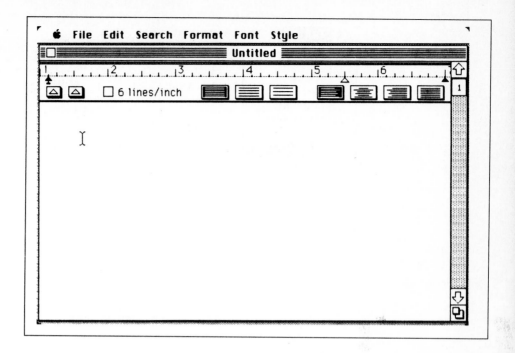

Figure 13.16b

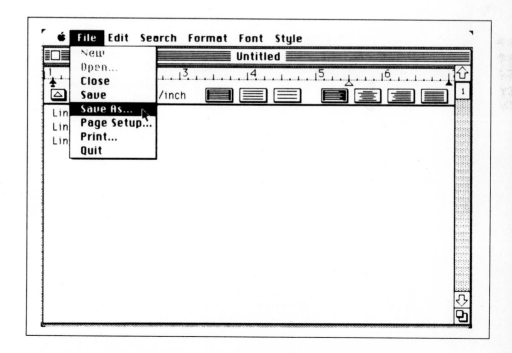

Figure 13.16c

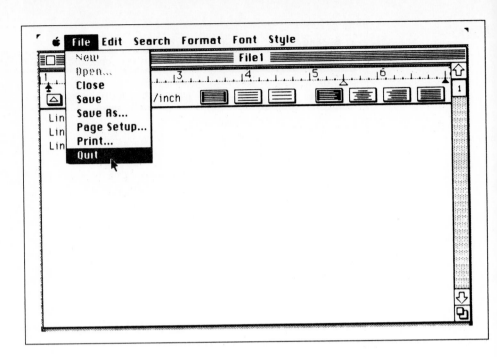

Figure 13.17

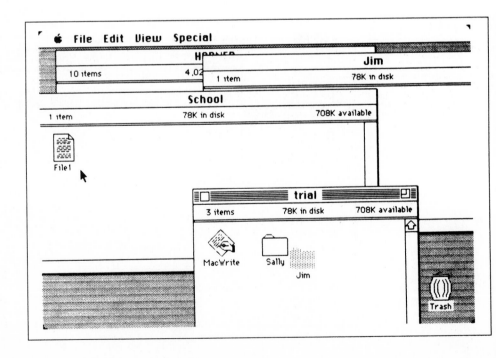

Figure 13.18

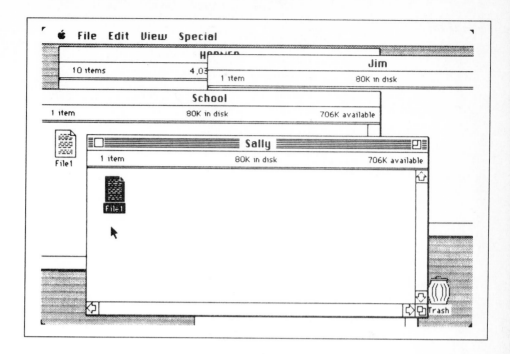

Figure 13.19

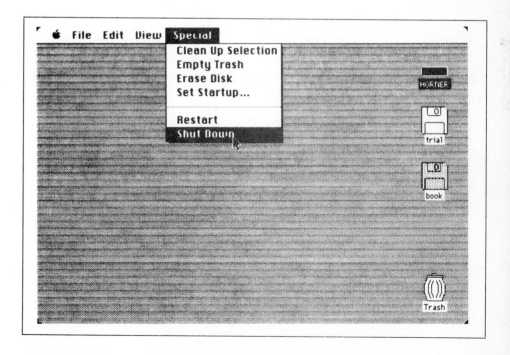

Figure 13.20

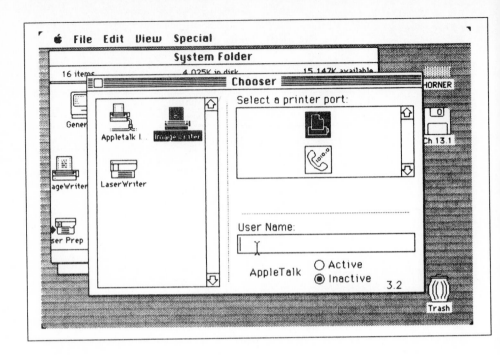

Note: By opening the *System Folder,* one can see which system capabilities and I/O drivers are available. By popping the *Apple* menu selection (extreme upper-left corner of the screen) and selecting *Choose,* the physical setup of the machine can be examined. For example, in Figure 13.20 the ImageWriter (printer) is connected to the printer port rather than the modem port (both are serial ports and may be used interchangeably). AppleTalk is disconnected. Changes can be made with the mouse.

The difference between an object-oriented, graphics-based user interface and a command-driven interface should be clear.

Exercises

1. Give at least two contributing factors that made the Macintosh popular.
2. Give at least two reasons for the Macintosh's slow rise to popularity.
3. Describe the user interface in one sentence.
4. Where is MS-DOS's boot information likely stored?
5. How is a disk volume's list of free blocks managed?
6. How are the directory entries for a disk volume managed?
7. How are a given file's data blocks known and managed?
8. Give at least two advantages of the SE and Mac II over earlier Macintosh versions.
9. Why is the SCSI (Small Computer System Interface) port an improvement over the serial port used in earlier Macintosh systems for hard-disk interfacing?
10. Find a text on the Macintosh and learn to make command files.
11. Why are pathnames not often seen by the casual user?
12. Find a text on the Macintosh and learn how to set up a system folder for use by some particular "turnkey" application.

13. Gain access to a Macintosh system and do the following:
    a. Boot the system
    b. Initialize several disks
    c. Make a system disk holding MacWrite and MacPaint
    d. On a nonsystem disk, create a tree of folders
    e. Use MacWrite to create several files in different folders
    f. Use MacPaint to create several files in different folders
    g. Transfer some files and folders to a blank (but formatted) disk

14 UNIX Operating Systems

The operating system known as **UNIX** was developed on and for minicomputers but it has the unique privilege of being the first operating system implemented on micro-, mini-, and mainframe computers from multiple vendors. UNIX has contributed significantly to the world of operating system design and implementation. Born in a research and development environment and nurtured in academic institutions, UNIX has become one of the most popular operating systems in the commercial marketplace. Developed by experienced programmers *for* experienced programmers, it has wandered beyond those bounds since the early 1980s. Designed to aid in the software development process, UNIX has been pushed into the everyday routine of nonprogramming users.

UNIX has its roots in the **Multics** project conducted at MIT. (Bell Labs participated in the project with General Electric and others for a time but then withdrew.) Ken Thompson (later joined by Dennis Ritchie and others) began the design of UNIX in the late 1960s to create a good programming environment for Bell Labs personnel like himself. The goals of the project were to build an *interactive programming environment with many tools and tool-building utilities* to assist in program development. The operating system was to be based on simple, elegant routines with efficiency taking a back seat to simplicity. The system was designed to encourage a particular programming philosophy: Solve large tasks by combining a number of simpler tasks. Three other characteristics now stand out: UNIX is portable, is device independent, and has a hierarchical file system.

The original version of UNIX was written in assembly language (PDP-7), but eventually it was rewritten in C (except for a small, machine-dependent core of assembly language routines) and implemented on PDP-11 systems from DEC. While UNIX was not the first operating system written in a high-level language, it was a leader in capturing the advantage of **portability** offered by such an approach.

Files and peripheral devices are treated essentially the same in this system, giving UNIX true **device independence.** The file system shows the guiding force of simplicity: All files are seen by UNIX as byte streams. UNIX supports no other file system structure; any required structure is added by the application routines. In general, the operating system itself supports a minimum collection of functions in all areas. Application-level tools supply the diversity of function as needed by users.

The command language of UNIX was built into a command language interpreter or shell (of which there are many). Unlike most operating systems of its time, UNIX treated each shell as an application program rather than part of the operating system. As a result, the shell is easily customized to fit the individual user.

Although interactive in nature, UNIX allows **shell scripts** (executable files of shell commands) and other programs to be executed as **background processes** with no intervention by the user. (Background processes are essentially batch processes, which may run **concurrently** with interactive processes.)

Most shells and the command language encourage **I/O redirection,** allowing input from wherever desired and output to wherever needed. Redirection and **pipes** (mechanisms for treating output from one process as input to another) encourage the UNIX philosophy of programming. **Filters** are simple programs that accept a stream of input, perform a single transformation on it, and then pass the stream on as output to the next process; entire applications may be created by piping between successive filters.

Until the early 1980s, Western Electric (Bell Labs' parent company) was a **monopoly,** protected by the federal government but restricted from competing in the commercial computer markets. Accordingly, UNIX was not groomed for the commercial market. In 1976 UNIX was licensed for use by colleges and universities. In 1978 Version 7 of UNIX was released to the academic world. When **divestiture** came in the early 1980s, college and university computer graduates already formed a large, trained cadre of UNIX enthusiasts within the commercial world. UNIX's success was guaranteed, in spite of the general unfriendliness of UNIX toward most users.

A number of UNIX operating systems are found today. **System V** is the "standard" as supported by AT&T at this writing and has been since 1983. Work done at the University of California at Berkeley has created **Berkeley 4.2bsd** (and 4.3) as a popular alternative. **XENIX** was created by Microsoft and licensed by Western Electric prior to divestiture. XENIX has been the predominant microcomputer version of System V UNIX and has brought a number of improvements aimed at the commercial market. XENIX is available for a number of minicomputers as well. Any number of UNIX clones, lookalikes, and workalikes can be found, particularly in the microcomputer world. Probably the best and most successful UNIX-flavored operating system is the **VAX VMS** by Digital Equipment Corporation.

User Interface: The Shell

The real interface to the UNIX operating system is the system service call. For nonprogrammers, the normal user interface is the **shell.** (Remember, "the shell" is a misnomer because there are many different shells.) The shell is a command interpreter executing as an application program. Users invoke the shell and its commands to accomplish the general tasks of process control, file manipulation, and information management. While any application program can act as a shell, two shells—the **Bourne shell,** and the **C-shell**—are in general use.

Bourne Shell

The (Steve) Bourne Shell, usually **/bin/sh,** was designed for program development and is excellent for creating and running shell scripts. It has more powerful flow control facilities in the form of **if/then/else, for/do/done, while/do/done, until/do/done, case,** and **break** constructs. A number of shell variables (**HOME, PATH, USER, MAIL, TERM, PS1,** and **PS2**) describe the user's environment for running the shell. A **.pro-**

file shell script in the user's home directory is executed at login time to establish the actual environment. A **trap** instruction allows the shell to react to predetermined conditions during execution. I/O redirection is a major feature of both the Bourne shell and C-shell.

C-shell

The C-shell (Bill Joy at Berkeley), often **/bin/csh,** was designed to adhere to the syntax of the C language and differs from the syntax of the Bourne shell. The C-shell was designed for interactive computing and, because of better process control and editing facilities, it is superior for interactive computing. Because of its design, however, it has less powerful flow control structures than the Bourne shell and is less helpful in writing shell scripts. The C-shell has its own set of shell variables for defining the shell environment. A **.login** file in the home directory is executed when the shell is invoked, and a **.logout** file in the home directory is executed at logout time. A **history** command allows the last few entered commands to be repeated, in some instances speeding up the command entry process. I/O redirection is essentially the same as for the Bourne Shell.

The **alias** facility allows the user to rename or redefine commands. For example,
    alias **l ls -al fileA**
allows the use of **l** to replace the longer **ls -al fileA.**

Shell
Commands

Commands in UNIX are of three general types. Some commands are built into the shell (**intrinsic** commands) and are not individual programs. Others (**extrinsic** commands) are simply compiled, executable programs that are loaded from the file system and executed. Still others are executable **shell scripts,** which are nothing more than files of shell commands. The repertoire of commands available to a given user is designed by the user himself or herself. Each user's shell has a **PATH** variable whose value dictates the search order used to locate nonbuilt-in commands stored within the file system. The default path may look like:
    :/bin:/usr/bin
Translation: Search the current (active) directory for the command name; if not found, search the public directory **/bin**; and if still not found, search the directory **/usr/bin.**

The commands, in conjunction with a shell, give the user an **extensible programming language** tailored to particular needs and styles. The two popular shells contain established **shell variables** whose values may be set (**PATH** is one). The user may establish other variables as needed. These two popular shells execute commands sequentially unless directed otherwise by selection and repetition.

The Command
Language and
Interface

The shell (meaning Bourne shell or C-shell for the rest of this discussion) is unusual in that it is **case sensitive.** Most commands are lower case, with shell variables upper case. The abbreviations that characterize command names are often cryptic and difficult to remember. Experienced programmers love them, but novices and infrequent users find them intimidating and frustrating. For example, the options list for a given UNIX command can be very long and difficult to remember. The formatting of arguments is not standard among commands or easily guessed in many cases. In other words, the UNIX command language is not easily learned and used by most people. UNIX supports the use of **wildcards** (including * and ?) for specifying command parameters. Arguments with wild cards are sometimes called **ambiguous** arguments, since they may represent one, two, twenty-two, or no actual parameter value (for example, ca* may represent cat, ca, cart, and so on, or it may represent no value with system meaning).

A current concern in UNIX circles is the line-oriented nature of the interface. Even though each user can tailor his or her shell to suit personal needs and tastes, many feel that the UNIX interface is antiquated. Projects to design alternative interface types have been common pursuits in the last several years. Menu-driven interfaces, iconic interfaces, and windowing are a few of the techniques beginning to appear. Some whole screen interfaces have come out of the **CAD/CAM** (computer assisted design and computer aided manufacturing) and **CAD/CAE** (computer assisted design and computer assisted engineering) packages developed to run on UNIX systems. (UNIX has been the most popular operating system for networks of engineering work-stations.)

Redirection and Pipes

Pipes and redirection are two important features of UNIX that are found in the shell. Every UNIX process has three files assigned to it at the time of creation: **stdin, stdout,** and **stderr.** For most processes, **stdin** is the keyboard, **stdout** the terminal screen, and **stderr** the director of error messages to the terminal screen (often the same physical destination as **stdout**).

Redirection of input or output is easily managed by UNIX. If a process is to take its input from some file other than **stdin,** the pointer to **stdin** is altered to point to the new file. For example, the command **cat** normally takes its input from the keyboard and places its output on the terminal screen. The command **cat <test** takes its input from the file **test** and writes the contents to the screen (in this case, **cat test** does the same thing). By changing the pointer from **stdout** to some other file, output can be redirected: **cat test >tempfile** copies the contents of **test** to the file **tempfile.**

The pair of commands

```
ls / >temp
wc <temp
```

writes a listing of the root file's directory into **temp,** passes the contents of **temp** to the wordcount process, and writes the results on the screen. Because of the nature of **wc,** the user sees a printout of the number of lines, words, and characters in the listing of the directory. The number of lines is the same as the number of files in the root directory. Since the output of **ls** has been redirected, the directory listing will *not* appear on the terminal screen.

The same result can be obtained by the use of a pipe:

```
ls / | wc
```

A pipe is essentially a system-managed file that acts as a read-once FIFO buffer. In the redirection example, a temporary file was created by the user. In the **pipeline** (two or more processes linked by pipes) example, the temporary file was managed by the system and was transparent to the user. Piping, like redirection, requires the reassignment of pointers from **stdin** and **stdout.** In many implementations, pipes are up to 10 blocks long, are managed as a circular read-once queue, and constitute a special file type managed by UNIX.

Since redirected output disappears from the terminal screen, UNIX has a **tee** command to allow the user to see the intermediate results when redirecting output to a file. For example,

ls / | tee temp

places the directory listing in the file **temp** while showing it on the video monitor. Recall that error messages go to **stderr**; because of this, error messages appear on the terminal screen even if the output is redirected or piped. If error messages were sent along with the output, they would likely disappear into files or into pipes.

UNIX Tools

UNIX delivers an operating system, but it also delivers much more in terms of the tools (utility routines) that accompany it. For example, there is online documentation and tutorial assistance through the commands **man** and **learn** and the files under **/usr/doc.** Interpersonal communications facilities are available through **biff, finger** (bsd UNIX only), **mail, mesg, news,** and **write.** Housekeeping utilities such as **cal, calendar, date, lock, pwd, uptime,** and **who** are also found.

Document Preparation

UNIX supplies text editors such as **ed** (line-oriented) and **vi** (screen-oriented). There is a form letter facility and text formatting commands for rough drafts (**pr, nroff**) and for typesetting (**troff**). Preprocessors (that is, filters) for these commands can format pictures (**pic, ideal**), tables (**tbl**), and equations (**eqn**) for insertion into the formatted document. Spelling, grammar, and style checkers are found in UNIX, along with indexing, bibliographical aids, and a thesaurus. Some limited graphics commands are available.

Information Management

Files may be compared using **cmp, comm,** and **diff** or searched for particular string patterns with **grep** and **egrep.** The **head** or **tail** of a file may be displayed, or the file may be **sort**ed. Duplicate file entries are removed with **uniq,** and the file's characters, words, lines, and pages are counted with **wc.** File contents may be displayed using **cat** and **more.** Directory contents may be seen using **ls.**

File System Management

Files may be created and altered by the use of text editors or other programs. In simple cases, the commands **cat** and **echo** can be used to create and edit files. Files may be copied by **cp,** renamed by **mv** (renaming in a hierarchical file system may mean moving to a different point in the tree), or deleted by **rm.** Nondirectory files may be linked to another name by **ln.**

Permissions for owner, group, and other users may be set by **chmod.** Since devices are treated as files, permissions for devices can be set similarly. Typically only the owner of the file or the **superuser** (system administrator) have the ability to do so.

Process Control

The running of jobs is assisted by a number of language translators. A linking loader is also included in the system. Jobs may be run interactively or in the background (by use of **&**); they may be started automatically **at** some time in the future or may be killed. A job's status may be examined by **ps** and its input and output redirected, piped, or split (**tee**).

Program Development

Besides the assemblers, compilers, interpreters, linking loaders, text editors, and others mentioned earlier, UNIX provides some powerful program development tools. Two pattern-scanning utilities known as **sed** and **awk** (particularly **awk,** which is really a programming language) allow developers to scan source code for a pattern and perform editing without invoking an editor (**grep** and **egrep** are also useful).

The **make** build utility is extremely useful when developing program systems. If one module in a large collection of modules making up an application system must be altered and recompiled, **make** will automatically determine which of the other modules must also be recompiled so as to remain compatible; **make** also automatically relinks the collection. For large applications, the automatic updating of all affected modules is a valuable safety net and time saver. This utility is really a part of the system configuration, rather than part of the tool set.

Two other well-known programs are the lexical analyzer **lex** and the parser-generator **yacc** (yet another compiler compiler). The functions performed by these two are similar to some performed by all interpreters and compilers, but their purpose is to help in the creation of parsers and translators. The use of **lex** and **yacc** is in keeping with the UNIX philosophy of using the tools available to minimize the amount of code written for new applications.

One additional feature that merits attention is **sccs** (source code control system). The sccs facility, a partner to **make,** maintains backup files on the development and alteration of all text (source code) files. Only the latest version of each file is stored, but an accompanying file chronicles the editorial changes indicating how to automatically backtrack and recreate any previous version. The editorial information deals with dates of alteration, users making the alterations, comments on the alterations or the particular version, users with permission to edit the file, and other error-checking information. The facility allows multiple version storage without storing a complete copy for each version.

Memory Management

The UNIX kernel has its own space in memory where its code image resides. It also maintains numerous tables and buffer mechanisms for controlling the processes, memory, and file system I/O. Systems vary greatly in terms of the number of permitted processes (fixed or variable?), the kinds and amounts of swapping done, and the use of paging and virtual memory techniques.

Every process in UNIX has its own virtual image and an in-memory image. The virtual image is partitioned into three segments: **text** (or code), **data,** and **stack**. Early versions of UNIX used a variant of the MVT mechanism with a first-fit placement strategy. The Berkeley model (starting with 4.0) introduced demand paging for UNIX. System V now also supports demand paging.

The text segment is customarily reentrant code that can be shared among processes in order to save main store. Although two processes might share a text segment, each has its own data and stack segments. In the MVT arrangement, it is common for the data and stack regions to start at opposite ends of a contiguous chunk of memory and "grow" toward each other.

Swapping

If the operating system needs more space in a swapping system, it selects a victim to be swapped out. A sleeping process is sought as a first choice. If no sleeping processes are in main memory, a ready-to-run process will be swapped out. In each case, the qualifying victim with lowest priority (**nice** value in UNIX jargon) is chosen. FIFO is used to break ties.

The victim is swapped out to a segment of the backing store established as the **swap region.** If a nonpaging implementation is used, a table or map of the swap region is maintained in main memory and is searched in a **first fit** manner for a place to put the victim. Victims' images are stored in contiguous segments of the swap region.

Ready-to-run processes held on the swapping store may be swapped in by the operating system. Processes are selected from the ready-to-run category on a FIFO basis. Priority usually plays no part in this decision.

Paging   For those implementations using demand paging, UNIX uses a form of the working set model. Page replacement is by LRU. Process images are held in a specific backing store location; swapping involves copying "dirty" resident pages to their designated locations. Swapping in this environment carries less overhead than in nonpaged implementations.

File Systems

The UNIX file system is **hierarchical,** with the root file being designated as /. Directory entries are simple, consisting of a two byte **inode number** and fourteen bytes for the file name. The inode itself is a data structure containing information about its file. Files come in three general types: regular, directory, and special. Special files are interfaces to device drivers: Remember that UNIX treats peripherals as files.

Each file system in UNIX has a characteristic pattern as seen in Figure 14.1. The **boot block** is present but may or may not be used, depending on whether the file system is intended as a root file system. The **superblock** contains information about the file system as a whole (Figure 14.2), along with caches for free inodes and free blocks. Free inodes are assigned when creating new files; the number of inodes, hence files, in

Figure 14.1

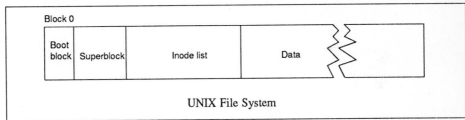

UNIX File System

Figure 14.2

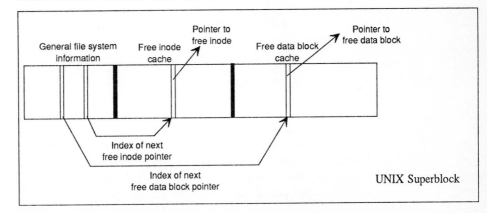

UNIX Superblock

the system is set during the creation of the file system. The inodes are stored immediately after the superblock. Data blocks take up the remainder of the file system's space; these blocks are normally multiples of 512 bytes.

Root File
System

Figure 14.3 shows a typical root file system in UNIX with its hierarchical directory scheme (as covered in Chapter 6). The directory **/bin** contains public commands (as does **/usr/bin**) that are either compiled code or shell scripts. **/usr** is normally the top directory for the users' file systems and normally contains the login or home directories for all users. **/lib** and **/usr/lib** contain system library (compiled) routines, while **/tmp** and **/usr/tmp** are used to create temporary workspace as required by various programs such as compilers and editors. **/dev** is the directory to the special files representing peripheral devices. **/etc** contains administrative commands for use by the superuser (for example, commands to mount and unmount file systems and to make new file systems), commands initiated by the operating system only (for example, **init**), and files logging system activity. **/mnt** is often found: It represents a dummy directory that exists as a mount point for other file systems. Mounting file systems to the root file system is a technique for extending the file system as needed for particular applications. Other directories and files may be found.

Figure 14.3

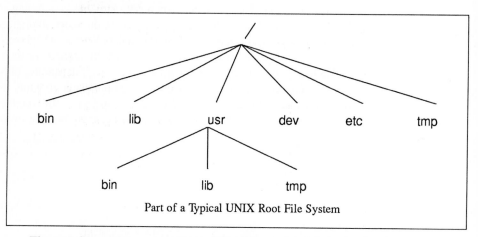

Part of a Typical UNIX Root File System

The root file system must contain **/bin, /dev,** and **/etc** in order for the boot process to work. Other portions discussed earlier may actually be mounted during the boot process. Once a file system is mounted, it appears to users to be a part of the root file system.

File Access
Control

Each file has a set of permissions associated with it. In fact, there are three sets of read, write, and execute (**r,w,x**) permissions: one each for **owner, group,** and **others.** The individual permission capabilities have normal meanings for ordinary files and special files.

Directories also have permission sets. To have read permission for a directory means that the directory may be read in the same manner as any file. In particular, a listing of the contents of the directory is permitted. Write permission allows the alteration of directory contents by adding directory entries, deleting entries, lining, and so forth. Execute permission allows the directory to be searched for a given file name.

(This facility is required when accessing a file whose pathname contains the directory in question or when making the directory the current working directory.) Therefore, a process may access a file if, and only if, it has correct permissions for every component of the pathname. To have access to the file itself is not sufficient.

Since peripheral devices are treated as files with I/O to them handled as read-and-write operations, the permission sets apply to peripheral devices as well.

Buffering/
Caching

Figure 14.4 illustrates the data structures used by the kernel to manage the file system. Each process has a **process file descriptor table** located in the user's **u-area.** Entries 0, 1, and 2 are respectively **stdin, stdout, stderr** (standard input, output, and error files automatically established for a process at creation). Each entry is a pointer to an entry in the system-wide **global file table.** Each entry in the file table contains information about an open file and includes a pointer to the file's entry in the **global inode table.** When a file is being shared, more than one file table entry will point to the same global inode table entry. Each entry in the inode table contains information about the

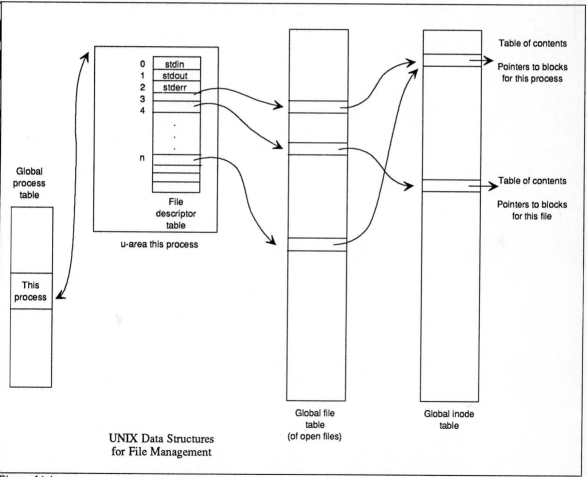

UNIX Data Structures
for File Management

Figure 14.4

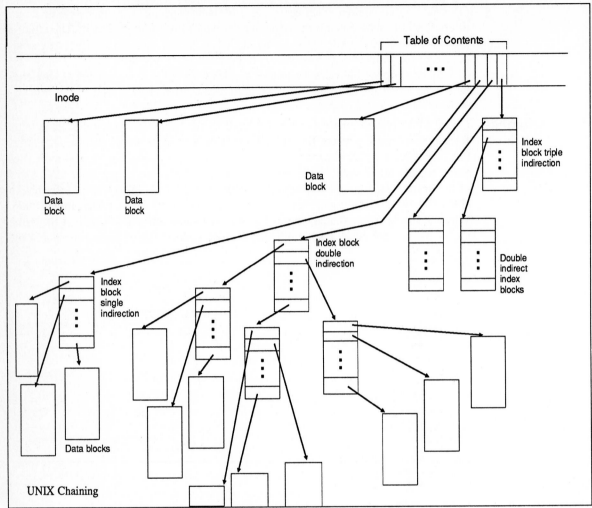

Figure 14.5

opened file, including information transferred from the disk version of the inode. Part of that information is an **inode table of contents**, often a set of thirteen direct, indirect, double indirect, and triple indirect pointers to the file's data blocks (as in Figure 14.5).

The file system cache mechanism is a hashed set of queues (linked lists) maintained according to a modified, **least recently used** strategy. When a request is made to read a block from a file, the cache is searched to see if the block is already in memory. If so, no disk I/O is required. Otherwise, a free block is found within the cache and the disk block read and transferred to it.

Free blocks in the cache are kept in a linked list within the caching mechanism. When a block is to be written to disk, it may be marked for **delayed write** and placed on the free list. The actual writing of the block to disk may not take place until a request for a free buffer requires its use, or the file is closed. Should the contents of the block be needed by a process before it is written to disk, the block is removed from the free list, and a disk I/O is saved.

One problem that UNIX faces is that the delayed write (which may be disabled in System V) may corrupt the file system if a crash occurs before the block is written out. Moreover, the correct inode information for an open file is maintained in the global inode table in main memory. The disk inode is updated every 30 seconds by **sync,** but a crash after a change to the file and before the inode updating can also corrupt the file system. Some claim that UNIX file reliability is a problem; yet recently, others claim that reputation is no longer deserved.

Peripheral Devices

Peripheral devices are treated as files, complete with a permission set. The system opens and closes devices very much like it opens and closes files, except that a device is typically opened by several processes and closed only when the last process closes it.

Devices are classified as **character** or **block,** depending on the minimal amount of data transferred at a time. Virtually all devices are interrupt-driven, with terminals being afforded a form of polling as well.

One of the major concerns with UNIX is the lack of control over when an interrupt will be serviced: No minimal service time can be guaranteed. That poses a problem for real-time applications and massive online data entry applications. In most cases, real-time process handling must be coded as part of the kernel. Such changes are difficult and expensive to make.

CPU Scheduling

UNIX is a process-rich operating system: A separate process is created for nearly every activity. For example, almost all shell commands, when executed, cause the creation of a new process. Processes exist in a hierarchical structure, each process (except for Process 0) a child process spawned by some parent. Figure 14.6 shows the possible states for a process in UNIX. Observe that application processes run in the **user mode** at times and in the **kernel mode** at others.

Figure 14.6

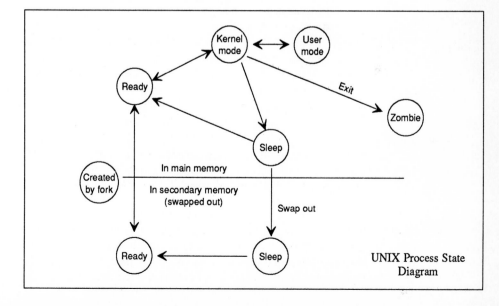

UNIX Process State Diagram

Figure 14.7

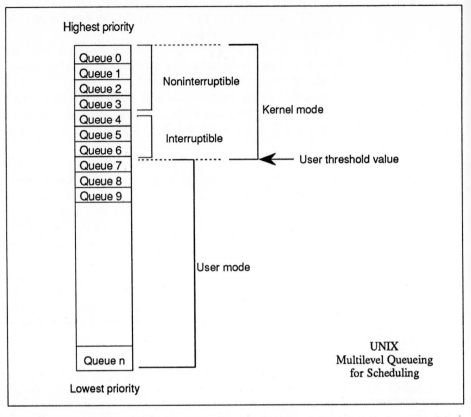

UNIX
Multilevel Queueing
for Scheduling

UNIX Scheduling	UNIX uses a **multilevel feedback queueing** mechanism with each queue managed in a **round-robin** fashion. The various levels are shown in Figure 14.7. The scheduler simply finds the highest level queue that holds a ready-to-run process and selects the first such process.

Processes running in a noninterruptible kernel mode have highest priorities, followed by those running in an interruptible kernel mode. The priority levels for these queues depend on the type of activity and are effectively rated according to the potential for a bottleneck to occur. Processes running in the user mode belong in one of several queues: Each queue is associated with a range of priority values and holds ready-to-run processes whose priority values fall in that range.

User processes are assigned a **threshold** value that is augmented by a **CPU service time** parameter. Receiving CPU service time lowers the priority. Periodically (about every second), **aging** is used to increase the priority of every waiting process by reducing the effect of the CPU service time parameter. For a process running in user mode, this priority value determines which queue holds the process.

Process Structure   A UNIX process is an instance of a program in execution. Its image is in three segments as described earlier: text (code), data, and stack. A process may share its code (UNIX code segments are reentrant) with another process but not its data and stack. Nor can one user process read or write data and stack information from another process. Every process except **Process 0** is created when a **parent** process executes a

fork system call. The new process is a **child** of the caller. Each process is assigned a Process ID (**PID**) at its inception.

The fork call creates an image that is essentially a clone of the parent's image. That is, the parent's text, data, and stack are duplicated for the child process and the system tables, and data structures are duplicated as well. If the child executes a program different from that of its parent (the normal case), its text, data, and stack segments are replaced by a new image for the program to be executed, and the system tables are updated accordingly. This replacement occurs as the result of an **exec** system call.

It is often necessary for processes to communicate with each other and for the system to communicate with processes. **Event waits** and **signals,** along with (named) **pipes,** are used for interprocess communication. System V IPC (InterProcess Communication) adds three capabilities: messages, shared memory, and semaphores. UNIX itself takes very limited action to deal with deadlock, preferring instead to live with controlled crashes in those rare occurrences. However, newer versions are improving synchronization for concurrent processes, and this negative assessment should be taken lightly.

The UNIX kernel maintains a number of data structures in order to manage processes. (See Figure 14.8.) There is a **global process table** with one entry per process. Additionally, the system establishes one local **u-area** for each process. The **u-**

Figure 14.8

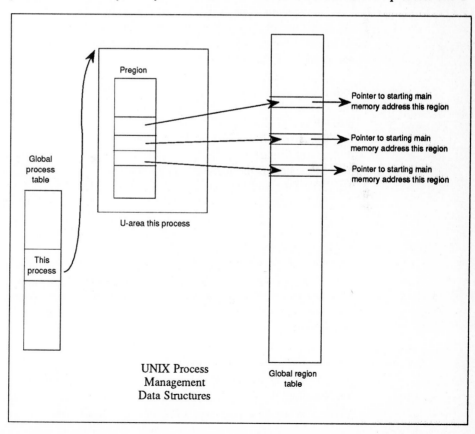

Pregion

Pointer to starting main
memory address this region

Pointer to starting main
memory address this region

Pointer to starting main
memory address this region

Global
process
table

U-area this process

This
process

UNIX Process
Management
Data Structures

Global region
table

area and global process table entry hold control and status information about the process, together with a pointer to the **per process region table (Pregion).** The Pregion (which may be a part of the **u-area**) contains the starting virtual address for each segment of the process's image and pointers (one per segment) to entries in the **global region table.** Entries in the global region table contain pointers to memory partitions holding the image segment in question. While the Pregion seems like an extra step of indirection, it does allow separate processes to point to the same main memory partition. This is how code segments are shared. For those UNIX implementations using paging, the diagram in Figure 14.8 must be augmented with page tables.

The **context** of a process must be saved (or restored) when switching the CPU between processes. A **context switch** can occur only when the CPU is in kernel mode. In UNIX, the context includes the values of the data structures mentioned earlier, the data structures involved in the buffering, caching, and managing of files, the machine register values, the values in the regions of its image, the associated values in the system stack, and so on. A switch between the kernel and user modes without a change of user process is called a **mode switch** and requires some of the same values to be saved.

Startup Like all systems, UNIX will not run until it is loaded and initialized. The details differ between systems, but the general mechanism looks like the following.

The **system console** is the starting point. The initial startup process directs the operator's use of the console so as to accomplish the bootstrapping activity. UNIX may be loaded from tape to disk during this part, or UNIX may be resident on a disk pack and need to be mounted.

In the event of loading from tape, as many as four tapes may be involved (boot, root file system, **/usr,** and updates). Loading the tapes onto disk and creating a UNIX file system that is mountable is an involved process. The system leads the operator through this process.

The boot block must be loaded into memory and executed; this is not a UNIX routine but a machine language routine specific to the host machine. Execution of the boot block begins the loading of the kernel into memory and the accompanying hardware, filestore, and software checks that are needed to validate the system and its configuration. Many of the details of booting that follow are implementation specific.

Process 0 is a "hand built" process created during bootup. It then spawns **init** (**/etc/init**) as Process 1. For the duration of the "run," **init** is the ancestor of every other process that is created. Process 0 eventually becomes the **swapper** process within the UNIX kernel. Next, **init** spawns the superuser shell on the console (the system is single user at this point). The superuser and the system go through the remaining steps to fully bring up UNIX as a multiuser system. It is **init** that spawns the shell process for each user logging onto the running system. In addition, **init** becomes the parent for any still executing children of a terminating process.

It is also necessary to bring the system down carefully. All executing processes must be terminated (**killed** in UNIX terminology) and a **sync** command executed to flush all buffers in the file system cache so file system integrity is maintained. Newer implementations of UNIX are less prone to file system corruption by improper shutdowns.

Networking

UNIX has a number of communications facilities. For interpersonal communication, there are commands such as **mail, write,** and **msg.** For interprocess communication, there are pipes and signals. For telecommunications and networking, there are a number of additional choices. In fact, UNIX has become popular as the controller for many networks; it has been used in virtually every popular network package and configuration extant.

The command **uucp** (UNIX to UNIX copy) allows the transfer of files between UNIX systems (including mail), while **cu** (call UNIX) allows a user on one UNIX system to logon to another UNIX system. For two-system communications like these, a local **client** process makes requests of a remote **server** process. Each process executes the required commands on its own machine. Other commands useful in a network or multisystem connection are **uux, uuname,** and **uustate.**

Since UNIX creates processes for virtually every activity, the networking of UNIX machines is a natural. To get service on a remote machine, a **server** process is established (the originating process is the **client**) to carry out the remote activity. Problems arise because networks are dissimilar physically and use different protocols, requiring the user to invoke network specific conditions. That is, networks as devices tend to violate the device independence so important to the UNIX philosophy. Later UNIX releases use **streams** to support device independent networking, while Berkeley versions employ **sockets.**

Streams

Device drivers of many types have fairly common traits: the need for a device control layer, a protocol layer, and a system interface layer. A stream is a full duplex communication connection between a process and a character-oriented device driver. A stream is implemented as a linked list of output queues for writing and a linked list of input queues for reading. Each module or layer has its own pair of input and output queues. Messages get from one end of the communications connection to another by being passed from queue to queue along the stream.

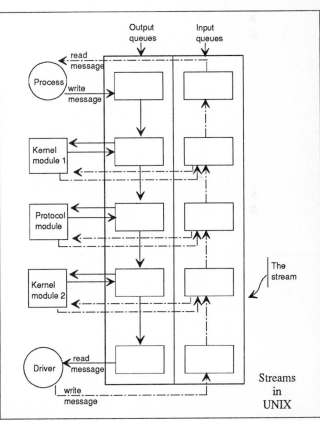

Figure 14.9

At each point, the associated module performs some transformation on the data before passing it on to the next queue, as in Figure 14.9.

Sockets   A socket is an end point for a communications path. A client process utilizes a socket on one end of the path, while the server listens at the socket on the other end. A socket is a part of the UNIX kernel and consists of three layers: the device layer (specific to the physical network), the protocol layer (specific to the network protocol being used), and the socket layer (interface to the kernel's system call structure). (See Figure 14.10.) The translation performed by each layer attempts to make network use transparent to the user and device independent.

Figure 14.10

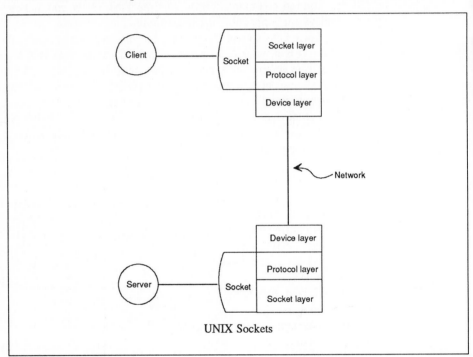

UNIX Sockets

Session with the Shell   The first normal user message in the UNIX multiuser environment is the request to login, followed by the request for a password. What follows are several segments from a UNIX "terminal session."

login: ast
Password:
Welcome to UNIX
$ who
geo tty0 Jul 01 14:57
ast   tty2 Jul 01 18:35
$ who am i
ast   tty2 Jul 01 18:35
$

The user logged in under the name *ast*. The password used is not shown: It is a normal security precaution for a typed password to *not* be displayed on the monitor. The $

prompt after the initial message indicates that a Bourne shell has been spawned for this user. The command *who* gives a listing of active users, the terminals being used, and the login times. The *who am i* command is helpful for forgetful users who have access to multiple login names and terminals. In the segment that follows, the user is attempting to change the password.

```
$ passwd
Changing password for ast
Old password:
New password:
Retype password:
Passwords don't match
$ passwd
Changing password for ast
Old password:
New password:
Retype password:
$
```

The user is requested to type in the old and new passwords, with the new password being repeated for verification. In the first case, the two versions of the new password did not agree. Observe that even here, no passwords appear on the screen. Continue with the session.

```
$ dir
dir: not found
$ pwd
/usr/ast
$ ls
.profile
$ ls -a
.
..
.profile
$ ls -l
-rw-r--r-- 1 ast 190 Jan 2 09:00 .profile
$ cd /user
$ ls
$
```

In this segment, a bad command name was entered, and the working directory was seen to be */usr/ast*. Since no change of directory command had been entered, */usr/ast* is the home directory. The listing of */usr/ast* (the default option for listing) shows only one file, *.profile,* which is executed at login time. The listing showing all entries in the directory (-*a* option) shows the listing for */usr/ast* itself (.) and its parent */usr* (..) in addition to *.profile*. The long directory listing (-*l* option) shows other information.

Note the following points: The file *.profile* is a regular file (the first -); the *owner* has read and write, but not execute, permissions (*rw-*); the owner's *group* has read only permission (r--); and the rest of the *world* has read only permission (the rightmost r--). There is one **link** (name by which the file is known) for this file owned by *ast*. The file has 190 characters and was last updated on January 2 at 9:00AM. The user changed the current or working directory to */user,* a directory with no children.

```
$ mkdir jim sally
$ ls -a
.
..
jim
sally
$ mkdir jim/school
$ ls jim
school
$ cd jim
$
```

Two directories, *jim* and *sally*, were created and attached to */user*, the working directory. Then a directory */user/jim/school* was created. Notice the use of defaults (current directory) and partial pathnames (*jim, jim/school*). The new working directory is now *jim* (*/usr/jim*).

```
$ ls /user >tempo
$ ls jim
school
tempo
$ ls | sort -r
tempo
school
$ cat tempo
jim
sally
$ cp tempo /user/sally
$ ls /user/sally
tempo
$ cp tempo tempr
$ ls
school
tempo
tempr
```

In the preceding segment, a listing of the files in */user* is redirected to go to the file *tempo* (*/user/jim/tempo*, actually). The next listing indicates what files *jim* now holds. A listing of *jim* is presented in reverse alphabetical order (*-r* option). The new file *tempo* is sent to the screen (*cat*) and correctly contains the listing for */user*. The file *tempo* is copied to the directory sally so that both *jim* and *sally* have a *tempo*. That same file is then copied to *jim* under the variant name *tempr*. Three distinct copies of the one file now exist. If linking (*ln*) had been used instead of copying (*cp*), there would be only one copy of the file, but all three names would be found in the directory system.

```
$ cat >file1
line 1
line 2
line 3
^d
$ ls
file1
school
```

tempo
tempr
$ mv file1 file2
$ ls
file2
school
tempo
tempr
$ rm /user/sally/tempo
$ ls /user/sally
$

The output from *cat* is redirected to *file1*. The (default) input to *cat* is from the keyboard and consists of three lines. The ^*d* is a control character that signals an end to the input to *cat*. The newly created file is now found in the current directory (*jim*). The name of that file is changed to *file2* (by *mv*). The only file belonging to the directory *sally* is deleted (*rm*).

$ cat >school/script
echo "hello from UNIX"
echo $PATH
date
echo $PS1
^d
$ cd school
$ sh <script
hello from UNIX
:/bin:/usr/bin:/user/bin:/usr/ast/bin:
Wed July 06 18:40:16 PST 1988
$
$

A new file script is produced in the directory *school* by using the *cat* command; next, four lines are entered. This is an example of a script file: It contains executable shell commands. By redirecting *script* as input for a new shell, the commands of the script file are executed. Observe the search sequence established for finding commands to execute. (First the current directory is searched; then the directories from left to right in the path are searched, until a command of the appropriate name is found.) The $ in *$PATH* indicates that the value of the Bourne shell variable *PATH* is to be echoed to the screen. (The command *echo PATH* would result in the four characters PATH being printed on the screen.) The extra $ printed when script is executed is from the *echo $PS1* command: *PS1* is the normal primary prompt, which is, of course, $. The script file can be made executable (so that it can later be executed) by typing *script*.

$ script
script: cannot execute
$ chmod +x script
$ script
hello from UNIX
:/bin:/usr/bin:/user/bin:/usr/ast/bin:
Wed July 06 18:42:29 PST 1988
$
$ PS1="ok "

ok

Setting the value of *PS1* customizes the prompt to *"ok"*.

ok wc script
    4 9 50   script
ok grep echo script
echo "hello from UNIX"
echo $PATH
echo $PS1
ok cd /user
ok ls j*
file 2
school
tempo
tempr
ok ls j?
j? not found
ok ls ji?
file2
school
tempo
tempr
ok

The file *script* is the input to wordcount (*wc*); *script* contains four lines, nine words, and fifty characters. The pattern matching *grep* found three lines in script having a match with the string *echo*.

The wild card * was used to gain a listing of every directory of the form *j** in */user* (the working directory at that point). Only *jim* fit the conditions. The form *j?* found no match, since the *?* is replaced by a *single* character. The form *ji?*, of course, found *jim* when searching */user*.

The preceding examples have only begun to scratch the surface of the shell command capabilities. Remember that the shell provides a sophisticated, block-structured programming language for creating commands and script files.

Exercises

1. Give at least four factors contributing to UNIX's success.
2. List several of UNIX's weaknesses.
3. Why is UNIX easily portable? Why should anyone care?
4. List two advantages and two disadvantages of the **ln** command to link nondirectory files.
5. Some say that it will be easier for UNIX to become the standard operating system for the newer micros (80386, 68020, and so on) than for MS-DOS to step up from a single-user system and maintain dominance. Why might this be true?
6. If you were AT&T, what kinds of changes would you make to UNIX?
7. What kinds of UNIX modules are likely to be machine dependent and written in assembly language?
8. Describe the UNIX shell in one sentence.
9. Compare/contrast the Bourne shell and C-Shell. Why might a developer use both?
10. If you were to design a windowing system for UNIX, what would you be likely to create?

11. Describe the terms pipe, filter, and pipeline.
12. Describe how and why the following set of commands might produce different results.
    a. sort file1.c file2.c >sortfile
        wc <sortfile &
        rm sortfile &
    b. sort file1.c file2.c | wc
13. Compare/contrast pathname and filename.
14. Compare/contrast root directory, home directory, and current (working) directory.
15. Describe the usefulness of . and .. directories.
16. What role do background jobs play?
17. How might **exec** be used other than as part of the spawning of a new process?
18. What does the image of a UNIX process look like?
19. If no paging is used, what kind of memory placement strategy does UNIX use? What kind of page replacement strategy is used for a paged implementation?
20. Describe the priority mechanisms involved in swapping UNIX processes into and out of main store.
21. Since the buffers in the file system cache are in kernel space, the data must be transferred between cache and user data segment, which is extra overhead. What advantages does the cache system offer to counterbalance this overhead?
22. Where is the UNIX boot information stored?
23. Describe the nature and role of an inode.
24. Describe the inode's table of contents in terms of knowing where the file's data blocks are located on disk.
25. The free block cache in the superblock contains the block numbers for several free blocks. One of those numbers points to a free block that has another list of free block numbers. Describe how you think this form of chaining might operate.
26. UNIX has an **lseek** service call to place the read/write pointer to any byte in the file. Describe how it might be used to create a record-oriented file mechanism for fixed length records. How might the service call be used to construct a variable length, record-oriented file system?
27. Discuss the pros and cons of delayed write. Do the same for read ahead. (If a block of file data is requested, the successor block is also read in anticipation.)
28. Discuss the mounting and unmounting of file systems. When might a request to unmount a file fail?
29. Describe the conditions under which a user might fail to gain access to read /usr/john/letter/business/karen.
30. How can a user interrupt a running UNIX process?
31. Interpret each field from the output of an **ls -l** command.

For the remaining exercises, find a book or manual that has a summary of the UNIX commands; then find a UNIX system and login.

32. Take a look at the root directory and at the directories contained in the root. Use the **man** command to obtain information about any command of interest. Use **learn** to find what else you can learn.

33. Edit the **.profile** script file to customize the welcoming statements, give the date, list all the current users, customize the prompt to something you like, and send a message telling anyone who will listen that you are logged in. The startup file should also set the terminal for accepting two-way communications with other users.
34. Create a script file that will remove all files ending in .c from the directory /usr/you/com. Make the file executable.
35. Redo Exercise 34, but present all such files, one at a time, to the user for a decision on whether to actually remove the file in question.

15 VAX/VMS Operating Systems

Introduction to VMS

It has been said that **VMS** (Virtual Memory System) is the best, most sophisticated implementation of the UNIX concept. While VMS no doubt has a strong UNIX flavor, it is unique to the VAX family of computers from DEC. The roots of VMS are intertwined with operating systems for DEC's very successful PDP-11 series from the early 1970s.

PDP-11

The **PDP-11** (Peripheral Data Processor) machines have 16-bit CPUs with main memory address capabilities to four megabytes (22-bit addresses). Because the program counter is 16 bits, the virtual-memory address space for a program is limited to 64K bytes segmented into eight 8K chunks of contiguous addresses. (This is one of the few cases in which the virtual address space is smaller than the physical address space.) The segmentation is dynamic, with the hardware memory management unit (**MMU**) managing address translation for virtual addresses. Swapping is used to manage those multiprogramming situations where main memory is too small. Some models allow up to 8K cache memory for speeding up processing. Disk packs used for secondary memory have capacities up to 500M bytes. Most of the PDP-11s run in two modes, **kernel** and **user,** with some having a third (**supervisor**) mode.

RSX-11

RSX-11 is a multitasking operating system for the PDP-11 series designed primarily for realtime applications such as factory automation, automatic data acquisition, process monitoring and control, and so forth. While RSX-11 supplies an interactive computing environment with normal applications packages, it is designed to give priority to realtime processes. Much of the user interface for interactive purposes is through the DEC Control Language (**DCL**).

Active programs are memory resident so that swapping and other overhead factors are kept to a minimum. The goal is to maintain the very best reaction times for realtime applications. There are 250 priority levels assignable to processes for scheduling purposes.

File management is handled through File Control Services (**FCS**) and Record Management Services (**RMS**). RMS manipulates logical records as data units, allowing the user a measure of freedom from the physical characteristics of the disk system.

These and other services form a layer of file-handling software sitting over the kernel. **DATATRIEVE** and **DBMS** (a **CODASYL**-compatible database management system) are two additional file-handling packages.

RT-11

RT-11 has goals similar to those of RSX-11. However, RT-11 is designed for single user applications. RT-11 makes a very compact, yet sophisticated, operating system available to the user. RT-11 has a series of increasingly sophisticated monitors available: Single Job monitor (**SJ**), Foreground/Background monitor (**FB**), and Extended Monitor (**XM**). FB includes the capabilities of SJ, and XM includes the capabilities of FB. XM also allows for an extended address space.

RT-11 allows for indirect command files (essentially macrocommands or script files) of DCL commands. RT-11 also has a job-control language **BATCH** for control of batch jobs.

RSTS/E

Perhaps the predominant PDP-11 operating system has been **RSTS/E**—an interactive, multitasking, multiuser operating system. The heart of the system is the collection of **runtime systems** (conceptually similar to command interpreters). Each runtime system is multitasking. The general runtime systems are **BASIC, DCL, RSX-11,** and **RT-11.** The latter runtime systems emulate DEC's other two PDP-11 operating systems while running under RSTS/E.

File system services are supplied by a layer of software that includes **FMS** (Forms Management System), **DMS-500** (Data Management Services), RMS, DATATRIEVE, and so on. RMS, in particular, gives the user device independent access to data. Sequential, relative, and indexed file organizations are supported, while sequential, random, and **RFA** (Record's File Address: individual records are located by their unique disk addresses) access methods are available. The file system is hierarchical and supplies file locking for disk blocks, groups of disk blocks, and entire files as required for concurrent file processing.

CPU processing is priority-based with 32 levels of externally assignable priorities. Overall, there are 256 levels of process priority possible. A round-robin algorithm is used when several processes have the same priority.

While designed as an interactive system, RSTS/E accepts jobs in batch mode using BATCH. DCL provides the standard user interface for interactive jobs through a subset called **CCL** (Concise Command Language).

Batch jobs and printer tasks are spooled to improve throughput. Code sharing is supported in order to make best use of the limited memory. Disk data is cached for improved I/O times. Errors and other system information are logged for administrative use. Networking is supported, primarily through DECnet/E.

VAX-11

In the late 1970s, DEC introduced the first of a family of 32-bit systems. The VAX (Virtual Address eXtension) family gave DEC a powerful next product to follow up the popular PDP-11 series. The larger virtual address space (4G bytes) and hardware—assisted management of paged virtual-memory techniques were centerpieces. Interactive processing was the driving design criteria, although batch processing was to be supported.

Compatibility with the PDP-11 series was to be maintained as much as possible. A **compatibility mode** essentially emulating RSX-11 was chosen. The operating system, VMS, was designed in parallel with the VAX hardware rather than being an afterthought. There is a subtle point hidden there: The VAX family would eventually consist of several different processors of differing capabilities, but there would be only one operating system across the entire line. Many consider VMS to be a souped-up, extended hybrid of RSX-11 and UNIX. In any respect, vertical and horizontal compatibility was a major consideration at DEC.

The 32-bit VAX-11 hardware units exist with up to 8M bytes of main memory. Memory management involves swapping and paging, with protections set at the page level. Code sharing is supported through global page areas. Virtual-memory address spaces can be up to 4G bytes in size. The CPU has an onboard 8K cache for buffering between it and main memory, an address translation buffer for speed-up address translation, and an instruction buffer for facilitating instruction fetches. I/O buffering uses free page frames (from the system pages in all but the latest versions).

Scheduling is a sophisticated, priority-based mechanism. Processes, when spawned, may exist as child processes or as independent processes detached from any terminal or other process. Interprocess communication uses **mailboxes** and **event flags.** To VMS, a process consists of an address space, a software context (**process header**), and a hardware context (**PCB,** primarily).

Figure 15.1

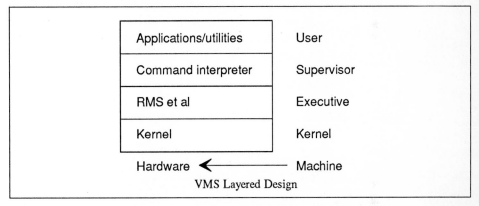

VMS Layered Design

The file system services allow for volume structuring and the usual protections expected of a UNIX-like system. RMS creates device independence for I/O in addition to extending DCL commands to offer the usual file-system services. RMS can even be used to manage mailboxes and terminals. The directory system is hierarchical.

The four layers of VMS (**kernel, executive, supervisor,** and **user**) are shown in Figure 15.1. For an executing process, each layer is known as an **access mode.**

Beyond VAX-11

Since the introduction of the first VAX-11, the VAX family has expanded. A series of **MicroVAX** machines has produced desktop VMS machines with speeds up to 2MIPS and beyond. A number of powerful (diskless) **VAX Stations** have appeared along with **VAX Servers** for use as boot nodes in VAX clusters (networks). The **8200** to **8700** (8xxx) series give DEC powerful computers falling into the performance categories of low-end mainframe units. The common ingredient is VMS.

The physical address space for the 8xxx machines runs to 1G bytes. The series starts with the 8250 (8M bytes of main memory). The 83xx machines hold a pair of tightly coupled 8250 processors using shared memory (**SMP**—synchronous multiprocessing). The 85xx machines support up to 80M bytes of main memory, while the 86xx offer up to 128M bytes. The 88xx systems are multiprocessor systems running dual CPUs (SMP, 128M bytes of main store). The top-of-the-line 89xx equipment sports multiprocessors (up to eight 87xx CPUs) and 1G bytes of main store. Again, VMS is the common ingredient: Newer VMS versions (such as 5.0) have been redesigned to take advantage of multiprocessing capabilities.

The User Interface

The real interface to the VMS operating system is the system call (service call). The normal end-user interface, however, is the command interpreter, which has DCL (DEC Command Language) built in. Users invoke the command interpreter to accomplish the general tasks of process control, file manipulation, and information management.

Unlike UNIX, the command interpreter is not an applications program but a part of the supervisor layer. The command interpreter is, nonetheless, extensible and easy for the individual user to tune.

Although interactive in nature, VMS allows **Com files** (executable files of interpreter commands) and other programs to be executed as **background processes** with no intervention by the user. Background processes are, of course, essentially batch processes and run concurrently with the user's interactive processes.

The interpreter and its command language do not encourage **I/O redirection** (allowing input from wherever desired and output to be placed wherever needed) as strongly as does UNIX. Nor does VMS support **pipes** (mechanisms for treating output from one process as input to another). Some redirection of input and output can be accomplished by *ASSIGN*ing *SYS$INPUT* (often the keyboard) and *SYS$OUTPUT* (generally the screen). However, VMS does not share the UNIX philosophy of building complex programs by combining a sequence of simple routines (filters), often in a pipeline.

DCL Commands

DCL (Digital Control Language) is the VMS programming language used for terminal and job control. Its commands are English-like and less cryptic than those of UNIX. Some commands are built into DCL. Other commands are user-compiled, executable programs that are loaded from the file system and executed. Still others are **Com files** which are executable files of interpreter commands. The repertoire of commands available to a given user is designed by the user himself or herself.

DCL, in conjunction with the interpreter, gives the user an **extensible programming language** tailored to particular needs and styles. There are interpreter variables, whose values may be set, and the user may establish other variables as needed. The interpreter executes commands sequentially unless directed otherwise by selection and repetition.

Several **wildcards** (including *) are available in DCL for specifying arguments created by pattern matching. Arguments with wild cards are called **ambiguous** arguments.

The Interface

The VAX command interpreter gives a line-oriented interface. Even though each user can tailor his or her version to suit personal needs and tastes, the interface is somewhat antiquated. As is the case with most popular operating systems, third-party vendors have created menu-driven interfaces, iconic interfaces, and windowing.

VMS uses a number of techniques to make DCL easier to learn and manipulate. Each command has an abbreviated form for more experienced users: Every DCL command can be given in four or fewer characters. Since there are numerous options and parameters for most commands, VMS makes liberal use of defaults. In addition, if the user omits one or more parameters, VMS will prompt for the missing values rather than giving an error message and aborting the attempt. This is a definite advantage for the newcomer and infrequent user.

Each user comes up running in a **home directory** within the hierarchical file system. The user can designate any directory to be his or her **current directory** (working directory) as needed.

VMS Tools

VMS does not come packaged with a wide range of tools for users. However, DEC and third-party vendors have made a large collection of tools available. More are being developed every day for this popular line of minicomputers.

Document Preparation

A number of text editors and word processors are available from DEC, and even more are available from third-party vendors. Text editors exist for both interactive and batch modes and may be either line oriented or full screen. **Runoff** (DSR) is a widely distributed text formatter. Typesetting facilities are also available. A forms management system (**FMS**) for creating on-screen forms is offered by DEC. As with most popular systems, third-party vendors have made hundreds of products available to compete with DEC products and to fill holes unserved by DEC.

Information Management

The usual file-manipulating services are also available in the form of service calls, or the user may choose to use the extended services of RMS. Files may be created, destroyed, altered, copied, and compared using RMS and DCL services.

File System Management

Files may be created and altered by the use of text editors, DCL commands, or other programs. For example, the command **CREATE** can be used to create simple files from the keyboard. Files may be copied by **COPY**, renamed by **REN**, or deleted by **DEL**.

Permissions for system, owner, group, and world may be checked by **DIR /PROT** and set by **SET PROTECTION.**

Process Control

An assembler, several compilers and interpreters, and a linker help get programs running. Jobs may run interactively or in BATCH mode. Process status may be checked by **SHOW PROCESS, SHOW WORKING_SET**, and other DCL commands. Programs can be started and killed. Execution can have a delayed start if desired. VMS handles realtime processes with the highest of priorities.

Program Development

Text editors, symbolic debuggers, compilers, libraries of functions (with a librarian), and a linker assist in program development. **PATCH** allows direct alteration of image files, which can then be run without recompiling, relinking, and so on. (Some question whether this is a necessary or even desirable feature in light of the fine collection of translators and linkers available to the developer.) **ANALYZE** checks object file formats against linker demands. **MESSAGE** and **MAIL** are two additional useful utilities. A Command Language Editor (**CLE**) allows users to alter existing DCL commands and add new ones. A code-management system (**CMS**) helps maintain histories of and relationships between modules created in large programming projects.

Memory Management

VMS memory management consists of two primary routines, the **pager** and the **swapper**. Figure 15.2 shows the conceptual subdivision of main memory into three primary regions. The VMS kernel resides in one of the three and maintains numerous tables and buffer mechanisms for controlling the processes, memory, and file system I/O.

Figure 15.2

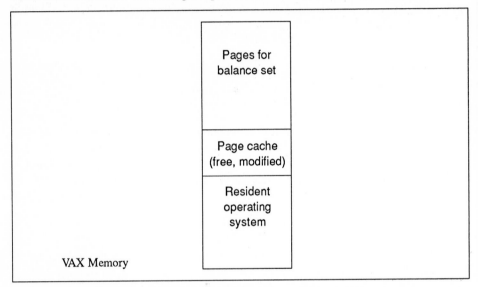

VAX Memory

Pages for balance set

Page cache (free, modified)

Resident operating system

A second primary memory region consists of frames holding pages from the working sets of memory-resident processes. This set of processes currently assigned to main memory is called the **balance set.** The balance set region from Figure 15.2, then, represents the page frames assigned to the working sets of the balance set.

The maximum number of processes allowed in the balance set represents the maximum level of multiprogramming without swapping. That value can be affected by the working set sizes of the active processes, and it can be adjusted by the system manager. If the number of processes exceeds the balance set limit, process swapping will be required.

Paging

The page size for VAX systems is 512 bytes, the same as the disk block size. Since virtual-memory address spaces may reach 4G bytes, working sets often represent a very small portion of the process's memory requirements. Working set sizes tend to fluctuate throughout the life of a process. VMS maintains global regions for pages that may be shared among processes and manages a page table for each process: The page table is itself paged.

The working sets for the balance set may or may not require all the available page frames. The pool of unassigned frames is called the **page cache.** Page cache frames come in two types: **free** (and unmodified) or **modified.** Free frames are available for use by the paging system, while modified frames hold a page that was modified by its process before being removed from the working set. Before a modified page may be considered free, its contents must be written to disk.

When a page fault occurs and the working set is below the maximum size, a frame is selected from the free list in the cache and overwritten with the needed page. (Actually, VMS tends to bring pages into frames in clusters to make the I/O process more efficient.) If a page fault occurs when the working set is at maximum size, a current page must be replaced.

Page replacement is local, since no frame is taken away from another process. However, the frame holding the exiting page (the victim is chosen by LRU) is removed from the working set, placed on the appropriate list from the page cache, and replaced by another frame (from the global page cache). The replacement strategy for frames is FIFO, altered by the following: If the page required by the fault can be found in the free list or modified list, its frame is returned to the working set without an I/O call. FIFO is used whenever the needed page is not found in the cache.

As just stated, free page frames are most often assigned to a process's working set and overwritten with a page from the virtual image. When frames are returned to the cache, they are free or modified. Modified frames are placed on the free list after they have been written to disk. Modified frames are not generally written to disk until either the modified list is too long, the free list is too short, or its process terminates and the associated files must be closed. A modified frame in the cache, then, is not reassigned until its contents have been written to disk (unless, of course, it is being recalled by its own process). The writing of modified page frames to the virtual images in swap space generally occurs in clusters to make the I/O more efficient.

A process starts life with a default working set size. The working set may grow in size, if required, until a first limit (working set **quota**) is reached. If further growth in the working set is needed, page frames may be "borrowed" until a second limit (working set **extent**) is reached. This borrowing clearly reduces the size of the page cache in general and the free list in particular.

Occasionally it is necessary to increase the number of free pages. Writing out the modified pages is the first activity to try. If that fails to generate enough free page frames, a general reduction in the working set sizes for the balance set is attempted. The next effort involves reclaiming borrowed pages given out in better times. Finally, processes may be swapped out.

Swapping

The swapper has a part in most of the activities for reclaiming page frames to increase the free list size. The swapper also has a hand in establishing a newly created process and in providing pages as I/O buffers. Its name, however, comes from its activities of swapping processes into main memory and out of main memory.

The decision of which process to swap in from secondary storage is relatively simple: Swap in the highest priority process that is ready to run. The balance set always contains the working sets for the highest priority, ready-to-execute processes. The choice of which process to swap out is more complicated and is based on the status of a process, its priority, and the amount of CPU time already received. Outswapping occurs when a process becomes unable to run. Outswapping also occurs to make room for a process that needs to be swapped into main memory. Recall that working sets, not entire process images, are being swapped.

The swapper is active if a process in the balance set moves out of the ready-to-run state or experiences one of several wait conditions, if the list of free pages in the cache needs increasing, or if a fixed period of time has passed without any activity on its part (a sort of "be suspicious when things are going too well" attitude).

File Systems

The VAX file system is hierarchical, with each directory entry containing the file name, type ID, and version number. At creation the file version number is 1; each time a modified version of the file is saved, the version number is incremented and the older version kept for archival purposes. Record management services (RMS) is available to give device independent access to peripherals. File system **volumes** (the major sub-units) must be mounted before being used. A volume usually consists of a single disk pack but may, in fact, span several disk packs. A volume contains a **master file**

Figure 15.3

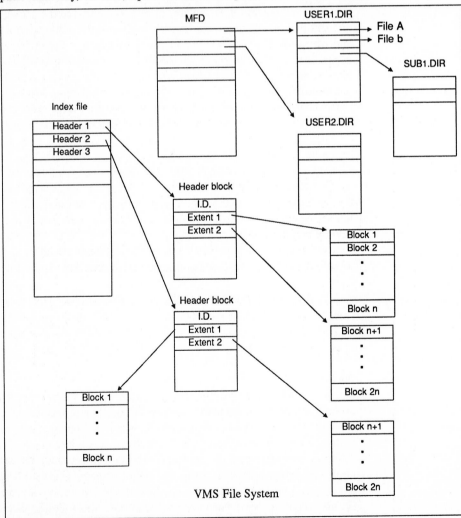

VMS File System

directory as the first level in the hierarchy. Several files are used by VMS just to manage the file system.

A block in a file system is 512 bytes in size. Blocks may be allocated in contiguous collections called **extents**. The **Storage Bit Map File** keeps track of the free/allocated blocks in the volume. A **Bad Block File** is maintained so that bad blocks on the disk will not be allocated. There is even a **Pending Bad Block File** for blocks that are suspect but not yet proven bad. Figure 15.3 shows the file system structure conceptually.

A directory's pathname includes a node name (invisible for the most part), a device name, and is enclosed by [ ]. For example, DUA0:[AST.JIM.SCHOOL] would be similar to the UNIX /USR/AST/JIM/SCHOOL or the MS-DOS A:AST\JIM\SCHOOL. A file TEMPO in SCHOOL would have the pathname DUA0:[AST.JIM.SCHOOL]TEMPO. TEMPO will have a type designation and a version number as well. A fuller specification might be DUA0:[AST.JIM.SCHOOL]TEMPO.PAS;3. For most purposes, the file type (PAS) and version number (3) are not required. The default version number is the latest one.

File Access Control

Each file has a set of permissions associated with it. In fact, there are four sets of read, write, execute, and delete (**R,W, E,D**) permissions: one each for **system, owner, group,** and **world.** The individual permission capabilities have normal meanings.

Directories also have permission sets. To have read permission for a directory means that the directory may be read in the same manner as any file. In particular, a listing of the contents of the directory is permitted. Write permission allows the alteration of directory contents by adding directory entries, deleting entries, linking, and so forth. Execute permission allows the directory to be searched for a given file name. This facility is required when accessing a file whose pathname contains the directory in question or when making the directory the current working directory. Therefore, a process may access a file if, and only if, it has correct permissions for every component of the pathname: To have access to the file itself is not sufficient.

Since peripheral devices are treated as files with I/O to them handled as read-and-write operations, the permission sets apply to peripheral devices as well.

File Organization/ Access Methods

RMS provides a set of system services for file management. As mentioned earlier, file organization techniques include sequential (record order matches the chronological order of writing), relative (fixed length records: record numbers represent offsets from the logical beginning of the file), and indexed (records are identified by key(s) rather than physical or relative positioning). RMS manages the tree-structured index for every indexed file.

The RMS access methods are sequential, random, and RFA. Sequential access can be applied to any file organization, producing the records in entry order, record number order, or indexed order. Random record access also applies to all organization types (sequential files must be of fixed length records): The application program determines the order of access. RFA is similar to the random access except that a record's unique file address is used for identification and location.

RMS files may be interactively manipulated and examined by DATATRIEVE. This gives unsophisticated users some control over their file systems without significant programming. Procedures (files of DATATRIEVE commands) can be packaged, however, and called by name. DATATRIEVE has a useful report-writing capability. Of course, third-party vendors have made many database packages available for running under VMS.

I/O   Much of the I/O for VAX systems is handled by Ancillary Control Processes (**ACP**), particularly for disk, tape, and network I/O. Each ACP handles multiple peripheral devices. The use of a buss structure, ACPs, and software creates a software answer to hardware I/O channels. A potential bottleneck for I/O can occur when an ACP must control both low-speed and high-speed peripherals, in spite of the ACP's cache mechanism.

A large part of the I/O effort in VMS comes from paging and swapping. Direct I/O uses DMA techniques to transfer data blocks to memory. I/O buffers simply consist of one page per block of data. The pages are selected by the paging mechanism from free pages in the *system space*. Buffered I/O is similar, except that a buffer must be designated in the process's space as well. (Data transfer between the two must occur.) The process's buffer is, of course, part of its working set. In a sense, direct I/O costs the user process less, since their working sets are unaffected: Later versions of VMS manage to charge users for direct I/O buffers. Figure 15.4 illustrates the layered approach to VMS I/O.

Figure 15.4

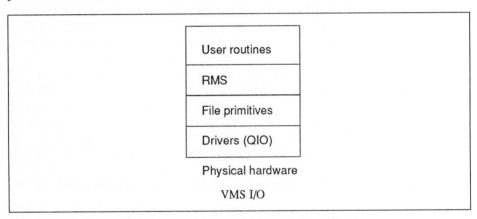

| User routines |
| RMS |
| File primitives |
| Drivers (QIO) |

Physical hardware

VMS I/O

CPU Management   VMS is a process-rich operating system. A separate process is created for most activities. The login of a terminal creates a process, a batch job creates a process, and DECnet requests generate processes. Any existing process can create child processes or unattached processes. Child processes share the parent's resources, while unattached resources are assigned their own set of resources. Processes exist in a hierarchical structure. Figure 15.5 shows the possible states for a process in VMS.

Scheduling   VMS uses a **multilevel feedback queueing** mechanism with each queue managed in an **FCFS** fashion. There are 32 levels assigned by priority. The scheduler simply finds the highest-level queue that holds a ready-to-run process and selects the first such process.

The highest-priority queues are given to realtime processes, middle-level queues to operating system processes, and lower-level queues to user processes. This pattern makes VMS a good operating system where realtime processes are important.

Figure 15.5

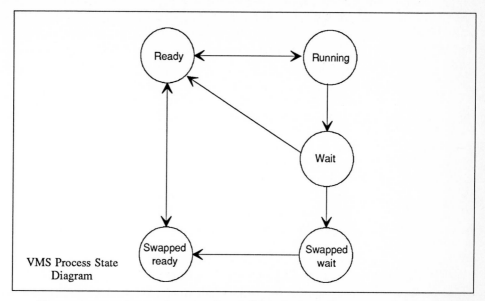

VMS Process State Diagram

User processes have a base or **threshold priority** value set at creation. During execution, processes also have a **current priority** value that varies but which always stays at or above the base value. As a process moves from waiting to ready status, its current priority is increased, the amount depending on the system event causing the status change. When the process is actually scheduled, its priority value is diminished. When the process gives up the CPU, it moves to the next lower-level queue (another lowering of its current priority value).

There are two CPU times associated with each process. The first is the time slice. The second is known as a **quantum.** A process will not be swapped out until it receives an accumulated CPU time equal to or greater than the quantum. It is a sort of guarantee that each process will receive some meaningful processing time before being swapped out.

The scheduling mechanism used by VMS is reminiscent of that used by IBM's VM operating system. (See Chapter 16.)

Process Structure

A VMS process is an instance of a program in execution. Its image is a virtual image of up to 4G bytes. A process may share its code with another process but not its data or its stack. Nor can a user process read or write data and stack information from another process.

A fork call creates an image that is essentially an empty shell into which the process may be swapped and to which pages may be assigned. If the created process is spawned as a child (the normal case), it shares the resources of its parent. If the created process is to be unattached, it receives its own set of resources. Clearly, the operating system must constrain the creation of unattached processes to prevent resources from being monopolized by a calculating or unwitting user.

VMS maintains a **PCB** (Process Control Block) for each process. The PCB contains most of the information detailing the context of the process. The scheduling queues are essentially queues of PCBs.

It is often necessary for processes to communicate with each other and for the system to communicate with processes. **Local event flags, mailboxes, asynchronous system traps (AST),** and **condition handlers** facilitate interprocess communication. ASTs are interrupts generated by a software request rather than a direct hardware action. ASTs are process specific rather than system generic in nature. Condition handlers are means of dealing with hardware and software exceptions by fixing the problem, passing the exception on to another handling routine, or allowing the process to continue execution without fixing the exception. Exceptions may represent errors, but they may not. At least one later version (version 5.0) was designed to improve the synchronization of concurrent processes with parallel processing in mind.

The context of a process must be saved (or restored) when switching the CPU between processes. The context for a process consists of hardware register values (**hardware context**) stored in the PCB and a **software context** (general information stored in the **process header**). A **context switch** can occur only when the CPU is in the kernel access mode.

Startup

Like all systems, VMS will not run until it is loaded and initialized. The startup procedure allows for system tailoring, environment modifying, and system upgrading. Several system-management utilities are provided: DEC has streamlined the boot/configuration process over the years by improving those utilities. DEC advertises the process as "self-installing" and "auto-configuring."

A User Environment Test Package (**UETP**) is available to test hardware and software components once the boot process is completed. UETP tests I/O drivers, VMS services (to include RMS services and PDP-11 compatibility mode), and system response to loading.

The system bootstrapping process is actually two separate bootstrap operations. For the 11/780, the console is used to execute several programs whose end purposes are to load the 64K **VMB** into memory from a floppy disk and then execute it. The programs executed by the console are actually PDP-11 programs running on an LSI-11 microprocessor. VMB determines main memory size, loads **SYSBOOT** from the system disk, and executes it. SYSBOOT configures the system, loads the operating system image, and transfers control to VMS. **INIT** takes over and completes the startup process by initializing memory management, the executive, and I/O components. Subsequently, INIT creates **STARTUP**, the first process to include a command interpreter. STARTUP calls **SYSGEN** to autoconfigure the system.

Networking

DEC supports quite a number of communications facilities. MS-DOS, CP/M, and Macintosh systems can act as **end nodes** (nodes that do not retransmit data) in a VAX network. There are gateway mechanisms to connect VMS machines with UNIX systems, networks using SNA (an IBM protocol), and CRAY supercomputers. VAX systems can be connected to CDC Cyber series machines. DEC equipment can be interconnected to IBM's DIOSS/370 (Distributed Office Support System) for office automation purposes.

DECnet is DEC's universal communications protocol that is well integrated into VMS systems. VMS systems may interconnect with Ethernet, X.25, MAP (Manufacturing Automation Protocol), and ISO/OSI networks. MAILGATE allows VAX equipment to access MCI's electronic-mail system. New packages are appearing continually. In most cases, **routing nodes** (nodes capable of retransmitting data not intended for it) must be VAX machines. End nodes need not be, however.

Some of the communication products include **X-Windows,** a public-domain product from MIT funded by DEC and IBM. X-Windows is a general-purpose, bit-mapped graphics display for use in client/server models. X-Windows is a user-level applications program that is network independent and whose use is relatively transparent.

Many of the DCL commands and RMS services can be used remotely with DECnet. Their use can be essentially transparent to the user. The general capabilities for VAX networks involve interprocess communication, file transfer, resource sharing, data packet routing, remote logon, remote system boot, and load balancing.

Session with the Command Interpreter

The first normal user message in the VMS multiuser environment is the request to login, followed by the request for a password. What follows are several segments from a VMS "terminal session."

```
Username: AST
Password:
Last interactive login on Sunday 17-Jul-1988 14:29
*************************************************************
* 7/15   VAX will be down 12:00pm - 4:00pm on 7/28   *
* 7/14   Macintosh training: "EWUHELP TRAINING" *
*************************************************************
MAIL ALL QUESTIONS/COMMENTS TO 'SYSMAIL'
You will hear good news from one you thought unfriendly.

$ SHOW USERS
                    VAX/VMS Interactive Users
                    23-Jul-1988 20:20:20.35
          Total number of interactive users = 3
Username      Process name      PID         Terminal
CSD3210101    CSD3210101        00000909    TXF3:
CSD3210115    CSD3210115        00000810    TXB4:
AST           AST               00000852    TXA3:
$
```

The user logged in under the name *AST.* The password used is not shown: It is a normal security precaution for a typed password *not* to be displayed on the monitor. The $ prompt after the initial message indicates that the command interpreter is running and a DCL command is expected. The command *SHOW* generates a listing: With the parameter *USERS,* the output includes job names (here, duplicates of user names), PIDs, and terminals being used. In the segment that follows, the user is attempting to change the password.

```
$ SET PASSWORD
Old password:
New password:
Retype password:
%SET_E_INVPWDLEN, minimum password length is 6; no change
$ SET PASSWORD
Old password:
New password:
Verification:
%SET_E_PWDNOTVER, new password verification error-no change
$ SET PASSWORD
```

```
Old Password:
New Password:
Verification:
$
```

The user is requested to type in the old and new passwords, with the new password being repeated for verification. In the first case, the user entered a short password: VMS insisted on a password of at least six characters. In the second case, the two versions of the new password did not agree. Success was achieved on the third try. In each case, no passwords appear on the screen. Continue with the session.

```
$ PED
%DCL_W_TVVERB, unrecognized verb-check validity/spelling
$ SHOW DEFAULT /DIR
  DUA0:[EWUFAC.CSD.AST]

$ DIR
DIRECTORY DUA0:[EWUFAC.CSD.AST]
CPU.PAS;1       CPU.EXE;1       CPU.LIS;1       CPU.OBJ;1
MFT.PAS;1       DISKIO.EXE;1    DISKIO.LIS;1    DISKIO.PAS;1
MVT.PAS;1       MVT.EXE;1       MFT.EXE;1       MFT.LIS;1
PAGING.PAS;1    PAGING.EXE;1    MVT.LIS;1       MVT.OBJ;1
PAGING.LIS;1    PAGING.OBJ;1    PAGING.LIS;1
Total of 19 files.
$ DIR CPU
Directory DUA0:[EWUFAC.CSD.AST]
CPU.EXE     1 CPU.LIS;1     CPU.OBJ;1       CPU.PAS;1
Total of 4 files.
$ SHOW PROTECTION
SYSTEM=RWE, OWNER=RWED, GROUP=R, WORLD=R
$ DIR /PROTECTION PAGING
Directory DUA0:[EWUFAC.CSD.AST]
PAGING.EXE;1    (RWED, RWED, RWED, RWED)
PAGING.LIS;1    (RWED, RWED, RWED, RWED)
PAGING.OBJ;1    (RWED, RWED, RWED, RWED)
PAGING.PAS;1    (RWED, RWED, RWED, RWED)
```

In this segment, a bad command name was entered, and the working directory was seen to be *EWUFAC.CSD.AST*. Since no change of directory command had been entered, *EWUFAC.CSD.AST* is the home directory. The listing for *EWUFAC.CSD.AST* shows a number of Pascal source files and some accompanying object files, executable images, and files of listings generated by the compiling process. Each file listed is a first version (*;1*).

Adding a file name to the *DIR* command returns the expected set of file names. Default protections assigned when files are created during this session are shown to be universal. The *PROTECTION* option for *DIR* shows the four sets of protection for individual files (in the following order: system, owner, group, world). The result of setting new protections is illustrated.

```
$ SET PROTECTION=(S:RWE, O:RWED, G:RWE, W:E)
_FILE: PAGING.PAS
```

The *_FILE:* is a prompt from VMS letting the user know that the file parameter was missing from the *SET* command. VMS tends to use this approach for coaching, rather than giving error messages.

```
$ DIR /PROTECTION PAGING
Directory DUA0:[EWUFAC.CSD.AST]
PAGING.EXE;1    (RWED, RWED, RWED, RWED)
PAGING.LIS;1    (RWED, RWED, RWED, RWED)
PAGING.OBJ;1    (RWED, RWED, RWED, RWED)
PAGING.PAS;1    (RWE, RWED, RWE, E)
```

The next segment concerns the creation of subdirectories for the file system.

```
$ CREATE /DIR [.JIM]
$ CREATE /DIR [.SALLY]
$ DIR
DIRECTORY DUA0:[EWUFAC.CSD.AST]
CPU.PAS;1      CPU.EXE;1     CPU.LIS;1    CPU.OBJ;1
JIM.DIR;1      DISKIO.EXE;1 DISKIO.LIS;1 DISKIO.PAS;1
MFT.PAS;1      MVT.EXE;1     MFT.EXE;1    MFT.LIS;1
MVT.PAS;1      PAGING.EXE;1 MVT.LIS;1     MVT.OBJ;1
PAGING.PAS;1 PAGING.OBJ;1 PAGING.LIS;1 SALLY.DIR;1
PAGING.LIS;1
Total of 21 files.
$ SET DEFAULT [.JIM]
$ CREATE /DIR [.SCHOOL]
$ DIR
DIRECTORY DUA0:[EWUFAC.CSD.AST.JIM]
SCHOOL.DIR
Total of 1 file.
$
```

Two directories, *JIM* and *SALLY*, were attached to *EWUFAC.CSD.AST*, the working directory. The working directory was then changed to *JIM* and a directory *SCHOOL* created as a subdirectory for *JIM*.

```
$ SHOW WORKING_SET
Working set    /Limit=169       /Quota=512         /Extent=2048
Adjustment enabled  Authorized Quota=512  Authorized Extent=2048
$ SHOW PROCESS
23-Jul-1988   20:40:33.17   TXA3:     User:AST
Pid 00000852   Proc name AST UIC[CSDFAC.AST]
Priority 4  Default file spec:_DUA0:[EWUFAC.CSD.AST]
Device Allocated: TXA3:
```

The previous section illustrates two other options that may be used with the *SHOW* command. *SHOW* and *SET* have many possible options.

In what follows, a three-line file is created directly from the keyboard (^z is Control-z). The output is then temporarily redirected to that same file: The only output requested is a directory listing. *TYPE* is then used to list the contents of the file onto the screen: The *VMS* characteristic of keeping multiple versions of a file is seen. *TEMPO.LIS;2* is shown. The VMS default is to use the latest version. The earlier version of *TEMPO* is called by explicit use of the version number.

```
$ CREATE TEMPO.LIS
LINE 1
LINE 2
LINE 3
^z
$ ASSIGN TEMPO.LIS SYS$OUTPUT
$ DIR
$ DEASSIGN SYS$OUTPUT
```

```
$ TYPE TEMPO
DIRECTORY DUA0:[EWUFAC.CSD.AST.JIM]
SCHOOL.DIR;1 TEMPO.LIS;2 TEMPO.LIS;1
Total of 3 files.
$ TYPE TEMPO.LIS;1
LINE 1
LINE 2
LINE 3
$ DEL TEMPO
%DELETE_E_DELVER, explicit version or wildcard required
$ DEL TEMPO.LIS;2
$ COPY TEMPO.LIS TEMPR.LIS
$ DIR
DIRECTORY DUA0:[EWUFAC.CSD.AST.JIM]
SCHOOL.DIR;1 TEMPO.LIS;1 TEMPR.LIS;1
Total of 3 files.
$ TYPE TEMPR
LINE 1
LINE 2
LINE 3
$ REN TEMPR.LIS TEMPE.LIS
$ DIR
DIRECTORY DUA0:[EWUFAC.CSD.AST.JIM]
SCHOOL.DIR;1 TEMPE.LIS;1 TEMPO.LIS;1
Total of 3 files.
$ SET DEFAULT [.SCHOOL]
$
```

The working directory is now *EWUFAC.CSD.AST.JIM.SCHOOL*. In what follows, a *.COM* file (command script) is created and executed.

```
$ CREATE SCRIPT.COM
$ WRITE SYS$OUTPUT "hello from VMS"
$ SHOW TIME
^z
$ @SCRIPT
hello from VMS
  23-Jul-1988 20:47:16
$ HI:=@SCRIPT
$ HI
hello from VMS
  23-Jul-1988 20:48:23
$ SUBMIT SCRIPT
Job SCRIPT (queue SYS$BATCH, entry 410) started
$
Job SCRIPT (queue SYS$BATCH, entry 410) completed
$
```

A new file *SCRIPT* is produced in the directory *SCHOOL* by using the *CREATE* command. Two lines are entered: Each line is an executable DCL command. The command *@SCRIPT* causes the two-line file to be executed. An alias (*HI*) for *@SCRIPT* can also call for execution. Finally, the file is submitted for batch execution.

```
$ SET DEFAULT [.--]
$ SHOW DEFAULT
DUA0:[EWUFAC.CSD.AST]
$ DIR M*T.*.*
DIRECTORY DUA0:[EWUFAC.CSD.AST]
```

```
MFT.EXE;1     MFT.LIS;1     MFT.PAS;1     MVT.EXE;1
MVT.LIS;1     MVT.OBJ;1     MVT.PAS;1
Total of 7 files.
$
```

Note how the .-- was used to back up two levels in the file hierarchy (from *EWU-FAC.CSD.AST.JIM.SCHOOL* to *EWUFAC.CSD.AST*). The wild card * was used to gain a listing of every directory entry of the form *M*T* regardless of the file type or version number. Seven files fit the conditions.

The examples in this session have only begun to scratch the surface of DCL command capabilities. Remember that the interpreter provides a sophisticated, block-structured programming language for creating commands and script files. Branching, looping, and much more are possible.

Exercises

1. Give several factors contributing to the success of VMS.
2. List several of the weaknesses of VMS.
3. To what extent are VMS applications easily portable? Why should anyone care?
4. Why is VMS unlikely to become a "standard" operating system?
5. If you were DEC, what kinds of changes would you make to VMS?
6. Describe the VMS command interpreter in one sentence.
7. If you were to design a windowing system for VMS, what would you be likely to create?
8. Compare/contrast pathname and filename.
9. Compare/contrast home directory and current (working) directory.
10. What role do background jobs play?
11. What does the image of a VMS process look like?
12. What kind of page replacement strategy is used for a paged implementation? What are the advantages and disadvantages of the global page replacement policy?
13. Describe the priority mechanisms involved in swapping VMS processes into and out of mainstore.
14. What is the purpose of the VMS quantum?
15. Discuss the mounting and unmounting of file systems. When might a request to unmount a file fail?
16. How can a user interrupt a running VMS process?

For the remaining exercises, locate a book or manual with a summary of the VMS commands, find a VMS system, and login.

17. Take a look at the root directory and the directories contained in the root. Use the **HELP** command to obtain information about any command of interest. Find out what facilities are available to help you learn about VMS.
18. Write a Com file to customize the environment welcoming the user so that it gives the date, lists all the current users, and shows the home directory. The file should be set up as a startup file.
19. Create a script file that will remove all files ending in ;3 from the home directory. Execute the file at your own risk.

20. Redo Exercise 19 but present all such files, one at a time, to the user for a decision on whether to actually remove the file in question.
21. Create a startup Com file that sets a number of aliases so that the user may use the following UNIX commands: **pwd, cd, who,** and **who am i.** Be careful that **cd .** and **cd ..** work.
22. Find out more about CODASYL.

16 IBM S360/370 Operating Systems

To many, the name IBM is synonymous with computers. IBM, however, was not the originator of the first commercially successful computers, nor was it the primary innovator of early technology. IBM has been, though, the most commercially successful company over the first 40 years of the digital computer industry. At least three factors contributed to that success: the **family concept** for computer systems, marketing ability, and **RAS.**

Computer systems are seldom purchased with the concept that they will fill organizational needs forever. There always comes a point when a different system is required and, when that time comes, there is a price to be paid for switching systems. If there is little or no compatibility between the old hardware and the new or between the old operating system and the new, programs will have to be rewritten, files will need to be reconstructed, operating system command sequences must be reexamined, and, in extreme cases, there may even be a requirement to change the way the organization conducts business. Such conversions can take a year or more, cause significant disruption to organizational activity, and cost hundreds of thousands or even millions of dollars.

In the mid-1960s, IBM announced the first commercially available family of computers—the **S/360 family.** IBM promised to deliver a range of machines having a compatible architecture and running the same operating system. Customers could purchase small S/360 machines, intermediate-sized S/360s, and quite large S/360s. As organizational needs outgrew a particular 360 machine, a more powerful member of the family could be purchased and current application programs moved to it with little or no conversion required. The family concept offered commercial users the ability to make data processing choices without worrying about unpredictable and uncontrollable conversion costs and interruptions lurking in their future.

IBM also delivered customer support at a level previously unknown in the computer industry. IBM prides itself on **RAS** (Reliability, Availability, and Serviceability). Customer support, compatible families of computers, and a powerful marketing division gave IBM a huge advantage during the mid-1960s, an advantage that has never been overcome by any competing computer manufacturer. Others produce units with similar or greater capabilities and often at a better price/performance ratio: Still, IBM leads.

IBM currently offers a range of families, from microcomputers to large mainframes. IBM also offers several different operating systems, rather than a single operating system as in the case of DEC's VAX family. However, each IBM operating system spans several families so that upward compatibility is available.

The 360/370 Family

The architecture of S/360 machines was carried over to the S/370 machines of the early 1970s. The 370 machines offered dynamic address translation, while the 360s offered only static address translation. Only the later S/360 machines provided for virtual memory capabilities, but S/370 machines were virtual memory machines from the start. S/370 machines retained the S/360 instruction set for compatibility reasons.

The 24-bit S/370 addresses matched those from the S/360 machines, giving a 16M byte virtual memory. Newer 370/XA (eXtended Architecture) hardware extends the virtual address space to 2G bytes with 31-bit addresses. The 370/XA machines can run in three modes: an S/360 mode, a 24-bit mode, and an extended 31-bit addressing mode.

S/370 machines can operate with 2K byte pages or 4K byte pages. They can also manage 64K byte segments or 1M byte segments. The hardware provides 4-bit keys for memory protection at the page level, and there is some hardware protection at the segment level. Hardware does all address translation for the paged segmentation. The 370 architecture is currently embodied in several individual families: the **9370 family,** the **43XX family,** and the **30XX family.**

The 9370 Family

This family of minicomputers has been dubbed *VAX killers* by some, in that IBM developed the 9370s for competition in the minicomputer arena. They are known as *departmental systems* as they occupy the mid-level in IBM's **connectivity strategy** for meeting the computing needs of large organizations. See Figure 16.1 for the computer use hierarchy.

Figure 16.1

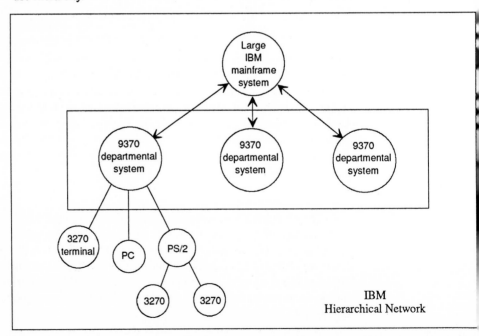

IBM
Hierarchical Network

The 9370, as the number scheme would indicate, is a 370 architecture system compatible with the larger mainframe units. Speeds up to 2.5 MIPS are found in the top-end 9370s. Main memory ranges from 8M to 16M bytes. The top-end machines are about five times as powerful as the low-end 9370s, offering customers some growth possibilities within the family. Networking of all sorts is supported: 9370s may be used effectively as network servers.

The 9370 family requires no special operator involvement for routine startup and shutdown activities. This is important if the system is to be a departmental system located where the work is, rather than being centered in data processing. The 9370 family supports the full range of mainframe operating systems running on 370 architecture machines.

Some feel the newer, more powerful microprocessor chips pose a threat to the 9370 family. Multiprocessor systems using 80386 or 68020 chips, for example, can easily match the gross power capabilities of the 9370s. Others see some conflict arising between the 9370 family and the S/3X (S/34, S/36, and S/38) family. The S/3X architecture is totally different from the 370 architecture and represents a unique IBM effort on the office automation and data processing fronts.

The 43XX Family

The 43XX family of mainframe 370 architecture machines includes the 4341, 4361, and the 4381. The 4381 is both the most powerful and the most current processor in the line. On the low end, the family overlaps the capabilities of the 9370 family, and on the high end, the line moves into the capacity of some less powerful members of the 30XX group.

The 43XX models are aircooled mainframes with a range of 2 MIPS to about 8 MIPS. Main memory can run up to 32M or 64M bytes. The top of the line 4381 is a dual processor machine. The 43XX systems support up to 24 I/O channels capable of moving data at 3M bytes/second.

The 30XX Family

The 30XX family of processor complexes sits at the top of IBM's 370 mainframe line in terms of power, size, and cost. The current focus by IBM is on various models of the 3090 line. (Others in the family are 3031, 3033, 3081, 3083, and 3084.) These machines all require water cooling.

The speeds for the 30XX family start at more than 7 MIPS and extend to over 16 MIPS. The 3090 model 400 is a four processor complex. Main memory may extend up to 128M bytes with **expanded storage** to an additional 512M bytes. A major function of expanded storage is the caching of pages to reduce the I/O calls for paging. Up to 96 I/O channels (3M bytes/second) may be incorporated.

Other companies are challenging IBM's 30XX line with offerings of their own. For example, Prime has models 9955II (5 MIPS), 6350 (12 MIPS), and 6550 (24 MIPS), which have grown up out of their minicomputer lines. Amdahl, a longtime maker of machines that are **plug compatible** with IBM mainframes has a model 5890 that competes in the 3090 world. However, IBM is, unquestionably, the leader in large mainframe installations.

Some Terms of Interest

In discussing IBM systems, a number of particular terms are bound to arise. While the terms are not all IBM-specific, they probably arise more in discussions about IBM equipment than any other. Short descriptions of several such terms follow.

Channels

Large data processing systems tend to be I/O-bound: IBM uses channels to release the processor from administering I/O. A channel is a complete but special-purpose micro- or minicomputer for handling I/O independent of the CPU. In effect, channels provide a measure of parallel processing.

Channels provide paths between main memory and peripheral devices for the transfer of data independent of CPU activity. The channel selects data paths and directs the data transfer, using its own memory for buffering.

Channels come in two general types: selector and multiplexor. A **selector channel,** while servicing multiple devices, dedicates its one subchannel to providing a path for high-speed, high-volume data transfer between memory and a single device at a time. A **multiplexor channel,** on the other hand, provides several subchannels or paths at a time by interleaving data transfer between main memory and several peripheral devices. Multiplexor channels are classified as **byte multiplexors** (data transfer for slower devices) and **block multiplexors.**

VSAM

VSAM (Virtual Sequential Access Method) is IBM's preferred access method for file systems within virtual storage situations. VSAM is an indexed approach based on one or more keys. The index structure is a tree, looking much like a B-Tree.

For virtual systems, VSAM is the replacement (not equivalent) of ISAM. Records may be referenced by key, by relative byte address (RBA), or by relative record number. The index mechanism is a dynamic mechanism (ISAM's is static) with both the index content and structure changing as records are inserted and deleted.

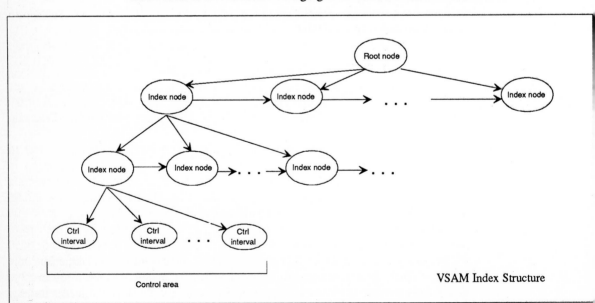

VSAM Index Structure

Figure 16.2

The smallest unit of contiguous allocation is the **control interval.** The index has one entry for each control interval, with each index record holding several entries. The collection of control intervals from a given index record is called a **control area.** (See Figure 16.2.) The insertion and deletion of records requires node splitting and rearranging of data records within a control interval.

VSAM is used to manage disk space for IBM operating systems. Each file system maintains a **master catalog** to identify the individual **user catalogs.** User catalogs are directories to the individual files (data sets). A job statement referencing any data set must identify (by name) both the data set and the catalog in which it is found.

Libraries of executable programs (**phases**) and job control language (**JCL**) procedures (**PROCs**) available to all users are maintained on the system disk **SYSRES.** The system directory in SYSRES locates files in four individual categories: **Source Statement Library, Core Image Library, Relocatable Library,** and **Procedure Library.** The Source Statement Library contains sublibraries of often used source code, while the Core Image Library contains **phases** (executable, linked object modules). The Relocatable Library holds object code modules that have not been linked. The PROC Library contains JCL PROC (macros, if you prefer) that have been **cataloged.**

JES

IBM's **Job Entry Subsystem (JES)** is a part of the job management system. The **job** is the major unit of work in batch-oriented systems. Jobs may be entered through a card reader, a terminal, or an active program. Jobs are composed of individual activities known as **job steps**; executing job steps are known as **tasks.** In some respects, job steps correspond to programs or subprograms, while tasks correspond to processes. (For MVS systems, there is another unit known as the **service request,** a special purpose activity performed on behalf of a job without the overhead of creating a task.) Two aspects of job management are job-to-job transitions and task-to-task transitions.

JES is the evolutionary product of earlier spooling mechanisms, and several varieties are found, some with very advanced job scheduling capabilities. Most perform some output spooling and help maintain journal files to support system restart. JES may read the job stream, scan for JCL accuracy, insert **PROCs** (catalogued macro commands) and send jobs to the appropriate queues. For multiprocessing systems, JES does some I/O resource allocation and processor workload balancing. JES has other capabilities as well.

Several Operating Systems

While the notion of a single operating system sounded great in the mid-1960s (and still does), getting all existing IBM customers to forego their investments and convert to the proposed **OS/360** was another matter. IBM made a Herculean marketing effort and created a great bank of software to simulate other operating systems (mostly IBM) on the S/360. Supposedly, customers could run their applications without significant conversion. Still, there was resistance.

IBM responded by creating several operating systems for the S/360, the most popular being DOS (Disk Operating System). Existing IBM customers, particularly those with smaller systems already running DOS, were enticed to move to the 360 machines. DOS/VS, DOS/VSE, and VSE/SP form a line of descendants for that popular batch-oriented operating system. Each is supported to some extent today.

OS/360 started with two versions, **OS/MFT** and **OS/MVT,** which evolved into **OS/VS1** and **OS/VS2** respectively. OS/VS2 gave rise to **MVS,** IBM's most popular high-end performer. OS/VS1 and OS/VS2 are still supported. Each of these related operating systems is also batch-oriented.

An operating system designed for interactive work was conceived in the latter half of the 1960s (**CP/67**) and evolved into the versatile and powerful operating system called **VM.** VM may become IBM's major operating system of the future.

DOS/VSE   As mentioned earlier, IBM's desire that all customers use OS/360 was met with little enthusiasm by those already running significant applications on some of the smaller IBM machines. As a consequence, DOS was made available on the S/360 as an **interim** operating system for small- to medium-sized business systems. Its popularity continued and evolved through **DOS/VS** to **DOS/VSE** (Virtual Storage Extended). The product continues today as **VSE/SP** (System Package) on smaller 370 architecture systems.

Originally, DOS supported two concurrent jobs, with VSE now supporting up to five concurrent application programs. VSE remains a batch-oriented operating system with layers of software added to make interactive computing possible. Up to 16M bytes of mainstore is supported, with virtual memory sizes up to 40M bytes. VSE supports a single (system) virtual memory image rather than a virtual image for each application program.

Figure 16.3

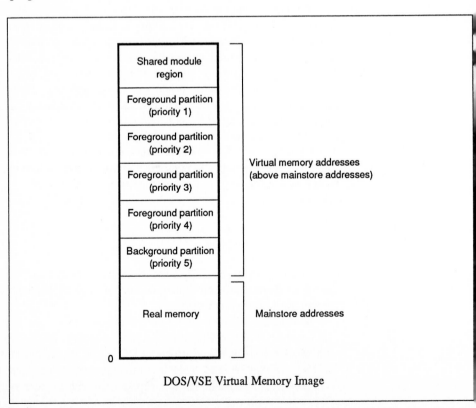

DOS/VSE Virtual Memory Image

Memory management. VSE provides paged segmentation for fixed partitioning. Application programs are paged from a single virtual memory image maintained by the system on the paging device. Paging is hardware managed, and hardware keys provide page-level memory protection for the different active jobs.

Figure 16.3 shows the general layout of the virtual image in DOS/VSE (VSE/SP is somewhat more complex). There are two general subdivisions: the **real address space** (those addresses coinciding with mainstore addresses) and the **virtual address space** residing on the paging device and partitioned into as many as five **fixed partitions.** There is also a region for routines shared among applications.

Each application partition has an associated job queue managed in an FCFS fashion, dividing the job stream into as many as five separate job streams. Each *partition* has an associated priority, which is automatically assigned to every job in its stream with the background partition usually representing the lowest priority level. The operator, however, can modify the priority settings to gain equal priority for all or some partitions.

Mainstore is segmented into three regions: the **supervisor** (operating system) sits in low memory, the **page pool** resides at the high end of mainstore, and application sections (typically one for each program running) are found in the middle. Each application section contains a PCB for the executing program (sometimes PCBs are associated with partitions rather than programs). In those cases where a routine must be totally memory resident, its entire image may reside in the section. Normally, an image is paged from the paging device using frames from the page pool.

DOS/VSE uses an interesting loading technique. When a partition is to be loaded with an application, the supervisor loads a **job control program** into the partition. The job control program does a number of housekeeping chores (to include locating the application program) and signals the supervisor when finished. The supervisor then overwrites the job control program with the application routine. Remember that this is a batch-oriented system: JCL statements are used to give instructions about the execution of a job and to break the job into individual tasks. It is the individual tasks that are loaded and executed one at a time.

CPU scheduling. CPU scheduling is a relatively simple, primitive task. The partitions are ordered by priority from highest to lowest (background partition). When the scheduler needs a program to dispatch, it simply searches for the highest priority *partition* holding a ready task. FCFS is employed when partitions have equal priorities.

I/O. From the programmer's point of view, I/O comes in two flavors: **PIOCS** (Physical I/O Control System) and **LIOCS** (Logical I/O Control System). PIOCS allows a programmer complete control of devices by writing channel programs. Generally, however, most applications programmers prefer to use the LIOCS where no writing of channel programs is required. Instead, the programmer simply writes a description of the file/device being accessed. LIOCS supplies the channel program necessary to complete the access.

File system. VSE uses **VSAM** (Virtual Sequential Access Method) for its own file system maintenance and supports VSAM as a user mechanism. VSE supports the typical array of file organizations (sequential, direct/random, partitioned, and ISAM) and the usual access methods. File protections and file system auditing measures are available.

User interface.   VSE is a batch-oriented system and, as such, makes extensive use of spooling. Spooling is used for (batch) job stream management and for much I/O. **VSE/POWER** (Priority Output WritERs) is a major IBM product in this category. On-line interactive computing capability is provided through **CICS/DOS/VS** (Customer Information Control System) and **VSE/ICCF** (Interactive Computing and Control Facility). CICS controls online communication between terminal and database. ICCF assists with interactive administration of the system and with interactive program development. ICCF allows terminal entry of code, data, and jobs.

The **Interactive Interface (II)** manages the user interface by way of **panels** (menus): Choices are made with a single keystroke and data is entered in a natural forms-oriented way. The II is easily tailored for a user's specific activities. Since experienced users often find selection menus too cumbersome, II offers a **fast path** option in which the entry of a single string (called a **synonym**) replaces tedious navigation through a sequence of panels.

The panels offer a security mechanism, as the system administrator, through user profiles, controls which panels are available to a given user. Since the user can access only what the panels allow, the administrator exercises a measure of control. This has an effect similar to that of a customized shell in UNIX.

Communications.   Networking capabilities are supported through two mechanisms: **BTAM** (Basic Telecommunications Access Method) and **VTAM** (Virtual Terminal Access Method). VTAM is used for SNA networks. VSE nodes in a network may communicate with other nodes running VSE, VM, or MVS. Local devices communicating with the VSE node may be RJE (Remote Job Entry) stations, PCs, terminals, or intelligent workstations. Figure 16.4 shows a network with a large central system and several VSE/SP nodes.

Figure 16.4

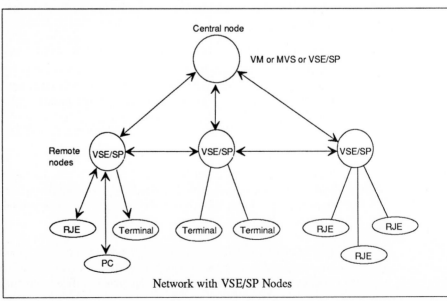

Network with VSE/SP Nodes

Startup. IBM states that VSE/SP installation takes about two hours. After that point, daily startup is nearly automatic, unless some fine tuning or reconfiguration is required. It is claimed that on smaller systems, an operator is not normally required.

VSE/SP may be installed with one, two, or three address spaces and from six to twelve partitions. (Note the differences from the DOS/VSE virtual memory.) These parameters are part of the **basic system environment:** VSE/SP comes with four predefined environments. Local system managers can alter the predefined environments anytime after initial installation.

To create a system from scratch, system disks must be formatted and VSE/SP loaded from tape to disk to create a startup or primitive system. When this startup system is booted, the Interactive Interface may be used for configuring. Additional software may then be added.

MVS   When OS/360 was created, two different OS/360 operating systems emerged. **OS/MFT** supported a fixed level of multiprogramming through fixed partitions of mainstore. **OS/MVT** supported a variable level of multiprogramming through variable partitioning of main memory. Neither incorporated virtual memory concepts.

Later S/360 models gave hardware support for virtual memory techniques, whereby OS/MFT became **OS/VS1** and OS/MVT evolved into **OS/VS2.** Each new version, like VSE, supported a single virtual image—OS/VS1 running OS/MFT in its virtual memory and OS/VS2 running OS/MVT in the single virtual image. Since hardware keys for protecting page frames consisted of four bits, only fifteen applications plus the operating system could run concurrently in a single virtual space.

By the mid-1970s, OS/VS2 gave way to **MVS** (Multiple Virtual Storage), where each user was given a personal virtual image in which to work. The limit of 15 concurrent applications no longer applied. MVS remains as IBM's high-end operating system, particularly for larger mainframes. MVS is batch-oriented by design. However, interactive computing is supported by user interfaces of several varieties. One such interface is **TSO** (Time Sharing Option), which is primarily used as a text editor for constructing and entering batch jobs. **CICS** (Customer Interactive Control System) runs as a task under MVS and offers true interactive computing. MVS can manage a set of up to 16 processors for multiprocessing.

As one might expect from an operating system with a long family history, a great deal of software is available for MVS. Software packages allow the system to be used for almost any desired purpose, thus MVS has a large base of corporate followers.

Memory management. Paged segmentation for MVS uses 4K byte pages, 1M byte segments, and a three-level scheme of page tables. Each **segment page table** is one page in size and contains entries for the 256 pages making up the segment. Each **intermediate-level page table** entry points to one of those segment page tables. Each **top-level page table** points to an intermediate-level page table. See Figure 16.5.

Since each page table is itself a page and requires a page frame when memory resident, it is eligible to be paged out when frames are needed. In practice, only low-level page tables are likely to be paged out and then only if each entry is currently inactive (that is, no page is in a working set). Each working set is a mix of **fixed pages**

Figure 16.5

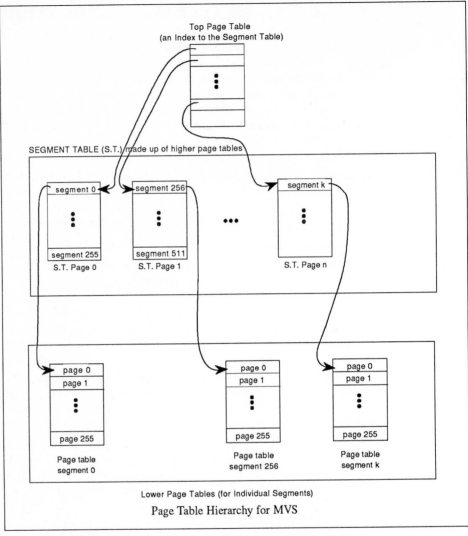

Page Table Hierarchy for MVS

(pages that remain memory resident during execution) and **transient pages** (pages subject to being paged out).

Page replacement is a form of **LRU.** Each page has a **reference counter, a reference bit,** and a **modified bit.** The reference bit is set whenever its page is referenced. At fixed intervals, the reference bit is checked by the operating system: If the bit is set, the reference counter is zeroed; otherwise the reference counter is incremented. In either case, the reference bit is cleared. When the free page frame list is too short, those pages with the largest reference counter values give up their frames to the free list. If possible, the system chooses nonmodified pages.

Another paging problem can occur: If too large a percentage of the system's page frames hold fixed pages, the available page frame pool may become too small and cause thrashing. A complex swapping mechanism is used to lower the percentage of fixed pages in such an event. Swapping generally adjusts the level of multiprogramming among various **domains** (groups of users/address spaces having similar requirements).

The virtual address space is 16M bytes (24-bit addressing) or 2G bytes (31-bit addressing in XA mode) for each user. In the 16M byte case, virtual memory is split evenly between the operating system and the application program. (OS/360 and its descendants are huge operating systems containing millions of lines of code.)

MVS/XA has two modes of operation: **24-bit addressing** and **31-bit addressing**. The 2G byte address space has two portions, the one using addresses up to the 16M byte point and a massive region above that address. The higher region is mapped to system and user portions similar to the subdivisions within the lower 16M bytes.

CPU scheduling.   Scheduling is a three-level proposition. At the highest level (of priority) are some **system-specific** and **time-specific** activities. The intermediate priority level includes system service requests that are **global** in the sense that more than one address space is affected. At the lowest priority level are the local service requests and task activities relating to a specific address space.

CPU dispatching for address spaces is also a priority system with three tiers. In the highest tier, address spaces are assigned **fixed priorities** (0 to 255) for the duration of execution. In the intermediate tier, address spaces are scheduled in a **round-robin** fashion. At the lower level, priority queueing is based on the average length of CPU time used at each opportunity: The higher the average CPU usage, the lower the priority.

Each address space can support local multitasking. Dispatching must consider not only the priority order among address spaces but a priority order within each address space as well. The local dispatching mechanism like the global one, is a three-level affair with the following levels: local service requests, tasks holding **locks,** tasks not holding locks. In summary, the queueing mechanism has three global queues, each internally managing three levels of priority.

Most hardware systems running MVS are multiprocessing systems. In general, tasks run on only one processor at a time; however, MVS is capable of supporting true parallel processing. Synchronization is managed by the use of **global** and **local locks** and by hierarchical resource allocation techniques.

The scheduling process is actually more complex than just described. The frontend facility **JES** is a combination high-level scheduler and output spooler capable of performing deadline scheduling and priority aging of waiting jobs. JES accepts the job stream, scanning each job for JCL errors. If there are no errors for a given job, required library routines are added and the job is placed into an appropriate queue (fixed priority, round robin, or other). JES also handles certain aspects of output spooling.

I/O.   In S/370 systems, physical I/O is handled through the I/O channel connecting the peripheral device to the CPU. In effect, the channels form a network through which the processor(s) communicate with peripheral devices. On XA systems, channels select and manage the paths to peripherals. On multiple CPU systems, one processor initiates an I/O request, the channel handles the request, and a (perhaps different) processor handles the request's completion. More of the burden of I/O is shifted from the processor(s) to the channels. A system can have up to 256 channel paths; a given device can be reached by up to eight paths.

As mentioned earlier, a **hierarchical** collection of global and local locks is used to synchronize the concurrent use of resources. The purpose of the locks is to provide **serialization** of those resources and to prevent deadlock. Locks are of two types: **spin** and **suspend.** When a spin lock prevents a task from gaining a resource, the task goes into a busy waiting loop, continually checking for the lock's release (and using valuable processor time in doing so). In the case of a suspend lock, the task is put on hold and relinquishes the CPU to another.

The hierarchical arrangement of the locks imposes some rules for their use. A task can generally hold only one lock at a given level. Each request for another lock (resource) must be for a lock at a higher level than the level of any lock presently held. A local lock must be held before a global lock may be requested. There are other constraints, but these essentially describe the deadlock prevention scheme.

File system.   The file system of MVS has a good number of organization and access types, many dating from its ancestors. The organization types are **sequential, direct/random, partitioned,** and **indexed sequential.** The access types are sequential (**BSAM, QSAM**), direct (**BDAM**), partitioned (**BPAM**), indexed sequential (**ISAM**), and virtual (**VSAM**). VSAM is the access method available across the entire line of IBM operating systems. MVS uses VSAM for its own file system management.

Files are called **data sets** in IBM terminology. Typical file manipulation functions such as creation, deletion, reading, and updating are supported. Data set **names** are partitioned into as many as three parts: user, file name, and file type (for example, CSDFAC08.RCVBL.PAS). The file system provides a number of backup services and auditing services.

Individual files may be protected by requiring passwords, and privileges may be set (**read without password, read with password, write with password,** and **write prohibited**). Files may be set by individuals for **private access** or **shared access.** Individual files may also be set by groups for **exclusive access by group members** or for **shared access** by users outside the group.

User interface.   The user interface afforded by **TSO** dates back to OS/MVT and the S/360 machines. TSO is primarily a means of coordinating IBM 3270 terminal communications among users and operators. User profiles offer a measure of security for the system. The command line interface appears typical of older mainframe interfaces.

Commands have abbreviated forms and defaults with wildcard capabilities. CLISTs offer the equivalent of command or script files for creating macrocommands and tailoring the system. **SPF** (Structured Programming Facility) creates a menu-driven environment for using MVS and greatly simplifies many activities. A split-screen facility is included, giving a limited windowing capability. There are menu types for selection, data display, and parameter entry.

CICS offers an interactive mechanism for database and data communication activities. CICS runs as a task and is essentially a realtime transaction processing layer that greatly simplifies the use of MVS services. CICS is used to manage jobs, tasks, and so on and to make MVS calls to manage the system's resources.

There is considerable software available for MVS systems, though none comes packaged with the price of the operating system. MVS/XA, the newest version of MVS for extended architecture machines, has many of the most useful data handling software modules packaged together as **DFP** (Data Facility Product).

Communication. MVS has a variety of communication and networking equipment and software available to it. At the lowest level is **BTAM-ES** (Basic Telecommunication Access Method—Extended Storage), which gives read/ write communications with peripheral devices.

ACF/VTAM (Advanced Communication Function/Virtual Terminal Access Method) is a fundamental networking software tool used with MVS in SNA networks. A typical mainframe node in an SNA network may consist of a host MVS computer and an **FEP** (Front End Processor) running **NCP** (Network Control Program). A collection of terminals and other peripheral devices communicates with the main computer through the FEP. VTAM defines a domain of address spaces (tasks) under MVS. In such an arrangement, the FEP absorbs a great deal of the processing normally handled by the CPU. The configuration may be used in a network with a single intelligent node or with many nodes having VTAM capability.

IBM has a large number of individual products to enhance networking in SNA and non-SNA networks alike. It is IBM's hope that customers will follow the SNA protocol.

Startup. The installation and startup procedures are very complex activities for MVS systems. (Remember that MVS systems are generally IBM's largest and most complex). The procedure is conceptually the same for all large systems: Operating system installation facilities come on magnetic tape, disk drives must be formatted and a minimal operating system copied over, that minimal operating system is booted, and then it is configured for the current site.

MVS systems have very extensive and sophisticated monitoring capabilities known as **SMF** (System Management Facilities). Detailed information is gathered on jobs, processor activity, paging, swapping, and disk drives. Performance information can be displayed and specialized reports can be generated using the **RMF** (Resource Management Facility).

VM

In the mid-1960s, a small group within IBM conceived and implemented a **virtual machine** operating system for the S/360 family. It was the first significant IBM effort to design a truly interactive operating system. **CP/67,** as it was known, had roots in the CTSS and Multics projects at MIT. In the early 1970s, the operating system was implemented on S/370 machines (as **VM/370**) to take advantage of improved hardware capabilities. Today the system is marketed as **VM/SP** (System Product) and **VM/HPO** (High Performance Option). VM has been implemented on the full range of IBM machines, from micros to the largest mainframes, and is likely to be the IBM operating system of the near future.

VM represented a radical departure from IBM's previous work in several ways:
- The system was to be interactive by design.
- It was designed by a small group.

Figure 16.6

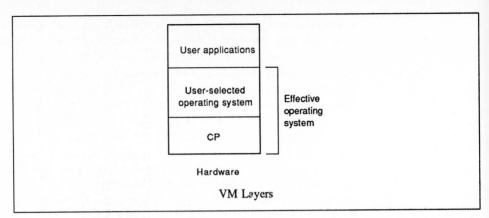

VM Layers

- It was created for in-house use to run other IBM operating systems during their development stages.
- VM was designed to supply each user with a complete, simulated machine.

At logon, a *complete, simulated hardware and software system* is created for the user. Most operating systems, of course, simply create a logon *process* that competes for time slices with all other active processes. The casual user will see no difference between the two methods of resource management, but users requiring an intimate knowledge of the operating system will see many differences.

CP.   Figure 16.6 illustrates the dual layered design of VM. The **CP** (Control Program) manages system resources and creates each user's virtual machine. The second layer represents the user's operating system of choice, any operating system capable of running on the machine being simulated by VM. Normally that operating system will be DOS, DOS/VSE, OS, IX/370 (IBM's UNIX), or MVS, although it can be VM itself, as shown in Figure 16.7. This ability allows organizations to upgrade to a large VM sys-

Figure 16.7

User 1	User 2	User 3a	User 3b	User 3c	User 4
		Applications	Applications	Applications	
Applications	Applications	MVS	CMS	MVS	Applications
MVS	DOS/VSE	CP			MVS
CP					
Hardware					

Multi-OS VM Installation

tem from one of IBM's other operating systems and then continue to run existing applications virtually unchanged.

Several different compatible operating systems may be running on one machine at the same time. Since each operating system shown (except CMS) is a multiuser system, the power of VM can be multiplied. *User1* may, in fact, be the billing department with fifteen employees running under MVS concurrently. *User2* may represent the sales department with five individuals running applications under DOS/VSE—and so on.

Each application that runs under CP control is a **guest** operating system. The CP presents to each guest operating system a simulated hardware configuration to include a virtual console, a virtual processor, a virtual memory, and virtual I/O devices. User access to VM is controlled by **privilege classes.** The Control Program does *not* manage a file system: That function is left to each guest operating system. The mapping required to translate between what is real and what is virtual is assisted greatly by the hardware.

The CP manages the processor(s), establishing a priority for each virtual machine and giving each a reasonable amount of service. Each guest operating system in turn

Figure 16.8

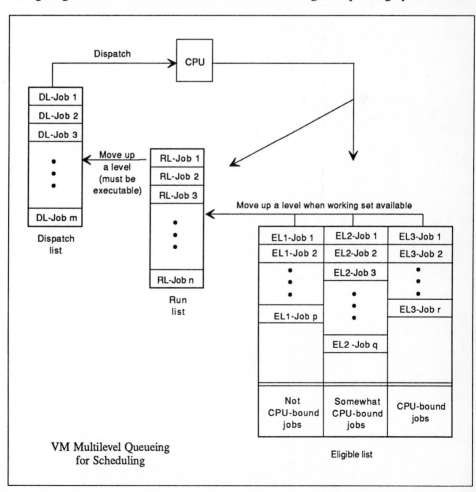

VM Multilevel Queueing
for Scheduling

apportions its CPU time among its currently running applications. The CP uses a complex three-level queueing mechanism. The highest level queue, the **dispatch list,** holds those tasks that will execute next. The **run list** is a queue of tasks whose next move is to the dispatch list. The **eligible list** (actually three separate lists, each characterized by the CPU-boundedness of its tasks) is the lowest priority scheduling queue. Figure 16.8 illustrates the scheduling system: Each task in one of the eligible lists is ready to run but may not execute until it moves level by level to the dispatch list. Each level is maintained in priority order with the priority being a combination of external priority, aging, and CPU-boundedness.

The CP manages mainstore by **paged segmentation** techniques. The Control Program itself has **resident** portions and **transient** portions, the transient portions being subject to paging. A complex paging scheme (a working set model) is used to present a **virtual mainstore** to each virtual machine running. On later systems, page swapping techniques have been implemented. In swapping systems, the **free page frame list** is augmented by the **swap list** (of the page frames previously used by swapped-out jobs) and the **flush list** (page frames held by jobs that are currently out of the queueing system but not swapped out). The swap and flush lists are maintained as a sort of cache, where required pages may be recovered without a disk access. Each page has an associated hardware key that is used to protect the main memory assigned to one virtual machine from contamination by another. Page sizes are either 2K bytes or 4K bytes with segment sizes either 64K bytes or 1M bytes.

The CP creates virtual devices for each virtual machine. A significant amount of address translation is required to accomplish this task. Spooling is, of course, the key to managing this activity, and hardware assistance is required.

Of special interest is the **minidisk** (virtual disk), a group of contiguous logical blocks from a disk pack. Each minidisk is seen by its guest operating system as an entire disk pack to be formatted and used as desired. Because each minidisk's allocation is contiguous, its size is difficult to increase: Generous first allocations are the norm. Since each minidisk's space is not available for any other purpose and since minidisks are almost never full, there can be a significant amount of "wasted" space in a VM disk system at any given time. The CP does not impose any file system structure on minidisks, although it does provide a password assignment for the security of each minidisk.

Each guest operating system runs as an application program under the CP. When the guest operating system executes in its kernel mode, it expects to be able to control the actual hardware. The need to execute privileged instructions in the kernel mode results in a call to the CP, which **simulates** the actual event and passes control back to the guest operating system. Interrupts are also handled differently: The CP inspects an interrupt and decides whether to handle it or (as usually is the case) pass it on to the guest operating system's kernel mode.

CMS. VM does come with its own operating system called **CMS** (Conversational Monitor System). CMS is a **single user,** interactive operating system whose command language shares a number of characteristics with UNIX, VMS, and MS-DOS. CMS takes care of the user interface and manages system calls. It is a complete layer of system utilities sitting on top of the CP. Since VM generates a virtual machine for each user, there is no need for CMS itself to support multiuser computing. Each user may run his or her own copy of CMS concurrently. What, in fact, VM offers is a (virtual) mainframe personal computer for every user.

CMS manages the nonhierarchical file system under VM (which the CP does not), and the CMS commands reside in that file system rather than being memory resident. Accordingly, its commands are easy to alter, add, and delete. This disk-based, interactive interface is effectively a **CLI** interface with extensions to make menu-driven interaction available as desired. The commands typically have abbreviated forms and defaults.

In keeping with the single-user nature of CMS, the operating system provides *no* file locking to protect in the case of concurrent use. CMS also provides no ability to assign privileges for individual files. One criticism of VM is that CMS does not provide adequately for the need for file sharing among groups of users.

While CMS is an interactive operating system, it does support the **CMS Batch** facility with two JCLs. The first, EXEC2, is a subset of the second, REXX. EXEC2 is a command interpreter for VM's JCL and is useful for small jobs. REXX, while more complex and difficult to learn, is a full, compilable programming language more appropriate for larger production batch jobs. CMS Batch establishes a complete virtual machine for the execution of each batch job submitted.

RSCS.   The Remote Spooling Communications Subsystem (**RSCS**) is IBM's primary (although not only) mechanism for incorporating communication techniques into VM. RSCS is actually a special purpose operating system running on a virtual machine assigned by the CP, and it is attached to communication equipment if remote devices or systems are involved. The major activity supported is that of data file transfer between virtual machines.

Data may be transferred between virtual machines on the same physical machine. In this case, the RSCS is the central node with all other virtual machines connected to it in a star configuration. As might be suspected, the CP's spooling system is used heavily. However, VM systems may be networked together by allowing the RSCS from one machine to communicate with the RSCS from another. Virtual machines on different real computers communicate through their respective RSCSs in a kind of connected star topology.

Startup.   The VM startup process may be simple (for microcomputer systems), somewhat complex (for intermediate-sized systems), or quite complex (in the case of larger mainframes). In the latter case, IBM provides a primitive VM starter system on tape. The primitive system must be transferred from tape to a formatted disk in a series of steps. Once the primitive system is booted from disk, it can be used to load and configure other elements so as to create the desired model of VM. In most cases, an experienced operator or system administrator is required for the startup procedure where system generation is performed. Subsequent startup is less complicated and is assisted by various menu-driven features of the operating system itself.

VM today.   VM is not a novelty. The ability to simulate a machine and run multiple operating systems is a powerful concept indeed. As stated earlier, customers can move to a larger, more powerful VM system from several other IBM systems and continue to run applications intact. Systems programmers and developers have the advantage of being able to design, implement, and test a new operating system (or a new version of an existing system) without needing to take over the entire machine: Other users can continue to operate as usual. The technique can even be extended to develop operating systems for nonexistent or nonavailable machines, so long as the target machine can be simulated by VM.

The primary drawback of VM is the sparseness of suitable application software: VM comes packaged without such software. The lack of software, while a temporary condition, means that most applications currently used have been developed under other operating systems and must use a guest operating system in place of CMS.

Other mainframe challengers to VM are appearing (for example, Amdahl's Multiple Domain Facility (MDF) for their 580 series of machines). The challenges come in the form of better efficiency: Guest operating systems typically operate at less than 80 percent of capacity under VM. Current efforts known as **processor partitioning** (a system's resources are partitioned and each guest operating system is given a partition) look to improve that efficiency. Such improvements to VM/XA are expected to answer these challenges.

S/3X   The S/3X series of machines (S/3, S/34, S/36, S/38, and SilverLake) represents a unique line of IBM machines totally different from the S/370 offerings. In particular, these machines are designed to be easy to use in an office or data processing setting by users who are not data processing professionals (for example, there is no system generation as such). They are not designed to be general purpose machines but are developed to work in an intelligent workstation environment. The series represents an intermediate-level offering in terms of size and capability.

S/36 units are intended for use in office automation applications with some data processing. S/36s may consist of up to eight processors and 7M bytes of mainstore. The larger, more powerful S/38 systems are intended for data processing applications. S/38s may be configured with up to 32M bytes of main storage. Machines from the series may be used as standalone units or may be networked by a variety of communications packages. They might be networked to other units in the S/3X family, to machines from the S/370 line, and to PCs.

The S/36 operating system **SSP** (System Support Program) utilizes priority queueing for jobs, virtual storage techniques for memory management, and spooled I/O. Most applications are written in RPG (Report Program Generator) or COBOL.

CPF (Control Program Facility) is the operating system for S/38 (Figure 16.9). It has a built-in relational database management system that uses record locking with multiple read capability for synchronizing reading and writing in the multiuser system. Main memory and disk storage are treated logically as a single unit. Paged virtual memory techniques are also used. No traditional partitioning of memory is available (batch and interactive jobs, however, are partitioned or separated in memory).

Most users are database users and take advantage of a menu-driven interface to manage data. The use of **data description specifications** represents a more primitive interface that may be required on occasion. As with all machines, there is also a control language that may serve as a programmer's interface to the system.

Figure 16.9

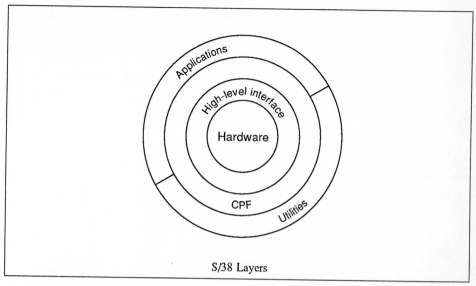

S/38 Layers

One of the most unique characteristics of these machines is their **object-oriented** and **capability-based** design. A significant part of the capability-based design and security measures are built into the hardware, making them less vulnerable. (See Figure 16.10.) A S/3X **object** is simply a named entity that has a list of attributes (to include behaviors) and an associated value. An object is referred to by name, regardless of its

Figure 16.10

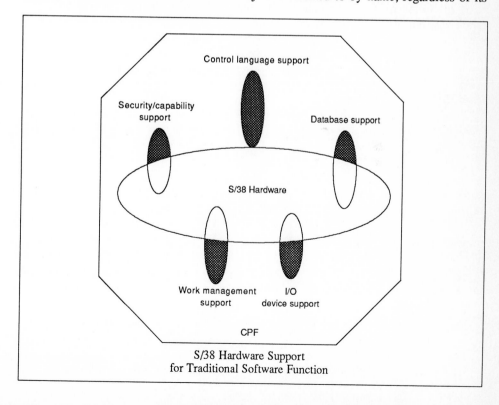

S/38 Hardware Support
for Traditional Software Function

type: This makes programmers' lives easier than might otherwise be the case. An object is created, destroyed, allocated, deallocated, moved, owned, named and renamed, accessed, and generally manipulated in keeping with its attributes. Objects are usually organized into libraries.

A **capability** for an object is, in effect, the list of actions to which the object may be subjected. Programming involves the use of actions on objects: Before an action may be carried out, it must be found in the capability list for the object being manipulated.

JCL

JCL is a batch-oriented programming language for controlling the operating system. JCL for VSE is simpler than JCL for MVS, primarily because MVS itself is a more complicated environment than VSE. JCL for MVS has a more extensive set of options, thereby making it more difficult to learn. As seen earlier, VM has two batch-oriented command languages available, EXEC2 and REXX.

JCL has been carried forward from the earliest days of batch processing. The terminology goes back to the times of **unit record equipment** (such as punched cards), where each instruction was considered to be an 80-character record. It is not uncommon to call a JCL instruction a "card" or a set of JCL instructions a "deck." Positioning of the instruction within the 80 "columns" plays a role in the interpretation of the instruction. The specific examples of JCL instructions used in this section come from VSE JCL.

JCL's General Nature

JCL commands are divided into three general categories:
- Separation and identification of jobs in the job stream
- Identification of individual tasks within each job
- Peripheral assignment

The general form for JCL statements is found in Figure 16.11.

Figure 16.11

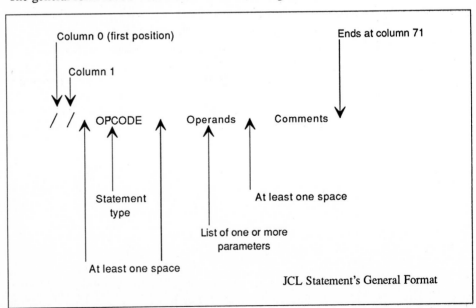

JCL Statement's General Format

Two Basic JCL Commands

JOB. The act of separating individual jobs in a job stream is simple: Insert a **JOB** card as the first statement at the head of the instruction stream, and insert the **terminating /&** instruction as the last. The following illustrates the stream for a job having no job steps (a condition not actually permitted):

```
// JOB JOBNAME
/&
```

Some installations require the insertion of certain accounting information in the operand section. Comments are always optional.

The space character is used as a **delimiter:** Never use a space in front of the //, to separate the slashes of //, or to separate the characters of /&. The following are JCL sequences for a one-step job and a two-step job respectively.

```
// JOB JOBNAME
// EXEC MYWORK
/&
```

and

```
// JOB JOBNAME
// EXEC MYWORK
// EXEC BOSSWORK
/&
```

EXEC. The **EXEC** command as used earlier identifies individual job steps. EXEC effectively calls each program from a **Core Image Library** and then loads and executes it. While the format of EXEC is straightforward, there may be additional operand parameters following the program name: Individual operands in a list of operands are separated by commas. The PROC= option allows the calling of cataloged sets of JCL instructions rather than executable core images.

Additional JCL Characteristics

JCL for MVS is much more complicated than that for VSE, with many more commands. Some of these commands are for looping and branching. Note that the DD (Data Definition) statement is important in MVS: One DD statement is required for each peripheral assignment. The format for JCL on MVS systems is somewhat different from that for VSE. In short, anyone wishing to use JCL has a great deal of work ahead in order to learn about JCL and its specific needs at his or her particular site.

Exercises

1. What is the significance of the *family of computers* concept? How was it important to IBM?
2. Talk to IBM representatives, or acquire IBM publications, so that you can find out what RAS means to IBM.
3. List several factors that have made and currently keep IBM the number one computer manufacturer.
4. Describe the typical user of the VSE line of operating systems.
5. Describe how the single virtual image has been used in VSE, VS1, and VS2.
6. Discuss priorities and scheduling for VSE.

7. Acquire the appropriate IBM literature, or find a knowledgeable user for each of the following. Describe the purpose, function and nature of each.
   a. VSE/POWER
   b. CICS/DOS/VS
   c. VSE/ICCF
   d. II
8. Make a guess about how multiple address spaces and the greater number of partitions are managed and used in VSE/SP. Then acquire the appropriate IBM literature, or find someone who knows about it, and compare your guess with the actual answer.
9. Show how the MVS three-tiered page table mechanism can handle up to 2G bytes in a virtual memory image.
10. Acquire the appropriate IBM literature, or find someone experienced in TSO in order to learn its purpose, function, and nature.
11. Find out the difference between expanded storage as an extension to mainstore and as an enlarged main store capacity. What does the difference have to do with addressability?
12. If the reference counter for an MVS page has a value of 7, what does that mean?
13. Find (through literature or experienced users) the significance of the IBM notion of domains.
14. Find a service request that is global in nature.
15. Find conditions under which a spin lock is preferred to a suspend lock. And vice versa?
16. Find out (through literature or a knowledgeable user) how the three eligible lists are used in VM's three-level queueing system.
17. Find the similarities and differences between VM's flush list and swap list.
18. Find out what processor partitioning is and how it may be used to improve performance in a VM setting.
19. Compare/contrast job, job step, and task. Compare/contrast job management and task management.
20. Describe several ways in which the S/3X systems are unique among the IBM offerings. What is the implication of their architectural differences from the S/370 machines?

Bibliography

Chapter 1 *Textbooks*

[1] Barron, D. W., *Computer Operating Systems,* Chapman and Hall, 1984, New York, NY, Chapters 1 and 2.

[2] Beck, L. L., *System Software,* Addison Wesley, 1985, Reading, MA, Chapter 6.

[3] Calingaert, P., *Operating System Elements,* Prentice-Hall, 1982, Englewood Cliffs, NJ, Chapters 1, 7, and 8.

[4] Davis, W., *Operating Systems: A Systematic View,* Addison Wesley, 1987, Reading, MA, Chapters 1–4.

[5] Deitel, H. M., *An Introduction to Operating Systems,* Addison Wesley, 1984, Reading, MA, Chapters 1 and 2.

[6] Finkel, R. A., *An Operating Systems Vade Mecum,* Prentice-Hall, 1986, Englewood Cliffs, NJ, Chapter 1.

[7] Gear, C. W., *Computer Organization and Programming,* McGraw-Hill, 1985, New York, NY, Chapters 1 and 6.

[8] Massie, P., *Operating Systems Theory and Practice,* Burgess Communications, 1986, Edina, MN, Chapters 1, 2, and 3.

[9] Peterson, J. L. and A. Silberschatz, *Operating System Concepts,* Second Edition, Addison Wesley, 1985, Reading, MA, Chapters 1 and 2.

[10] Yuen, C. K., *Essential Concepts of Operating Systems,* Addison Wesley, 1986, Reading, MA, Chapters 1 and 8.

Chapter 2 *Textbooks*

[1] Andrews, M., *Principles of Firmware Engineering in Microprogram Control,* Computer Science Press, 1980, Potomac, MD.

[2] Beck, L., *System Software,* Addison Wesley, 1985, Reading, MA.

[3] Hayes, J., *Computer Architecture and Organization,* McGraw-Hill, 1987, New York, NY.

[4] Hwang, K. and F. Briggs, *Computer Architecture and Parallel Processing,* McGraw-Hill, 1984, New York, NY.

[5] Stallings, W., *Computer Organization and Architecture,* Macmillan, 1987, New York, NY.

Chapter 3   *Textbooks*

[1] Finkel, R. A., *An Operating Systems Vade Mecum,* Prentice-Hall, 1986, Englewood Cliffs, NJ, Chapter 7.

[2] Massie, P., *Operating Systems Theory and Practice,* Burgess Communications, 1986, Edina, MN, Chapter 3.

[3] Peterson, J. L. and A. Silberschatz, *Operating System Concepts,* Second Edition, Addison Wesley, 1985, Reading, MA, Chapters 2 and 12.

Articles

[4] Brunt, R. F. and D. E. Tuffs, "A User-Oriented Approach to Control Languages," *Software-Practice and Experience,* Vol. 6, No. 1, January 1976.

[5] Carrol, J. M., "Presentation and Form in User- Interface Architecture," *BYTE,* Vol. 8, No. 12, December 1983.

[6] Good, M., "Etude and the Folklore of User Interface Design," *Proceedings of the ACM SIGPLAN SIGOA Symposium on Text Manipulation, SIGPLAN Notices,* Vol. 16, No. 6, June 1981.

Chapter 4   *Textbooks*

[1] Bach, M., *The Design of the UNIX Operating System,* Prentice-Hall, 1986, Englewood Cliffs, NJ, Chapters 3, 4, and 5.

[2] Bull, M., *The Pick Operating System,* Chapman and Hall, 1987, New York, NY, Chapters 1 and 2.

[3] Deitel, H., *An Introduction to Operating Systems,* Addison Wesley, 1984, Reading, MA, Chapter 13.

[4] Dennon, J., *CP/M Revealed,* Hayden Books, 1982, Rochelle, NJ.

[5] Folk, J. and B. Zoellick, *File Structures: A Conceptual Toolkit,* Addison Wesley, 1987, Reading, MA.

[6] Norton, P., *PC-DOS: Introduction to High Performance Computing,* Brady Communications, 1985, Englewood Cliffs, NJ.

[7] Smith, D. and G. Barnes, *Files and DataBases: An Introduction,* Addison Wesley, 1987, Reading, MA.

[8] Worth, D. and P. Lechner, *Beneath Apple ProDOS,* Quality Software, 1984, Chatsworth, CA.

Articles

[9] Birrell, A. and R. Needham, "A Universal File Server," *IEEE Transactions on Software Engineering,* Vol. SE-6, September 1980.

[10] Codd, E., "A Relational Model of Data for Large Shared Data Banks," *Communications of the ACM,* Vol. 13, No. 6, June 1970.

[11] Shapiro, E., "Text DataBases," *BYTE,* Vol. 9, No. 12, December 1984.

[12] Svobodova, L., "File Servers for Network-Based Distributed Systems," *Computing Surveys,* Vol. 16, December 1984.

Chapter 5   *Textbooks*

[1] Comer, D., *Operating Systems Design,* Prentice-Hall, 1984, Englewood Cliffs, NJ, Chapters 11 and 12.

[2]   Gear, C. W., *Computer Organization and Programming,* McGraw-Hill, 1985, New York, NY, Chapters 4 and 8.

[3]   Lister, A. M., *Fundamentals of Operating Systems,* Macmillan, 1979, New York, NY, Chapter 6.

[4]   Milenkovic, M., *Operating System Concepts and Design,* McGraw-Hill, 1987, New York, NY, Chapter 2.

Articles

[5]   Laub, L., "The Evolution of Mass Storage," *BYTE,* Vol. 11, No. 5, May 1986.

[6]   Teorey, T. J. and T. B. Pinkerton, "A Comparative Analysis of Disk Scheduling Policies," *CACM,* Vol. 15, No. 3, 1972.

Chapter 6   *Textbooks*

[1]   Calingaert, P., *Operating System Elements,* Prentice-Hall, 1982, Englewood Cliffs, NJ, Chapter 2.

[2]   Deitel, H. M., *An Introduction to Operating Systems,* Addison Wesley, 1984, Reading, MA, Chapters 7 through 9.

[3]   Massie, P., *Operating Systems Theory and Practice,* Burgess Communications, 1986, Edina, MN, Chapter 8.

Articles

[4]   Bays, C., "A Comparison of Next-Fit, First Fit, and Best Fit," *Communications of the ACM,* Vol. 20, No. 3, March 1977.

[5]   Denning, P.J., "Virtual Memory," *ACM Computing Surveys,* Vol. 2, No. 3, September 1970.

[6]   Pohn, A. V. and T. A. Smay, "Computer Memory Systems," *IEEE Computer Magazine,* October 1981.

[7]   Sluta, D. R. and I. L. Traiger, "A Note on the Calculation of the Average Working Set Size," *CACM,* Vol. 17, No. 10, October 1974.

[8]   Spirn, J. R. and P. J. Denning, "Experiments with Program Locality," *AFIPS Conference Proceedings,* Vol. 41, 1972.

Chapter 7   *Textbooks*

[1]   Comer, D., *Operating Systems Design,* Prentice-Hall, 1984, Englewood Cliffs, NJ, Chapters 4–7.

[2]   Deitel, H. M., *An Introduction to Operating Systems,* Addison Wesley, 1984, Reading, MA, Chapters 3, 4, 10, and 11.

[3]   Massie, P., *Operating Systems Theory and Practice,* Burgess Communications, 1986, Edina, MN, Chapter 6.

[4]   Peterson, J. L. and A. Silberschatz, *Operating System Concepts,* Second Edition, Addison Wesley, 1985, Reading, MA, Chapters 4 and 9.

Articles

[5]   Bunt, R. B., "Scheduling Techniques for Operating Systems," *Computer,* Vol. 9, No. 10, October 1976.

[6]   Curtois, P. and D. Parnas, "Concurrent Control with Readers and Writers," *CACM,* Vol. 14, No. 10, October 1971.

[7]   Dijkstra, E. W., "Cooperating Sequential Processes," *Technical Report EWD-123,* Technological University, Eindhoven, The Netherlands, 1965.

[8]   Dijkstra, E. W., "Hierarchical Ordering of Sequential Processes," *Acta Informatica,* Vol. 2, No. 1, 1971.

[9]   Doherty, W. J., "The Effects of Adaptive Reflective Scheduling," *IBM Research Report RC3672,* Yorktown Heights, NY, 1971.

[10] Ritchie, D. M. and K. Thompson, "The UNIX Time-Sharing System," *CACM,* Vol. 17, No. 7, July 1974.

Chapter 8

Textbooks

[1]   Deitel, H., *An Introduction to Operating Systems,* Addison Wesley, 1984, Reading, MA, Chapters 4, 6, and ll.

[2]   Finkel, R., *An Operating Systems Vade Mecum,* Prentice-Hall, 1986, Englewood Cliffs, NJ, Chapters 8 and 9.

[3]   Hwang, K. and F. Briggs, *Computer Architecture and Parallel Processing,* McGraw-Hill, 1984, New York, NY, particularly Chapter 1.

[4]   Shaw, A. and L. Bic, *The Logical Design of Operating Systems,* Second Edition, Prentice-Hall, 1988, Englewood Cliffs, NJ, Chapters 2, 3, and 4.

Articles

[5]   Curtois, P., F. Heymans, and D. Parnas, "Concurrent Control with 'Readers' and 'Writers,'" *CACM,* Vol. 14, No. 10, October 1971.

[6]   Dijkstra, E., "Hierarchical Ordering of Sequential Processes," *Acta Informatica,* Vol. 2, No. 1, 1971.

[7]   Dijkstra, E., "Cooperating Sequential Processes," *Programming Languages,* Academic Press, 1968, New York, NY.

[8]   Hoare, C., "Monitors: An Operating System Structuring Concept," *CACM,* Vol. 17, No. 10, October 1974.

[9]   Holt, R., "Some Deadlock Properties of Computer Systems," *ACM Computing Surveys,* Vol. 4, No. 4, September 1972.

[10] Lamport, L., "Mutual Exclusion Problem (Parts I and II)," *Journal of the ACM,* Vol. 33, No. 2, February 1986.

[11] Paseman, W., "Applying Data Flow in the Real World," *BYTE,* Vol. 10, No. 5, May 1985.

[12] Patil, S., "Limitations and Capabilities of Dijkstra's Semaphore Primitives for Coordination Among Processes," Technical Report, MIT, February, 1971.

[13] Peterson, G., "Myths About the Mutual Exclusion Problem," *Information Processing Letters,* Vol. 12, No. 3, June 1981.

[14] Tanenbaum, A. and R. Van Renesse, "Distributed Operating Systems," *Computing Surveys,* Vol. 17, December 1985.

[15] Walker, P., "The Transputer," *BYTE,* Vol. 10, No. 5, May 1985.

Chapter 9

Textbooks

[1]   Black, U., *Data Communications and Distributed Networks,* Second Edition, Prentice-Hall, 1987, Englewood Cliffs, NJ.

[2]   Chorafas, D., *Personal Computers and Data Communications,* Computer Science Press, 1986, Rockville, MD.

[3]   Deitel, H., *An Introduction to Operating Systems,* Addison Wesley, 1984, Reading, MA, Chapter 16.

[4]   Peterson, J. and A. Silberschatz, *Operating System Concepts,* Second Edition, Addison Wesley, 1985, Reading, MA, Chapter 13.

Articles

[5]   Feng, T., "A Survey of Interconnection Networks," *IEEE Computer,* Vol. 14, No. 12, December 1981.

[6]   Johnson, J., "Putting Broadband into Perspective, *Telecommunications,* December 1984.

[7]   Metcalfe, R. and D. Boggs, "EtherNet: Distributed Packet Switching for Local Computer Networks," *CACM,* Vol. 19, No. 7, July 1976.

[8]   Mier, E., "The Evolution of a Standard EtherNet," *BYTE,* Vol. 9, No. 12, December 1984.

Chapter 10
Textbooks

[1]   Calingaert, P., *Operating System Elements,* Prentice-Hall, 1982, Englewood Cliffs, NJ, Chapters 7–8.

[2]   Davis, G., *Management Information Systems,* McGraw-Hill, 1974, New York, NY, Chapters 8–13.

[3]   Krause, L. and A. MacGahan, *Computer Fraud and Countermeasures,* Prentice-Hall, 1979, Englewood Cliffs, NJ.

Articles

[4]   Denning, D. and P. Denning, "Data Security," *ACM Computing Surveys,* Vol. 11, No. 3, September 1979.

[5]   Gaines, R. and N. Shapiro, "Some Security Principles and Their Application to Computer Security," *Operating System Review,* Vol. 12, No. 3, July 1978.

[6]   Parnas, D., "The Influence of Software Structure on Reliability," *Proceedings of International Conference on Reliable Software,* April 1975.

[7]   Popek, G. and C. Kline, "Encryption and Secure Computer Networks," *ACM Computing Surveys,* Vol. 11, No. 4, December 1979.

Chapter 11
Textbooks

[1]   Condon, R., *Data Processing Systems Analysis and Design,* Reston, 1978, Reston, VA.

[2]   Davis, G., *Management Information Systems,* McGraw-Hill, 1974, New York, NY, Chapter 16.

[3]   Ferrari, D., *Computer Systems Performance Evaluation,* Prentice-Hall, 1978, Englewood Cliffs, NJ.

[4]   Sauer, C. and K. Chandy, *Computer Systems Performance Modeling,* Prentice-Hall, 1981, Englewood Cliffs, NJ.

[5]   Zmud, R., *Information Systems in Organizations,* Scott, Foresman, 1983, Glenview, IL, Chapters 9–13.

Articles

[6]   Boyle, B., "Software Performance Evaluation," *BYTE,* Vol. 9, No. 2, February 1984.

[7]   Carroll, J. and M. Rosson, "Beyond MIPs: Performance Is Not Quality," *BYTE,* Vol. 9, No. 2, February 1984.

[8] Donelom, W., "Project Planning and Control," *Datamation,* Vol. 22, 1976.

[9] Houston, J., "Don't Bench Me In," *BYTE,* Vol. 9, No. 2, February 1984.

[10] Marvit, P. and M. Nair, "Benchmark Confessions," *BYTE,* Vol. 9, No. 2, February 1984.

Chapter 12   *Textbooks*

[1] Davis, W. S., *Operating Systems: A Systematic View,* Third Edition, Addison Wesley, 1987, Reading, MA, Chapters 5, 8, and 14.

[2] Letwin, G., *Inside OS/2,* Microsoft Press, 1988, Redmond, WA.

[3] Massie, P., *Operating Systems Theory and Practice,* 1986, Burgess Communications, 1986, Edina, MN, Chapter 13.

[4] Norton, P., *Programmer's Guide to the IBM PC,* Microsoft Press, 1985, Redmond, WA.

[5] Petzold, C., *Programming Windows,* Microsoft Press, 1988, Redmond, WA.

Articles

[6] Haugdahl, J. S., "Local Area Networks for the IBM PC," *BYTE,* Vol. 9, No. 13, December 1984.

[7] Larson, C., "MS-DOS 2.0: An Enhanced 16-bit Operating System," *BYTE,* Vol 8, No. 11, November 1983.

Chapter 13   *Textbooks*

[1] Lu, C., *The Apple Macintosh Book,* Second Edition, Microsoft Press, 1985, Redmond, WA.

[2] Rose, C. (ed.), *Inside Macintosh* (3 vols.), Addison Wesley, 1985, Reading, MA.

[3] Waite, M., R. Lafore and I. Lansing, *Microsoft Macinations,* Microsoft Press, 1985, Redmond, WA.

Articles

[4] Crawford, C., "The Mac Plus," *BYTE,* Vol. 11, No. 12, November 1986.

[5] Williams, G., "The Apple Macintosh Computer," *BYTE,* Vol. 9, No. 2, February 1984.

[6] Williams, G. and T. Thompson, "The Apple Macintosh II," BYTE, Vol. 12, No. 4, April 1987.

[7] Zehr, G., "MMU for 68000 Architectures," *BYTE,* Vol. 11, No. 12, November 1986.

Chapter 14   *Textbooks*

[1] Bach, M., *The Design of the UNIX Operating System,* Prentice-Hall, 1986, Englewood Cliffs, NJ.

[2] Foxley, A., *UNIX for SuperUsers,* Addison Wesley, 1985, Reading, MA.

[3] Frank, B., *UNIX System Administration,* Harcourt Brace Jovanovich, 1987, New York, NY.

[4] Halamka, J., *Real World UNIX,* Sybex, 1984, Berkeley, CA.

[5] Kernighan, B. and R. Pike, *The UNIX Programming Environment,* Prentice-Hall, 1984, Englewood Cliffs, NJ.

[6] Sobell, M., *A Practical Guide to the UNIX System,* Benjamin-Cummings, 1984, Menlo Park, CA.

[7] Waite, M., D. Martin, and S. Prata, *UNIX Primer Plus,* Howard W. Sams, 1983, Indianapolis, IN.

Articles

[8] Bourne, S., "An Introduction to the UNIX Shell," *Bell System Technical Journal,* Vol. 57, No. 6, October 1978.

[9] Ritchie, D., "The UNIX Time-Sharing System: A Retrospective," *Bell System Technical Journal,* Vol. 57, No. 6, October 1978.

[10] Ritchie, D. and K. Thompson, "The UNIX Time-Sharing System," *CACM,* Vol. 17, No. 7, July 1974.

Chapter 15 *Textbooks*

[1] _____, *VAX Hardware Handbook,* DEC, 1980, Maynard, MA.

[2] _____, *VAX Architecture Handbook,* DEC, 1981, Maynard, MA.

[3] _____, *VAX Software Handbook,* DEC, 1982, Maynard, MA.

[4] _____, *PDP-11 Software Handbook,* DEC, 1982, Maynard, MA.

[5] _____, *RSTS/E PDP-11 Operating System,* DEC, 1983, Maynard, MA.

[6] Kenah, L. and S. Bate, *VAX/VMS Internals and Data Structures,* Digital Press, 1984, Bedford, MA.

Chapter 16 *Textbooks*

[1] _____, *Systems and Products Guide,* IBM, White Plains, 1987, NY.

[2] _____, *IBM VSE/SP General Information,* IBM, 1986, White Plains, NY.

[3] _____, *MVS/SP Version 2 General Information Manual,* IBM, 1986, White Plains, NY.

[4] _____, *IBM System/370 System Summary: Processors,* IBM, 1986, White Plains, NY.

[5] _____, *A Guide to the IBM 4381 Processor,* IBM, 1986, White Plains, NY.

[6] _____, *9370 Information System: Introducing the System,* IBM, 1986, White Plains, NY.

[7] _____, *IBM System/38 Introduction,* IBM, 1986, White Plains, NY.

[8] _____, *IBM System/38 Control Program Facility Concepts Manual,* IBM, 1984, White Plains, NY.

[9] Ashley, R., J. Fernandez, and S. Beamesderfer, *JCL for IBM VSE Systems,* Wiley Press, 1986, New York, NY.

[10] Davis, W., *Operating Systems: A Systematic View,* Addison Wesley, 1987, Reading, MA, Chapters 10–12 and 17–20.

[11] Hanson, O., *Design of Computer Data Files,* Computer Science Press, 1982, Rockville, MD, Chapter 7.

[12] Yuen, C., *Essential Concepts of Operating Systems Using IBM Examples,* Addison Wesley, 1986, Reading, MA.

Index